A Latin American Existentialist Ethos

SUNY series in Latin American and Iberian Thought and Culture
Rosemary Geisdorfer Feal, editor
Jorge J. E. Gracia, founding editor

A Latin American Existentialist Ethos
Modern Mexican Literature and Philosophy

STEPHANIE MERRIM

Published by State University of New York Press, Albany

© 2023 State University of New York

All rights reserved

Printed in the United States of America

No part of this book may be used or reproduced in any manner whatsoever without written permission. No part of this book may be stored in a retrieval system or transmitted in any form or by any means including electronic, electrostatic, magnetic tape, mechanical, photocopying, recording, or otherwise without the prior permission in writing of the publisher.

For information, contact State University of New York Press, Albany, NY
www.sunypress.edu

Library of Congress Cataloging-in-Publication Data

Name: Merrim, Stephanie, author.
Title: A Latin American existentialist ethos : modern Mexican literature
    and philosophy / Stephanie Merrim.
Description: Albany : State University of New York Press, [2023] | Series:
    SUNY series in Latin American and Iberian thought and culture | "In
    order to engage a host of constituencies, this book translates into
    English all non-English material (except for obvious cognates and
    poetry, for which [the author] provide the original plus a literal prose
    translation)."—Preface. | Includes bibliographical references and index.
Identifiers: LCCN 2022037724 | ISBN 9781438493190 (hardcover : alk. paper) |
    ISBN 9781438493206 (ebook) | ISBN 9781438493183 (pbk. : alk. paper)
Subjects: LCSH: Mexican literature—20th century—History and criticism. |
    Existentialism in literature. | Philosophy, Modern, in literature.
    Mexico—Intellectual life—20th century. | LCGFT: Literary criticism.
Classification: LCC PQ7155 .M47 2023 | DDC 860.9/97720904—dc23/eng/20230119
LC record available at https://lccn.loc.gov/2022037724

10 9 8 7 6 5 4 3 2 1

Contents

ACKNOWLEDGMENTS	vii
NOTE ON TRANSLATIONS	ix
CHAPTER ONE Engaging Existentialism: Transformative Possibilities and Local Agendas	1
CHAPTER TWO The Mexican Existentialist Ethos	33
CHAPTER THREE The Seminal Mexican Existentialism of Rodolfo Usigli's Theater	75
CHAPTER FOUR Excavating Comala: The Existentialist Juan Rulfo, the Grupo Hiperión, and *Lo Mexicano* in *Pedro Páramo* (1955)	105
CHAPTER FIVE "Christs for All Passions": José Revueltas's *El luto humano* [Human Mourning]	129
CHAPTER SIX Rosario Castellanos's Freedom	155
NOTES	187
WORKS CITED	217
INDEX	235

Acknowledgments

Previously published portions of this book, in somewhat different form, have appeared as "'Living and Thinking with Those Dislocations': A Case for Latin American Existentialist Fiction," *Hispanic Literatures and the Question of a Liberal Education*, special issue of *Hispanic Issues On Line*, vol. 8, fall 2011, pp. 93–109; "The Existential Juan Rulfo: *Pedro Páramo*, Mexicanness, and the Grupo Hiperión," *MLN*, vol. 129, no. 2, 2014, pp. 308–29, copyright ©2014, the Johns Hopkins University Press; "'Los Cristos de todas las pasiones': The Latin American Existentialism of José Revueltas's *El luto humano*," *Revista Hispánica Moderna*, vol. 69, no. 2, 2016, pp. 193–209; "Mexican Existentialist Ethics and the Pragmatic Authenticity of Rodolfo Usigli's *El gesticulador*," *Revista Canadiense de Estudios Hispánicos*, vol. 43, no. 2, 2019, pp. 375–401. I gratefully acknowledge permission from each of the above publications to reprint my work herein, as well as permission from Teresa Clifton, whose photograph of the *Monumento a la Revolución* is reproduced in chapter 3.

Warmest thanks go to Rebecca Colesworthy, my extraordinary editor at SUNY Press, and to Aimee Harrison, who went beyond the call of duty in designing the book's cover. They, and the rest of the people I have worked with at SUNY Press, have been models of expertise, professionalism, and cordiality.

Note on Translations

In order to engage a host of constituencies, this book translates into English all non-English material (except obvious cognates and poetry: for poetry I provide the original plus a literal prose translation). I quote published translations of works in languages other than Spanish. Translations from the Spanish, including the prose versions of poetry, are mine. However, again in the hope of reaching a broad readership, each chapter on literature is anchored in a particular text that has been translated into and published in English; for these "anchor" texts, as well as Octavio Paz's repeatedly referenced *El laberinto de la soledad*, I quote published translations and provide page references for both the translation *and* the Spanish original, as listed in the bibliography. *In all cases, the italicized page number in such double citations refers to the published translation*, which at times has been silently modified into a more literal or precise rendition.

Chapter One

Engaging Existentialism

Transformative Possibilities and Local Agendas

> O my soul, do not aspire to immortal life,
> but exhaust the limits of the possible.
>
> —Pindar, *Pythian* iii
> Albert Camus, Epigraph to *The Myth of Sisyphus* (1942)

Camus's epigraph invites his readers into an "absurd" universe of shaken absolutes, a contingent world that, fearsome as it is, scintillates with possibilities for meaning-making. The philosopher holds out the prospect that life "will be lived all the better" (*Myth* 535) when, accepting the lack of absolutes or givens, we confer meaning on the world in consciousness and good faith. He neatly states that it is "a matter of living and thinking with those dislocations" (532). Simple as Camus's directive may sound, whether or how to embrace the existentialist worldview it announces roiled into axial issues of Western postmodernity at large. For a postcolonial, largely God-anchored Latin America, Camus's clarion calls at once have special purchase and entail special challenges. Existentially oriented Latin American philosophers, essayists, and creative writers of the twentieth century rallied to the challenges of dislocation in all their magnificent complexity. Exploring "the limits of the possible" within the spheres of their own locations, they constructed the maps of meanings and values—a distinctive existentialist spirit, an ethos—that this book investigates.

"Oh *my* soul," says Camus (emphasis added): trained on individuals in their lived contexts, existentialism lends itself to anecdotes, *petites histoires*, personal stories. I will therefore take the liberty of glossing a couple of the personal epiphanies on Latin American existentialism that gave life to *A Latin American Existentialist Ethos*. The first flashpoint came about several years ago when I was preparing a class on João Guimarães Rosa's 1962 *Primeiras estórias* (translated into English as *The Third Bank of the River and Other Stories*).[1] As I thought about the crowd that revives the existentialist crusader of the Brazilian author's story "Darandina" ("Much Ado" in *Third Bank*), a poem by the Peruvian proto-existentialist César Vallejo came to mind. Vallejo's simple parable, "Masa" [Mass] (*España, aparta de mí este cáliz*, 1939), an inspirational reflection on the Republican struggle in the Spanish Civil War, is a paean to loving solidarity. "Masa" has everyone on earth joining together in heartfelt emotion, "tanto amor" [so much love], to bring a fallen warrior back to life. The poem's last lines read,

> Entonces, todos los hombres de la tierra
> le rodearon; les vió el cadáver triste, emocionado;
> incorporóse lentamente,
> abrazó al primer hombre; echóse a andar . . . (610; ellipsis in original)

> [Then, everyone on earth surrounded him; the corpse looked at them sadly, profoundly moved; he got up slowly, embraced the first man; started to walk]

From the unexpected convergence of Guimarães Rosa and Vallejo arose the revelation that much of Latin American existentialism appeals to community and, in the enduring backlash against positivism detailed below, to emotion.

The second flashpoint occurred after I realized that in thinking about Latin American existentialism I had not, ironically enough, taken sufficient account of Mexico, my favorite intellectual haunt. I soon became engrossed in the Mexican existentialist Grupo Hiperión, whose still-antipositivist philosophical investigations enfold two further hallmarks of the Latin American existentialist ethos: identity and ethics. When I then began to glimpse the connections between the Grupo Hiperión and the *literary* works written in its milieu, the flashpoint turned into an exhilarating, runaway experience. As a result, I have centered this book on Mexico, thanks to its dynamic conjugations of both literature and philosophy and of identity, ethics, and community.

Pulsating behind the entire ensemble is a formidable issue, another clarion call that demands consideration. I refer to the fact that the overarching narrative of Latin American literary existentialism, on its own and as it relates to existential philosophy, has basically gone unarticulated. The chapter at hand ventures to frame that narrative in broad strokes. "Engaging Existentialism: Transformative Possibilities and Local Agendas" scopes out key interfaces between European existentialism and Latin American existentialist projects; paying close attention to existentialism's transformative potency, it traces the developments that the philosophical current was singularly positioned to enable, and *did* enable, in Latin America; it attends to the motors, from philosophy to literature, of Latin American existentialism.[2] The Latin American foundations in place, we move into ever more local terrain: the platforms of the Mexican context and, finally, the specific building blocks of *A Latin American Existentialist Ethos.*

The itinerary I have just sketched out merely tenders an, I hope, helpful orientation to the several threads of chapter 1. As such, it only hints at the true spirit of Camus and of all things existentialist. For beneath even the most technical philosophical aspects lies the passion of existentialism itself and the passions it catalyzes in Latin American writers. To those passionate opportunities we now turn.

An Engaging Existentialism

In 1999 the renowned French theorist Jean Baudrillard brashly wrote: "We have thrown off that old existential garb . . . . Who cares about freedom, bad faith, and authenticity today?" (73). One might well wish away the notoriously abstruse garb of Jean-Paul Sartre's philosophical works, which can obscure the living passions of existentialism. Apart from that and with due respect to Baudrillard, it is easy to deny that the root concerns of existentialism could ever cease to engage hearts and minds. Freedom, bad faith, and authenticity among them, they implicate us on deep, vital levels of our lives. They reach out to the individual as an individual, to the individual trying to forge a life in a world without guideposts, or at least a world that places established, normative guideposts in question. Existentialism of every ilk wants to jolt us into awareness of the choices we make and of our freedom to make them. It wants to shake us out of a mechanical existence, to destabilize us, awaken and prime us for happiness. In the oft-quoted but always compelling words of Camus, "the struggle itself towards the heights is enough to fill a man's heart" (*Myth* 593).[3]

That existentialism inalienably speaks to the core of our lives and why she believes it does was the message that Simone de Beauvoir strove to convey when in 1947 she published the essay "What Is Existentialism?" in *France-Amérique*. An implicit partner piece to Camus's *Myth of Sisyphus* and overt companion piece to Sartre's *Existentialism Is a Humanism* (1946), Beauvoir's essay matches the latter text's humanistic, down to earth register. In chorus with both male giants of French existentialism, Beauvoir lucidly attempts to rescue the maligned philosophy from allegations of pessimism. "What Is Existentialism?" at the same time effectively transmits signature features of Beauvoir's own bounteous existential program. Too frequently overshadowed by Sartre's massive feats, Beauvoir's expansive and grounded agenda will materialize into a heartbeat (a generally de facto but still telling one, as shall become clear) of various projects that my later chapters survey.

Listening, then, for many good reasons to Beauvoir's seductive rendition of existentialism, we hear her declare the movement "a practical and living attitude posed by the world today" that proposes "a concrete human attitude" (*Philosophical Writings* 324). Existentialism, like Christianity and Marxism, wishes to apprehend "the totality of the human domain" (324). It follows, as Beauvoir states in consonance with her recently published philosophical work *The Ethics of Ambiguity* (1947), that existentialism "strives to hold both ends of the chain at the same time, surpassing [dépassant] the interior-exterior, subjective-objective opposition" (325). Beauvoir's existentialism then disrupts a pernicious opposition, the all too often competing interests of ethics and politics. She maintains that because the individual "has reality only through his engagement in the world" (325), existentialism seeks "a reconciliation of those two reigns whose divorce is so nefarious to men in our time: the ethical reign and the political reign" (325). Freedom is the prime mover of all such dislocations: "By freely taking his own freedom as an end within himself and in his acts, man constitutes a kingdom of ends" (326). An existential warrior like Camus, Beauvoir revolts against absurdity, avowing that "the task of man is one: to fashion the world by giving it a meaning" (325). A world thus fashioned, she concludes, shimmers with promise, not hopelessness.

Beauvoir's sanguine apologetics usher us into the appeals of existentialism for Latin America. A recent uptick of interest in existentialism thanks in a significant measure to post-continental philosophy's more global sights has brought front and center the movement's relevance to so-called Third World issues.[4] As Lewis R. Gordon, whose investigations of existentialism and Africana thought have contributed to the resurgence, observes: "Existential philosophy addresses problems of freedom, anguish, dread, responsibility, embodied agency, sociality, and liberation" (7). Latin American authors did not fail to seize with a vengeance on these enabling positives of existentialism, further lured by certain of its other most consequential staples: the weight that existentialism places on a self-determined existence as versus a predetermined essence, authenticity, commitment, activism, and new ways of envisioning religion. Beyond existentialism's core note of freedom, it was Martin Heidegger's *Dasein*—being-there, being-in-the-world—that principally galvanized Latin American thinkers. Dasein, a "lived context of concern" (Gordon 10), dovetails not only with Sartre's notion of human beings in "situation" (i.e., in a particular context) but also with Spaniard José Ortega y Gasset's influential "I am myself and my circumstances, and if I do not save them, I do not save myself" (*Meditaciones* 77). A transnational watchword, Dasein offered Latin Americans both a mandate and modus operandi for inquiring into their own specific, lived contexts. Famously emerging for Sartre from the contemplation of an apricot cocktail, phenomenological existentialism had attuned the French philosopher to the thing in itself (Beauvoir, *Prime* 112); for Latin Americans, existentialism grew into a means of taking the measure of their own possibilities, of assuming the "practical and living attitude" that Beauvoir's situated existentialism champions.

It is therefore symptomatic that one of the first Latin American formulations of an existential philosophy, devised by the Argentine Carlos Astrada (1894–1970), quickly grasped and capitalized on Dasein's emancipatory promise. Astrada, who had studied with Heidegger, injected Heideggerian thought into Argentina starting with *El juego existencial* [The Existential Gambit] (1933). The Argentine philosopher's "humanism of freedom," elaborated in various works, views man as forging his essence from his existence in a concrete sociohistorical setting.[5] The humanism of freedom then proposes to rescue and affirm the "full man," an individual who activates his full *humanitas*, the entirety of his immanent human capabilities. Astrada's version of existentialism accentuates not only its drawing power for Latin Americans in situation but also its role in paving the way for subsequent activist Latin American modes such as liberation theology.

More to our purposes, Astrada's existential "humanism of freedom" stood on the cusp of a movement that would soon permeate and energize the hemisphere's philosophy. Surfacing in the 1930s when students of Heidegger like Astrada returned home, Latin American existential philosophy reached its apogee in the 1940s and 1950s. From initial hubs in Argentina and Mexico, it spread to the Caribbean, Central America, and other parts of Latin America.[6]

Elements integral to the Latin American philosophical and political context dramatically enhanced the magnetism of existentialism for these various locations. Existentialism initially gained traction in a philosophical milieu dominated by reactions against a formidable European import, positivism. Not confined to philosophy, positivism infiltrated Latin America during the nineteenth-century period of nation building as an organ of the state and as a developmental program intended to launch post-Independence nations into modernity. The "order and progress" positivism's motto heralds gave it enormous currency for post-Independence Latin America, and the European import maintained a tenacious grip on the maturing nations. One thinks of the positivist Porfirio Díaz's thirty-one-year dictatorship of Mexico (1876–1880, 1884–1911) and the positivist Getúlio Vargas's regime in Brazil (on and off from 1930 to 1954), the longest of any Brazilian president. In Latin America, positivism largely equated to the anti-metaphysical, anti-religious, mechanistic philosophy of the French Auguste Comte (1798–1857). Comte's positivism debunks religion and metaphysics as obsolete, inadequate vehicles to knowledge. It replaces them with determinism, empiricism, and the enshrining of reason. Everything was to be subordinated to, reduced to, science. And science entails laws, regularities, discipline, logic, materialism, the scientific management of the state. In keeping with its scientific, hegemonic ambitions, Latin American positivism sought to exile religion and displace the Catholic church.[7]

A soul-numbing positivism of alien origins soon became anathema to Latin American thinkers. Around the start of the twentieth century, in a colossal defining moment for Latin American philosophy, a tidal wave of Latin Americans formed by positivism disowned it. The revolutionary surge of antipositivism that fanned out through the former colonies included works by the Argentine Francisco Romero and Alejandro Korn; the Brazilian Raimundo Farias Brito; the Mexican José Vasconcelos and Antonio Caso; the Peruvian Alejandro Deústua; and the Uruguayan Carlos Vaz Ferreira (Gracia and Millán-Zaibert 18–19). Altogether, they constituted the first generation of *professional* Latin American philosophers, the "first in their several countries to dedicate themselves wholly to philosophy" (Sánchez Reulet xiii). In other words, antipositivism both mobilized hemispheric activity and spurred the genesis of modern Latin American philosophy.[8]

From this genesis, this watershed moment, sprung potent structures of feeling that created bridges to existentialism and Latin American identity. "Structures of feeling," in fact, obtains quite literally here insofar as against the absolute dominion of logic, reason, and science, antipositivists advocated emotion and a comprehensive approach to human existence. Revealing the cracks in a positivism that presented itself as a totalizing system, against absolute knowability and the devaluation of religion the antipositivists pitted the mysteries of the spirit and spirituality. As Aníbal Sánchez Reulet notes: "From various sides, and in different tones, they criticized the scientist concept of reality, the naive progressivism, and the dogmatic narrowness of the positivists," to defend, instead, "the rights of human freedom" (xiii). Antipositivism's robust endorsement of human freedom slides into line with that of existentialism, creating improbable bedfellows. Unnatural as a partnership between existentialism's placing of God in question and an assault on positivism's discrediting of religion may seem, existentialism so zealously opposed positivism's valorizing of reason and determinism as to allow the burgeoning trend to make common cause with antipositivism. Hence, naturalized into the territory of Latin American philosophy, existentialism would serve as a latter-day weapon in the war on positivism that continued to ripple vigorously through the twentieth century.

The ripple effect gained momentum from the role of antipositivism in triggering Latin American self-definition. Perhaps most important, José Enrique Rodó's essay *Ariel* (1899) channeled antipositivism into a pilot yet singularly long-lived crystallization of modern Latin American identity. The Uruguayan Rodó takes the title, narrative frame, and central symbols of his book-length essay from Shakespeare's *The Tempest*. Setting the essay in the aura of a bronze statue that depicts Ariel at the moment he is freed from servitude, Rodó rewires Shakespeare's scenario into a multiplex drama of resistance. The Uruguayan writes in the wake of the Spanish American War that saw Spain lose its colonies and under the specter of mounting US imperialism. Rodó accordingly looks to North America as the menace over against which Latin America must urgently assert its identity; he revamps Shakespeare's uncouth Caliban into the US and the pure, airy spirit, Ariel, into Latin America. As this characterization might suggest, for Rodó the US represents the embodiment not just of imperialism but also of positivist ideologies. Throughout *Ariel*, teacher Próspero exhorts his pupils to free themselves from the ways of Calibán, or "Nordomanía": utilitarianism and sensuality without ideals, materialism, and idolatry of capitalism, science, and progress. Rodó's antipositivist script, a cultural nationalism, denominates the superior humanism of the Greeks, Christian spirituality, leisure, idealism, love, and honor as the salient values of Latin America. In casting Ariel as "the noble and soaring element of the spirit . . . the ideal to which human selection aspires, erasing from superior man the tenacious vestiges of Caliban" (24), Rodó urges a life ruled by the spirit.

Again, the stakes considerably higher now thanks to the coupling of spirituality with identity politics, an inherent disconnect between existentialism and Latin American philosophy looms. How to reconcile a mode of thought premised on existence with one premised on (a God-given) essence, nevertheless, was not a Gordian knot, an intractable dilemma. For one thing and almost needless to say, there is no single existentialism but manifold existentialisms. There are existentialisms that speak to the left and the right, the revolutionary and the conservative, the atheist and the believer. Predictably, the abundant strains of Christian existentialism flourished in Latin America. European Christian existentialists Søren Kierkegaard, Gabriel Marcel, and Max Scheler exercised a particular attraction for Latin American philosophers.[9] From the first and onward, despite the addition of Sartre's entire corpus to the Vatican Index of Prohibited Works in 1948, existentialism won fervent Latin American adherents.

For another, Latin American existentialist philosophers entered into sinuous, impactful negotiations with Christianity. Religious and nonreligious existentialists acceded to the entrenched purchase of Christianity in their countries and redeployed theology in the humanistic, ecumenical form of values. They combated the moral wasteland of positivism, "an ethical dead end" (Gracia and Millán-Zaibert 17), by reterritorializing, *transvaluating*, Christian theology into the secular realm.[10] Jesus Christ's ministry of love and ductile theological axioms like the Golden Rule of doing unto others as one would have them do unto oneself lent themselves to an all but unimpugnable earthly credo. Argentine creative writer and essayist Julio Cortázar, a high priest of secular Latin American existentialism, enunciates the crux of the phenomenon in his *Teoría del túnel* (1947; in *Obra crítica*). He states: "If Christian axiology represents man's highest ethical stance, existentialism maintains that stance, but weans it from theology" (113).

God could be bracketed out and what remains of a Christianity divested of supernaturalism—that is, a post-metaphysical Christianity—advanced as desiderata for a postmodern Latin America. The existential repurposing of theology to this end, case studies of which I present in chapter 2 and chapter 5 vis-à-vis Mexico, lines up with what we now understand as postsecularism. Postsecularist Jürgen Habermas, for instance, emphasizes the need to invigorate modernity with renewed awareness of theologically based moral phenomena, translating them into a secular idiom accessible and useful to all citizens (Mendieta and VanAntwerpen 4).[11]

The translation of Christianity into a secular scripture that would work to the benefit of all citizens indexes existentialism's larger calling for

Latin America as, in my view, a *theater of values*. Existentialism provided a liberating force field, a critical opportunity to forge a situated value system that could mesh with yet stand apart from religion and, moreover, from nationalistic ideologies in countries prey to dictatorships and nationalistic propaganda (we may think of Juan Domingo Perón's Argentine popularism, 1946–1955).[12] An existentialism beholden neither to partisan ideologies nor to the state could constitute an independent realm, a clean slate on which to erect a national, rather than nationalistic, value platform. One might appropriately object that freedom and the positing of values are fundamentally at odds. Indeed, this is where Latin American "situations" put pressure on European existentialisms and lead to distinctive New World enactments of them. As identity, politics, and history exert their weight on Latin American existentialism, they shape it into a vehicle for an imagined community that can replace, or at least righteously supplement, an official imagined community.

By the same token, existentialism allows Latin Americans to salve two wounds of a militant nationalism, insularity and provincialism. While purveying agendas that have specific relevance to and viable transformative potential for their own locations, Latin Americans inscribe their works in a Western current that reimagines the human condition in toto. A Latin American existentialism in dialogue with its European manifestations reverberates into the domain of universals. All told, it effects a rooted cosmopolitanism that mediates between the international or universal and the local or identity politics (on rooted cosmopolitanism, see Appiah, ch. 6).

Eduardo Mallea's early *Historia de una pasión argentina* (1937) brings into a paradigmatic synergy a host of the factors that bear on Latin American existentialism. Mallea wrote the book-length essay in the midst of Argentina's "infamous decade," during which the country suffered a military coup, electoral fraud, the rise of fascism, and the incipient great economic depression. A Mallea writhing with despair for his nation opens the book with these lines: "After spending years trying to assuage my affliction, given the present state of my country, our country, I feel the need to shout out my anguish. This work is born of that anguish" (19). The supremely anguished Mallea immerses himself in the angst-ridden soul searching of Christian existentialist Søren Kierkegaard. Throughout the *Historia* Mallea layers Kierkegaard's searing moral conscience and summons to authenticity onto the Latin American antipositivist repertoire. Of signal consequence, he routes Kierkegaard's burning mindfulness into an overall assessment of Argentina, which means that almost immediately upon arrival in Argentina existentialism consorted with identity discourse. Mallea evaluates the authenticity versus the inauthenticity of an Argentina that, akin to Kierkegaard's visible and invisible Church (*Practice* 211–24), the Latin American essayist limns as *two* Argentinas. He deplores the inauthenticity of a soulless, bourgeois, "visible Argentina" (that inheres mostly in the city), addicted to bad faith, materialism, progress, utilitarianism, conformism, arid erudition, and a lack of spirituality. Mallea entreats his compatriots to adopt as their model the authentic "invisible Argentina" (that inheres mostly in the countryside), characterized by sincerity, ideals, tradition, individualism, ideas, and genuine faith. With this, it is clear, Mallea embeds existentialism in the profile of Latin America that Rodó's *Ariel* had seeded.[13] Seven years after the military takeover of Argentina, Mallea engages existentialism for a resistant but apolitical secular scripture that carries a homegrown identity formation in tow.

A Literature of Possibilities

In 1932 Ortega y Gasset's journal, *Revista de Occidente*, published Mallea's novella, *La angustia* [Anguish]. The Argentine author went on to write more than thirty volumes of fiction, as far as I know the first substantially existentialist Latin American literature. Well before Sartre's *Nausea* (1938), it can be said, Mallea had activated the special fit between imaginative works and existential philosophy that would catapult the former into a prime stage for the latter. Literature proved not merely to be apposite to existential philosophy, a lively paraphilosophical adjunct, but almost fungible with it. Camus remarks that it "would be impossible to insist too much on the arbitrary nature of the former opposition between art and philosophy" (*Myth* 570). Furthermore—as undoubtedly occurred to philosophers Beauvoir, Camus, Kierkegaard, Sartre, and so on when they spanned disciplines—creative endeavors are uniquely suitable to the designs of existential philosophy. An existentialist manifesto titled "Why Literature?" might include these bullet points, previews of what Mexican literature will bring to life for us:

- Literature can disseminate ideas to a broad, nonspecialist public in an accessible human register (as versus the forbidding lexicon of Heidegger et alia).

- Literature can dramatize individual lives as they evolve in concrete situations.

- Literature can encompass the total individual, including a person's actions, thoughts, feelings, body, and becoming. It can capture what Colin Davis calls the "density of lived experience" (150).

- Literature is a consecrated, powerful venue for privileged existentialist themes such as angst, agency, and responsibility.

Primordially, I believe, the manifesto would underline that literature can animate the exercising of freedom, and do so in free, open-ended ways. If back in 1959 Hazel Barnes christened creative ventures shot through with the subject matter of freedom, no less than with the freedom hardwired into artistic endeavors, a "literature of possibilities," the rubric has a distinct pertinence to Latin American fiction.

In saying this, I have in mind that existentialist fiction counts among its Latin American practitioners a raft of the hemisphere's most free-thinking and free-writing, salient mid-twentieth-century writers: Julio Cortázar, Ernesto Sábato, and David Viñas from Argentina; João Guimarães Rosa and Clarice Lispector from Brazil; Alejo Carpentier from Cuba; Rosario Castellanos, Carlos Fuentes, and José Revueltas from Mexico; Mario Vargas Llosa from Peru; Juan Carlos Onetti from Uruguay. As these authors engaged a literature thronging with possibilities, they collectively revitalized the discursive landscape in ways that Vargas Llosa's *Entre Sartre y Camus* [Between Sartre and Camus] (1981) retrospectively pinpoints. The book's essay "El mandarín" surveys what Sartre meant to young Latin American writers. According to Vargas Llosa, in the long run the French thinker helped pull them away from hackneyed folkloric tendencies as well as from a superficial regionalism laden with Manicheanism and naturalism (116). Closer to the moment, Sartre enlivened them to projects beyond the fantastic literature then rampant in South America. Vargas Llosa caustically submits that Sartre unblocked South American writers, rescuing them from the preciosity of Jorge Luis Borges & Company: "Sartre could also save one from esteticism and cynicism. Thanks to Borges, back then our literature gained great imaginative subtlety, an extraordinary originality. But, as an influence, Borges's genius could be lethal: it produced little Borgeses, imitators of his affronts to grammar, his exotic erudition, and his skepticism" (117). If not, Vargas Llosa grants, as skilled a writer as Borges, Sartre taught a generation of Latin Americans that "literature can never be a game," that "writing was the most serious thing in the world" (117). The world, tangible worlds, thrummed outside

Borges's labyrinths, and, for Vargas Llosa, Sartre prodded Latin Americans to meet them with a situated, committed literature.[14]

While Borges's ingenious *ficciones*, a mixture of literature and essay, aim to impart an electric charge of unreality, Latin American existentialist fiction delivers thunderbolts of reality.[15] Yet it falls neither into vulgar realism nor into didactic thesis-fiction. The aforementioned existentialist writers instead rely heavily, for example, on irony, dialogism, first-person narrators, shifting narrative points of view, and extreme structural complexity to infuse their creations with the flux of existential becoming. Beauvoir's "Literature and Metaphysics" (1946) catches the gist of these narrative maneuvers in contending that the metaphysical novel permits writers "to evoke the original upspringing [jaillisement] of existence" (*Philosophical Writings* 274), an organic jaillisement that can offset the clash between advocating freedom and prescribing values I referred to above. Sartre's *What Is Literature?* (1948) reinforces the freedom bound up in authentic literature, a counterforce to the deterministic thesis novel. Sartre writes that "reading is a free dream" (49); "it is false to say that the author *acts* upon his readers; he merely makes an appeal to their freedom" (159). Sartre and Beauvoir's maxims for the literary disclosure of existence predict Cortázar's novel *Rayuela* [Hopscotch] (1963), whose "Table of Instructions" leaves its audience free to choose between two reading itineraries—a reminder that existentialist literature paved the way for the experimentalism of the so-called Latin American Boom. Several authors participated in both currents. Writ even larger, existentialist literature fostered a postmodern esthetic. When existentialist literature does want to convey something of a worldview, it is a postmodern one, best served by complexity and challenge, by questions in lieu of answers.

However much it strayed from Borges, Latin American existentialist literature did keep faith with his battle cry in "El escritor argentino y la tradición" [The Argentine Writer and Tradition] (1953).[16] "We Argentines, we South Americans in general," Borges declaims, "can wield all European themes, wield them without superstition, with an irreverence that can have, and already has had, fortunate consequences" (273). Duly irreverent, the majority of Latin American existentialist fiction pushes off from, and frequently pushes back at, constructs that Western existentialist philosophy and literature supply. "There is no such thing as existentialism," professes Cortázar, "there are just existentialists" (*Obra crítica* 114). Latin American existentialist authors scan Western existentialism and discover in it templates for remarkably diverse agendas. They interpellate the vast terrain knowledgeably and expertly, with a predilection for Western writers who straddle literature and philosophy (Camus, Fyodor Dostoevsky, Kierkegaard, the Spanish Miguel de Unamuno and, of course, Sartre).[17] Sartre may broadly appear to command Latin American existentialist literature, but in fact that corpus responds to a bundle of models. An agile, and as Borges enjoins, iconoclastic playing field, it mixes and matches at will.

Cortázar's breakthrough novella "El perseguidor" [The Pursuer] (1959) offers a window onto the irreverent, productive eclecticism of Latin American existentialist literature. Cortázar confessed that in "El perseguidor" he divorced himself from his former perfectly crafted, Borges-inspired tales, because "I was a bit sick and tired of seeing how well my stories turn out." Thus, structurally "El perseguidor" appears to meander; further, it parts ways with Borges to enter the turf of Jack Kerouac's exuberant, then-fresh Beat Generation novel *On the Road* (1957). Culture-spanning and cutting-edge, "El perseguidor" goes existential. Again in Cortázar's words, the novella tackles "an existentialist problem, a human problem." He adds: "I wanted to stop inventing and stand my own ground, to look at myself a bit. And looking at myself meant looking at my neighbor, at man" (Harss and Dohmann 223–24). Cortázar's resulting inquiry into a human problem revolves around the interactions between protagonist Johnny Carter, a visionary jazzman based on the North American saxophonist Charlie Parker, and narrator cum antihero, Bruno, a cerebral French jazz critic.

As each of the primary characters reaches out to the other, his other, the two are entangled in a love-hate battle fraught with Sartrean energies. Johnny, an existentialist Christ figure for the Beat Generation, pursues Bruno in a crusade to wrest him from bad faith, an emotion-squelching rationality. Transfixed and conflicted by the oracular jazzman ("this angel who is like my brother . . . this brother who is like my angel" [228]) who yearns to live permanently in an authentic *durée* [duration], Bruno pursues Johnny.[18] Bruno's narrative of the two men's relationship—"El perseguidor" per se—and Bruno's exploitative biography of Johnny on which the narrative comments are both infected with a Sartrean neurosis. They teem with the malignancies that according to Sartre's *Being and Nothingness* (1943) and attendant works characterize human relationships as we attempt to objectify the "other" who threatens our freedom. Disputes with this Sartrean philosophical complex, I note, become a fulcrum of Mexican existentialism. Objectifying, essentializing, and belittling the crusader Johnny, Bruno strives to reduce him to a thing, the Sartrean "in-itself." Bruno's misprisions betray the heart of Johnny's pursuit, his struggles to remain authentic, "faithful unto death" (as one of the novel's epigraphs declares) to his quest. Johnny's authenticity, grotesquely troped in the saliva that runs out of his mouth when he talks and plays the sax, is a nausea that the jazzman confronts, expels, rejects.

Conspicuously stocked with Sartrean moves as it is, "El perseguidor" does bring another existential interlocutor into the conversation. Cortázar's discovery of his "neighbor" also involved a gravitation towards the Algerian Camus, whose affirmative, non-nihilistic attitudes the Argentine author praised. Camus, Cortázar writes in his 1950 essay "Situación de la novela," "progresses from proud negation to confrontation and ultimately to connection" (*Obra crítica* 285). Cortázar threads "El perseguidor" with nods to Camus, from the Arab neighborhood where Johnny lives, setting of his and Bruno's final showdown, to descriptions of Johnny as plague-ridden.[19] More momentously, Cortázar associates his tragic hero with that of Camus, Sisyphus. In Bruno's estimation: "the efforts Johnny has made to change his life, from his failed suicide attempt to using marijuana, are what one would expect from someone as lacking in greatness as he. I think I admire him all the more for that, because he's really the chimpanzee who wants to learn to read, a poor guy who hits his head against the wall, isn't convinced, and *starts all over again*" (252; emphasis added). As usual, Bruno resists Johnny's greatness. The paradox that is Johnny—nearly divine/agonizingly human—lies outside the binary categories of the ultra-logical jazz critic, so Bruno not only objectifies but also animalizes and infantilizes Johnny. Bruno's jaundiced perspective aside, the quote evokes Camus's rendition of Sisyphus. Camus refashions the classical Sisyphus who each day hauled a boulder up the mountain, only to fall back to its bottom and start over again, into an emblem of a conscious revolt against absurdity. In consciousness, Camus's Sisyphus accepts his travails, knowing "the whole extent of his wretched condition" (*Myth* 591). "This universe henceforth without a master seems to him neither sterile nor futile . . . . One must imagine Sisyphus happy" (593). The French existentialist's Sisyphus chooses to live, with passion and joy, in a godless world.

What, then, is the Sisyphean condition of Cortázar's Johnny? Simply put, Johnny plays his music and makes his God ("Perseguidor" 264)—evanescently. His music hurls Johnny into a sublime, hyper-authentic state, which evaporates when he ceases to play. Thereafter, Johnny lands back in a world of complacent reason that he singlehandedly labors to redeem from bad faith. Described as hauling a boulder (or a cross), constantly gesturing into the air, Johnny has assumed a Sisyphean mission. However, unlike Camus's hero, *Johnny is not happy*. Camus writes: "From the moment absurdity is recognized, it becomes a passion, the most harrowing of all. But whether or not one can live with one's passions, whether or not one can accept their law, which is to burn the heart they simultaneously exalt—that is the whole question" (*Myth* 510). Johnny lives in the shadow of just that question and, sadly, collapses under the burden of his Sisyphean task. His lonely battle with time and inauthenticity kills the jazzman, who drinks and drugs himself to death. Johnny wants to be saved from his becoming, Christ-like vocation, and misery. Hence the other epigraph to the novella, "Oh make me a mask," with its evocations of Wormwood from Revelation 8:10–11, which reads: "And the third angel sounded, and there fell a great star from heaven, burning as it were a lamp, and it fell upon the third part of the rivers, and upon the fountains of waters. And the name of the star is called Wormwood: and the third part of the waters became wormwood; and many men died of the waters, because they were made bitter" (*Bible*). Johnny, both biblically inflected and a living personification of the absurd ("un absurdo viviente"; "Perseguidor" 249), is that star. He crashes and burns. A Sisyphean martyr, Johnny is heroic and authentic but not happy.

Johnny's sorry state leads us to the unfortunate critical state of affairs I mentioned at the outset of this chapter and, as we will see in a minute, may well explain it. Namely, that despite the abundant possibilities built into Latin American existentialist literature, the body of works has not received its due. Displaced by Magical Realism, the Boom, and the Post-Boom, existentialist fiction appears predominantly to have been edged off the critical map. Canonical writers aligned with Latin American existentialism, obviously, still garner attention. Nevertheless, scholarship tends to absorb them into the rubrics just listed, or into feminism, identity politics, or politics per se. The big-picture story of Latin American literary existentialism, I repeat, has mainly gone untold. While some articles do address the existentialist dimensions of specific texts, as far as I can tell attempts to consolidate and elucidate the field per se stalled after the 1970s, years that witnessed two book-length, albeit limited, studies, *An Existential Focus on Some Novels of the River Plate* by Rose Lee Hayden (1973) and *Three Authors of Alienation: Bombal, Onetti, Carpentier* by Michael Ian Adams (1975).[20] The latter book's foregrounding of alienation returns us to Cortázar's Johnny. Lonely and undone, the character points to a likely explanation for the genre's relative neglect: a widespread tendency to equate existentialism with alienation and negativity, which has produced a disheartening literature eminently capable of alienating the reader.

The negativity of "El perseguidor," tempered by the grandeur of Johnny's quest, pales in comparison to that of other signature South American existentialist texts. Utterly engulfed in doom and gloom, the human adventures they portray resound with the sense of abandonment that Sartre extracts from Dostoevsky's *The Brothers Karamazov* (1879): "Dostoevsky once wrote: 'If God does not exist, everything is permissible.' This is the starting point of existentialism. Indeed, everything is permissible if God does not exist, and man is consequently abandoned, for he cannot find anything to rely on—neither within nor without" (*Existentialism Is a Humanism* 28–29). The propensity to dramatize imprisonment in a no-exit, no-answer state of forlornness permeates Latin American existentialist fiction, dragging it down and sometimes justifiably out of sight.

In that regard Mallea's existentialist fiction serves up a curious object lesson. An editor of the Buenos Aires literary supplement to the newspaper *La Nación* from 1931 to 1955 who exercised a "benevolent dictatorship on Argentine literature" (Rodríguez Monegal, *Narradores* 251), Mallea was more lionized in his time than Borges himself. Yet, as the Modern Language Association International Bibliography attests, Mallea has by now to a considerable degree faded from view. And not, one might reckon, unfairly. His monotonous, exorbitant novels (*Simbad*, for instance, runs to 750 pages), with their endless indictments of alienation from a mechanistic Buenos Aires and anguished protagonists incapable of escaping inauthenticity and solitude, steep their readers in despondency. Perhaps enticing because innovative when first introduced, Mallea's dismal narrative has not stood the test of time and may have given existentialist fiction a bad name.

Two urban South American existentialist novels that have justifiably retained their currency nonetheless so brutalize the reader's sensibility as to render the texts ineluctably abhorrent. Fueled by Dostoevsky's prototypical existentialist novel *Notes from Underground* (1864), the texts showcase deracinated individuals whose futile struggles with an absurd world reap heinous violence. Eladio Linacero of Onetti's novella *El pozo* [The Well] (1939) carries Dostoevsky's underground man to a shocking extreme. As an adolescent, Linacero convinces the innocent young Ana María to enter a gardener's hut, musing that if she had not entered it "I would have to love her for the rest of my life" (12). Then, pinning Ana María down, twisting her breasts, and seeking the most odious caress (12), Linacero hideously violates her. This episode of appalling sexual and textual depravity marks the character's vacating of ideals and absolutes, a dislocation that effectively rebirths Lin-*acero* into a *cero*, a zero. Ana María dies shortly afterwards, but Linacero lives on in forlornness, unable to fill the void with a meaningful existence and shackled to a wretched urban reality he cannot transcend. For its part,

Ernesto Sábato's harrowingly similar novel *El túnel* (1948) perpetuates *El pozo*'s scapegoating of the woman (both novels tellingly name her María), in whom male antiheroes impossibly seek respite from ontological insecurity. *El túnel* locates the alienated underground man in Buenos Aires and afflicts him with the Sartrean malady of objectifying the other, exacerbated into a lethal poison. The novel's sadomasochistic protagonist Juan Pablo Castel subjects his lover to the abuse that tragically culminates in her murder and his imprisonment, literal and figurative.

Such doom and gloom texts rife with disincentives can thwart the most compelling vindications of Latin American existentialist literature. It would be as abusive as the texts themselves to downplay the violence that the two authors wreak on their female characters. The drives of Latin American existentialism, though, prompt us not to dismiss out of hand even thoroughly repugnant texts—because they may have a different story to tell, one that participates in the theater of values discussed above. And that, I would argue and will illustrate, turns out to be the case for Latin American existentialist literature. When we attempt to tease a value-rich story out of Onetti and Sábato's novels, as well as the preponderance of Latin American existentialist literary texts, they yield pleas for *emotion and community*. In other words, an antipositivist privileging of feeling over reasoning and an appeal to a transvaluated Golden Rule, which "El perseguidor" has already evinced, pervade works by leading writers. Writers of tremendously varied persuasions working from diverse templates, they militate for the same two incentivizing values.

Revisited as players in a theater of values, Sábato's *El túnel* and Onetti's *El pozo* shape shift arrestingly. Their characters' dire perversion resonates with that of Dostoevsky's patently flawed underground man and demands to be construed as ironic. Read in the supple mode they betoken, the two River Plate novels gesture fervently to love and human solidarity, loudly berated as goals not achieved. Sábato's novel, a melodramatic gloss of Onetti's short but highly cryptic text, voices their shared message at its start. Castel announces that he recounts his crime from his jail cell in a last-ditch petition to humankind for understanding: "I'm moved by the faint hope that someone will understand me, EVEN IF ONLY ONE PERSON" (12). Authentic ties with others have heretofore eluded him for reasons that his ensuing confession thunderously exposes. A Castel incapable of dealing with emotion, we learn, has unshakably resorted to logic in the bad faith effort to rationalize his feelings and subjugate the threatening chaos of love. Foreclosing love and breeding a crime of passion, his logic has ravaged human ties. It is hard to imagine a more scathing denunciation of reason.

El túnel's predecessor, *El pozo*, orchestrates the problematic of emotion and community by focusing ways *out* of the underground, the trifecta of writing, love, and communication. Linacero proposes to write the story of a soul (9), a narrative based not on facts but on feelings and dreams, because facts "are always empty, they are receptacles that will take the shape of the emotions that fill them" (29). Unable to implement this new poetics of the emotions, his account ends up mired in events, reduced to narrating failed loves and failed acts of communication. Linacero's exposition of his unsuccessful attempts to communicate with the prostitute Ester and the poet Cordes, significantly enough, occupies over half the novella. Meanwhile, the text floats the hope of overcoming alienation through communitarian efforts in the person of the Marxist Lázaro (i.e., Lazarus), an activist whom Linacero grudgingly acknowledges as a superior human being (44). That Lázaro, together with Linacero's other two interlocutors, brand him a failure gives rise to the exquisite images of night overpowering the protagonist that close the text.[21] Leaving the poignancy of Linacero's defeat engraved on the reader's mind, they unmask the magnitude of his loss, the irony latent in his apparent resignation to it.

Socratic irony, Kierkegaard observes, can follow two protocols. One "can ask without any interest in the answer except to suck out the apparent content by means of the question and thereby to leave an emptiness behind." Or, "one can ask with the intention of receiving an answer containing the desired fullness" (*Concept of Irony* 36). Onetti and Sábato's ironic texts clearly opt for a fullness that bespeaks desired values. The values at stake, it is important to register, need not always find expression in irony or in doom and gloom. Those who identify existentialism with unrelenting horrorscapes need only look, for example, to the Brazilian João Guimarães Rosa.

Guimarães Rosa envelops the eccentric new saints of *Primeiras estórias* in a buoyant, positive aura. Literalizing the existentialist absurd, Guimarães Rosa mounts comic spectacles that glorify madmen, the antithesis of reason. The hero of "Tantarum, My Boss," reminiscent of Don Quixote, jubilantly roars through the countryside on an ostensible expedition of madness and death. The nameless protagonist of "Much Ado" climbs a palm tree at the hub of a public square. There he performs a metaphysical burlesque, stripping naked and shouting wild pseudo-Nietzschean aphorisms. Nevertheless, both he and Tantarum deviate from Nietzsche's superman, for the two heroes advocate not elitism but community. Society pursues these madmen, who, imbued with the courage Guimarães Rosa reveres, pursue society right back.

Mesmerizing, they entice the masses, win disciples, and grow community along with their selves. When the flailing protagonist of "Much Ado" loses courage and potency, the furor of the masses revives him; Tantarum's antic marauding ends in a Last Supper, a communal celebration of life that is a fitting last act for the life of the saintly protagonist. Guimarães Rosa, in sum, lets us picture Sisyphus happy *and* ensconced in a Latin American value system.

Mexican Platforms

Mexico's lived context of concern, its Dasein, propels the country into the electric arena for value formation, existential philosophy, and existentialist literature to which the rest of my book attends. The staggering dislocations and transformations Mexico underwent in the twentieth century occasioned rigorous self-examination, *prises de conscience* that furnished an especially auspicious climate for existentialism. As Mexico's proliferating limit situations, testing grounds for authenticity, gear existentialism's enabling positives to local agendas, they accomplish what Camus requires of absurd creation: "I ask of absurd creation what I required from thought—revolt, freedom, and diversity" (*Myth* 587).

Revolt, freedom, and diversity flow from twentieth-century Mexico's unique historical circumstances, a motor of all the texts we will consider. All the texts site themselves in a panorama that has its own rhythms, its own pressure points. And the dynamics of the panorama, as our works articulate them, invariably launch from a ground zero, the Mexican Revolution (1910–1920). According to conventional wisdom, the Mexican Revolution awakened a sleeping giant. A Mexico splintered into regions, classes, ethnicities, and ideologies came together to overthrow Porfirio Díaz's dictatorship. This the Revolution unquestionably accomplished, in tandem with mobilizing social reform. Notoriously chaotic, awash in bloodshed and factionalism, the Revolution did not in any case master or slake the forces it had released—an unfinished business that fell to subsequent regimes. Mexican scholar Ana Santos Ruiz well expresses what innumerable others have concluded: the Mexican Revolution "was a disruptive, chaotic, and violent event, which only later was apprehended, delimited, and parsed into phases, with the aim of making it intelligible, neutralizing its unrestrained violence, and constituting a new social pact" (426). Then and now Mexican rulers invoke the originary moment of the Revolution, construe it by their lights, and claim finally to realize its goals. The colossus lives on under the guise of what officials tend to vaunt, propagandistically, as a permanent revolution (Hurtado, "Dos mitos" 275).

President Plutarco Elías Calles's administration (1924–1928) arguably enacted the first monumental recycling of the Revolution. With the alleged intent of continuing the Revolution while restoring law and order, Calles egregiously broke faith with the 1910 insurrection. His administration slacked off redistribution of land to peasants, suppressed labor movements, and encouraged foreign investment. Further, instead of restoring stability, Calles rekindled chaos. Attempting to limit the power of the Church, he sparked the bloody Cristero Wars (1926–1929) that reaped some 90,000 casualties. Outlawed by the zealously anticlerical president, defended with bloody fanaticism by its adherents, the Church suffered devastation on every side. At the end of the Cristero Wars and his formal regime, ostensibly to unite the divergent sectors of the Revolution, Calles institutionalized it. He established the PNR, the Partido Nacional Revolucionario [National Revolutionary Party], forerunner of the PRI, the Partido Revolucionario Institucional [Institutional Revolutionary Party] that maintained a hegemony over Mexican politics until 2000. The PNR then became a weapon for the shadow regime Calles implemented through his handpicked successors. True to the letter of the law prohibiting reelection but not to its spirit, in the era now known as the "Maximato," "Jefe Máximo," or Supreme Chief, Calles stealthily controlled Mexico behind a series of puppet leaders who generally did his bidding: presidents Emilio Portes Gil (1928–1930), Pascual Ortiz Rubio (1930–1932), and Abelardo Rodríguez (1932–1934).

President Lázaro Cárdenas assumed office in December of 1934 and at long last shut down the Maximato. In June of 1935 Cárdenas reorganized his cabinet, purging it of Calles loyalists. He dispatched Calles to exile in 1936. The strongly left-leaning Cárdenas went on to institute sweeping changes that honored the reformist objectives of the Revolution. He distributed more land than all of his predecessors combined and organized much of the redistributed land into collective agricultural *ejidos* that paralleled Indigenous agrarian structures. To aid the Indigenous peoples, Cárdenas founded the Departamento de Asuntos Indígenas [Department of Indigenous Affairs] and vocational schools. Mexico was to be for Mexicans, so he took the bold step against imperialism of nationalizing the foreign-owned oil industry in 1938. Cárdenas similarly supported organized labor and revamped Calles's PNR into the PRM (Partido de la Revolución Mexicana [Party of the

Mexican Revolution]), which made ample provision for labor and peasant confederations. Tzvi Medin's influential *Ideología y praxis política de Lázaro Cárdenas* stresses that Cárdenas's government recovered the Revolution for the classes the war had ideally aimed to serve; his regime was a time of copious promise. However, Medin concedes that the end of the Cárdenas sexennium dashed some hopes it had bred. On a number of occasions after 1938 Cárdenas veered to the right and clashed head-on with labor syndicates (see Medin, *Ideología*, ch. 9; Negrín, ch. 4).

Diminished at the end of his administration, Cárdenas's program still supplied the next two presidents, Manuel Ávila Camacho (1940–1946) and Miguel Alemán Valdés (1946–1952), with a lightning rod in contrast to which they would define their regimes. The radical Cárdenas gave way to the moderate Ávila Camacho, who directed his efforts at abating the polarizations the previous regime had engendered. Alemán picked up Ávila Camacho's campaign for national unity and worked it into a wide-ranging new "revolution" that utterly recast both the original one and that of Cárdenas. "Mexico," said Alemán, "has had its revolution," so new ones must replace it (qtd. in Alexander 5). In stream with that notion, Alemán undertook to erect a modern Mexico predicated on industry, commerce, and consumerism. Tight government control of the economy and labor unions, import substitution industrialization, foreign investment in Mexico, and revitalizing cities formed the cornerstones of the economic miracle Alemán sought to engineer. Literally towering accomplishments such as the construction of high-rise tourist hotels and the Universidad Nacional Autónoma de México (UNAM) campus accrued from Alemán's strategy, as did a new brand of nationalism, the *Mexicanidad* that my next chapter treats.

Alemán's modernizing yet at heart conservative revolution achieved many of its successes at the expense of the social reforms that the original Revolution had instigated. As eminent Mexican economist Jesús Silva Herzog put it in 1949, Alemanismo amounted to the "death knell of our last great social movement" (qtd. in Martínez 36). Alemán having chosen growth over the equitable distribution of wealth (Alexander 80), the prominence that Cárdenas had once accorded to the redistribution of land and the agricultural collectives ceded to the backing of lucrative private property, a *neolatifundismo*. Likewise, rather than on the rural peasantry and the poor, the mid-century economic miracle concentrated on the urban middle class. An upwardly mobile middle class held tremendous potential for the consumerism that had fortified the US and could do the same for Mexico.

Alemán thus elevated the middle class previously seen as reactionary, tacitly appointing it the new revolutionary sector (Santos Ruiz 263). Yet in his *Las batallas en el desierto*, a 1981 novella that takes place during the Alemán era, the clear-sighted José Emilio Pacheco pronounces judgment on the affluent society this third major avatar of the Revolution vowed to deliver. According to *Las batallas*, for ordinary Mexicans Alemán's utopian plan had devolved into inflation, crime, destitution, corruption, "the unbounded enrichment of a few and the misery of almost everyone" (11), and a flood of foreign products intended to "whiten Mexicans' tastes" (12).

The Mexican literature created in the actual throes of the post-Revolutionary period—Calles's through Alemán's presidencies—trains an equally clear-sighted eye on the Revolution and its metamorphoses. Mariano Azuela's classic *Los de abajo. Novela de la Revolución Mexicana* [The Underdogs. Novel of the Mexican Revolution] (1915) empowered fiction to critique the Revolution, a job that literati have avidly shouldered. From Martín Luis Guzman's novelistic exposé of Calles, *La sombra del caudillo* [The Shadow of the Strongman] (1929), to Carlos Fuentes's expansive denunciation of the Revolution's aftermath, *La muerte de Artemio Cruz* [The Death of Artemio Cruz] (1962), and beyond, countless literary works deplore the unfulfilled promise of the movement, hoping to impact the insidious permanent revolution.[22] It follows that post-Revolutionary literature would not lack doom and gloom, that grim scenarios would not pertain solely to existentialism but also accord with the tenor of the communal Mexican situation.

To wit, Agustín Yáñez's landmark novel *Al filo del agua* [The Edge of the Storm] (1947) swathes in darkness its contemplation of pre-Revolutionary Mexico from a post-Revolutionary outlook. At the leading edge of the modern Mexican novel thanks to its marriage of avant-garde literary techniques and a sociohistorical impetus, the noir *Al filo* cries out for modernity itself. Yáñez ascribes Mexico's deferred entrance into modernity to the hidebound religion that imprisons his compatriots, a dogmatic piety that throttles the life spirit. The dystopian *Al filo* transpires between 1909 and 1910 in a small, virtually medieval town in Jalisco. Crushing free will, the town's fanatical religious zeal has suffused it with repression, hatred, and insanity. When winds of change—Liberalism, Spiritism, Socialism, Freemasonry—begin to encroach on Jalisco, they make minimal inroads into the hermetically sealed preserve. The Revolution, too, finally arrives, albeit to the same effect. Displaying the lawlessness and untrammeled violence to which *Los de abajo* gave voice, the Revolution that appears in *Al filo del agua* is a necessarily savage, cathartic stage in an evolving process.[23]

A Latin American Existentialist Ethos: Modern Mexican Literature and Philosophy

The life-denying Catholicism of Yáñez's apocalyptic novel throws into relief the need for the life-affirming stance that existentialism, even when projected through a glass darkly, can offer Mexico. To unfold what existentialism opened to Mexico and how Mexican thinkers availed themselves of it is precisely the aim of my book. I have also had keenly in mind the neglect of Latin American existentialist literature, lamentable for the reasons that preceding pages have laid out. Aligned, these two drivers resulted in the parameters I have brought to bear on the literary territory of *A Latin American Existentialist Ethos: Modern Mexican Literature and Philosophy*.

The book assembles what I like to think of as a *portable* version of Mexican existentialist literature. Portability here does not imply collapsibility, the loss of cultural specificity. Rather, it implies mobility: transporting cultural phenomena from one place to another and finding an apt means of doing so. With regard to the project upon us, "portable" reflects my desire to encourage the study and teaching of existentialist literature, not just by Spanish-speakers but also by English-speakers. That desire has materialized into the criteria for the literature to be treated here (the fact that relatively few philosophical texts have been translated precludes application of the criteria to them). I have focused on premier twentieth-century Mexican authors one or more of whose works have been translated into English; each chapter is anchored in a translated text and fans out to others, translated or not, that illuminate it. For the sake of intercultural portability, I have also chosen to focus on teachable texts, that is, relatively short works, manageable for students. Yes, the criteria constrain—they certainly do not make for a literary history of Mexican existentialist works—but I believe they allow us to probe crucial developments in and faces of modern Mexican existentialist literature. I look forward to seeing other scholars fill in the literary historical blanks.[24]

Coming pages, then, delve into works by Rodolfo Usigli (1905–1979), Juan Rulfo (1917–1986), José Revueltas (1914–1976), and Rosario Castellanos (1925–1974). While the inclusion of Usigli and Rulfo in the ranks of existentialist writers will likely surprise the reader, some bemusement is perhaps expectable given the relative neglect of existentialism. We are typically not accustomed to reading these authors through an existentialist lens, an enterprise that can yield fresh perspectives on their storied texts. In any event, by no means are Usigli and Rulfo, or the other authors discussed herein, *only* existentialists. They do, on my readings, inscribe their works in existential lines or coincide with those lines, but neither they (I presume) nor I would define them solely as existentialists. Just the opposite: Usigli, Rulfo, Revueltas, and Castellanos extend their sights to an array of matters as diverse as the Mexican arena itself, indeed to the matters most alive in their situations. That each of our authors orchestrates a particular center of gravity, vitalized by a particular configuration of existentialism, renders Mexican existentialist literature an always shifting, always revealing adventure.

Withal, the existentialist authors at issue exhibit striking commonalities. Voracious, encyclopedic readers, they wield heterogeneous domains of knowledge. Matching European existentialists, they propagate their ideas in fiction and in essays, sometimes reams of them (hence the weighty role that essays play in my analyses). Activist writers, none of the Mexican authors believes that the Revolution accomplished its goals. Castellanos laments: "No, it all came down to a mere catharsis for the outcasts who, exhausted into inertia, only left ruins and desolation, mourning and sadness" (*Juicios sumarios*, in *Obras II* 504). As Castellanos implies and as one might expect from the vicissitudes of the Mexican situation, dark scenarios abound in their works. Activists goaded by defaults on the Revolution, the authors are drawn to Cárdenas and, in terms of Usigli and Revueltas, to Marxism. Marxist or not, they agitate for radical causes and embrace iconoclasm. Existentialist literature's oft-decried predilection for matters shocking and unpalatable helps license Mexican authors to air in the public forum controversial subjects such as feminism, homosexuality, and rape.

Usigli, Rulfo, Revueltas, and Castellanos also dialogued with one another. As well-informed Mexican intellectuals, the later authors read the earlier ones, commented on them in essays, and mounted intertextual discussions with them in their literary works. Members of interlocking cultural circles, they met in person. The personal contact that seemingly disparate authors whose writing lives peaked at different times enjoyed further catalyzed transactions between their works. For instance, Castellanos, whose feminism left her something of an outlier to the male group, studied with Usigli in 1954 (Seale Vásquez 33). She and Rulfo spent 1954–1955 at the the official hub for writers, the Centro Mexicano de Escitores, in the same cohort of fellowship recipients (Schwartz 60). Moreover, all of our authors had commerce, both personal and intellectual, with Octavio Paz, author of the luminous treatise on Mexican identity, *El laberinto de la soledad* [The Labyrinth of Solitude] (1950).

This fact introduces the overriding dimension of the four authors' shared imaginary along with one of their overriding interventions in the collective conversation: a profound investment in Mexican identity. Committed writers, they leveraged literature and essays to make their mark on the Mexican identity discourse that had proliferated long before Paz's *Laberinto*. "I have always wondered," says Carlos Fuentes, "if any other country has been as preoccupied with its national identity as ours has" (*Tiempo mexicano* 62). Why national identity has such surpassing relevance to and currency in Mexico finds ready explanations. A history of colonialism compounded by proximity to the US, a more exigent scare figure for Mexico than for Rodó's Uruguay, always already threw Mexican identity into question. The Mexican Revolution intensified the preoccupation. The first of its kind in post-Independence Latin America, the Revolution had cast the eyes of the world on Mexico and the eyes of Mexico on itself. Accompanied by the burst of nationalism that immediately produced Manuel Gamio's *Forjando patria (pro-nacionalismo)* [Forging a Homeland (Pro-nationalism)] (1916), the Revolution ignited Mexican identity discourse. Mexican intellectuals, notes Henry Schmidt, so closely yoked *lo mexicano*—"Mexicanness"—to the Revolution that two were "virtually synonymous" (67).[25] The political and social turmoil that succeeded the Revolution added fuel to the fire. Absorbing a panoply of disciplines, the quest to locate the differentia specifica of lo mexicano had itself by the time Paz wrote *Laberinto* burgeoned into a defining aspect of Mexican thought.

Importantly, the polemics of lo mexicano do not, as one might expect from them, first and foremost celebrate Mexico. In the main they eschew predictable nationalistic apologetics. The polemicists write otherwise, with the cardinal objective of diagnosing their country's ills. As distinct from the triumphalist foundational discourse of the US (e.g., the self-made man, American exceptionalism), that of lo mexicano labors to ferret out the nation's problems and failures. It is a practical, therapeutic instrument bent on diagnosing maladies in order to remedy them. The monumentalizing of failures in the name of self-knowledge and self-healing, however, can implode. A "cage of melancholy," to use Roger Bartra's pungent epithet, the anatomizing of the Mexican dwells vigorously, sometimes exclusively, on negatives; fixated on inadequacies, the discourse of lo mexicano can end up pathologizing its subjects. Whether, as Bartra's book of the same title would have it, complicit with a hegemonic State that blazons its ability to remedy the deficiencies the texts expediently broadcast, or emanating from autonomous critical voices, Mexican identity discourse performs a strategic, strategically melancholy, essentializing. An "artificial entelechy" (Bartra 17), in net effect it leaves Mexican identity predicated on nonidentity, that is, on neuroses and the instabilities that elicited them.[26] Down the line we will see Mexican philosopher Emilio Uranga magnify an unstable, precarious identity into an emblem of the non-Western condition.

Amid the riot of Mexican identity discourse, two texts have special status for our purposes and in general. Both of them anatomize the Mexican in would-be therapeutic, pathologizing terms, and both of them have incited controversy. The first milestone identity text is Samuel Ramos's *El perfil del hombre y la cultura en México* [Profile of Man and Culture in Mexico] (1934), "an essay on characterology and the philosophy of culture" (10). Ramos wrote *Perfil* at the close of Calles's Maximato, an era in which according to Mexican philosopher Leopoldo Zea "all the defects and qualities of the Mexican became apparent" (*Conciencia* 38). *Perfil* gleans its hallmark of Mexican (non)identity, the inferiority complex, from Alfred Adler's psychoanalytical *The Neurotic Constitution* (1921). In Ramos's words: "Psychoanalysis allows us to unearth dark forces from the Mexican soul that, disguised as aspirations towards lofty goals, in reality work to debase the individual" (*Perfil* 16). Whereas Adler views the inferiority complex as originating in individual childhood trauma, Ramos attributes its Mexican incarnation to colonialism. Spanish domination, he argues, foisted Mexicans into the position of children in thrall to superior foreign parents, an orientation not fully abandoned after Independence. Up to his time, Ramos avers, Mexicans have measured their achievements by European, rather than Mexican, standards and have found themselves lacking. *Perfil*'s fabled chapter "Psicoanálisis del mexicano" tenders the lower-class, urban, male *pelado* as the quintessence of the ongoing pathology. The pelado displays a number of traits related to an inferiority complex: verbal braggadocio, overwrought machismo, jealously guarded self-protection, and a defensiveness that easily explodes into violence.

Ramos, in sum, deals Mexican identity a series of harsh blows. He mitigates them by assuring his fellow Mexicans that they are not innately or truly inferior. They just need to take cognizance of their own potential and have the courage to be themselves. These caveats notwithstanding, *Perfil* incurred criticism so severe that its author ceased publishing for several years (Leidenberger 231).

In 1950, writing from Paris, Octavio Paz entered the fray of identity diagnostics with *El laberinto de la soledad*. Paz awaited the Mexican reception of his work with bated breath (Santí 45), and well he might have for many reasons, including the intimate relationship between *Laberinto* and the controversial *Perfil*. Intent, like Ramos, on rooting out the tensions and repressions that have contorted Mexican identity, Paz psychoanalyzes "the" Mexican. As does *Perfil*, *Laberinto* unravels the pathologies of Mexicans consigned by their colonial past to defensive postures. *Perfil*'s flamboyant urban pelado morphs into *Laberinto*'s inner-city Mexican-American *pachuco*, who manifests the fractured identity that, for Paz, haunts both Mexico and Greater Mexico. Paz's heavy debt to Ramos was not lost on Mexican intellectuals of the time. Judging that *Laberinto* insufficiently acknowledges its kinship to *Perfil*, several parties accused Paz of plagiarism.[27] Confessedly or not an archive of sorts, *Laberinto* also evinces traces of Ortega y Gasset's 1929 work on Argentinians' surrender to masks ("La pampa . . . promesas"), the discussions of masks in Mexican José Fuentes Mares's *México en la hispanidad* (1940) and in Ramos's *Hacia un nuevo humanismo* [Towards a New Humanism] (1940), and of the inferiority complex in Argentine Ezequiel Martínez Estrada's renowned *Radiografía de la pampa* [X-ray of the Pampas] (1933). Bartra aptly observes that *Laberinto* "collects the ideas of all its predecessors" (20).

Yet *Laberinto*—an act of postcolonial mourning and melancholia, conceivably recirculating others' ideas and certainly derivative of the thorny *Perfil*—has ascended into iconicity. Over a million copies of *Laberinto* have sold in Spanish alone, and the text continues to provoke heated debates (Hurtado, "Octavio Paz" 239). At least internationally *Laberinto* has coalesced into the face of Mexican identity discourse, "possibly the book about Mexico that is most taught elsewhere" (Sánchez Prado, *Naciones* 239), "a kind of Baedeker guide to the spirit of the nation" (Hurtado, "Dos mitos" 269). Christopher Domínguez Michael, author of *Octavio Paz en su siglo* [Octavio Paz in His Century], partially credits *Laberinto*'s "preeminence among Spanish-American works that interrogate national characteristics" to Paz having surpassed his predecessors "*as a writer*" (168; emphasis added). As Domínguez Michael suggests, in *Laberinto* Paz marshals his poetic talents and fashions his arguments with consummate eloquence, which endows the essay with transcendent suasion.

We will repeatedly visit *Laberinto*, a touchstone for the authors under study, and in so doing both compound and complicate the book's iconic status. At this entry point, a sketch of the premises that have garnered such outsize mimetic capital is in order. *Laberinto* represents Mexicans as shaped by a history of subjugation, victimization, and violence. Paz derives a paradigm for the Mexico thus historically conditioned from a sexualized reading of the Conquest. *Laberinto*'s paradigm hinges on Malinalli (aka Doña Marina/La Malinche), Hernán Cortés's Indigenous translator and the consort whom he threw over for a Spanish wife. Paz infamously baptizes Malinalli "la Chingada" [roughly, She who has been screwed over] and Mexicans from the Conquest on, "children of la Chingada." Violated and orphaned, Paz holds, Mexicans retreat into solitude. They camouflage themselves with masks of conformity, forms "we have neither created nor endured, masks" (*Labyrinth* 34; *Laberinto* 170), which hide their true being, obstruct true intersubjectivity.

Whence the fundamental dialectic that *Laberinto* plays out in terms of both history and *mentalités*: "In a certain sense the history of Mexico, like that of every Mexican, is a struggle between the forms and formulas that have been imposed on us and the explosions with which our spontaneity avenges itself" (*33*; 168). Specifically, Mexicans only accede to spontaneity and remove their masks in privileged historical moments like the Revolution (an "authentic revelation of our true nature" [*135*; 279–80] after a long romance with positivism) and more routinely in the communal fiestas that restore an "original state of formless and normless freedom" (*53*; 188). According to Paz: "If in our daily lives we hide ourselves, we discharge ourselves in the whirlwind of the fiesta" (*53*; 188). A purging of tensions, fiestas are the counterweight to a pathologized modus vivendi and arguably somewhat pathological unto themselves, because, as Paz concludes, Mexicans have not discovered the Form that would reconcile freedom with order (340), solitude with communion and community.[28]

Lo mexicano, write Carlos Alberto Sánchez and Robert Eli Sanchez in their introduction to the Oxford University Press *Mexican Philosophy in the 20th Century: Essential Readings* (2017), "is perhaps the most controversial notion in 20th-century Mexican philosophy" (xxxiv). Between Ramos's *Perfil* and Paz's *Laberinto*, the Mexican existentialist *Grupo Hiperión*, active from 1948–1952, cuts into the debate and cuts the wide swath on its home scene that my study for the first time tracks from philosophy to the *literature* written in Hiperión's orbit.[29] Guillermo Hurtado, an outstanding exegete of Hiperión, tells us that the group aspired to "do philosophy in original and authentic ways, as Mexican existentialists" whose object of study was neither humans in the abstract nor Europeans but Mexicans themselves ("Introducción" xii). Hiperión's principal members were Ricardo Guerra (1927–2007), Jorge Portilla (1918–1963), Salvador Reyes Nevares (1922–1993), Joaquín Sánchez MacGrégor (1922–2008), Emilio Uranga (1921–1988), Luis Villoro (1922–2014), and Leopoldo Zea (1912–2004), the group's chief organizer and promoter. The Hyperions disseminated their reflections on lo mexicano in a barrage of lectures and articles that made their way into distinguished periodicals and books, such as the influential book series "México y lo Mexicano" that Zea founded.

Young mavericks, the Hyperions particularly—but far from exclusively—conscripted for their meditations on lo mexicano the newest-wave existentialism, Sartre's. What happens to Sartre's European existentialism when appropriated by the periphery and put to work for Mexican identity by philosophy and fiction is a gripping transformation that my book seeks to elucidate.[30] *Chapter 2*, "The Mexican Existentialist Ethos," walks into the transformation as it obtained in philosophy. Scrutinizing the Grupo Hiperión, the chapter argues that Mexican identity issues dispose its constituents towards *ethics*, which impels them to supplement early Sartrean existentialism. Like that of Simone de Beauvoir, but in the Mexican domain flowing from Mexican philosopher Antonio Caso (1883–1946), Hiperión's existentialism leans into altruism, intersubjectivity, and community. Altogether, chapter 2 frames a broader than usual, more Mexican genealogy for Mexican existentialist philosophy, a literally generous constellation of concerns.[31]

This constellation of concerns asserts itself in the inaugural stirrings of Mexican existentialist literature, which I locate in Rodolfo Usigli's polemical play *El gesticulador* [The Gesticulator] (written in 1938, debuted in 1947), a linchpin of modern Mexican theater. Let me pause here to mention one last aspect of my modus operandi. After chapter 2, I generally work with the philosophers whom the literary authors themselves cite and attempt to read philosophy as the creative writers presumably did. That is, *not* (with the exception of Rosario Castellanos) as professional philosophers who dedicate their lives to puzzling through the intricacies of existential philosophy per se, but as writers who essentially filter it through their own prism. Consequently, *chapter 3*, "The Seminal Mexican Existentialism of Rodolfo Usigli's Theater," looks at how Usigli wraps both his pre-Sartrean existentialists of choice and the pragmatism circulating in his environment into a interrogation of absolute truth, expressly as it relates to post-Revolution Mexican politics. Usigli's political thinking, which the chapter traces through his essays and early plays, leads him to reimagine Calles's disingenuous "Revolutionary Family" propaganda campaign correctively and existentially. Though laced with the equivocations that distinguish Usigli's provocative stagecraft, *El gesticulador* campaigns for community, altruism, and a supple authenticity suited to a post-factual political climate. Both impulses—undecidability and a salutary ethos—reemerge in Hiperión Uranga's vision of Mexican identity.

Chapter 4, "Excavating Comala: The Existentialist Juan Rulfo, the Grupo Hiperión, and *Lo Mexicano* in *Pedro Páramo* (1955)," as its title indicates, takes us into the mid-twentieth-century literature that coexisted with Hiperión. Uranga once declared that Hiperión's mission resounded "throughout Mexican culture, feeding the theories and perspectives of philologists, literary critics, historians, poets, novelists, painters, etc." (*Análisis* 64). Rulfo's novel *Pedro Páramo*, like other texts I examine, corroborates Uranga's claim. Therefore, while *Pedro Páramo*'s dialogue with Paz's existentially inflected *Laberinto* comes into the mix, chapter 4 unearths other existentialist pulsations of Rulfo's masterpiece. These include Zea's picture of Mexican history as haunted by an unresolved past and especially Villoro's *Los grandes momentos del indigenismo en México* [Major Moments of Indigenism in Mexico] (1950), a passport to the novel's racial politics. In the air, if not, as is impossible to ascertain, direct sources for *Pedro Páramo*, the Hyperions' formulations not only shed light on the novel's most tantalizing enigmas, they and Rulfo's photographs also unlock its advocacy for an authentic, Indigenous *México profundo*.

The writers studied in the final two chapters tackle Sartre head-on—and pivot from him so as more fully to constitute existentialism as a vehicle for Mexican identity, ethics, and community. *Chapter 5*, " 'Christs for All Passions': José Revueltas's *El luto humano* [Human Mourning]," addresses these issues in Revueltas's text, a prizewinning novel on Mexico from the Revolution to Cárdenas's era. *El luto humano* (1943) performs startling, far-reaching conjugations. Under the auspices of *religare* (bind together; the origins of the word "religion"), the novel brings into synergy existentialisms, Christianity, Marxist activism, and the theorizing of national identity. Going a step further, the chapter demonstrates how the elements that Revueltas's *religare* unites pervade Latin American existentialism and constitute much of its *differentia specifica*. If, as chapter 3 maintains, Usigli seeds a Mexican existentialism, chapter 5 holds that *El luto humano* seeds a Latin American one, which comports, for example, with works by Brazilian and Argentine intellectuals.

Chapter 6, "Rosario Castellanos's Freedom," bears witness to the author's incremental migration from Sartre to Beauvoir in the name of feminism and communitarian ethics. The chapter traces Castellanos's negotiations, personal and philosophical, with freedom in venues ranging from the intimate (letters to her partner Ricardo Guerra, one of Hiperión's staunchest Sartreans) to the public (essays, journalism, novels, a play, and some poetry). The love triangles that trouble the Mexican writer's own life and that populate Beauvoir's works in fact set Castellanos on the roads to freedom. Taking its cue from the *ménages à trois*, chapter 6 charts the drift of Castellanos's thinking via triangulations: Castellanos—Guerra—Sartre; Simone—Jean-Paul—Olga, referring to the love triangle that Beauvoir's novel *She Came to Stay* (*L'Invitée*, 1943) and memoir *The Prime of Life* (*La Force de l'Âge*, 1960) depict; and Castellanos—Sartre—Beauvoir.

Castellanos's trajectory, like the trajectory of my book, is a healing one. Both edge away from Sartre's noxious thesis in *Being and Nothingness* and *No Exit* (*Huis Clos*, 1945) that "hell is other people" as well as from Ramos's and Paz's pathologizing. They rarely traffic in happiness, but they do expand the limits of the possible and break through from apparent no-exit situations into productive models for identity, ethics, community, and freedom.

Chapter Two

The Mexican Existentialist Ethos

In his obituary for Jean-Paul Sartre, Octavio Paz notes that the French philosopher had made just one short trip to Mexico, which he was not all that eager to discuss with the author of *El laberinto de la soledad* ("Memento" 115). Sartre's reticence to discuss his visit to Mexico, it turns out, was symptomatic of his overall bent: he favored Cuba, a hotbed of revolutionary activity, over a post-Revolutionary Mexico. Undeterred by Sartre's relative lack of interest in their country, long before the French writer's death a cluster of Mexican intellectuals had brought his incandescent philosophy home, to their home. From 1948 to 1952 the Grupo Filosófico Hiperión acted with and on Sartre's existentialism, intently fitting it to the Mexican context. At heart, Sartrean existentialism transfigured Mexican thought, and Mexican thought reconfigured Sartrean existentialism.

The Mexicanizing of Sartre that Hiperión transacted has everything to do with the scale of the word "ethos." To speak generally of an ethos, the *New Oxford American Dictionary* tells us, is to speak of "the characteristic spirit of a culture, era, or community as manifested in its beliefs and aspirations." In the time-honored Aristotelian art of persuasion, ethos constitutes an appeal to ethics. As the chapter on which we embark will corroborate by unveiling Mexican existentialism's specifically Mexican lineage, both senses of the word "ethos" are central to Hiperión's project. The imperatives of Mexican identity move Hiperión into a profound engagement with homegrown philosophical forebears who promoted the values of altruism, intersubjectivity, and community. Sartrean existentialism takes on new life in Mexico as an eclectic, even heterodox, avatar of the French philosopher's thought. In

Hiperión we find emblematic, self-aware philosophical interactions between the periphery and the metropolis.

"The Mexican Existential Ethos" works to bear out these claims on the granular level that as a newly inclusive genealogy of Hiperión they require. Here, I key in on the history of ideas in Mexico and do the philosophical heavy-lifting vital to *A Latin American Existentialist Ethos* as a whole; our creative writers, too, will partake in their own dynamic ways of the ethos that Hiperión crystallized. The weighty—and, I hope the reader will agree, exciting—work of the chapter makes for a formidable agenda. Overall, the chapter unravels the intricate web of philosophical affiliations by articulating the strands of the Mexican existentialist ethos and then pulling the strands together. Part One therefore begins with an ample, fairly standard introduction to Hiperión. It next takes a near-epic journey into less charted territory, the networks of Mexican thought that inform Hiperión's positions on ethics. In Part Two the strands coalesce, as we are able to view Hiperion's existential value system on its own as well as over against the many forces it places in alignment and in tension. Finally, for those who have braved the journey, I promise that Part Two's last section, on the question of Hiperión's complicity with President Miguel Alemán's problematic *Mexicanidad*, will deliver a pungent coda to our inquiries.

Part One

Movers and Shakers

Although the dedicated activities of Hiperión lasted only four years, the group's outsize aspirations, intellectual vivacity, and impact on Mexican culture overspilled its limited run. Hiperión's "legacy has remained in the philosophical consciousness of Mexico" (Sánchez, *Contingency* 13), thanks in no small measure to the group's pathbreaking merger of French existentialism with the philosophy of lo mexicano, Mexicanness. The Hyperions began with a focus on the former but soon discovered in situationally oriented existential philosophy the theme that would define their endeavors: knowledge of what constitutes Mexicanness, self-knowledge ("autognosis"). Hyperion Emilio Uranga confirms that the group explored, on philosophical grounds, "the essence of the Mexican, that is, his particular way of life, the radical project of existence that pertains only to him and that distinguishes him from the Spaniard, the North American, and the European" (*Análisis*

64).[1] The philosophical investigations of the movers and shakers bursting into prominence aimed to have a transformative effect on Mexican society. True to prior Mexican identity projects like that of Samuel Ramos in 1934, the transformation would be therapeutic, and, true to Sartrean existentialism, liberating (Hurtado, "Introducción" xx). Such were the grand enthusiasms of Hiperión, which the group assiduously translated into concrete, public form.

In materializing its program, Hiperión counted on a spectrum of luminaries. Christian-leaning existentialists Luis Villoro and Jorge Portilla (Villoro, "Génesis" 241), as well as emerging and established intellectuals stood at the center of the initiative. Hiperión's core philosophers ranged from the group's leader, Leopoldo Zea, and Villoro, both born in 1912, to Portilla, almost thirty years old in 1948, to Joaquín Sánchez MacGrégor and Emilio Uranga, in their mid-twenties, and Ricardo Guerra, only twenty-one at the start of Hiperión. The group's age range notwithstanding, Hiperión crusaded with the untrammeled fervor of youth. Its "almost irresistible magnetism" (Valero Pie 373) drew in prior master essayists such as Alfonso Reyes and Samuel Ramos. Anthropologists, sociologists, legal scholars and creative writers, including José Juan Arreola, Rodolfo Usigli, and Agustín Yáñez, partnered with the group that launched into a panoply of enterprises.

Hiperión made its inaugural appearance in the spring of 1948 with a conference on French existentialism that took place at the Instituto Francés de América Latina (IFAL). From there, burgeoning and institutionally validated, Hiperión channeled its efforts into lecture cycles at the UNAM. The fall 1949 lecture cycle at the UNAM demonstrates the group's broad compass. Addressing the theme of "What is the Mexican," the cycle featured talks by Guerra ("Mexico: Image and Reality"), Portilla ("Community, Greatness, and Misery of the Mexican"), Ramos ("An Idea of the Mexican Soul"), Salvador Reyes Nevares ("The Two Americas: Motives and Motivations"), Uranga ("Discretion and Dominance in the Mexican"), Villoro ("The Double Aspect of the Indian"), Yáñez ("Decent People and Lowlifes [pelados]"), and Zea ("Responsibilities of the Mexican") (Bieber 284). Winter courses at the UNAM under the rubric of "The Mexican and His Culture" followed, and, as Zea says, laid "total siege to Mexican man and his culture" (*Conciencia* x). In keeping with the courses' goals, Zea and several members of Hiperión founded the Centro de Estudios sobre el Mexicano y sus Problemas in 1952 (Santos Ruiz 30).

Hiperión expanded its circuitry into general philosophical conferences, radio broadcasts, and, above all, publications. The journal *Filosofía y letras*, sponsored by the UNAM's philosophy department, served as a leading venue for Hiperión; between 1948 and 1953 nearly every issue of the journal treated matters germane to the group (Santos Ruiz 153). Newspapers' literary supplements disseminated accounts of Hiperión's program oriented to a lay public. Less ephemeral than newspapers, many of them classics still reissued today, are the works that Zea published in the landmark book series he directed from 1952 to 1955, "México y lo Mexicano." Zea's mission statement for the series positions it as a clearing house for "all manner of efforts to capture our being, the meaning of our actions, and the spirit that drives them" ("Advertencia" 8). Within a year, the series had yielded eleven books, among them the works by Zea, Uranga, and the Hyperions' mentor, José Gaos (1900–1969) that we will be considering.

It was in fact largely to Spanish exile José Gaos's purveying of au courant European philosophy that Hiperión and the Mexican existentialism the group had thus spiritedly animated owed their existence. Ignacio Sánchez Prado observes that Gaos's arrival in Mexico "gave rise to the most important transformation of thought Mexico experienced in the twentieth century. Under his influence, to a significant degree the field of philosophy took on the themes and problems that concern it to this day" (*Naciones* 178). The sway on Mexican intellectual life of this redoubtable mover and shaker derives from a transatlantic nexus.

In the late 1930s and early 1940s, after the defeat of the progressive Republican cause in the Spanish Civil War, Mexico absorbed thousands of Spanish refugees. Under the good offices of President Lázaro Cárdenas and his emissary Daniel Cosío Villegas, Mexico not only opened its academic preserves to an influx of Spanish intellectuals but also created a new institution for them, the Casa de España that evolved into the venerable Colegio de México. In 1938 Gaos, former rector of the Universidad Central de Madrid and preeminent disciple of José Ortega y Gasset, reached Mexico, where he was welcomed into the Casa de España. A grateful Gaos coined the term "transterrados" that came to characterize his generation of exiled Spanish intellectuals. As he observed, "we do not feel like we are exiled [desterrados] but transterrados," that is, in a kindred climate (qtd. in Valero Pie 182). Gaos would go on principally to teach at the Colegio de México and the UNAM for more than twenty years and warmly to reward his adoptive country for its generosity by dynamizing Mexican philosophy.[2]

Curiously enough, Gaos's impact rested little on a published corpus of original thought. A foremost authority on Gaos, Aurelia Valero Pie, refers to his "relative agraphia" (111), which spawned a turbid, prolix style. That Gaos, as he himself told Uranga, "martyred himself every time he had to write a page" (Uranga, *Astucias* 101), also stymied his ability to formulate an ownmost project, a philosophy utterly his own—all the more grievous for a man determined to take the discipline of philosophy in Mexico by storm. Gaos cultivated influential contacts, compiled anthologies, wrote numerous articles, letters, and journal entries. He promised full-scale, original books. Yet the Spanish emigrant only mustered, informally, an exiguous philosophy that he called *personalismo*. Gaos's personalismo, not entirely without reason, held up his personal intellectual trajectory as a microcosm of the current intellectual landscape. After retiring, Gaos published a couple of books that, to his disappointment, mainly went unnoticed. Valero Pie dubs him a philosopher in search of a philosophy (137). Gaos's prime forums, therefore, lay elsewhere, namely, in pedagogy and in transmitting others' ideas.

Gaos poured his lifeblood and pride into his students. He taught all of the Hyperions and, briefly, Paz (Stanton, "Lectura" 304); Gaos directed the theses on Mexican positivism that would catapult his star pupil, Zea, into eminence and thus leadership of Hiperión.[3] However much the Hyperions pulled away from Gaos, dealing their mentor a sorely felt blow, the education they received from him remained crucial to their endeavors. The transcontinental philosopher instructed the Hyperions in a sweep of areas, from the history of philosophy in general and Hispanic thought over the ages, to historicism, Marxism, phenomenology, and select existentialisms. Gaos evenhandedly took the measure, positive and negative, of each area. Materially, though, he privileged the recent European modes he regarded as necessary to enliven a stagnant Mexican philosophical milieu. In a 1939 letter from Mexico Gaos wrote: "philosophical activity, however you may define it, does not exist here" (qtd. in Valero Pie 83). For the Spanish intellectual, to invigorate the Mexican milieu meant steeping his pupils in Ortega y Gasset's *circunstancialismo*, the primordial orientation of philosophy towards lived circumstances.

Ortega y Gasset's circunstancialismo synchronized with Martin Heidegger's Dasein—and it was Heidegger's philosophy that afforded Gaos the limelight. Over the decades, Gaos made his widest mark on the lettered city through translations, his chief locus of publication. While he rendered into Spanish thousands of pages by Hegel, Husserl, Kant, Kierkegaard, Scheler, et alia, his translation of Heidegger's *Being and Time* crowned Gaos's writing career. After more than twenty years' labor, in 1951 Gaos published *El ser y el tiempo*, the first translation into any language of Heidegger's massive work, and a companion volume, *Introducción a* El ser y el Tiempo *de Martín Heidegger*. Gaos's classes had provided a laboratory for the monumental achievement. His students recall the courses he imparted in which twice a week they scrutinized Heidegger's work line by line, guided by their teacher's commentary (Valero Pie 119). Gaos never presented himself as a Heideggerian per se, but his tutelage, says Carlos Sánchez, propelled "the Germanization of the modern Mexican mind" ("Heidegger" 443).[4]

Not just the Germanization but also a renewed Mexicanization, as it were, of the Mexican mind: from Gaos, albeit originally an outsider, the Hyperions reaped a knowledge of Mexican philosophy together with the stimulus to grow it. Steadily familiarizing himself with the rich intellectual history of his adopted homeland, an impressed Gaos plunged students into their own philosophical traditions through seminars on seventeenth- and eighteenth-century Mexican thought. In his polemical *En torno a la filosofía mexicana* [On Mexican Philosophy] (1952), Gaos also undertook to theorize the subject, generating a call to action that he sent out to his pupils, specifically to the Hyperions. The book begins with the inflammatory assertion that Mexican philosophy does not exist because it is too derivative to qualify as actually Mexican. Gaos immediately defuses the provocation, a mere paper tiger, by refuting the belief that a philosophy must be entirely autochthonous to warrant the denomination "Mexican." First, amid a three-page pileup of quotes from Ortega y Gasset, Gaos contends: "There is no such thing . . . as an 'eternal idea'" insofar as any idea "is irremediably attached to the situation or circumstance that activates it and regulates its function" (19), and neither absolutes nor universals obtain for the historically eclectic Mexican situation. A paradigm shift then allows Gaos to nullify his initial taunt. One can deem a philosophy Mexican "even when it is not [totally] original," if Mexicans have rendered it more original or more Mexican (14). Hand in hand with the paradigm shift, Gaos trenchantly decries the inapplicability of European categories to Mexican culture. He objects to the cultural "imperialism" of a European historiography that assumes the universality of its categories and imposes them on other cultures (39). Presumptions of universality, says Gaos, lead Europeans to measure other cultures' histories by alien standards, norms that can result in a condemnation of non-European endeavors as lacking in "substance" and "originality" (39).[5]

After a lengthy excursion into the history of Mexican philosophy, reconfigured in accord with the particular Mexican Dasein, at the end of *En torno a la filosofía mexicana* Gaos throws down the gauntlet to the Hyperions. "Oh, young Hyperions," he exclaims, "what a weighty task falls to you: responsibility not only for the future of Mexico's philosophy but also for that of its past" (86). The Hyperions stepped up to the greater challenge that Gaos in essence posed. To advance Mexican philosophy Gaos had enjoined circunstancialismo, Dasein, and a discriminating absorption of foreign knowledge, all of which catalyzed the Hyperions' brash new wave orientation. Yet, mavericks that they were, the Hyperions abided more by the spirit than the letter of Gaos's curriculum. For their turn to Sartre flew in the face of Gaos's aversion to the French philosopher's existentialism, which he deemed a copy of Heidegger's, with an added dose of "existential psychoanalysis" (Díaz Ruanova 133), and which he declined to probe in either his teaching or writing. As Uranga observes, Gaos's winter courses "unequivocally" condemned "any deviation from Heideggerian orthodoxy" ("Dos existencialismos," *Análisis* 174). Gaos, once the conduit for the latest thinking, had lapsed into an anachronism (Valero Pie 451). The Hyperions stridently exploited the void that Gaos had created. While down the line some of them acknowledged Gaos with appreciation, as Hiperión took shape its members swerved from disciples to parricides who assailed their Heideggerian mentor.[6]

"Dos existencialismos" [Two Existentialisms] (1949; in *Análisis*), a manifesto for the Grupo Hiperión authored by its brilliant enfant terrible Uranga, marries a generational declaration of independence *from* Heidegger and Gaos with a declaration of allegiance *to* Sartre. "Dos existencialismos" forms a sequel to a programmatic essay that Uranga had presented the year before in Hiperión's second round of lectures on French existentialism at the IFAL. Titled "Maurice Merleau-Ponty: Fenomenología y existencialismo," the earlier talk portrayed French existentialism as fundamental to Hiperión's intent to "carry out a concrete analysis of the Mexican mode of being" (224). Gaos had recriminated the Hyperions' espousing of Sartre, which Uranga now, in "Dos existencialismos," brands as their proud "value judgment" unrestrained by the niceties of "diplomatic behavior" (176). Somewhat tongue in cheek (we might hope), the 1949 piece harshly takes Gaos to task and doubles down on the merit of French existentialism. As its title signals, the essay delimits two existentialisms, one championed by Gaos and predicated on Heidegger's *Being and Time*, and another that "acknowledges Sartre's *Being and Nothingness* as its most systematic source of inspiration" (173). For years, says Uranga, to be an existentialist in Mexico was to be a Heideggerian, a state of affairs that the Hyperion sarcastically attributes in part to fear of offending Gaos (173–74). Discounting further objections to Sartrean existentialism (its recent emergence, its foreign provenance), Uranga issues his and Hiperión's battle cry. Heidegger is "outdated" (174) and Sartre the most auspicious philosopher on the horizon, because he promises theories of social relations, pedagogy, history, morality, and man (175).

In espousing Sartre, the Hyperions affronted far more than José Gaos. For reasons that Uranga only began to name, the general tide in Mexico ran against French existentialism. Put bluntly, "Sartre" was a dirty word for the brunt of Mexicans familiar to any degree with his work. Hiperión's Portilla informs us that Sartre has been condemned as a "professional immoralist" (97), a facile judgment that could stream from the most popularly available face of the French philosopher, his plays staged in Mexico (e.g., *Dirty Hands*, *No Exit*, and *The Respectful Prostitute* [Santos Ruiz 142]). Oswaldo Díaz Ruanova, who experienced the milieu firsthand, remarks: "In those years, the thinking that a restless Sartre issued from his Parisian boulevards got bad press . . . . Existentialism seemed to be synonymous with nihilism, fatalism, pessimism, even with licentiousness and bourgeois decadence" (57). Beyond popular opinion, intellectuals from both ends of the spectrum had similar grievances with Sartre. Díaz Ruanova details the contempt in which Marxists and the extreme right held the notoriously scabrous Sartre (57).

The question therefore arises of why Hiperión so resolutely swam against the various adverse tides. Mere "mavericking," a desire to be on the cutting edge? Whereas Ana Santos Ruiz (whose critiques the last section of this chapter examines) ascribes such motivations, and more iniquitous ones, to Hiperión, we can readily surmise that the group had a philosophically honorable rationale for instrumentalizing Sartrean existentialism. As Uranga no doubt had in mind when he blazoned Sartre's singular relevance to the "concrete analysis of the Mexican mode of being," the Hyperions encountered in French existentialism innovative, potent ways of thinking about Mexican identity. Zea, an adept synthesizer of Hiperión's concerns, glosses the phenomenon. He explains that the new European philosophy "justifies the aspirations of Mexican philosophers" because it has "expanded the scope of philosophical problems" to include authenticity, freedom, the ability of humans to forge their own lives (man "is not something already made, but something making itself") and to forge their lives within the parameters of a distinct situation (*Conciencia* 11). The last topic Zea cites, the powerhouse of the Sartrean "situation"-cum circunstancialismo-cum Dasein, implicates others—Guerra declares, quoting Sartre: "Freedom only exists in situation, and the situation only exists in freedom" ("Sartre" 309)—and gave Hiperión its prime mover, its bedrock. Entirely cognizant that "our *situation* is not the same as Jean-Paul Sartre's," that Mexican philosophy "need not respond" to the same issues "as contemporary European philosophy" (Zea, "La filosofía" 161), the Hyperions assumed responsibility for their situation and existentialized Mexican identity discourse.

In so doing, Hiperión trod the fine line between the ontological and the ontic intrinsic to its project of capturing, as we heard Uranga state some pages ago, "the essence of the Mexican, that is, his particular way of life." Sartre's *Being and Nothingness* geared Hiperión to ontology, the metaphysics of being ("the essence of the Mexican"). On the other hand, taking responsible stock of the concrete Mexican situation fed into the ontic, which relates to real existence, facticity ("his particular way of life"). The Hyperions sought to bridge the disciplinary divide. They would commence with "the systematic description of Mexicans' mode of life, character traits, gestures, works of art and literature, and especially, history" in order to distill from them the "dynamic nucleus" of Mexican being (Hurtado, "Introducción" xv). The Hyperions, in short, posited that their *situated existentialism* would vault from the ontic to the ontological. Yet when enacted, as Gaos was quick to point out, Hiperión's hybrid methodology evinced disturbing flaws. Gaos argued that to meet the requisites of ontology, the Hyperions fell into essentializing. That is, they insouciantly lumped all Mexicans into *the* Mexican, with little regard for location, gender, race, or class—a deeply problematic shortcoming and a well-founded critique on Gaos's part, though it does not cancel out Hiperión's philosophical accomplishments. The emigrant philosopher at the same time punches holes in the ontological dimensions of the Hyperions' labors. According to Gaos, their project, so engrossed in the description of Mexican life, was essentially ontic. It followed from there, Gaos complained, that universals got lost in the profusion of Mexican specifics.[7]

Deliberately or myopically, Gaos's latter objection misses the revolutionary approach to universals bound up in Hiperión's existentialized identity discourse. The group's name references the Greek god Hyperion, son of earth and heaven, and we have just seen that the Mexican philosophers boldly aim to fuse the concrete with the metaphysical. More bold yet was their assault on the lofty realm of universals, the "eternal ideas" that Gaos himself had challenged. With various tools of a situated existentialism at their disposal, the Hyperions resolved to extrapolate from the Mexican Dasein, from the particular, sweeping ontological characteristics. Villoro announces the recalibration objectively, noting an impetus from "the particular and concrete to the universal and abstract—and not the other way around" (*Grandes momentos* 18). Zea raises the ante: "Let us not aim merely to arrive at a Latin American truth, but instead to arrive at a truth that is valid for all men" (qtd. in Villoro, "La cultura" 212). In thus outreaching to universals, the Hyperions grow a situated existentialism that dissolves polarities into a rooted cosmopolitanism.[8]

Uranga carries his fellow Hyperions' shared subversive design to its ultimate philosophical consequences. In *Análisis del ser del mexicano* [An Analysis of Mexican Being] (1952), he writes: "It is not a matter of constructing lo mexicano . . . as human, but the other way around: to *construct the human as Mexican* (45; emphasis added). Uranga embeds his radical pronouncement in an aggressive contestation of the "deplorable 'generalization'" whereby when philosophy speaks "of man in general, in truth it refers to European man" (67). He opposes this tendency to generalize from—to ontologize—"European man" by delineating two ontological states, the substantial and its alternative, the accidental.

Pivotal, dense concepts whose names belie the meanings Uranga assigns them, these two terms require some unpacking. In Uranga's system, the substantial—read: the European, including Mexico's former master, Spain—possesses fatal flaws. The substantial presents as a plenitude, a fixed, stable, suspect "finished reality" (Lipp 120) rife, one could say, with the fallacies of Sartre's "in-itself," thingness. Yet nearly all Western tradition, writes Uranga, "has endowed being with the meaning or sense of the substantial," a "being for substance" (*Análisis* 41), by regarding the substantial as the standard, the ideal, the sine qua non. To fall short of the mark is to be, by literal definition and as a lack, insubstantial (lacking in substance, as Gaos remarked). This brings us to the accidental, which Aristotle's *Metaphysics* (book 4, part 2) sets against the essential, the unchanging. For Uranga, the accidental—read: Mexican and other non-European ontologies—is the opposite of the substantial. Thus, the accidental is contingent and mutable. A "Third World" focused existentialist, Uranga privileges accidentality, not just as a more inclusive but, significantly, as a more *human* ontology. He sets Mexican "accidentality" over against the European master narrative and its "boastful substantiality" (43). In sum, despite the seemingly negative vibrations of the word "accident," Uranga exalts accidentality, a truly, authentically human mode of being. Two decades before Jacques Derrida's "White Mythology," Uranga has struck at the pretensions to universality of metropolitan philosophical norms.[9]

With due nods to Uranga, Zea's *Conciencia y posibilidad del mexicano* (1952) draws out the powerful ideological implications of Hiperión's existentialism in general. Published at the tail end of the group's activity, as the second book in the "México y lo Mexicano" series, *Conciencia* is at once a digest of and an apologetics and a swan song for Hiperión.[10] *Conciencia* inserts Hiperión in a stock existentialist repertoire. The touchstones of that repertoire as construed by Mexican philosophers (situation, responsibility, choice, freedom, existence vs. essence, authenticity, and bad faith) all figure in the campaign of Hiperión to raise Mexican consciousness that *Conciencia* itself memorializes. Unexceptional as Zea's baseline is, *Conciencia* wrests from it a muscular decolonizing argument. World War II, Zea's at first Spenglerian argument runs, placed Europe in crisis and decentered the Western world. No longer can an immaculate Europe see itself as the "benefactor of humanity in an absolute sense" (*Conciencia* 7). Shaken by crisis, consigned to solitude, adds Zea, Europe has recognized its fraternity with more peripheral nations. French existentialism itself, in his view, stems from the post–World War II European prise de conscience. The new philosophical turn provides an instrument for "comprehending the humanity of man" (53). We note here a sharp reversal of the solitude that Paz's *Laberinto* attributes to Mexicans themselves as well as Zea's finessing of existentialism into a reflection of Europe's kinship with the margins, which renders the Sartrean mode less foreign, *almost* native to Mexico.

Concomitant with Europe's displacement from centrality, Zea maintains, more peripheral nations have come to the fore and to a new sense of self. Now on an equal footing with Europe thanks to shared experiences of limit situations (for the "first time we find ourselves in the same situation as Europeans" [52]), the erstwhile margins realize that they "are not as backward, nor bereft of values, as they had supposed" (51). Mexico in particular, which has successfully weathered the revolutions of Independence and 1910, holds "a privileged place in this new consciousness" (6). Envisaging Europe's decline and the Americas' post–World War II ascendancy, Mexicans can see themselves with new eyes, eyes that discern the "soaring human spirit that [Mexico] possesses despite all its errors and failures" (51). Zea expounds on the *inversion of values* that the revisionary outlook has brought about: "An inversion of values that focuses on man's capability to adapt and readapt to the circumstances reality presents" (69). By virtue of Mexicans' consummate elasticity, what had formerly appeared to be errors and failures now appear as authentic grapplings with a situation.

A positive, emancipatory conception of lo mexicano that verges on triumphalism patently scaffolds the Hyperions' agenda. Encouraged by the economic boom and political stability under Miguel Alemán, matters more tangible than the post–World War II weltanschauung, the Hyperions marked their distance from the entrenched negativity of Mexican identity discourse. In *Conciencia* Zea scrutinizes Plutarco Elías Calles's era, which fostered the pathologizing of Mexicans that Samuel Ramos's 1934 *El perfil del hombre y la cultura en México* had exemplified. Ramos (and the Calles-era Yáñez and Rodolfo Usigli), says Zea, intuited "an 'authentic' reality, a Mexican reality" but could only see "its negative aspects" owing to overreliance on foreign standards (49). For his part, Zea concentrates on what will help him and his compatriots "consider ourselves, as we already have begun to do, confident, complete, firm, open, optimistic, and possessed of the capabilities that, until just recently, we thought we lacked ("La filosofía" 191). Similarly, in "Optimismo y pesimismo sobre el mexicano" Uranga writes: "All the lucubrations that have obtained up to now have been set aside . . . while other appraisals are coming center stage that let us speak of an atmosphere of hope" (*Análisis* 150). He announces straight out: "We have arrived at a point in which the theory of lo mexicano and an optimistic theory of the Mexican have utterly converged" (150). Imbued with optimism and resisting cultural imperialism, the Mexican existentialism that had taken its stimulus from Sartre eschews his disposition to nausea, forlornness, and similar brooding topics.[11]

This is not to say that the Hyperions wholly abandoned brooding, in the tenor of Ramos's *Perfil*, on the ills of the Mexican condition. Rather, as a corollary to their optimism, they too at times diagnosed the features of Mexicans that in keeping now with *existentialist* criteria needed rectification. Uranga, Portilla, and Zea especially target *desgana*, an apathy that entails a raft of traits inimical to the authenticity the Hyperions desired for Mexico: indolence, sentimentality, dreamy self-absorption, passivity, and indifference to others' hardships (Uranga, "Ensayo," in *Análisis* 114–17; Portilla 130–31; Zea, *Conciencia* 134). Desgana, for Uranga, is the "antipodes of generosity" (*Análisis* 116). To dwell in desgana is to shun the existentialist exercising of freedom and responsibility that had enabled the Hyperions to replace a sense of inferiority originating in colonialism with confidence in Mexico's postcolonial superiority (*Análisis* 5). In thus executing a therapeutic diagnostics according to its own criteria, Hiperión entered into a gradated relationship with *Perfil*, one which leaned more towards evolution than complete revolution. *Perfil* had set forth the mission Hiperión wholeheartedly assumed: Mexican identity discourse, writes Ramos, "has not launched from its logical starting point: knowledge of Mexican man" (*Perfil* 86). Yet the negativity of *Perfil*, including a near-blanket disregard of Mexicans' saving graces and a failure to indicate what a Mexican culture divested of the inferiority complex would actually look like, clashed with Hiperión's modus operandi.[12]

Uranga's watershed "Ensayo de una ontología del mexicano" [Essay on an Ontology of the Mexican] (1951; in *Análisis*) and kindred *Análisis del ser del mexicano* read *Perfil* through Hiperión's optic. In a diplomatic spirit, for once, Uranga recognizes the perspicacity of Ramos's analyses and states that the inferiority complex "undoubtedly . . . explains numerous aspects of Mexican life" (*Análisis* 69). Uranga will not dismiss the inferiority complex. He will, he says, perfect Ramos's study by distinguishing the concept of "inferiority" from that of "insufficiency" (*Análisis* 69). The two are often conflated, but "inferior" appraises quality (inferior/superior) and "insufficiency" can appraise adequacy to a given context. Food, for example, can be inferior in quality but still sufficient to meet specific dietary needs. From the prosaic example of food, Uranga moves to his philosophical bullseye. The residue of the colonial situation has exacerbated Mexicans' perception of their insufficiency to the point that, despite the distinctions between the two conditions, Uranga's compatriots are apt to view their culture as *both* inferior and insufficient vis-à-vis Europe. Insufficiency, Uranga underscores, does not necessarily equate to inferiority. Acquiescing to inferiority is just one among the set of postures that the sense of insufficiency can occasion—and the most insidious, for it can lead to the resignation and paralysis of such attitudes as desgana ("Mexicans evade desgana, the feeling of insufficiency, by choosing inferiority" ["Ensayo," *Análisis* 117]). Uranga offers a more productive reaction to insufficiency. A Mexican can have faith in his ability to "achieve sufficiency through his actions" and thus "attain on his own the sufficiency he lacks" (*Análisis* 72). With this achievable, factic "conquest of 'sufficiency'" (*Análisis* 72), Uranga has maneuvered the inferiority complex into consonance with Hiperión's practical, transformative ambitions.

A methodological gear change from *Perfil* allows Uranga at once to shed redemptive light on Ramos's and on his fellow existentialists' rosters of Mexican lacks. In concert with Hiperión at large, Uranga walks away from the kind of psychoanalyzing that had bred *Perfil*'s insistence on Mexicans' inferiority complex to search for a "system that would rid us of the monster" Ramos had exposed (Uranga, *Análisis* 107). Uranga's *Análisis*, consistent with Hiperión's assault on putative universals, goes ontological in ways that turn the tables. If, as Uranga advised above, Mexicans may palliate their dis-ease by applying themselves to sufficiency, they cannot, and should not, aspire to the ontological condition of substantiality.[13] "*[A]ll interpretations of man as a substantial creature strike us as inhuman*" (*Análisis* 45); insubstantiality stands for what is authentically human, a far cry from inferiority (*Análisis* 84). Thus, with a masterful gambit that forms a linchpin of *Análisis del ser del mexicano*, Uranga connects *insufficiency* to *accidentality*. The nature of insufficiency, the author discloses, greatly exceeds inadequacy to a given situation. Deep down, insufficiency comprises experiential fallout from the precarious yet salutary ontological state of accidentality, a message pumped from the ontological to the ontic (see Sánchez, "Heidegger" 451).

From this ontological perspective the psychological characteristics commonly ascribed to Mexicans, be they positive or negative (including an inferiority complex), radiate from their ontological "proximity to the accident" (*Análisis* 47).[14] Mexicans' "emotivity," for instance, "expresses or symbolizes in psychological terms their ontological condition" ("Ensayo," *Análisis* 114). Uranga here puts to ontological work the inversion of values that in *Conciencia* Zea associates with historical circumstances. From their respective vantage points, Zea and Uranga share the goal of supplying the capital, absent from *Perfil*, for an empowered consciousness. Accidentality is neither a prison house nor a determinism. It just *is*, and, in Uranga's analytic, to own it fully is to live the human condition authentically.

The Mexican Existentialist Arena

Above and beyond Ramos's *Perfil*, the Hyperions had entered an arena laden with philosophical drives that could bear on their venture. As the Hyperions well knew, the Mexican intellectual arena bristled with homegrown philosophical energies relating to identity and foreign ones akin to them. Hiperión would amalgamate the moving parts, some of them conflicting with Sartre, into a unique coalition—a supple, multiform Mexican existentialism attuned to the project of building a value-rich country fit for the "privileged place" historical circumstances had bestowed on it. Guillermo Hurtado praises Hiperión for enriching Mexican identity discourse by turning not just to Sartre but also to such Mexican philosophers as Antonio Caso ("Introducción" xiv); it is the chief objective of this section to set up the *ethical* prescriptions for Mexico, like those of Caso, with which Hiperión engages. However, we first attend to Hiperión's most clear and present competitor, a force to be reckoned with, as Hiperión did: Octavio Paz qua existentialist.

Already familiar with Heidegger from his studies with Gaos, as Mexican ambassador to France during the years he was writing *Laberinto* Paz immersed himself in the latest existentialism.[15] Albert Camus won Paz's admiration (*Itinerario* 88–90), Sartre less so. Paz's love-hate relationship with Sartre, on the one hand, acknowledges the passionate, inhabited commitment to life's big questions that had molded the French philosopher into an indispensable beacon for the whole postwar generation ("Memento" 119). On the other, Paz takes exception to Sartre's philosophical writings for their lack of originality, their dependence on Heidegger ("Memento" 118).

Heideggerian and/or Sartrean, *Laberinto* reverberates with existentialist constructs. If it can be hard to parse out the origins of Paz's philosophy, it is easy, indeed nearly requisite, to translate into an existentialist idiom the general lines of *Laberinto* that we surveyed in chapter 1. *Laberinto* thus recoded proves to answer Dasein's siren call and revolve around alienation, authenticity, and inauthenticity. That is, the basic dialectics of the text arguably respond to the three existentialist staples: living in a state of alienation, Mexicans suppress their "authentic" (a word Paz continuously employs) being, and retreat into the self-protective masks that betoken inauthenticity. Paz appraises the overall history of Mexico along the same lines: "The whole history of Mexico, from the Conquest to the Revolution, can be regarded as a search for our own selves, which have been deformed or disguised by alien institutions, and for a Form that will express them" (*Labyrinth 166*; *Laberinto* 311–12). Concretely, Paz views Mexico as oscillating between eras of inauthenticity in which the nation cleaves to foreign forms, like the positivist epoch of Porfirio Díaz, and of authenticity, like that of the Mexican Revolution.

Paz's foregrounding of alienation and inauthenticity holds out little hope for the micro-level, human relations. In *Laberinto*, alienation and the fetishizing of Form occasion Mexicans' dread of their fellow humans beings' penetrating gaze ("we are frightened by other people's glances" [*35*; 170]), in response to which Mexicans attempt to disappear others ("we also pretend that our fellow man does not exist" [*44*; 180], we "nullify him" [*45*; 180]).[16] Perpetrating acts of consummate bad faith, Mexicans also disappear *themselves* (the Mexican "is afraid of others' looks and therefore he withdraws, contracts, becomes a shadow, a phantasm" [*43*; 178]). Thus, as Paz would have it, Mexicans shut themselves in and down, all of which forecloses authentic intersubjectivity. Paz returns to the plight of intersubjectivity, broadening its scope to the universal human condition, at the end of *Laberinto*. He concludes the 1959 and subsequent editions of *Laberinto* with an appendix titled "La dialéctica de la soledad" [The Dialectics of Solitude], or, as Enrico Santí christens the appendix, a "meditation on love" (122). Love may be the appendix's theme, but the disquisition lays out the blockages to that emotion. "In our world," Paz declaims, "love is an almost inaccessible experience. Everything is against it" (*197*; 343). Only solitude, "the profoundest fact of the human condition" breeds awareness of the "lack of another" (*195*; 341) that can lead to communion/community. *Laberinto*'s final flourishes dishearten. Nevertheless, they cannot surprise, for they unfold inexorably from Paz's own demoralizing, existentialist gaze on his compatriots.

Shot through with existentialism, profoundly engaging identity, *Laberinto* overlapped with Hiperión, and Paz may have seen the group as something of a rival. He would later dissociate himself from the home-based existentialists by contrasting his own historical, social, and psychological interests with theirs in ontology ("Vuelta" 421). This reductive characterization of Hiperión hints at Paz's contemporary actions vis-à-vis the group. When Paz returned to Mexico in 1953 he kept up relationships with some Hyperions, especially Uranga, but collaborated with the *Revista Mexicana de Literatura* rather than Zea's important "Mexico y lo Mexicano" series (Reeve, "Making" 44). Moreover, although the 1959 revised edition of *Laberinto* incorporates Zea, who by then had swung from creating a Mexican to a pan-Latin American philosophy, Paz dispatches Hiperión's collective exertions with a few equivocal words. While lauding their avidity, he laments the narrowness of their focus.[17]

At least for our purposes, the fault lines between *Laberinto* and Hiperión have little to do with the reservations Paz professes. The Grupo Hiperión that balked at the unrelieved negativity of Ramos's *Perfil* would, as we will see, have their quarrels with the bleak *Laberinto*.[18] In any case, neither singly nor jointly could these two texts claim sole ownership of meditations on lo mexicano. A hallowed, alternative discourse on the palpitating subject lay at the ready and would spill over into Hiperión—that of an affirmative ethics based on altruism set in motion by Mexico's first professional philosopher, Antonio Caso (1883–1946). Having served as director of the Escuela Nacional Preparatoria, rector of the national university when it reopened in 1910 after the Reform, director of the Facultad de Filosofía y Letras at the UNAM (1930–1932), and a prolific author and inspired teacher throughout, Caso was a benchmark for the Mexican intelligentsia.

Caso's leading role in the Mexican reaction against the official doctrine of Porfirio Díaz's long dictatorial regime, positivism, triggered the philosopher's meteoric career. In 1902 in the Teatro Arbeu, Mexican Secretary of Education Justo Sierra pronounced the landmark "Discurso" commonly known as "Dudemos" [Let Us Doubt], which questioned the absolute epistemological sovereignty that positivism had awarded science. The founding of the humanistic Ateneo de la Juventud [Athenaeum of Youth] by Antonio Caso, Pedro Henríquez Ureña, Alfonso Reyes, and José Vasconcelos followed in the speech's wake. The Ateneo mounted an attack on positivism, spearheaded by Caso's 1909 lectures on the philosophy. In line with the general tendencies of the Latin American philosophical sea change, to the anti-metaphysical, anti-spiritual, anti-esthetic cast of Comtean (cum Porfirian) positivism, the Ateneo opposed the profile that Hiperión Villoro neatly summarizes: the Mexican institution "privileged metaphysics over science; action, moral or esthetic, over technology; the human being over the State; the impulses of emotion or will over the excessive cult of reason" ("Génesis" 235). José Enrique Rodó, crusader for the noble, pure Latin American spirit, afforded the Ateneo one of its guiding lights (Hurtado, *Búho* 68). Ramos, a student of Antonio Caso, reports that the more than one hundred quite disparate participants in the Ateneo shared an inclination to moral issues (*Historia* 134).[19]

Improbably, the attention to moral issues that the antipositivist Ateneo marshaled took its cue from a wayward direction in Auguste Comte's system, his "Religion of Humanity." Towards the end of his life, Comte published the *System of Positive Polity, or Treatise on Sociology, Instituting the Religion of Humanity* (1851–1854), a four-volume opus in which the philosopher labors to endow the scientific State he had conceptualized with a form of spirituality. A Comte mourning his devoutly Catholic beloved, Clotilde de Vaux, leans in to spirituality and devises a positivist religion that negotiates the seeming oxymoron by devirtualizing Catholicism. The "Religion of Humanity" substitutes an abstract "Humanity" for "God" and preserves such mechanisms of Catholicism as prayers and rituals. Along with cultic Christian practices, Comte safeguards Christian values, most notably altruism. The word "altruism," coined by none other than the French philosopher, reflects the weight he attached to living for others (*altrui*) instead of for the self. In Comte's thinking, both the fabric of social relations and the moral fiber of a society depend on altruism. "Altruism was centrally about promoting other people's interests, and morality was the triumph of altruism over egoism" (Scott and Seglow 15). Inviting altruism into his secularized Religion of Humanity, Comte construes the principle scientifically and formalistically, as emotion tempered by reason.

The coinage of altruism aside, Comte's incursions into religion earned him little but scorn from his contemporaries. Had Comte, John Stuart Mill wondered, lost his mind (Stehn 52)? Nonetheless, the Religion of Humanity held a special allure for Mexico and gained traction there. As a template for *transvaluation*, Comte's schema spoke to a modernizing Mexico that, from Benito Juárez's nineteenth-century Reform onward, had been wrangling with Church versus State. Still largely Catholic, now pushing back at positivism, the Mexico-in-the-making could benefit from the form of transvaluation the "crazy" Comte envisioned: the transfer of religious values and practices to a secularized State. Evidence that dimensions of the more outlandish Comte proved less outlandish for Mexican intellectuals surfaces early on in the educational stronghold of positivism, the Escuela Preparatoria Nacional founded in 1868. Charles Hale explains that although its first director, Gabino Barreda, certainly did not wish to implant the Religion of Humanity per se in Mexico, the curriculum he designed for the school implicitly adopted some of the later Comte's premises. Hale cites Barreda's credence in "replacing religion with a proven or positive religion, based on the worship of a real God, humanity, rather than an imaginary one" and in altruism "as the principle of morality" (148). Alexander Stehn adds that the subsequent generation of positivists, given over to the Darwinian and Spencerian aspects of Porfirian ideology, ignored "Barreda's dream of educating Mexicans into altruism" (56).[20] Therefore, what Justo Sierra and the Ateneo had "doubted" was not Comte's transvaluation but the negation of its ethical bent.

Antonio Caso's masterwork, *La existencia como economía, como desinterés, y como caridad* [Existence as Economy, Disinterest, and Charity], epitomizes that ethical bent. *Existencia* was Caso's lifelong project, and a porous one. He first published the work in 1916, augmented it in 1919, and revised it substantially in 1943, so shortly before his death and the inception of Hiperión (I list the edition[s] in which the lines I cite appear).[21] In each version Caso updates *Existencia* to the current philosophical climate. Hence, whereas the first two editions of *Existencia* pit Henri Bergson and Arthur Schopenhauer against positivism, the 1943 version adds discussions of Edmund Husserl's and Max Scheler's works, among others. Still, the three principal lines of *Existencia*, announced in its title, remained firmly standing over time and embody the propulsions of Caso's whole philosophy (Krauze 42). In essence they contrast: (1) Economy, the biological imperative of survival and the utilitarian self-interest that are the cornerstones of positivism; (2) Disinterest, the partial transcendence of "economy" through the surpluses of play and esthetics; (3) *Caridad*, the noble transcendence of "economy" through selfless love for one's fellow human beings; best translated as "altruism" because "caridad" here greatly surpasses simple acts of charity.

As caridad qua altruism attests, though formed in positivism and then predominantly veering away from it, Caso retained an esteem for Comte. "Personally, I will always deem it an honor to have been trained in the vigorous philosophical tradition of Auguste Comte, one of the most solid, powerful pioneers of the history of thought!" he once exclaimed ("Ramos y yo" 147). By opposing altruism to egotism and valorizing "Charity" as the final stage of a teleological progression, *Existencia* makes common cause with

Comte's social vision. More than straightforward common cause, by replacing science as the outcome of the three-stage progression for humanity (from the theological stage to the metaphysical and then the *scientific* stage) that Comte's original positivism had famously ordained, Caso enthrones Comte's revered altruism. Yet, as the religious resonances of the word caridad suggest, *Existencia* enters territory anathema to Comte. Caso rescues altruism from scientific interpretations of it, bringing an unabashedly Christian caridad back into the picture. "God is love" and the "essence of Christianity is charity," pronounces Caso (*Existencia* 114; 1919, 1943).

In Caso's humanistic Christianity—transvaluated but effectively Christian—altruism encompasses everything from interpersonal to metaphysical drives.[22] It begins in the Golden Rule of do unto others as you would have them do unto you, "love of one's fellow human beings, the first and singular truth . . . the only virtue; honoring the rule and the prophets" (*Existencia* 114; 1919, 1943). Coterminous with *agape*, charity "consists in going outside oneself, giving oneself to others, offering oneself, serving, and lavishing oneself on others without fear of depletion" (17; 1916). This Christian generosity begets community, an Augustianian "city of God" on earth (117; 1943). Rosa Krauze, a leading authority on Caso, states: "Caso recognized that human fulfillment . . . is impossible without the collective" (178). Lastly, given that Caso elevates charitable acts into a vehicle for achieving salvation (*Existencia* 111; 1919, 1943), altruism provides a springboard from the city of God on earth to the actual heavenly city.

When Caso, with more care towards the Earthly City than towards salvation, deems charitable acts a necessary *pre*condition of faith ("Faith is impossible without charity" [18; 1916 and passim]), he opens a gateway to existentialism. If faith need not generate agape, but the other way around, the onus falls on how we make the world, how we exercise free will. Charity, he says in *Existencia*: "Is not proclaimed but practiced, *made*, as is life" (18; 1916, 1919, 1943). Then, in 1944, with a Heideggerian slant, Caso writes: "From the perspective of a transcendent philosophy, everything we do gains meaning from human freedom. We are freedom itself, freed from iniquity, be it individual or social" ("Trascendencia y libertad" 172; 1944). While Heidegger's emphasis on freedom and Dasein command Caso's respect, as one might expect the German philosopher incurs Caso's displeasure for having abandoned divine transcendence ("San Agustín y Heidegger" 170; 1944).[23] Caso diverges from Heidegger and rarely touches on French existentialism, but, as one might also expect, he fervently admires Christian existentialism. The 1919 edition of *Existencia* (by intense implication) and that of 1943 (outright) display a Kierkegaardian Caso, captivated by a "perfectly essential," interiorized Christianity, a "radically new and eternal Christianity, singular and triumphant; the Christianity of John, with its two privileged lessons: love of one's fellow human beings and eternal life" (114; 1919, 1943). A Kierkegaardian existentialism that charges human beings with choosing God and buttresses an altruistic Golden Rule goes to the very heart of *Existencia*.

Existencia, in toto, adumbrates an ethical core for human society, and Hiperión (as "Hiperión and Values" below details) folds Caso's ethics into the core of its being. Absent from *Existencia*, however, is the matter of Mexican identity so vitally present to Hiperión. *Existencia*, pure philosophy, operates on the level of abstract desiderata, without coming down to Mexican ground. Caso's *El problema de México y la ideología nacional* (1924) fills in the gap and yields a paradigm for an ethically involved Mexican identity discourse. A tacit companion piece to *Existencia*, *Problema* applies the earlier work's antipositivist, Christian humanist agenda to a Mexico beset by disunity, the eponymous "problem of Mexico." Mexico's extraordinary diversity, Caso asserts, has failed to meld into a national community. Instead, from the "immense evil" of the Conquest for Indigenous peoples (69) henceforth, never resolving past problems, Mexico has remained splintered. And a splintered Mexico cannot constitute a democracy: "Full democracy demands . . . racial unity, uniform treatment of all; and such uniformity, such unity, has never existed in Mexico" (70). The final essays of *Problema* outline how a post-Revolutionary Mexico can unite in spirit to generate an "ethical democracy" (Hurtado, *Búho* 80).

Among the final essays, the ardent "México: ¡Alas y plomo!" [Mexico: Wings and Lead!] has left an indelible mark on the country's intellectual life. The enduring purchase of Caso's exhortation in "¡Alas y plomo!" that his compatriots abandon foreign models, flying high while keeping their feet on earth, has already entered our sights at several points. No less consequential, I believe, is the ethical program that *Problema* advances in the two essays that bracket "Alas y plomo." As the two essays map out ways in which Mexico can come into its own, they blur the line between advocating Christianity per se and advocating secularized Christian values. Acclaiming Catholicism as a constructive idea to which Mexico should hew, the essay titled "Ideas que construyen e ideas que destruyen" [Constructive and Destructive Ideas] calls for a restoration of religion. Caso hastens to stipulate, silently invoking Kierkegaard, that Mexico should cleave not to the institutionalized Church but to Christianity's root values: "Not Christ the King, but Christ the people [pueblo]: here we have the dictum and the action that can save us. The most urgent lesson for us to preach is the forgiveness of offenses and love for one's fellow human beings" (84). By these teachings so integral to the Mexican spirit, rather than by any foreign political ideology, the country should be guided. Caso, Hurtado tells us, replaces discrete political ideologies with a collective ethic.[24] Accordingly, the penultimate yet culminating essay of *Problema*, "¡México: Hazte valer!" [Mexico: Make Yourself Worthy!], focuses on patriotism, an overarching "consciousness of the Mexican collectivity" (*Problema* 89). For Caso, a patriotic collective consciousness must stem from Mexico's spirituality, as versus the nation's extrinsic features. The love Saint Francis preached, a positive value that subsumes all other positive values, will in Caso's judgment form the basis of a cohesive national imaginary that befits a cohesive, democratic country.

In *Hacia un nuevo humanismo: Programa de una antropología filosófica* [Towards a New Humanism: Plan for a Philosophical Anthropology] (1940), Caso's student Ramos launches his teacher's insistence on values and spirituality into the secular, phenomenological zeitgeist of the then-contemporary philosophical milieu. Several years after the vexatious *Perfil*, Ramos rejoins the public arena with a work that strives to impact the scene and, in the bargain, rehabilitate its author's reputation. Decamping from the contentious ontics of *Perfil*, in *Hacia* Ramos shifts his purview to the less fraught, abstract realm of axiology, the metaphilosophy of values.[25] Only one passage anchors *Hacia* to the context from which it emanates. Well into the book, Ramos proclaims that "in our country," values "have lacked firm principles, always operating in a completely arbitrary manner" (60). Nor does Ramos, from his axiological viewpoint, endorse specific values or specifically champion Christianity. Rather, the message that Mexicans could glean from *Hacia* resides in its familiar privileging of a spiritual, humanistic climate. Ramos writes that "the backbone of modern culture is the spiritual meaning of life" (4). Herein, of course, lies a strong continuity with Caso. Nonetheless, setting himself apart from the old guard, Ramos explicitly inscribes his work in the philosophical anthropology of Max Scheler's *Man's Place in Nature* (1928), translated into Spanish by Gaos in 1938. Scheler's supradisciplinary philosophical anthropology trains a spotlight on human existence as a "particular and irreducible" phenomenon (*Hacia* 37), and aims to take in the whole of it. Ramos parlays Scheler's itinerary into an "anthropological axiomatics" (39) that centers on human consciousness, circumstance, awareness of death, freedom, and choice (40–43).

When in his apostrophe to Mexico Ramos states that "all efforts to correct our flawed value judgments, propagating the conviction that human life possesses intrinsic values" that have "an inalterable reality" will be beneficial (60), the philosopher refers not to axiomatics but to the axiological dialectic he culls from Scheler. Ramos, like Scheler, sees values as strung between inalterable Kantian ideals and their realization in reality. For the "anthropological" *Hacia*, human beings mediate the two pillars of this Janus-faced axiology: "The world of values and the world of reality are complementary spheres. Man mediates between the two worlds. He can posit values that will underlie his actions and then fulfill those values in the world" (66). The equipoised dialectic of *Hacia* counters Caso, whose dogmatic anti-idealism Ramos had belittled in 1927 ("Antonio Caso" 164). In any event, the younger man's philosophical anthropology highlights the life of values in situation, a matter equally apposite to Caso and to phenomenology. Humanistic values, ultimately, are social entities incarnated in "community" by individuals given over to their being-for-others, that is, to altruism (*Hacia* 65, 68, 87).

As Ramos, intent on human existence as "particular and irreducible," makes his case for a moral reform divested of attachments to religion, he frames what one might go so far as to call an existentialist platform sans Sartre. At the least, Ramos carves out a space that the most atheistic, Sartrean Hyperions could occupy unproblematically. It stands to reason, then, that 1948 finds Ramos, conceivably on the strength of *Hacia* appointed director of the UNAM's Facultad de Filosofía y Letras in 1945, aligning with Hiperión. At Hiperión's first conference, Ramos defends the group's philosophical adherence to a concrete situation. Ramos urges Mexicans to exchange an inferiority complex for the responsibility to circumstances that became Zea's mantra. Hiperión proceeded to incorporate the now quite influential Ramos into its activities, while, as we know, significantly diverging from *Perfil*. A third, augmented edition of *Perfil* published in 1951 reveals a Ramos who expresses optimism for Mexico and its promising youth.

A greater source of forward momentum for Hiperión is the group's much less ambivalent relationship with Ramos's teacher and his sometimes model, Caso. The very name "Hiperión" reflects Caso's "México: ¡Alas y plomo!" And the very origins of Hiperión, in an undergraduate study group its members baptized "El Ateneo" (Santos Ruiz 181), relate to Caso. In 1946, upon Caso's death, Zea assumed that scholar's chair at the UNAM. The next year witnessed an homage to Caso at the UNAM in which Gaos, Ramos, Uranga, and Zea, among others, participated. Published as *Homenaje a Caso* (1947), their contributions all honor Caso as an antipositivist who freed Mexican philosophy from various constraints, including prohibitions on spirituality. Beneath the conference's key theme, the importance of Caso for the proto-Hyperions (just a year before their formal debut) makes its appearance. Uranga and Zea pay tribute to Caso, a Mexican tutelary figure. Uranga encourages his peers to cultivate a "true dedication to the philosopher's thought" (220). Zea, clearly having the incipient Hiperión in mind, hails Caso as "the paladin of the doctrine that is now growing" (107). He asks that his generation, which strives to "make Mexican reality a worthy object of philosophical reflection," consider Antonio Caso its master (108).

Zea's requests bring us up to the advent of Hiperión and bring to a close the anatomizing of the Mexican existentialist force field in which Hiperión operated. Taking stock of the force field, it has emerged as a complex yet largely harmonious one, a finely wrought entity with interlocking pieces in which values play a signal role. Conversely, looping back to Sartre we hit a dissonance or roadblock, that being the underdeveloped, well-nigh mute ethics of the French philosopher's early works. This claim requires serious attention—and a brief prelude, on the indispensable question of with *what* Sartre Hiperión was in dialogue. After all, the late 1940s were a moment in Sartre's trajectory, in general and for Mexicans, not the whole Sartre. By the late 1940s Sartre's major published works consisted of *Being and Nothingness* (1943); the Bildungsroman novels, *Nausea* (1938) and two volumes of *The Roads to Freedom* trilogy (1945); the plays mentioned above; and the monographic *Existentialism Is a Humanism* (1946), *Anti-Semite and Jew* (1946), and *What Is Literature?* (1947). He had written but not published the *Notebooks for an Ethics* (written 1947–1948, published posthumously in 1983). The magnum opus that Sartre would denominate a sequel to *Being and Nothingness* (Anderson 86), his *Critique of Dialectical Reason* (1960), lay in the future. Now, as far as I can tell, of the preceding Sartrean repertoire *Being and Nothingness*, *Existentialism Is a Humanism*, the novels, the plays, and *What Is Literature?* most galvanized the Hyperions. The Hyperions are principally in conversation with these works, from which they could garner an ample picture of Sartrean ethics, or the lack thereof.

Let us recall that in "Dos existencialismos" Uranga alludes to an imminent, not actual, Sartre. Uranga's exact words read: "From whatever position Sartre adopts, theories of social relations, pedagogy, history, morality, and man will *immediately follow* (*Análisis* 175; emphasis added). Uranga, vaunting his allegiance to Sartre, puts a positive spin on the philosophy of ethics that Sartre heralded but had not thoroughly delivered by the late

1940s. Strictly speaking, Uranga adduces the last paragraph of *Being and Nothingness* (henceforth, *BN*). There Sartre poses questions about situated freedom, and he closes the book by remarking: "All these questions, which refer us to a pure and not an accessory reflection, can find their reply only on the ethical plane. We shall devote to them a future work" (628). Sartre hereby acknowledges ethics as a project *a fare*, and by the time of Uranga's "Dos existencialismos" the French philosopher had not yet written the promised book (though he was penning the *Notebooks*). The inroads Sartre *had* made into ethics, as a scan of them that begins with *BN* should suffice to demonstrate, were inchoate and riddled with gaps.

BN, it is only fair to register, purposely keeps ethics in abeyance so as not to depart from ontology. Sartre declares: "Ontology itself can not formulate ethical precepts. It is concerned solely with what is, and we can not possibly derive imperatives from ontology's indicatives. It does, however, allow us to catch a glimpse of what sort of ethics will assume its responsibilities when confronted with a *human reality in situation*" (625–26). The divide between ontology and ontics that Hiperión in its own way endeavored to soften underlies Sartre's rationale. *BN* somewhat mitigates the divide through the notion of the "ethical anguish" that arises from awareness that a priori ideals and complacent "everyday morality" must cede to values forged from our own free existence (38). Only our existential freedom determines our values: "*nothing* makes values exist—unless it is that freedom which by the same stroke makes me myself exist" (94). The ethical anguish and freedom that we "glimpse" through the cracks in *BN*'s ontology foreshadow the unequivocal support of a personal value system that Sartre activates, to philosophical and moral peril, in his outright meditations on ethics.

He starts them in the same year that *BN* was published. Sartre's first play, *The Flies* (1943), despite strenuous efforts to the contrary, opens a window onto the vulnerabilities of his ethics. *The Flies* showcases an Orestes reimagined from Aeschylus's play into an existentialist hero who deposes the gods' value system, replacing it with a personal moral code. To save his community, Sartre's Orestes murders Clytemnestra and Aegisthus, overlords of a life-denying, tyrannical regime. "I am my freedom," Orestes cries (117); he refuses to display remorse for having exercised his freedom through a vigilante justice that he characterizes as "doing what is right" (102).[26] The play's audience can hardly help but agree. Sartre has so stacked the deck against the depraved tyrants and in favor of the Christ-like Orestes that a personal moral code resulting in vigilante murder appears unassailable. *The*

Flies' internal logic, its passion, mask the ethical quandaries inherent in Orestes's bloody justice. As often happens with Sartre, as soon as we step outside his works' suasive frames ethical complications assert themselves.

The most frontal, accessible, and widely circulated elucidation of ethics that Sartre had formulated by the time Hiperión began, *Existentialism Is a Humanism* (1946), compounds rather than resolves the quandaries. Responding to charges of nihilism, Sartre's lecture transformed into a book does not shrink from sounding the dangerous notes of existential freedom and autonomous morality ("You are free"; no "general code of ethics can tell you what you ought to do" [33]). *Existentialism Is a Humanism* works to defuse the threat through a portrait of the humanistic ethics that can ensue from freedom. Whence Sartre's much-cited credo in the 1946 treatise, which recalls the communitarianism of *The Flies*: "When we say that man chooses himself, not only do we mean that each of us must choose himself, but also that in choosing himself, he is choosing for all men" (24).[27] Sartre confidently avows: "We always choose the good, and nothing can be good for any of it unless it is good for all" (24). Anticipating the question of why any given individual should presume to decide "for humanity as a whole," Sartre invokes one's inborn "full and profound" sense of responsibility (25). Thus, while outreaching to the possibility of creating "a human community" (51) for "all men," Sartre has drilled down on individual subjectivity.

The preceding exposition of *Existentialism Is a Humanism* (henceforth, *EH*) should amply indicate that the book suspends ethics in a vague, open-ended subjectivism. Such aporias, naturally, have not escaped Sartrean scholars. They corroborate what Sartre denies in *EH*, namely, that his ethics can boil down to doing whatever one likes (*EH* 44). Let us listen to a few piercing summations. Paul Vincent Spade deduces that Sartre's position "allows all ethical codes, and requires none of them—not even authenticity. But that is just to say that there is no such thing as an 'existentialist ethics'—that is, an ethics that follows naturally from the ontology of *Being and Nothingness*." Thomas Flynn weighs in with: "Sartre was a moralist but scarcely a moralizer." Sonia Kruks wonders "what Sartre's notions of value and moral consciousness might contribute to ethics in the more traditional sense of the search for general precepts of good or right conduct," and concludes, it "is hard to know what kind of ethical judgments we could ever make about this total freedom" (60–61). All told, Sartrean scholars worry that *EH*'s ethics amount to a freedom that can easily give way to moral anarchy.

Part Two

HIPERIÓN AND VALUES

The pressures on Mexican existentialism that Part One has tracked leave little doubt that a precarious moral compass, not to mention moral anarchy, held little attraction for Hiperión. On the contrary, the exigencies of identity and transformation combined with Mexican philosophy's sedimented ethical disposition powerfully draw Hiperión into the sphere of morality. We now arrive at the denouement of the plot—what happens when Hiperión brings all the energies together. And what happens, within philosophical bounds, is not short on drama. The Hyperions rush in where angels, or Sartre, fear to tread and devise an ethics for Mexico inscribed in an existentialist framework. Capitalizing on the gaps in ethics that eventuate from the French philosopher's commitment to ontology as well as from the aporias in his ethical thinking, Hiperión supplements Sartre. Zea underscores the latitude to forge their own approach of which the Hyperions availed themselves. Because existentialism "is simply an instrument for capturing the reality of Mexican man," not a "doctrine to which we grant absolute credence," it allows the Mexican intellectual "his own assessments," which "must be abstracted from the specific reality he faces" (*Conciencia* 54). In effect and in brief, the fractures in Sartrean ethics clear a space for Hiperión to occupy, a seeding ground for a distinctive Mexican value system. Hiperión's capacious existentialism sees no disjunction between freedom and advocating particular values.

Which values? The first, as we might imagine, is altruism, or, in the existentialist parlance of the time, intersubjectivity. The term "intersubjectivity" has become so diffuse that a clarification is in order. Hiperión's sense of intersubjectivity bears the stamp of French Christian existentialist Gabriel Marcel (1889–1973), a portion of whose works Villoro translated.[28] Marcel affords philosophy the scintillating "idea of being open towards others: that openness I have called inter-subjectivity" (*Man Against* 24). His Christian existentialist intersubjectivity carries in tow the array of religious norms that Caso's altruism encloses (e.g., the Golden Rule, agape, caritas). Like altruism, Marcel's intersubjectivity encompasses one to one and one to the whole of society relationships.

The second key value Hiperión promoted, integrally related to the first, then combats a fragmented Mexico purportedly awash in solitude by visualizing the whole of its society as an interlinked *community*. The sense of community that pervades Hiperión's writings, too, comports with theology. In 1 Corinthians 12, Paul delineates a religious collectivity: "For as the body is one, and hath many members, and all the members of that one body, being many, are one body: so also is Christ (*Bible*, 1 Cor. 12:12), and "there should be no schism in the body; but that the members should have the same care one for another" (12:25). 1 Corinthians 12 lends itself as easily to transvaluation as to ethics. Then again, Galatians 5:13 reminds us that a theologically informed communitarianism such as Hiperión's need not default on freedom: "For, brethren, ye have been called unto liberty; only use not liberty for an occasion to the flesh, but by love serve one another." The City of God, the Earthly City, and Sartre's classless City of Ends thereby slide into plausible alignment.

Reading Sartre from the perspective of an ethical agenda, certain Hyperions maintain a hearty solidarity with him, as did Uranga in "Dos existencialismos." Rather than abandon the writer whose zeal for freedom, engagement, and situation had electrified them, they seize on Sartre as a lightning rod and stretch his hermeneutic to fit their concerns. Carlos Sánchez's 2016 book, to my knowledge the first study to pinpoint the communitarian thrust of Hiperión, observes that Mexican thinkers accepted "existentialism as a conceptual matrix for the reinterpretation of their reality" and urgently attempted "to locate an existentialist morality somewhere in the existentialist literature" (*Contingency* 19).[29]

Joaquín Sánchez MacGrégor does exactly that in his contribution to Hiperión's premiere, "¿Hay una moral existencialista?" [Is There an Existentialist Morality?] (1948). His lecture and article register the widespread perception of immorality, or, at best, an "uncertain moral content" in Sartre's works (268), a vagueness regarding ethics that Sánchez MacGrégor ascribes to Sartre's preoccupation with ontology: "In effect, Sartre's doctrine is an 'ontology of freedom,' not an ethics for reality" (275). Undaunted, Sánchez MacGrégor continues the efforts to finesse Sartrean ontology into an ethics begun, he says, (not by Sartre but) by Francis Jeanson and Simone de Beauvoir (276). He spotlights Sartre's paramount ethic of freedom, in which "freedom is the absolute principle and value, the alpha and omega of existence" (278). Sánchez MacGrégor then augments *EH*'s circumscribed notion of intersubjectivity ("The other is essential to my existence, as well as to the knowledge I have of myself"; see *EH* 41–42). The Hyperion comments that existants realize their freedom in the midst of concrete situations, "always attending to the freedom of the *other*" (278; emphasis in original). Allegedly based on Sartre, the fuller-bodied ethics that Sánchez MacGrégor puts forth inflects care for the other.

"Here I mean to explain Sartre, not to refute him" (103), writes Jorge Portilla in "La náusea y el humanismo," his presentation at Hiperión's 1947 conference. True to his word and eager to illuminate a value-rich Sartre, Portilla's commentary performs an elaborate dance with *Nausea* and *EH*. Portilla reads *Nausea*, somewhat idiosyncratically, as an existential pilgrim's progress from solitude to community. For Portilla, *Nausea*'s protagonist Roquentin evolves from the "absolute solitude" that the discovery of existence foists on him into the "center of a small community" (112) that the novel he proposes in *Nausea*'s last pages to write will create by reaching out to others.[30] Camus's 1938 review of *Nausea* (perhaps unbeknown to Portilla) detects "something rather comic in the disproportion" between Roquentin's fraught, protracted awakening to contingency and the awakening's quick resolution in a proposed novel (202); by contrast, Portilla aggrandizes *Nausea*'s tenuous finale into a harbinger of the "eminently moral" program (113) that Sartre comes closer to solidifying in *EH*. Portilla extracts from *EH* certain "cardinal concepts" of a Sartrean ethics: responsibility, freedom, choice, a secular value system (113–14), and the "possibility of creating a human community" (117). Portilla's indulgent apologetics for Sartre, like Uranga's, cites *BN*'s as yet unfulfilled promise of an ethics. Unlike Uranga, however, Portilla has substantiated that Sartre's extant works themselves display a far from "innocuous" investment in ethics (118).

Mexican philosophy, attentive to the dynamics of a rooted *cosmopolitanism*, tends to do important work for its country in texts unmoored from the immediate context, that is, in philosophical meditations of a universal nature. Caso's *Existencia*, Ramos's *Hacia*, and Portilla's essay demonstrate this tendency. Luis Villoro's contributions to Hiperión, for their part, first gravitate to the cosmopolitan and then to the Mexican. His initial essays take on pure philosophy, in 1950 Villoro produces *Los grandes momentos del indigenismo en México*, and subsequently, of course, the many works in each of the two veins that made him a towering figure in Mexican philosophy. If over his long, prolific career Villoro set his hand to disparate subjects, he retained throughout a profound dedication to ethics—in the main to ethical intersubjectivity, respect for others.[31] Of all the Hyperions, Villoro seems to be the person who most concertedly builds on Caso's altruism.

Villoro's debut with Hiperión propels Mexican existentialism into commerce with Marcel's and Casos's principles of intersubjectivity. In "La reflexión sobre el ser en Gabriel Marcel" [Gabriel Marcel's Reflections on Being] (1948), Villoro contemplates Marcel's ontological arguments, which for the Hyperion extol the bridges that unite "being in general to human beings, their concrete existence" (290).[32] Only by establishing such bridges through love, charity, and *disponibilité* (availability to others), writes Villoro of Marcel, can one realize the plenitude of Being (290–94). Caso enters the scenario sideways. Interestingly enough, completely independent of each other, often writing concurrently, Caso and Marcel developed remarkably similar arguments (on the commonalities, see Krauze 231–44). The symbiosis between Villoro and a lesser-known Mexican philosopher, Alberto Menéndez Samará, reveals a more direct link with Caso. Villoro's 1949 article "Génesis y proyecto del existencialismo en México" outlines Menéndez Samará's *Menester y precisión del ser* [Mission and Rationale of Being] (1946), a book dedicated to Caso. The article establishes that Villoro shares Menéndez Samará's, as well as Marcel's, advocacy for love, overcoming the self/other binary, and for the collectivity.

Villoro's "Soledad y comunión" [Solitude and Communion] (1949) then provides a veritable how-to guide for achieving the nonobjectifying communion with others that its author regards as the "primordial nucleus of any authentic community" (38). The Hyperion's treatment of his essay's title subjects is worlds away from Paz's impending *Laberinto*. After surveying the evolution of our current immersion in solitude (25), Villoro spurs his readers to community and interpersonal communion with a philosophical argument inspired by Marcel, as above, and by Scheler's *The Nature of Sympathy* (1923). The two thinkers bolster Villoro's stirring case for a communion, or sympathy, with others that does *not violate their freedom*. Villoro posits an I-Thou love that "frees us from the prison of egocentrism" (41) and rejects "any impulse to enslave the other" (45). Acting otherwise renders love impossible: "Love moves us to appropriate the other, but at the same time it demands that the other remain independent; because if for even a moment the other ceases to be irreducible, the loving partnership disappears; rather than with two alterities face to face, we are left with singular solitudes" (44–45). Villoro's portrait of a noncoercive intersubjectivity at once bonds with Sartre, in favoring freedom, and disowns him, in rejecting objectification.

The preceding two essays allow us to grasp the raison d'être of Villoro's milestone work on attitudes towards the Indigenous-other, *Los grandes momentos del indigenismo en México*. *Grandes momentos*, which began its life in 1949 as Villoro's MA thesis directed by Gaos, details misprisions of the Indigenous worlds. The work traces the history not of the Indigenous peoples per se but of *indigenismo*, the evolving, generally problematic positions on the Indigenous peoples that foreigners in Mexico and non-Indigenous

Mexican intellectuals have espoused from the colonial period onward. Villoro spells out the book's mission: "This book strives to respond to one question: what being has been attributed to the Indian and occupied Mexican consciousness? We are not interrogating what the Indian actually is, but instead what is revealed when people take him as their subject" (13). Employing a phenomenological method, *Grandes momentos* tells an existentialist story. It recounts the history of an inauthentic "*false* consciousness" (9) that for centuries has objectified Indigenous others. As it lays bare constructions of the Indigenous peoples arrived at *without* the subjects' actual involvement in the process, *Grandes momentos* becomes an exposé, an encyclopedia of defective intersubjectivity (my chapter 4 examines the important *Grandes momentos* in more depth).

By contrast, a text we have already met, Zea's *Conciencia y posibilidad del mexicano*, applauds Mexican intersubjectivity, and morality and community. The inversion of values discussed above sets the stage for Zea to document the specifically Mexican ways of life from which one can extrapolate a commendable value system not only for Mexicans but also for other nations in similar circumstances (32, 70). Zea's chapter 3, "Comunidad y moral" [Community and Morality] offers up the special texture of Mexican community as one exemplar. The fact that the 1952 *Conciencia*, unlike Villoro's "Soledad y comunión," now coexists with *Laberinto* throws Hiperión's distinctive approach to Mexican community into relief. Zea's third chapter draws heavily on Portilla's "Comunidad, grandeza y miseria del mexicano" [Community, Greatness, and Misery of the Mexican] and acclaims Mexican *personalismo*. Neither *Laberinto*'s bacchanalian community nor in the least Gaos's method of the same name, Zea's and Portilla's personalismo denotes the real human ties that supersede loyalties to abstractions such as the government or the law.[33] Mexican community rests on "relationships of concrete individuals'" such as friendship and kinship, albeit sometimes with the downsides of political bribes and cronyism (*Conciencia* 67). The personalismo burgeoning under the auspicious current conditions will, if Miguel Alemán's regime fulfills the promise Zea sees in it, overthrow prior alienation, masks, and the lack of true intersubjectivity (33). When Mexico realizes the shining possibility, Zea concludes with brio: "This society of ours, despite all its defects . . . may give rise to a truly human form of community" (67). To get there, Mexico need only assimilate the understanding of itself that *Conciencia*, wedded to existentialism, has brought to the fore.

Gauging the present state of their country's mores, other thinkers involved with Hiperión navigate a course between panegyric to and critique of Mexican community. Portilla's deep-seated commitment to values elicits both standpoints. In the essay on which Zea's *Conciencia* drew, "Comunidad, grandeza y miseria del mexicano," Portilla grants that Mexican community does in fact honor "existence" as "co-existence" (130; Marcel's *co-esse*). Portilla's book, *Fenomenología del relajo* (relajo has "no straightforward equivalent in English" [Sánchez, *Suspension* 6]) then examines the agents who obstruct community. Portilla's *Fenomenología*, published after his death by Villoro and others, undertakes to set Mexico on an "authentic path . . . to community" (14). It does so circuitously, through the figure of the obstreperous Mexican *relajiento* who makes a mockery of values, or "seriousness," in public, stoking a negative "intersubjectivity" (23).[34] "The meaning or sense of relajo," writes Portilla, "is that of suspending seriousness. In other words, suspending or destroying the subject's adherence to a value offered up to his freedom" (18). On Portilla's interpretation, as relajientos defy seriousness and court chaos, they spectacularize the need for authentic, generous values (see Sánchez, *Contingency*, chs. 1–2).

The chaotic community that relajientos instigate recalls Paz's fiesta, an unhinged form of collectivity and co-existence. As this implies (for we do not know when Portilla composed *Fenomenología*) and *Conciencia* evidences, Paz may have distanced himself from Hiperión, but Hiperión did not fail to engage with *Laberinto*. Salvador Reyes Nevares and María Elvira Bermúdez, for example, interlace Paz with Hiperión intellectuals like Uranga and Zea. Reyes Nevares, in *El amor y la amistad en el mexicano* [Love and Friendship in the Mexican] (1951), and Bermúdez, in *La vida familiar del mexicano* [Mexican Family Life] (1955), a major early study of Mexican gender relations, compose sociological exposés of alienation defined à la *Laberinto*. The two authors, however, eventually pivot away from Paz's obstructions and towards intersubjectivity. Reyes Nevares lauds Mexicans' signal capacity for egalitarian friendship, which contravenes the affective power plays that dominate *Laberinto*. Stretching Reyes Nevares's encomium of friendship, Bermúdez holds out hope for gender equality in Mexico, a "true friendship" and "authentic solidarity" that would represent an organic outgrowth of her native land's convivial nature (130). Bermúdez's enlightened, pioneering work resonates uncannily with Beauvoir's *The Second Sex* (1949), particularly in terms of women's complicity with the patriarchy. Yet Bermúdez mentions neither Beauvoir nor Sartre, instead appearing only to polemicize with *Laberinto*.

The Hyperions' expansive calculus of Mexican community and intersubjectivity, we see, has absorbed Paz, incorporated Marcel et alia, and temporized with Sartre. In the aggregate, these slippages from Sartre betoken a further disconnect between Hiperión and the French philosopher, an incommensurability even more fundamental than his inadequate ethics. I refer to Hiperión's break from the early Sartre's model of human relationships as a power-mongering war, a model that Villoro's special pleading for intersubjectivity in "Soledad y comunión" patently opposed. In chapter 1, I characterized the dark Sartrean model as the objectification of an other who threatens our freedom. Hiperión's value-platform now abundantly in view, I want to take a thicker measure of the Sartrean complex and bring home how dramatically it goes against the grain of Mexican existentialism.

"Hell is other people" ("L'enfer c'est les autres"): the chilling slogan from Sartre's play *No Exit* (*Huis Clos*, 1944) has pervaded the popular consciousness as the sum total of his position on human interactions. The truism, while not entirely inaccurate, sensationalizes the narrative of human relations *BN* weaves in "First Attitude toward Others: Love, Language, Masochism," the first section of part 3, chapter 3, "Concrete Relations with Others." We meet an encapsulation of that narrative, distilled to its most commanding essentials—the essentials most anathema to Hiperión and to the literary writers in Hiperión's sphere—in this paragraph on the gaze of the other:

> Everything which may be said of me in my relations with the Other applies to him as well. While I attempt to free myself from the hold of the Other, the Other is trying to free himself from mine; while I seek to enslave the Other, the Other seeks to enslave me. We are by no means dealing with unilateral relations with an object-in-itself, but with reciprocal and moving relations. The following descriptions of concrete behavior must therefore be envisaged within the perspective of *conflict*. Conflict is the original meaning of being-for-others. (*BN* 364)

Why conflict and enslavement? According to Sartre (we should remember that he writes in the midst of the German Occupation), human relations are a struggle of wills, and at issue is whether one will be a subject or object. When I, qua any individual, am regarded by an other, the viewer's gaze acts as a mirror that endows me with being as a subject *and* threatens to obliterate me into an object, assimilated into the other's consciousness. In Sartre's never too transparent words: "By virtue of consciousness the Other is for me simultaneously the one who has stolen my being from me and the one who causes 'there to be' a being which is my being" (364). A conflict ensues in which I struggle to recover my being by possessing the other's consciousness, and the other struggles to possess mine. Again in Sartre's words: "My project of recovering my being will be realized only if I get hold of this freedom and reduce it to being a freedom subject to my freedom" (366). The battle of wills, it almost goes without saying, offers no viable template for relationships between equals or for intersubjectivity.

Love itself falls victim to the battle of egos. In Sartre's logic, internally coherent no matter how debatable the larger premises on which it rests, love would naturally collapse into masochism and sadomasochism, drives that befit the war of subjectivities. Further, when Sartre interrogates romantic love per se he burdens it with tortuous convolutions, more no-exit scenarios. They accrue from the fact that Sartrean ontology, grounded in freedom, demands a special kind of possession: the Sartrean lover wishes to possess the beloved *as a freedom*. Hence, "the Other's freedom should determine itself to become love" (367). A fair enough prospect, perhaps. But in the coercive universe of *BN*, in order to achieve it the lover impinges on the beloved's freedom. The Sartrean lover will strain to become the beloved's "whole World" (367), to "be placed beyond the whole system of values posited by the Other" (369). Only in this manner can the lover avoid succumbing to the other's gaze (369). Yet the assault on the other must needs persist and the other resist. Under the sway of World War II, *BN* upholds radical freedom, each person's absolute, indestructible freedom under any circumstances, including torture (403). It follows that another's freedom can never be fully possessed.

The fatal attractions and resistances of human relationships that *BN* depicts lead one to ask what kind of "we," in the sense of solidarity and community, Sartre's framework accommodates, or if it accommodates any such "we" at all. Here Heidegger's ontological *Mitsein*, "being-with-others," comes into play. For Heidegger, Mitsein broadly and nonprescriptively designates the ontological circumstance that we share the world with other people. Dasein and Mitsein are coterminous, Heidegger indicates in *Being and Time* (1927): "So far as Dasein is at all, it has Being-with-one-another as its kind of Being" (163). The last section of *BN*'s "Concrete Relations with Others," entitled " 'Being-With' (Mitsein) and the 'We,' " overlays on Heidegger's Mitsein constructions of the "we" and the "us" none too propitious for solidarity. In short, *BN* diminishes the "we" into a mere act of perception, an "I" and an "Other" that a spectator's gaze constitutes from outside as a "we" (e.g., 413). The "us" likewise results from the gaze of a third party who witnesses a group unite against an oppressor. Hatred, more than love, compels the "us," and the "we," Sartre professes, is something of a fiction (413).[35]

Incrementally, "Concrete Relations with Others" has dismantled the core elements of intersubjectivity. Under the constraints of the Sartrean worldview, even Garcin's pleas in *No Exit* for altruism and solidarity go for naught (29). *BN* leaves intersubjectivity, as well as the values connected to it, mutilated, practically disappeared, and thus in a state antithetical to Hiperión.[36] Juliana González Valenzuela, a latter-day Mexican philosopher who studied with Eduardo Nicol, precisely (if de facto) identifies the Sartrean biases that were so adverse to Hiperión's pursuits. She writes in *Ética y libertad* (1997): "Insofar as existentialism does not establish what constitutes true *community* and genuine interhuman *communication* . . . and insofar as it does not account for 'love' in its proper ontological and radical sense, strictly speaking *existentialism does not establish an ethics*" (22). Available to Hiperión itself was Marcel's scathing critique in "Existence and Human Freedom" (1946) of Sartre's nihilistic default on "genuine community, the community of love or friendship" (*Philosophy* 74). Therefore, no matter how much Hiperión stretched Sartre, Mexican existentialism had to, and did, push beyond him. Frontally or tacitly, as text or subtext, Hiperión breaches Sartean pathological relations with the other, transforming Sartre's ontological Mitsein into an ethics. Hiperión effectively seizes on Sartre as both a model and a counter-model. The group effectively pits one profile of Sartre (freedom, situation, engagement) against another (problematic ethics/intersubjectivity).

Mobilizing an eclectic, altruistic existentialism, Hiperión has channeled the limited Sartrean moment of the 1940s into a fertile moment for the *theater of values* that, I maintained in chapter 1, was existentialism's larger calling for Latin America. As Hiperión did so, it not only forcibly strayed from Sartre but also moved into unwitting lockstep with Beauvoir and Camus. Although Beauvoir and Camus certainly did not cut as large figures on the Mexican horizon as Sartre, their existentialisms strikingly resemble what Hiperión independently enacted.[37] Beauvoir and Camus, repudiating the meaninglessness of life, forge an existential ethics. The two philosophical warriors impress on their readers that, Sartre notwithstanding, existentialism *can* generate an ethics that quite literally embraces the other, singularly and collectively. The metaphysical rebels tease out of existentialism a loving embeddedness in the world resplendent with, and enlarging upon, the authentic intersubjectivity Marcel's philosophy expounds. At heart, I submit, *Hiperión wanted Sartre to be what Beauvoir and Camus already were*. That

Beauvoir and Camus's individual slates of values, which I will now explore much more briefly than they deserve, parallel Hiperión's makes the two French philosophers' works something of a missed opportunity for Mexican existentialism. Conversely, the possible missed opportunity foregrounds the razor-sharp acuity of Hiperión's transactions with Sartre.

Whereas the early Sartre gestures to ethics, Beauvoir confronts them. "No ethics is implied in existentialism. I have sought, for my part, to extract one from it," she declared in 1945 (qtd. in Simons, introduction 3). Beauvoir confronts them head-on in *Pyrrhus and Cineas* (1944) and, shortly after, in *The Ethics of Ambiguity* (1947). These works, like Sartre's *BN*, grapple with Mitsein. The ethics Beauvoir advances, however, restore magnanimous life to the "we" that *BN* bankrupted. Beauvoir's overriding conviction that subjectivity "cannot exist without intersubjectivity" (Kruks 92), spurs her to probe Mitsein and to imagine it not as a locus of conflicts but as a wellspring of generosity and solidarity.[38] Beauvoir stakes out her territory in *Pyrrhus and Cineas*, published just a year after *BN* and, like *BN*, written during the German Occupation. Jumping off from Voltaire's directive in *Candide* that we cultivate our garden, *Pyrrhus* inquires what exactly *our* garden is. Surely, according to Beauvoir, its boundaries exceed our own little plot of earth, and indeed may encompass the whole world, wherever injustice reigns. "Our" garden thus vastly expanded raises the matter of "our" neighbor. *Pyrrhus* reminds its readers that the "disciples of Christ asked: who is my neighbor?" (91).[39] Beauvoir invokes compassion and responsibility in her reply that we *make* our neighbors, we make the other our brother or sister. Our consciousness, the "for-itself" (the *pour-soi*), disposes us to cast aside the distinction between self and other: because "I am not a thing, but a project of self toward the other, a transcendence," I "can call the other mine" (93).

Part 2 of *Pyrrhus* delves into the problematics of calling the other mine, the threat of abrogating the other's freedom that it poses. Eminently mindful of intersubjectivity's dangers, Beauvoir repeatedly enjoins that we approach others as a freedom and that we respect their freedom with a "lucid generosity" (124). "Respect for the other's freedom is not an abstract rule. It is the first condition of my successful effort," she writes (136). And a successful effort can only proceed from what Beauvoir calls the "appeal," answerability to the other in a reciprocal recognition of freedom. The appeal and generosity combine to heighten awareness that one's own projects may not coincide with those of one's neighbors. "What is good for different men differs . . . . One cannot stop at this tranquil solution: wanting *the* good of *all* men" (127). With this, Beauvoir deconstructs Sartre's credence that any given individual can purport to arbitrate "for the whole of mankind."

Beauvoir has mapped out an intersubjective, moral territory in which it would be difficult for the Sartre whom we have met thus far to live. The years after *Pyrrhus*, in any event, find Sartre at work on the *Notebooks*, which augured his self-stated "conversion" from ontology to the ethical praxis that informs the *Critique of Dialectical Reason*.[40] According to Kruks, Beauvoir supplies the missing link between the early and later Sartre. It was Beauvoir "alone, starting in *Pyrrhus and Cineas*, who began to make the case for that independence of freedoms which a synthesis of existentialism and Marxism must be able to demonstrate" (Kruks 98–99). Meanwhile, Camus and his compelling ethical repertoire had exploded onto the scene. In likely dialogue with Camus's indomitable Sisyphus (*The Myth of Sisyphus*, 1942), Beauvoir places her 1944 text under the aegis of a Pyrrhus who, in victory or failure, keeps on trying.[41] For Beauvoir and his general readership, Camus had further riveting messages on ethics to impart. His novel *The Plague* (1947) redefines the disease as a lack of consciousness of others, of the individual. It chronicles the "path of sympathy" (225) that will combat the pestilence: friendship, compassion, love for all, being and doing good, community, solidarity, and taking the side of the victim. "What interests me," says character Jean Tarrou, battler of the plague, "is learning to become a saint," a "saint without God" (225). Analogously, Camus's ethical program in *The Plague* bows to Christianity by recruiting its tenets for a secular moral universe. Little wonder, then, that in *Entre Sartre y Camus* the Peruvian Mario Vargas Llosa chose Camus over Sartre as his lodestar.

Hiperión faced a different predicament. Rather than wrestling with Camus versus Sartre, the Mexican intellectuals tangled with Sartre cum Paz. Paz's renditions of the gaze, self-protection, love, and so on, had Mexicanized the Sartrean war of subjectivities. Moreover, *Laberinto* launched the occluded intersubjectivity and erratic community of Mexicans into near-inescapable points of reference. *Laberinto* kept Sartre's dark vision alive, relevant, and circulating widely in Mexico. Hiperión, in contradistinction, had charted an empowering, affirmative path away from both Sartre and Paz.

Although Hiperión disbanded in 1952, the path the group charted did not evanesce. Conveying transvaluation into postmodernity, the postsecularism of Villoro's *El poder y el valor: Fundamentos de una ética política* [Power and Value: Foundations of a Political Ethics] (1997) and of Hurtado's *Dialéctica del naufragio* [Dialectics of a Shipwreck] (2016) reembodies Hiperión's signature concerns with community and intersubjectivity. Each by his own lights—Villoro emphasizing aspects of traditional Indigenous communities that can serve as models for Mexico, Hurtado how faith, hope, and charity can reinvigorate democracy—the two works sustain Hiperión's ethical compass. Villoro ends his work with a peroration reaffirming the "true values" of "freedom, authenticity, responsibility, equality" (380) and "the desideratum of love: to fulfill oneself by affirming the other" (381). His peroration, which Beauvoir would celebrate as a full-fledged appeal, emblematizes the ongoing currency of Antonio Caso and Hiperión. The thrust towards altruism that Villoro and Hurtado share, so rooted in the Mexican philosophical ethos, still impels them to crusade for authentic community.[42]

Conclusion: Weaponizing *Lo Mexicano*?

Upon taking office as president in 1946, Miguel Alemán Valdés trumpeted his doctrine of *Mexicanidad* to the Congreso de la Nación. "The Mexicanidad that we acclaim as the guiding light of our National Program," Alemán blazoned, "is the awareness that we ourselves—thanks to our resolute work ethic and our moral and spiritual convictions—hold the solution to our own problems" (qtd. in Martínez 105). Alemán appropriates the term "Mexicanidad" from Agustín Yáñez, who had employed it in 1942 as a designation for the "authentic attributes" of Indigenous religions that still vitalize Mexican culture (*Mitos* xi). Twisted from Yáñez's usage, Mexicanidad equipped Alemán's bourgeois "revolution" with its ideological and rhetorical foundations. The propagandistic, ebullient nationalism of Mexicanidad rallied the country to erect a modern Mexico, technological and intensely capitalistic. Alemanismo's modern Mexico, supposedly transcending partisan ideologies, would prioritize the needs of the country over discrete interests. In practice, as I discussed in chapter 1, this entailed deprioritizing land redistribution. It also entailed neutralizing outliers like communist and labor movements that threatened to disrupt the polity ostensibly united in the PRI, which had adopted Mexicanidad as its party line. Finally, Mexicanidad involved a dynamizing of the Mexican mentality (Santos Ruiz 297), a summons to a work ethic, action, and responsibility. Bundling together all the foregoing initiatives, the doctrine of *Mexicanidad* weaponized *lo mexicano* for Alemanismo.

Whether Hiperión, whose abundant optimism and exertions to raise Mexican consciousness we have witnessed, was complicit with Mexicanidad therefore demands consideration. To what degree are Mexicanidad and lo mexicano one in the same? Ana Santos Ruiz's *Los hijos de los dioses: El* Grupo filosófico Hiperión *y la filosofía de lo mexicano* [The Children of the Gods: The Philosophical Grupo Hiperión and the Philosophy of Lo Mexicano] (2015) tackles the issue exorbitantly, brilliantly, and vehemently. Her 486-page, prizewinning book, the longest study of Hiperión, links up with Roger Bartra's *La jaula de la melancolía* [The Cage of Melancholy] (1987) to expose Hiperión's alleged unsavory collusion with Mexicanidad.[43] Piece by piece, Santos Ruiz unveils Hiperión's "contribution to the creation of a hegemonic culture that upheld and justified the patterns of domination that the period reinforced" (433). Although at times she hedges her bets (e.g., "I should underscore that the Hyperions did not conceive of themselves as a group of organic intellectuals, but their work effectively supported the political and economic regime" [443]), Santos Ruiz mercilessly indicts Hiperión.

In her Marxist-leaning script, Hiperión, avid for fame, exploited its connections with the university, which was newly in favor with the government. Leveraging university resources, the group staged a huge campaign of self-promotion that included affiliating itself with renowned thinkers like Ramos and with French existentialism primarily to enhance its own status. Hiperión's philosophy of lo mexicano adopted Ramos's *Perfil* and broadcast the inadequacies of Mexicans in ways that meshed with Alemanismo's expedients. The Hyperions, partial to mestiz@s and the bourgeoisie, disregarded Indigenous peoples. Co-opted and upwardly mobile, the Hyperions refrained from criticizing the government and, indeed, angled for government jobs. In sum, for Santos Ruiz Hiperión's lo mexicano was directly and indirectly in bed with Alemanismo's Mexicanidad, the official story.[44]

Sustaining an elaborately documented, exceptionally articulate critique for nearly five hundred pages, Santos Ruiz's account mounts a persuasive attack on Hiperión. As I hope readers of my account will recognize, Santo Ruiz's study contains valid observations along with tendentious spins on them. For instance, arguably unremarkable, normal matters I have laid out, like Hiperión's alliances with previous Mexican thinkers, become objectionably abnormal, highly suspect, from her perspective. In the utterly non-Sartrean no-exit scenarios that Santos Ruiz assembles, Hiperión cannot escape suspicion: praising or finding fault with Mexicans, championing a united community or fomenting class interests, Hiperión reportedly has a tainted ulterior motive.

Given that even before Santos Ruiz scholars responding to Bartra had contested the putative coalition of Hiperión and Alemanismo, my account finds itself in good company. If, in Hurtado's estimation, certain aspects of the "philosophy of lo mexicano" were "*in tune with* the official story," "it would be incorrect to say that the philosophy of lo mexicano was planned by a government office," was intended as "a political program," or functioned as a "legitimating ideology." Instead, Hurtado continues, lo mexicano "aimed to address certain deep concerns of Mexicans—concerns which may well be called existential" ("Introducción" xxxii–xxiii). An article by Zea's former student Tzvi Medin, "La mexicanidad política y filosófica en el sexenio de Miguel Alemán. 1946–1952" (first published in 1990, reissued in 2017), arrives at similar conclusions. "As a platform for launching Mexico towards a new stage in its history, [Hiperión's] heightened consciousness in fact parallels the vision of [Alemán's] ruling party" but is not causally related to it, because Hiperión "explicitly presented itself as continuing the philosophical thought" of Caso and Ramos, among others.

Perhaps the most telling retort to Santos Ruiz's outlook is Ricardo Guerra's "Una historia del Hiperión," a 1984 retrospective of the group to which he belonged. Guerra locates Hiperión in the "important years" of Alemán's administration, when "the Mexican bourgeoisie was affirmed and firmed up the country's development," "an era of great nationalism" (16). Hiperión, Guerra grants, was a moving part of the context. However, from Guerra's post-Hiperión, Marxist standpoint his former group did *not* meet the needs of the Alemán moment. Caught up in academic philosophizing, Guerra maintains, Hiperión was unable to furnish the down-to-earth socioeconomic and historical analyses relevant to the material development Mexico was undergoing (17). Santos Ruiz, not passing up an opportunity to impugn Hiperión, cites Guerra's statement that Hiperión's theories "in no way accorded with the reality or concrete needs of the Mexican, with Mexican history, or with the country itself at that moment"(Guerra, "Una historia" 17), in spite of the damage it does to her thesis on the group's complicity with Alemanismo (Santos Ruiz 43).

On balance, it seems that we can understand Hiperión fairly enough as part and parcel of the fabric of its times. I would happily leave things there were it not for an aspect of Santo Ruiz's methodology that strikes at what "The Mexican Existentialist Ethos" has endeavored to illuminate as well as fuels her vitriol on Hiperión. To wit, *Los hijos de los dioses*, self-statedly "a sociopolitical history of ideas and intellectuals" (13), construes Hiperión more as a social than a philosophical project; in so doing, it *brackets out Hiperión's philosophical depth and amplitude*. The absences from the bibliography of Santos Ruiz's book plainly tell the tale. Primary texts by Sartre and Heidegger, not to mention Beauvoir, Camus, Marcel, and Scheler, make no appearance in the bibliography's twenty-four pages. When Santos Ruiz attends to Sartrean existentialism, I note, she does so through catchphrases and others' writings. Caso's *La existencia como economía, como desinterés, y como caridad* shines for its complete absence. Disappearing or marginalizing major pieces of Mexican existentialism's gestalt and coming at Hiperión as a social project aligned with Alemanismo yields a slanted, reductive view of the group that primes it for the negative judgments with which Santos Ruiz freights her book.

I take as a case-in-point the treatment of values in *Los hijos de los dioses*. Given Santos Ruiz's focus on Alemanismo's efforts to reshape Mexican society, values matter for her book, and she deals with them extensively as they relate to the politics of subject formation. Existentialism, she says, endowed Hiperión's philosophy of lo mexicano with "the surgical instrument" necessary to bring about a "moral transformation" in keeping with Mexicanidad (136). The "prophylactic dimension" of Hiperión's philosophy "strove to consolidate nationalism, understood as the acceptance of a series of values, codes of conduct, and projects on which the political regime was also insisting" (136–37). The Mexican "new man" (136) that a compromised Hiperión reputedly had a hand in fashioning would overcome desgana along with the host of pathological traits on which, according to Santos Ruiz, Hiperión harps. Energized, transcending an inferiority complex, the new man would be poised to create and consume Mexican goods.

What is exceedingly wrong with Santos Ruiz's picture, I think, is that it makes no room for *doing good*. *Los hijos de los dioses* effaces the altruistic, humanistic ethics Hiperión had adopted in covenant with its forebears. Impoverishing the group's ethos, Santos Ruiz strips Hiperión of the very values that distinguish it from Mexicanidad's modernizing, capitalistic agenda. The circuitry between Hiperión and Alemanismo that *Los hijos de los dioses* takes as its subject voids the higher motivations the philosophy of lo mexicano so strenuously advocated. A value system thus reduced appears, all too easily, as an instrumentalized, weaponized one. Santos Ruiz has exorbitantly interrogated Hiperión's philosophy of lo mexicano but not its full, capacious philosophical scale.

The circuitry between Mexican existentialist philosophy and literature to which the rest of this book is devoted reinforces, rather than obfuscates, the capacious ethos that Hiperión embodied. Avant la lettre or contemporaneously, the literary texts we investigate embrace both the philosophical spectrum and the value-orientation into which Hiperión breathed life. When the existentialist literary works under study dramatize identity, ethics, and community, they do, like Hiperión, push beyond Sartre and situate themselves over against Paz. They also push beyond Hiperión in arresting ways. It was incumbent upon Hiperión, keen on revolutionizing Mexican philosophy and society, to issue programmatic statements; the literature to which we turn wields the matters at stake for Hiperión sinuously and unpredictably, layering on productive complexities. If Hiperión was in some measure beholden to Alemanismo, the creative works militantly assert their independence from hegemonic pressures, their iconoclasm.[45] Last but certainly not least, our authors take Mexican identity to places Alemanismo proscribed and that Hiperión rarely entered. Rodolfo Usigli dives into the hypocrisies of post-Revolutionary politics, Juan Rulfo into Indigenous autonomy, José Revueltas into Marxism, and Rosario Castellanos into feminism. Pluralizing forces, our authors advance what Uranga described as the radical promise of Hiperión's existentialism: to make Mexico a "wide-open plaza, an all-embracing space for humanity in its plenitude" (*Análisis* 55). The writers who occupy coming pages look back at the Indigenous past, the Revolution, and political platforms with a forward-looking eye that envisions a more generous Mexico.

Chapter Three

The Seminal Mexican Existentialism of Rodolfo Usigli's Theater

el hacer bien, y el engañar bien [good actions, and good deceptions]
—Miguel de Unamuno, *San Manuel Bueno, Mártir* (1931)

In 1947 Rodolfo Usigli's now classic play *El gesticulador*, a hard-hitting indictment of post-Revolution Mexican morality and politics, finally reached the stage after a nine-year delay. Just three years later, the Mexican public came face to face with a second debut of the play almost as momentous as the physical one when Octavio Paz's *El laberinto de la soledad* delivered a watershed, soon to be commanding, account of *El gesticulador*. Paz's account inscribes *El gesticulador* in the lines of the continental existentialism that he and Usigli had encountered when they worked together in Mexico's Paris embassy from 1945 to 1946. This simple fact gives rise to a set of intriguing paradoxes. Usigli harbored no great fondness for French existentialism; he wrote *El gesticulador* in Mexico in 1938, before the heyday of post-Christian existentialism; still, Usigli's play, unmoored from absolutes as it is, can be considered the first *literary* existentialism to arise in Mexico, and Paz's existentialist approach to the drama a rightfully abiding one. Usigli's claim that his stagecraft gave birth to a genuinely Mexican theater heightens the stakes exponentially (*Teatro completo* 3:497).[1]

I propose to take the paradoxes to heart and to root them in the Mexican context that they beg. This chapter elucidates the heterogeneous drives of Usigli's *actual* scene of writing, drives that—as they crosscut Mexican philosophy, Mexican politics, and the author's evolving stagecraft—bring about the inception of literary existentialism in Mexico. Building such an architecture reveals another, truly daunting, complication in *El gesticulador*: how Usigli's morally slippery play can possibly make common cause with the ethical strain of Mexican philosophy and, what is more, lay tracks for the ethical existentialism forged in the arena of identity discourse that the Grupo Hiperión was propagating at the exact time *El gesticulador* first appeared on the Mexican stage. In the long run, illumination will come from Usigli's framing of pragmatic authenticity and his post-Maximato agendas, but in a moment we will begin to see that the undecidable, aporetic nature of Usigli's theater allows inimical impulses to occupy the same space, both irreducibly and productively.

Existentializing Dynamics

In addition to paradoxes, Paz's celebrated monograph introduces an array of issues that bear on the foregoing panorama. For one, *Laberinto* cracks open some of the ethical complexities of truth when seen through an existentialist lens, in general and in *El gesticulador*. Existentialism underpins much of *Laberinto*, and the chapter that contemplates Usigli's play, "Máscaras mexicanas" [Mexican Masks], displays Paz's au courant existential pedigree in spades. The masks that according to Paz Mexicans erect to protect themselves from the hostile gaze, the alienation that incites masking, the love of Form that powers it, and the repression that masking presupposes all reverberate with scare word of Sartrean existentialism, inauthenticity. Curiously enough, the only redeeming quality of masks in Paz's chapter involves the existential possibilities of *lies*, of "dissimulation" (*Labyrinth* 40; *Laberinto* 175). Rather than condemning lies, Paz teases out their potential for authenticity. Lies, he argues, can entail an existential becoming, the positing and achieving of a desired self when the mask fuses with the face.[2]

On Paz's reading, *El gesticulador* (henceforth, *EG*) offers a superb case-in-point of redemptive existential becoming. *Laberinto* maintains that Usigli's protagonist César Rubio lives his lie of being the original revolutionary, General César Rubio, *authentically*: "Through dissimulation we come closer to our model, and sometimes the gesticulator, as Usigli saw so profoundly, becomes one with his gestures and thus makes them authentic. The death of Professor Rubio makes him what he wanted to be: General Rubio, a sincere revolutionary and a man capable of giving the stagnating Revolution a fresh impetus and purity." Therefore, "we can arrive at authenticity by means of lies" (*41*; 176). In unreservedly endorsing Rubio's ability to finesse, as Unamuno would say, "good actions, and good deceptions" (*San Manuel* 136), Paz renders the lies of Usigli's character not just existential but also unqualifiedly positive, a model existential development.

Here we run into something of a betrayal on Paz's part. Much as Usigli may have appreciated his friend's favorable reception of the beleaguered *EG*, Paz's categorical interpretation could raise the playwright's hackles because the mechanisms of *EG*—and indeed, the very bedrock of Usigli's conception of the theater—militate against singular interpretations. Polemical and undecidable, *EG* refuses to take a totalizing position on Rubio's lies, his impostures. Every stance that *EG* tenders, we will see, has a counter-stance that keeps it in question, bouncing. The slippage between "gall" and "valor" in the following sentence encapsulates the polemic that *EG* unfolds. Rubio's rival for the office of governor, Navarro, says to him, "I don't know how you could have had the gall . . . , the valor to get involved in a farce like this" (*Imposter 99*; *EG* 189; ellipsis in the original). Definitively resolving the slippage between shameless and valiant lie, purveying an unequivocal or singular position on the issues at hand, would contravene Usigli's signature *theater of ideas*, which dynamizes the theater into an agora, a public forum intended to provoke debate (Swansey 50). In the footsteps of George Bernard Shaw, Henrik Ibsen, and Anton Chekov, Usigli mounts a theater of ideas characterized by "debate within a play and outside it" (*Corona* 55) that can form community (*TC* 3:803). He believes that an *idée fixe* is a dead idea. Characters come and stay alive "insofar as they challenge, or defend, new ideas; they are ideological or *ideistic* characters," always mobile (*Corona* 56). All told, Usigli creates an aporetic theater that any treatment of his works, including the present one, does well to heed.[3]

Articulating his aporetic practices led Usigli to weigh in on French existentialism, a subject that he discusses solely in terms of Sartre's and Camus's theater. The same essay in which Usigli defines his own theater of ideas, "virtually the only modern form of theater" (*Corona* 55), finds him immediately contrasting it with another modern form of theater, French existentialist theater as the Mexican playwright understood the movement. Perpetually an unabashed contrarian, Usigli excoriates Sartre's plays. He views them as the opposite of dialogical, that is, as theater *à these*; he denounces the French existential efforts as unoriginal, anti-dramatic, and propagandistic by virtue of their slavish adherence to promulgating a "thesis" (*Corona* 25).

Elsewhere, Usigli lambastes existentialist theater for depriving characters of complex dimensionality, instead predetermining them, making them "statue-like beings" (*TC* 5:183–84, 218).

Usigli's immoderate, jaundiced appraisals belie the fact that his own dramaturgy turns on the element of choice so intrinsic to French existential theater, philosophy, and literature. All of these posit as an article of faith that only through free choice can the existant forge a self, a life, and a value system. In attempting, not unexistentially, to express "the conflicts and destinies of men condemned to live on this planet" (*Corona* 56), Usigli's plays invariably derive their motor as well as their electricity from characters bound up in choosing. Thematically and structurally, his theatrical productions depend on gripping choices of all sorts, political, ethical, or romantic. The drama of choice percolates from the protagonists, often male, to the female characters, where it trains a spotlight on the changing roles of Mexican womanhood (Meyran 48), on women's self-determination. Up to the last minute of each play and trailing into its aftermath, what paths the characters will choose remains hanging. With this, Usigli unwittingly fulfills the desideratum for an authentic existential literature that Simone de Beauvoir proposed in a 1946 essay, well before Usigli's programmatic *Corona*. Beauvoir's "Literature and Metaphysics," which we met in chapter 1, counteracts manifesto-like novels such as Sartre's *Nausea* (and her own poorly received 1945 novel, *The Blood of Others*) by decoupling the philosophical novel from the thesis novel. The thesis novel, she believes, abrogates the characters' and readers' freedom. Beauvoir contends that to achieve a worthy philosophical literature authors must surrender their individual agendas and replace the tendentious portrayal of theses with a dialogical modus operandi, as does Fyodor Dostoevsky. The self-willed death of the author, she says, will create an "authentic adventure of the mind," a lived experience of choice for reader and author alike (*Philosophical Writings* 272).[4]

EG's tragic denouement, in particular, vigorously differentiates it from thesis play and intensifies the authenticity of the adventure by dealing a death blow to potential judgments that the drama champions Rubio's lies wholesale. If, as Paz has led us to believe, César Rubio's lies have morphed into actions so admirable, so salutary, why must he die and his dreams for Mexico immediately evanesce, co-opted by the demagogue Navarro as he appropriates the César Rubio whose murder he had plotted? The play certainly keeps its audience bouncing, confounded. Nonetheless, the preponderance of evidence Usigli assembled in and around *EG* valorizes the anomalous moral code that underwrites Rubio's imposture. Crediting the good faith of Rubio's anagnorisis as the General, multiple statements in *EG* shake the public out of a morality predicated on absolutes and sway it towards the protagonist's relativized one. Compelling statements in *EG* to that effect include:

> [RUBIO to political boss Navarro]: I am not César Rubio, but I know I can be him, do what he wanted to do. I know that I can do good for my country, stopping thieves and murderers like you from taking over . . . . I started out with a lie, but I have become the real thing, without knowing how, and now I'm sure. Now I know my destiny: I know that it is to fulfill the destiny of César Rubio. (*102*; 192)

> [RUBIO to his wife Elena]: The fact is, Elena, there's no lie anymore; it was necessary at first, so that the truth could come out of it. But now I'm the real thing, self-possessed, don't you understand? Now I feel as if I were the other César . . . I'll do everything he could have done, and more. (*109*; 197; ellipsis in the original)

The excessive, though always revealing, apologetics for *EG* that Usigli amasses in his essays further support the "false" Rubio. "It cannot be said," writes Usigli, "that the false César Rubio, absolved of his lie, transfigured by his faith in the vitality of the Revolution and dying for it, is a negative" (*TC* 3:534). And the most forthright: "It is crystal clear that my play does not reproach the two César Rubios, neither the true nor the false one, but instead the Navarros of this world" (*TC* 3:550).

The preceding battery of quotes bespeaks a destabilizing of truth and a jettisoning of ready-made, or bad faith, morality so imperative to Usigli that he promotes it in *EG* at the risk of overriding his protocol of undecidability. Remaking morality and discarding absolutes also feed into Usigli's conceptualization of lo mexicano at large, another of the author's stomping grounds. A strong example for our purposes is the suite of essays Usigli composed on the seventeenth-century dramatist Juan Ruiz de Alarcón. Usigli began the essays in 1939, and he revised and published them in 1967 as *Juan Ruiz de Alarcón en el tiempo* [Juan Ruiz de Alarcón in Time]. The essays confront the stock question of whether to consider Alarcón, raised in Mexico and transplanted to Spain, Mexican or Spanish. Usigli goes dialectical. In what for recent scholars is a textbook definition of the colonial criollo, he deems Alarcón bicultural, a cultural voyager born in the colonies but aspiring to the metropolis (e.g., *JR* 2, 11). Suspended between two nationalities, the in-between Alarcón foretells the present-day anguished Mexican (*JR* 2, 3). When Alarcón fulfills his dream and settles in the metropolis, he desires wholly to inhabit the forms of Golden Age drama. However, Usigli discerns in the transculturated author a forward-looking impetus to break out of Spanish forms.

Such structures of feeling manifest themselves, among several ways, in a disruption of rigid, categorical Spanish morality. Usigli pictures Alarcón spurning "the theological vices and virtues" (*JR* 3) that the missionary religious dramas he attended as a youth in Mexico imperiously expounded. Superseding facile moralizing, Alarcón brings a "modern morality" to the stage, an ambiguous, relativized "new ethics" that "totally infuses theater with a *humanized* Christian morality" (*JR* 3; emphasis added). Whence Alarcón's magnificent play *La verdad sospechosa* [The Suspicious Truth], which renders the lies of fabulator Don García almost irresistibly alluring and assigns the liar a quite restrained punishment.[5] As Usigli comments on *La verdad sospechosa*: "It is not exactly moralistic, though it may be axiomatic;" if "it were moralistic, it would *genuinely* punish Don García for lying, instead of making him a true artist" (*JR* 8). Usigli, who so admired Alarcón that he resigned as head of the Bellas Artes theater division in order to direct a play by the early modern dramatist, also stated that he wanted to write an adaptation of *La verdad sospechosa* to be called *La verdadera mentira* [The True Lie] (*TC* 3:294). Though Usigli never accomplished his plan to the letter, *EG* accomplishes it in spirit. Read alongside Usigli's essays on Alarcón, *EG* proves to concretize the breakout structures of feeling latent in *La verdad sospechosa*, to Mexicanize them, and thereby to restore the Mexican side of Alarcón's transatlantic identity.

Philosophical Drives

As Usigli weds Mexican identity to a destabilized morality, it comes unavoidably into view that placing the dramatist's oeuvre over against the signature aspects of Mexican philosophy, existentialism, and identity discourse yields, not answers, but the daunting complication I mentioned at the outset. Namely, how can the aporetic Usigli, with his ex-centric, almost post-factual notion of truth, relate to the moralistic Antonio Caso and his mid-twentieth-century successors? The warm friendship between Usigli and Caso softens but does not materially resolve the conundrum, which engenders other similarly thorny ones, such as the following.[6] On the shoulders of which philosophical giants, on what bases does the seminal existentialism of Usigli—an autodidact and omnivorous reader—rest? What breed of existentialism and ethics does Usigli, a dramatist rather than a philosopher per se, generate for his country? I will now hold up the pragmatic and existential relativizing of truth that inhered in the philosophical horizon of Mexico in 1938, the year of *EG*'s genesis, as a first way to address the raft of questions.

Advents like Gregory Pappas's edited collection *Pragmatism in the Americas* have substantiated the hemispheric reach of early North American pragmatism, which, on the face of it, would seem to be an unlikely lodestar for Mexican philosophy. After all, philosophical pragmatism crested around the time of the Spanish-American War and, thanks to its valorizing of practical consequences as the sine qua non of truth, gained an association with positivist utilitarianism. Antonio Caso and Pedro Henríquez Ureña, nevertheless, seized on pragmatism and tooled it into a vehicle for the Ateneo de la Juventud's humanistic project, validating the international current. Pragmatist William James in particular suited their needs. Scientist as well as believer in Christianity and in the sway of human experience, James could mediate between worldviews. Thus, in *La existencia como economía, como desinterés, y como caridad* Caso characterizes pragmatism as "a synthetic point of view that, while respecting experiential data, honoring it fully, also strives—with no contradiction whatsoever—to preserve the highest values of culture and humanity, idealism's standpoint on existence, religion, and morality" (56–57; 1943). He bifurcates pragmatism into its merely "economic" Comtean manifestations and its beneficial "charitable" strains.[7] Predictably, love and action—"Only he who does good is good" (*Existencia* 102; 1919, 1943)—surface as prime draws of pragmatism for Caso.

Henríquez Ureña's 1908 lecture for the Ateneo injects a third party and an aberrant ethics, both crucial to Usigli, into the mix. Titled "Nietzsche y el pragmatismo," it accords with Caso's revisionary sense of pragmatism as, in Henríquez Ureña's words, "anti-intellectualism" (i.e., against Kantian abstraction), "humanism," and "pluralism" (61). The talk then pivots, in sentences larded with emphases, to the "surprising coincidences" between James and Friedrich Nietzsche (63), neither of whom affected the other. James, Henríquez Ureña observes, transfigures truth: "For pragmatism, truth is not an absolute value, a fixed, invariable unit of measure. Rather, an idea *becomes* true; truth is an event, a process: it is *verified*" (67). Nietzsche had already introduced the tendency: "What matters, Nietzsche has said, is not that something *is* true (in the *static* sense of intellectualism), but that one believes something to be true" (69). An extreme anti-intellectualist, Nietzsche had waged flat-out war on conventional values (63). The conjunction of James and Nietzsche leads Henríquez Ureña to ask, equally deconstructively and pragmatically, if truth might not thrum with ambiguity (70).

As construed by Henríquez Ureña, Nietzsche bridges pragmatism and a godless existentialism. Now, the prologues to Usigli's one theatrical foray into religion, *Corona de luz* [Crown of Light] divulge Usigli's personal rupture with the Church (17) and praise existentialists for humanizing God (59–60). Then again, the essays that Usigli appended to *EG* oppugn the Christian God who in Mexico is Spanish-identified and/or prey to government machinations (*TC* 3:485–86). Having thus disavowed the institutionalized Church, Usigli would naturally gravitate to existentialists, the destabilizers and interrogators of Christianity. We can therefore consider the fact that towards the end of his life Usigli declared Nietzsche the philosopher who most attracted him (qtd. in R. Rodríguez 68). Usigli analyzed Nietzsche's *The Birth of Tragedy* but beyond that did not elaborate much on the attraction.[8] Ramón Layera and Guillermo Schmidhuber have, examining correlations between Usigli's historical plays and Nietzsche's theories of the historian, the artist, and truth. The two scholars' discussions, augmented by Usigli's reference in the 1943 edition of *EG* to "the candor that Nietzsche identified as a characteristic of the pure artist" (*TC* 3:489), strongly suggest the dramatist's familiarity with Nietzsche's "On Truth and Lying in an Extra-Moral Sense" (1873). A seminal encapsulation of Nietzsche's later philosophy, the short essay would beckon to Usigli as a beacon for *EG*, especially owing to the German philosopher's involvement with "simulation," "dissimulation," and the creative mind.

To wit: setting the stage for twentieth-century existentialism, Nietzsche's essay rehearses his focal contention that there is no inborn structure, morality, or truth to the world. What pass as truths are "illusions" (250), palliative fictions manufactured to make life bearable and to enable civilization. The rational individual professes—simulates—truths because they discharge an instrumental function. Arthur Danto explains that Nietzsche "advanced a pragmatic criterion of truth" in which truth basically means "the facilitation of life" (54); as numerous scholars have investigated, Nietzsche and James intersect in accepting the expedient nature of truth.[9] The German philosopher then explores expedient truth's ramifications. Within the realm of pragmatic illusions, Nietzsche argues, society tags as objectionable lies anything patently self-serving or damaging to others (Nietzsche 248). Conversely, standing apart from the herd, artists—"liberated" intellects, "intuitive" individuals

(255–56)—dissimulate. That is, they *dis-* or *un*-simulate. Harbingers of the life-affirming, value-flouting *Übermensch*, creative minds embrace the manufactured nature of so-called truths and creatively play with serious matters. By "smashing and scorning the old conceptual barriers," the free intellect imbued with passion confirms "the domination of art over life" and conveys "an exalted happiness" (256). Hyperconscious, intuitive individuals may suffer, at times more than rational beings, but they hide their suffering in a "mask with a dignified harmony of features" (256).

One can easily visualize the allure of Nietzsche's essay for Usigli. Reading it *as* an artist with an eye to Rubio *qua* artist, Usigli (and Paz as well?) would gain sustenance from the dissimulator capable of overleaping conventional ethics and possessed of a visionary, salutary, *authentic*, zeal. Withal, the most full-bodied template available to Usigli in 1938 for his specific designs would have to be Miguel de Unamuno's then-recent novella, *San Manuel Bueno, Mártir* [Saint Manuel the Good, Martyr]. Enormously influential in Spain and Latin America, *San Manuel* presents a scintillating trifecta of literature, proto-existentialism, and ethical dilemmas. The novella, furthermore, bears the stamp of William James's humanistic pragmatism. Unamuno once proclaimed James "the modern thinker to whom I am most drawn" (Urrutia 95), and Jaime Nubiola identifies Unamuno as "the first to spread pragmatist ideas in the Spanish-speaking world" (26).[10] James, the Christian believer, and Unamuno, the tragic *agonista* who yearns to believe, share an image of truth not as propelling action and passion but as resulting from them. Hence, in tandem with James and Matthew 7:16, Unamuno avows: "The truth is whatever feeds generous inclinations and engenders fertile works; the lie is whatever stifles noble impulses and breeds sterile monsters. By their fruits ye shall know men and things" (*Vida* 92). Unamuno's credo, a plainsong that reaches across time and space, also harmonizes with Nietzsche and Caso.

And, of course, with Usigli. The links between *San Manuel* and *EG* are virtually unmistakable. Don Manuel, the eponymous priest of Unamuno's parable, martyrs himself in life by purveying to his congregation an efficacious, *pragmatic* lie—a belief in the existence of the Christian afterlife that he excruciatingly doubts. Like César Rubio, whose imposture aspires to build a better Mexico, Don Manuel perpetrates a fiction for the sake of his community's well-being: "The most important thing . . . is that the village is happy, that everyone is happy to be alive" (*San Manuel* 107). Outcomes and ethics thus prevail over metaphysics, the praxis of Christian morality over absolute truth. It follows that in the name of the greater good and with words transposable to Usigli's protagonist, Don Manuel spurns the label of hypocrite: "Pretending? Pretending, no! This isn't pretending! As someone once said, drink Holy Water, and you'll end up believing" (122). The two gesticulators skirt demagoguery by placing weight on results, not rhetoric. Don Manuel wears the disguise of an orthodox priest, Rubio that of a former revolutionary; both lay claim to authenticity by living their roles to others' benefit and to perfection. In sum, despite having sundered truth from absolutes, the humanistic pragmatism circulating in both authors' milieux bequeathed them a field for ethical actions and communitarian values.

Political Drives

Coupled with Unamuno, drawn to Nietzsche's artist, in *EG* Usigli Mexicanizes their commingled pragmatism and proto-existentialism, firmly binding the two currents to the political "situation" of 1938. "In Mexico," *EG*'s César Rubio militantly asserts, "everything is politics . . . politics is in the air, it's everywhere" (*26*; 127; ellipsis in the original); "it connects everything"; the politician comprises "the axis of the wheel" (*91*; 182). In net effect, for Usigli politics is everything in Mexico and a driving force of his corpus. With vehemence and unflagging tenacity, Usigli's dramas and essays tackle the Mexican politics he regards as "the most active force in our lives," one so potent, he believes, that it has replaced religion (*TC* 3:499). Usigli's oft-stated ambition singlehandedly to launch modern Mexican theater, it stands to reason, could not and would not eschew politics: "Forging a Mexican-style theater without a political basis would probably be more difficult than forging a revolution, or a dictatorship, without generals" (*TC* 3:514). It also stands to reason that the inalienable role of politics in Mexico and for Usigli would push them into the writer's other analytics, such as his stance on truth. That is indeed what happens, to powerful result. Politics so saturate Usigli's thinking as to become the prime mover, in ways obvious and subterranean, of his early works' engagement with *authenticity*, arguably surpassing frontal existential sources. Hence, at least in part, the canted dealings of Usigli with French existentialism referred to above.

Usigli's marriage of politics and philosophy has two essential implications that the rest of this chapter aims to bear out. First, that the earliest creative stirrings of existentialism in Mexico arise to a significant degree organically and autochthonously, from the living post-Revolutionary context as interpreted by the polemical Usigli. Second, that from his inaugural plays onward, culminating in *EG*, Usigli's literary-political activism blazes a trail not just for an innovative Mexican theater but also for Hiperión's innovative, distinctively Mexican existentialism.

The sinuous trail that Usigli blazes towards both outcomes has an obvious foundation: *EG* demands to be read through a political lens. The play's subtitle, "A Play for Demagogues," elicits the reading, and the contempt for demagogue Navarro and his local party that *EG* exhibits requires it. Wary of others' interpretations, Usigli has repeatedly spelled out the cores of the play, politics and lying. For example, and centrally: "Demagogy is nothing more than Mexican hypocrisy systematized in politics" (*TC* 3:461), and "both implicitly and obviously, *El gesticulador* presents the struggle between the truth of the original Revolution and the lie in which those who, immoral and incapable of constructive thinking, have shrouded it, exploiting the Revolution for self-interested, corrupt purposes" (*TC* 3:532–33). Usigli's overview of the play's two hearts brings *EG* down to brass tacks. But the fact that from 1935 to 1936 Usigli entered the political realm to serve enthusiastically as the press secretary of Lázaro Cárdenas, who from 1934 to 1940 battled the legacy of Plutarco Elías Calles, opens up fresh vistas on *EG*'s central concerns. These vistas have everything to do with Usigli's post-Maximato political agenda, which, as I will now corroborate, his essays and earliest plays flesh out. Usigli's political thinking, as broached in his *Tres comedias impólíticas* [Three Impolitic Comedies] (*Noche de estío* [Summer Night], *El Presidente y el ideal*, and *Estado de secreto* [State of Secrecy]; all composed between 1932 and 1935), and *Alcestes* (composed in 1936) critically impact the seminal existentialism of *EG in its own situation*.[11]

Usigli's first works scrutinize the "Maximato"—the brief administrations of Emilio Portes Gil (1928–1930), Pascual Ortiz Rubio (1930–1932), and Abelardo Rodríguez (1932–1934) in which Calles continued to prevail behind the scenes as the "Jefe Máximo," Supreme Chief—and the challenges Cárdenas initially faced. The author's leftist tendencies conditioned his allegiance to Cárdenas. Albeit as dialogical as his plays, Usigli's political writings contain surprisingly unambiguous affirmations of Marxism. Thus, after leveling one of his usual critiques at communist leaders' vainglory, Usigli observes in 1947: "Having pointed out some of the leftists' defects, I must add that, for me, it is they who establish the only tolerable, broad, and healthy political atmosphere." The panegyric to leftists into which he erupts passionately adds: "In them we find the activity of the spirit, the fervent desire for freedom, and, truly, the very life force of man, the hope that discontent will be productive" (*TC* 3:507–08). A realist, Usigli deems communism ("a path lacking god, economy, and land" [*TC* 3:361]) impossible in the Mexico he knew, where it clashed with another monolithic force, entrenched Catholicism. As *Alcestes* will confirm, despite Usigli's enthusiasm for the left he urges moderation, a rapprochement between the two giants. In something of the same spirit and ruefully contemplating the chaos of the Mexican Revolution, he advocates a revisionist socialism that depends not on the proletariat but on each class defining itself and taking action.[12] Usigli sees socialism as inevitable (*TC* 3:381) and exhorts Mexico to lead the way for Latin America (*TC* 3:371).

Such attitudes naturally pitted Usigli against Calles, whom he regarded as a demagogue and a strongman (*TC* 3:462). They led him to join Cárdenas's team for a brief period. When in 1936 Usigli resigned as head of Cárdenas's press department, he did so with reluctance, from fear that the supposedly imminent publication of his *Tres comedias impolíticas* would compromise the president's administration (R. Rodríguez 59).[13] The former press secretary also accepted the opportunity to study theater at Yale University in 1936–1937 on a Rockefeller Foundation grant reluctantly, loath to forsake the effervescent climate of Cárdenas's regime. It was a time, Usigli tells us, of renovation, "an awakening of general interest in public affairs, a sudden desire for trust and service, as a direct reaction to the prolonged indifference" the previous regime had inspired (*TC* 3:363) that found Cárdenas, "a more realistic president than others by virtue of being more idealistic" (*TC* 3:488), at a critical juncture as he struggled to eradicate the Maximato.

From Mexico before his departure and continuing in the US, Usigli engineered his theatrical works to be players, so to speak, in the post-Maximato arena. The scripts he devised then partake of the *teatro de revista*, or vaudeville revue, that Usigli admired (e.g., *TC* 3:556, 590; also Swansey, ch. 4). A traditional, popular genre in Mexico and a venue for political critique, true to its name the teatro de revista passes review on the burning issues of the day, catalyzing debate. And, for better or worse, the *Tres comedias impolíticas* were bound to stir up dangerous debate. As Usigli has attested and various scholars seconded, "my three impolitic comedias clearly portray Cardenismo and Callismo."[14] The thin subterfuges that the *im*politic plays employ hardly camouflage their biting commentaries on the insidious residue of the Maximato and the vexed transition to Cárdenas. None of the inflammatory works was performed in the period. *El Presidente y el ideal* has never reached the stage (Meyran 35).

Conceivably the most disruptive of the three comedias, *El Presidente* (written in 1935) unveils the main planks of Usigli's partisan platform. Indeed, Usigli, the then press secretary, "signs" the play by sporadically figuring himself in it as a "Young Enthusiast" of the president, a supporter who may be writing an opus titled, yes, *El Presidente y el ideal*. Calles's and Cárdenas's avatars loom far larger in the play, an updated version of Martín Luis Guzmán's 1929 *à clef* novel on President Álvaro Obregón's assassination (a deed, often imputed to Calles, that cleared the way for the Maximato), *La sombra del caudillo* [The Shadow of the Strongman].[15] For its part, *El Presidente* deals with the surreptitious machinations of a Calles-like former president to destroy his idealistic Cárdenas-like successor, twice compared to Francisco Madero, who precipitated the Mexican Revolution by calling Porfirio Díaz to task (275, 302). *El Presidente*'s disjointed, farcical vignettes, reminiscent of the teatro de revista, one by one submit to the audience the real-life changes in land distribution, religion, labor, and education that Cárdenas initially rolled out. As the dark comedia proceeds, the Calles henchmen who have infiltrated the new president's administration systematically sabotage his initiatives. *El Presidente* therefore amounts to a mise-en-scène and an apologetics for Cárdenas's early battles, a spectacle of the nearly insuperable obstacles the man of the people faced.

Socialist education emerges in *El Presidente* as the most daunting obstacle. Now perhaps a footnote to Mexican history, in the 1930s and 1940s the charged matter of education incensed the nation, embroiling Calles, the Maximato, and Cárdenas. Academic reform came to the fore and to friction as Calles, once a schoolteacher, incited Rodríguez to sponsor a program of socialist education that had little to do with Marx and much to do with Calles's virulent anti-clericalism (Buchenau 165). Not unexpectedly, Usigli censured the sham socialism that the Calles-Rodríguez axis touted as they promoted their educational agenda (*TC* 3:361–62). Calles's campaign resulted in the 1934 revision of Article 3 of the Mexican Constitution. The revised Article 3 mandated a pedagogy divorced from religious doctrine that would lead to a rational understanding of the world (Medin, *Ideología* 181). Vague in definition and much more so in implementation, the socialist education program that Cárdenas inherited confounded teachers, enraged the pope, and sparked the frenzied tragedies Rosario Castellanos depicts in her novels on Chiapas.[16] Yet the leftist Cárdenas saw possibilities in the venture he inherited from Calles, and propagated it. Characterizing socialist education as "an orientation towards new forms of social life and justice" (Cárdenas, qtd. in Lerner 192), Cárdenas endowed the reforms with a more legitimate Marxist grounding than had Calles.

This fraught heritage clarifies *El Presidente*'s deceptively *anti*-socialist treatment of the pedagogical reforms, for the farcical play revels in mocking the educational initiative that induces phobic, histrionic reactions in a public threatened by the bogeyman of a misunderstood socialism. The backlash against the originally Callista scheme works to the advantage of *El Presidente*'s Calles proxy. His loyalists gleefully watch the president's men defend an agenda that intensifies hostility towards the idealistic leader. The supporters of the president thereby fall into a trap that subverts the educational platform they seek to implant; over the course of the play, comparable ambushes undermine each facet of the president's program. Yet his supporters obstinately persevere. As such, the cruelly ironic scenario that *El Presidente* exposes indicts Cárdenas's friends and enemies alike, shedding further light on Usigli's decision to step down as press secretary.[17]

Problematic in terms of the president's men, the play safeguards Cárdenas himself. *El Presidente* revolves around the question of whether the president under ever-increasing pressure will renege on his ideals. The text ultimately confirms the leader's probity. Although Usigli does not forego his typical ambiguous, discussion-rousing ending, he subtly insinuates the downfall not of the idealistic president but of his corrupt predecessor. When newspaper headlines (prophetically, as it turned out, given that Cárdenas exiled Calles in 1936) announce the expulsion from Mexico of an unnamed "Jefe Máximo" of the Revolution, the smile of the Usigli figure, the "Young Enthusiast," clues us into the identity of the exiled leader (*TC* 1:350). Even more strategically and redemptively, the Cárdenas stand-in never appears on stage. "My predominant idea," Usigli comments, "was only to set the figure of the idealistic president on stage through allusions, announcements of his arrival, peoples' opinions, etc." (*TC* 3:419). As the dramatist brackets out his favored president, exculpating him, he orchestrates a portrait of the publicity campaigns that, as Usigli knew all too well and as Navarro's hijacking of César Rubio at the end of *EG* underscores, can derail a righteous leader.

Tensions around political idealism cross into Usigli's *Alcestes*, written far from the fray and constraints of the Mexican scene. He composed *Alcestes* in New Haven in March of 1936, after the *Tres comedias impolíticas* and between *La última puerta* [The Final Door] and his first family-centered play, *El niño y la niebla* [The Boy and the Fog] (*TC* 3:294). Clumsy as the play Usigli wrote in four days admittedly is, he informs us that "*Alcestes* contains all the main elements of *El gesticulador*" (*TC* 3:295). Alcestes, a young politician and a forerunner of *EG*'s Miguel, crusades for absolute, uncompromised truth. The play immediately sets its central tensions in motion with first lines that read: [PEDRO to Alcestes] "Frankly, my dear friend, it seems to me that you take things far too seriously and take them to immoderate extremes, extremes that only exist in your mind" (*TC* 1:121).

Alcestes, obdurate and rigid, consistently chooses to reject the savvy advice of his friends that he bend his principles, that the end will justify the means: [GILBERTO to Alcestes] "Have you no sense of self-preservation? What you call a lie is also termed tolerance, diplomacy, *savoir vivre*, reverence for human relations" (*TC* 1:164). Pedro adds: "I am an honorable man, Alcestes, and I don't go to these extremes" (*TC* 1:165). Gilberto and Pedro here debut the *pragmatic* authenticity that will mark *EG*.[18]

Laudable, one might say, on the most abstract ethical level, Usigli's Alcestes chiefly cuts a ridiculous figure. Beyond Alcestes's refusal to temper his principles in order to achieve his larger goals, his spouting of the patriarchal attitudes towards women that Usigli often combats and the character's inconstancy in personal relationships devalue him.[19] Compounding its protagonist's abasement, the subtitle of *Alcestes* proclaims the play to be a "Transposition of J. B. Poquelin de Molière's *Le Misanthrope* to a Mexican milieu" (*TC* 1:121). Molière's 1666 satire, which focuses the same ethical dilemma as Usigli's, ends up mocking its protagonist, also named Alcestes, as a diehard and consigning him to solitude. In the centuries-later words of Usigli's Pedro to his Alcestes, "logically, your talent and good will should bring you closer to others, not distance you from them; it should help you understand them rather than condemn them" (*TC* 1:166), we hear a twinning of the two misanthropes that mutually stigmatizes them.

The line just quoted expresses a belief in *civilité*, civic life, that acquires special weight when we take to heart Usigli's announcement that *Alcestes* transposes *Le Misanthrope* "to a *Mexican* milieu" (emphasis added). Usigli's subtitle directs our sights to Mexico and, notably diverging from *Le Misanthrope*, to politics. In that vein, *Alcestes* returns to the scenario of *El Presidente*, the deleterious effects of Calles's agents on Cárdenas's regime. The president in *Alcestes*, like Cárdenas in 1935, endeavors to purge his cabinet of Calles's loyalists, but to no avail. Demagogue Núñez del Río, a Callista official whom Alcestes's compulsion to tell the truth has egregiously offended, continues to influence the president and eventually brings Alcestes down. Usigli's drama embeds this scenario in the broader one of Alcestes's attempts to establish a political party that could save the president he admires from foes and salvage the civic life of Mexico.

Alcestes may be ridiculous, but his political program is not, which heightens the pathos of the intransigence that keeps him from carrying it out. Just when Cárdenas was striving to transform the Partido Nacional Revolucionario, the fictional Alcestes plans to found the Partido de la Razón Nacional ("in opposition to the PNR of the early 1930s," notes Usigli [*TC*

3:300]). The Partido de la Razón Nacional will faithfully support its leader (*TC* 1:130) and at the same time "bring a moderating element to Mexican life that will incorporate the productive ideas of all Mexican intellectuals (*TC* 1:149), principally Marxists and Catholics. While Alcestes's checks and balances commendably aim to keep the ruling party honest, his plan has its flaws. As his friends point out, it lacks a guiding ideological force (*TC* 1:150) and misanthropically emphasizes reason over human relations (*TC* 1:166). Alcestes fights back by professing allegiance to the ideals of socialism (*TC* 1:167).

It takes little imagination to understand *Alcestes* as a second, more ambitious, theatrical manifesto of Usigli's post-Maximato thinking. With the insight he had developed at some remove of time from the first work and the freedom entailed in a much greater remove of space, Usigli expands on *El Presidente*, insinuating himself as still, from the US, a player in a situation he has not abandoned. Furthermore, Usigli shapes *Alcestes* into a *speculum principis* that tenders advice to Mexico's president. The Alcestes in whom scholars have perceived traces of the ineffectually idealistic political candidate José Vasconcelos (Schmidhuber 51; Swansey 85), bears a dual message for Cárdenas. On the one hand, Alcestes indicates that an unyielding commitment to absolute principles can prove counterproductive in Mexico. Next, consistent with Usigli's own efforts as press secretary to inform the president of all points of view (*TC* 3:533), the play covertly urges Cárdenas not to let his socialism run rampant and squelch the ecumenical exchange of ideas that would let the politician truly be "the axis of the wheel." Much as *Alcestes*'s pragmatism defaults on *El Presidente*'s robust endorsement of idealism, both plays block easy answers. Between them, they plant doubts that the corrupt, polarized topography of Mexican politics will accommodate either idealism *or* cooperation.

From the Family to the Revolutionary Family

Self-exiled to the US, Usigli persisted in his attempts to forge a constructive, "purely Mexican form of theater." He realized that *Alcestes*, brutally satirical and pedantic, lacked the fellow feeling necessary to compel a broader public (*TC* 3:295). Studying international theater at Yale, Usigli gleaned a new staple of his dramatic repertoire that allowed him to humanize the Mexican issues of his times—family plays centered on the home. *El niño y la niebla* (written in New Haven right after *Alcestes*), *Medio tono* [Half Tones]

(Usigli's first family play to reach the stage; written in 1937 and performed that year), *Otra primavera* [Another Spring] (written 1937–1938), and *La familia cena en casa* [The Family Dines at Home] (written in 1942) exemplify these advents. Like the post-Maximato dramas, the four works exert pressure on *EG*, itself a family drama but a far more politically engaged one; these plays seed *EG*'s (re-)vision of Calles's treacherous Revolutionary Family, the platform for Usigli's merger of politics and existential rebirth.

The four breakthrough plays have a common core. Focusing on truth, on the unleashing of truth, they ask: Can middle class or bourgeois families vanquish the genteel civility of half truths, the *medio tono*, and finally voice what the families have repressed? Demonstrating that they can, Usigli sites the plays entirely in the home, which he consecrates as a space propitious to speaking the unadulterated truth. Within the confines of the home, Usiglian families often literally fight their way towards candor and undergo trials that strengthen rather than destroy them (Beardsell 7). More than merely restore the families to peaceful lives, the trials occasion transformative awakenings to greater authenticity and love. The prises de conscience that the older generation experiences in *Medio tono* open their eyes to the promise of the younger one; those of the parents in *Otra primavera* to their own possibilities for rejuvenation as they rekindle their marriage; those of the mother in *Familia* to new familial and social purpose. Whereas the four plays derive major momentum from the choices of romantic partners that young women make to avoid purposeless lives, *Medio tono* and *Otra primavera* also rescue fathers, a philanderer and a man suffering from dementia, respectively. Usigli's tributes to the family, in sum, afford its members "another spring," a veritable existential and moral rebirth.

The throes of rebirth propel characters to the outer limits of the private sphere. Each play ends with certain of its reinvigorated characters *about to* cross the threshold from the home into the public sphere, where they intend to enact a vital project.[20] Usigli's mobile theater of ideas, like Sartre's novel of an awakening, *Nausea*, ends with beginnings. The dialectics of the public versus the private spheres that the Mexican author introduces in his family dramas render the home contingent, liminal. Long before their finales, however, plays such as *Medio tono* and *La familia cena en casa* had already infused the home with explosive energies by mapping the public sphere onto the private. That is, they catapult the home into a space where the heated political topics of the day are freely vented. Again mirroring the teatro de revista, a welter of topics, from communism to labor, democracy, conservatism, abortion, the Revolution, patriarchy, international relations, and so on, provide fodder for debate in the private sphere. The home and family slide into microcosms of Mexico, testing grounds ready to be taken public.

For the family, or himself, to take their politics fully public in Mexico, Usigli had already learned, was a high-risk enterprise. Heeding the lessons of his previous compositions, Usigli omits from his family plays the à clef layers of the *Tres comedias impolíticas* and *Alcestes*. To be sure, *Medio tono* revolves around a communist rally, but the fictional characters simply are who they are, and the play delivers a life-enhancing *existentialist* message.[21] Usigli's first family plays, by the same rationale, suspend his dealings with the Maximato. The author's political activism, in any event, could not be restrained for long: the oblique à clef elements that crowd into *EG* revive Usigli's post-Maximato agendas.

Usigli begins by stating that *EG* takes place in a generalized "today," but later the play supplies the date of circa twenty-four years after 1914, which means circa 1938, during the Cárdenas administration (*Imposter 36*; *EG* 136). This sleight-of-hand alerts us to the protocol of caution that Usigli, back in Mexico and writing his first political play since his return, adopts in *EG*. To sidestep the hazardous blatancy of the 1930s plays, Usigli has *EG* encrypt, mix, and match its terms, starting with the subtle replacement of schoolteacher Calles with university professor Rubio. Veiled as they may be, certain encryptions speak volumes. The assassination of *EG*'s César Rubio by an alleged religious zealot signals the 1928 murder—rumored, we remember, to be Calles's handiwork—of the Jefe Máximo's predecessor, Álvaro Obregón, by the mystic, José de León Toral. In 1930 Pascual Ortiz *Rubio*, who ventured to resist Calles's influence, suffered a failed assassination attempt likewise sometimes imputed to the Jefe Máximo and Portes Gil (Buchenau 157–58). That in 1934 Calles put out feelers for a comeback and from exile attacked *Cárdenas* as a demagogue (Buchenau 180–83; 185) lends urgency to the coded, anti-Calles script of *EG*.

As if the foregoing were not enough, secondary characters in *EG* evoke personages of the era. Harvard professor Oliver Bolton would remind contemporary audiences of the American Carleton Beals, one of several foreign journalists Calles enlisted to publicize his regime (Buchenau 133), and/or of the American historian Herbert E. Bolton, author of treatises on the inalienable relations between the US and Mexico (Schmidhuber 57; Meyran 116). As his enthusiastic supporter, Rubio's daughter Julia conjures up Calles's daughter Tencha, who "played the role of First Lady during her mother's last years and remained Calles's principal confidante up to his death" (Buchenau 198). Estrella, a delegate of the national party won over by Rubio's dedication to the people, squares with Cárdenas in their mutual efforts to overhaul the PNR. *EG*'s local party delegate Treviño brings to mind Manuel Pérez Treviño, an anticommunist who belonged to Calles's team of elite generals (Medin, *Ideología* 219).

The disparate, orphaned à clef pieces that stud *EG* with evocations of Calles and Cárdenas, I now aim to establish, index a submerged design, a wellspring that joins the scattered pieces and charges *EG* as a whole. I refer to the metaphor and machinery of the Revolutionary Family propaganda campaign, which accompanied Calles's launching of the PNR and extended well beyond it.[22] The Revolutionary Family was an overarching vision for post-Revolutionary Mexico, a vision that revived, redeployed, and betrayed the Mexican Revolution, thereby epitomizing the "self-interested, corrupt purposes" (Usigli, *TC* 3:533) anathema to Usigli. As he escalates in *EG* from the family to the Revolutionary Family, Usigli imaginatively revamps Calles's self-serving publicity campaign into an altruistic one that will serve the common good.

The first Mexican president to capitalize on modern mass media and to exploit it, as Usigli notes, "for the opportune circulation of his initiatives" (*TC* 3:367), Calles undertook in live and radio speeches to rewrite the Mexican Revolution (Buchenau xxiv). The Maximato's propaganda campaign affronted cultural memory by transmogrifying the ungainly Revolution into a solid front, reembodied in a PNR that could unite the country going forward. Diametrically opposed to the disunity and fragmentation of the Revolution itself, this post-factual initiative recasts the war as a single fabric, a unified, politically expedient Revolutionary Family. According to the idealized Revolutionary Family, a Freudian family romance of sorts, the revolutionary father led his children—Mexican peasants, Indigenous peoples, and the working classes—in a common battle against dictatorship. A mythologized revolutionary mother, a "saint and sufferer, whose moral superiority and spiritual strength acted as glue for the ultimate stability of the family—and by extension the nation" (Zolov 5), assisted the mythologized paterfamilias. The imagined community of the Revolutionary Family envisaged the PNR as the " 'family home' in which postrevolutionary 'squabbles' were resolved" by the president, a stern, benevolent father (Zolov 4). The PNR would at once be synonymous with the counterfeited Revolution, the Revolutionary Family, and Mexican identity.

But where to find the father in the none too perfect real leaders of the Revolution? We think of Pancho Villa, often impetuous and violent; Venustiano Carranza, an unpopular, unpopulist (O'Malley 71), notoriously

Machiavellian schemer; and Emiliano Zapata, a force of nature to whose radical ideas on land reform Calles was averse. The solution: the Revolutionary Family script melded leaders who in actuality had opposed, even assassinated, one another, conflating them into one supreme, multifaceted father figure. Whitewashed and mythified, each one became a father. All together, they formed the collective father of the Revolutionary Family. Through these maneuvers Zapata "acquired a 'Christ-like martyred image,' whereas his arch enemy, Venustiano Carranza, became known as 'the Father of the 1917 Constitution' and a 'symbol of law' in the official discourse. Victors and vanquished thus shared the stage as national heroes, their images and (perhaps less successfully) memories sanitized and represented as official history: the unified Revolution."[23] Finally, in a remarkable *coup de théâtre* on a vast public stage, Calles promoted himself as *the* Revolutionary Father, heir to and culmination of a teleological process. Claiming "the diverse legacies of Madero, Zapata, Carranza, Villa, and Obregón as his own," Buchenau observes, enabled the relatively uncharismatic Calles to fan a personality cult that continued to qualify him as Jefe Máximo long after his incumbency (170).

The symbolic Revolutionary Family was soon literally set in stone. Designed by Carlos Obregón Santacilia and sculpted by Oliverio Martínez de Hoyos, the *Monumento a la Revolución* built in the 1930s still towers over Mexico City's Plaza de la República. A mausoleum for several Mexican presidents, in a pungent re-conflation of revolutionary "fathers" it now contains the bodies of Calles *and* his nemesis, Cárdenas. Originally, though, the monument celebrated the pillars of Mexican nationalism: Independence, the nineteenth-century Reform, and agrarian and labor laws (Olsen 79). The resulting sculptural groups placed beneath the dome breach Mexican commemorative tradition. Rather than depicting Mexican leaders, they contain abstract figures modeled in an art deco, geometric style (see fig. 3.1).

Most important for our concerns, colossal trinities of a father, mother, and child comprise three of the four groups (in then-patriarchal Mexico, men alone would perforce symbolize the fourth, labor laws). Lobbying strenuously for the edifice, Calles and President Rodríguez had oriented it to the Revolutionary Family, alleged cardinal pillar of modern Mexico. The depersonalized structure, "the Revolution converted into a monument" (T. Benjamin 131), would reify for posterity a Revolution that Calles had usurped, deranged, and institutionalized.[24]

An official ceremony that afforded "a suitable conclusion to Rodríguez's administration" (Olsen 80) inaugurated the still-unfinished monument on

The Seminal Mexican Existentialism of Rodolfo Usigli's Theater | 95

Figure 3.1. *Monumento a la Revolución*, detail. Photograph by Teresa Clifton.

November 20, 1934. Usigli himself attended the ceremony and vented his ire at it in the conclusion to the voluminous essay "Una comedia shavian. *Noche de estío*" [A Comedy à la Shaw. Summer Night] (written between 1933 and 1935). Sarcastically reprising a slogan hawked at the inauguration, Usigli accuses the monument of marking not the endless life of the Revolution but its death. "We find proof," he writes, "that the Revolution came to life (died) on November 20, 1934, in the inauguration of this monument to the Revolution of Yesterday, Today, Tomorrow, and Forever" (*TC* 3:376); "the Mexican Revolution is now truly dead: it has a mausoleum" (*TC* 3:378). Usigli explicitly maligns the Revolution-qua-family: "The Revolution of Today is a family, the head of a dynasty in which, like the Greek passing of the torch, children succeed their parents in usufruct of leadership positions, contracts for public works, exploitation of gambling dens, buying and selling elections, and the acquisition of national and foreign businesses" (*TC* 3:377). The outraged cognizance of Calles's propaganda machine that Usigli here displays—one would expect no less from Cárdenas's soon-to-be press secretary and the author of *El Presidente y el ideal*—furnishes a smoking gun, an indispensable backdrop for *EG*'s reenactments of the Revolutionary Family.

For, with the aim of rerouting the Revolutionary Family from demagoguery into service of the collectivity, *EG* at once mimics and rewrites the objectionable script with which Usigli was painfully familiar. He doubles down on the rebirth to more authentic lives that family members underwent in his earlier plays and politicizes it through the figure of César Rubio.[25] Both incarnations of César Rubio target the revolutionary father, fulcrum of Calles's campaign. The original Rubio, the general, "the one individual who explains the Mexican Revolution, who had a total concept of the Revolution" (*36–37*; 137), compensates for what Usigli regards as the insurrection's lack of leadership and political vision (*TC* 3:463). Having broken with Huerta, Carranza, Villa, and Zapata (*35*; 136), *EG*'s invented hero worthy of the designation problematizes each figure whom the PNR had mystified into a holistic father. Rubio is "the only revolutionary leader who is not a politician [Carranza?], a mere militarist [Villa?], or a blind force of nature [Zapata?]" (*37*; 137). In other words, while Usigli appropriates the notion of a grand revolutionary father, he endows him with a totally corrective profile, implicitly critiquing Calles, father of the revolutionary father. The reborn Rubio, the imposter, represents a constructive, healing amalgamation. Usigli's gesticulator looks like Zapata (*16*; 118), shares Zapata's social commitment, possesses Carranza's strategic intelligence, has Villa's vitality, and operates from the north. In fact, the second Rubio takes Zapata's south to Villa's north, symbolically uniting the fractured landscape of the Revolution.

Wreaking ever more comprehensive damage on the Maximato script, *EG* marshals the interplay of the public and private spheres immanent in the family dramas. The wider imprint of the Revolutionary Family in *EG* assumes the following contours. Rubio's family is dysfunctional, demoralized, riven. Whether reflecting the true state of the PNR, or, more likely, the nation as a conflictive family, the Rubio clan has reached a point of crisis. From the very outset, family members tell the naked truth. Yet truth will not bring rebirth to the Rubios. Only the father can do so. And he can do so only by leaving the private sphere (while the play is in motion instead of at its final moment), and entering the public sphere of politics. *He must become the leader of Usigli's new Revolutionary Family, not just of his own.* By leaving the home to campaign, Rubio heals the nation-as-family. After Harvard professor Oliver Bolton mistakenly outs Rubio as the real general, Rubio the politician places his trust in the "populace" that spurs him to action and embraces it as his new, public family (e.g., *68*; 162 and *91*; 183).

The former professor's historical knowledge of the Revolution, formerly dead currency, regains its power when mobilized for the public good to the effect that Rubio unites the people, divergent leaders, and the party in common cause. The last of the cascading benefits that accrue from the inside/outside synergy has the politician Rubio, "the pulse, the very heart of everything" (*91*; 183), also uniting the private and public domains. He exits the home and returns to it reenergized; as Rubio converts his home into a campaign headquarters, the public sphere invades and reinvigorates the private one. Its threshold crossed, its boundaries dissolved, the home that started out as a shadow version of a troubled Mexico realizes its full, authentic potential.

Repurposed and inserted in the private sphere per se, the Revolutionary Family provides templates for the modern woman. Rubio succeeds in awakening his daughter Julia to a better life, albeit of somewhat bizarre proportions. At first he tries to coax the young woman into self-respect by peculiarly complimenting her "admirable body" (*25*; 126). Later, her father's consecration as a public figure regenerates Julia's love for him, galvanizing her into his most ardent champion. Unlike the other family members, Julia attends her father's public rallies (*119*; 204) and dreamily envisions her life with him when he is elected governor. She tells her mother, Elena: "I will lay out his clothes every morning so that he will not be able to touch his tie or feel the suit on his body without touching me or feeling me. With you, he will discuss his ideas, his plans, all his decisions, and when he carries them out he will be seeing and touching you" (*120*; 205). Highly unnatural, the near-incestuous interactions between father and daughter are naturalized by the play's transactions with the Revolutionary Family. The taboo of incestuous love signals that Julia, like her father, must break out of the home. Hence Julia's successful seduction by the *revolutionary* father, leader of a political initiative that gives her life a greater meaning (as well as material benefits, for the play keeps her motives bouncing). Julia, who sees herself as all ugly face, not beautiful body (*25*; 126), will obtain a deeper beauty by uniting with the body politic. She falls in love with, wants to "marry," the father of the Revolutionary Family. So enamored is Julia with her father's communitarian activism, so in thrall is she of a revitalized love for him, that she wishes to make the leap from revolutionary child to new revolutionary wife.

Julia's expression of that wish to Elena throws into relief the play's scrutiny of the revolutionary mother. Party spokesperson Estrella initiates it in the second act when he recites the official version of the revolutionary mother to an Elena distressed by her husband's imposture and trying to extricate him from politics. "You, madam, must remember the Mexican woman's glorious tradition of heroism and sacrifice." He cites the "symbol of Mexican womanhood, the soldadera" (*82*; 174), clearly seen as a camp-follower, not a fighter. Elena wrestles with her conscience and convinces herself to accept César's lie because it will benefit the family she loves (*114*; 201). Despite her moral misgivings always loyal, long-suffering, and heroically devoted to family, the traditional Elena embodies the revolutionary mother, as limned by Zolov above. Therein, for Usigli, lie her shortcomings. Elena is a realist with a limited perspective, limited to the family. Intransigently circumscribed to the private sphere, she cannot accept the husband who as a public figure will no longer require her to tend to his needs. When Rubio is elected governor, she says, "it will be as if he were dead to me" (*120*; 205). The logic of the play would then have it that Julia steps in as substitute "wife" of the father. She will help him serve the public good in the outside sphere unpalatable to Elena. Youth and "passion" (*16*; 118), Julia will realize the progressive Usigli's ideal for a modern Mexican womanhood, a reimagined revolutionary mother.[26]

The Mexican Existentialist Hero:
Pragmatic Authenticity and Emilio Uranga's *Zozobra*

EG accords the Rubios' other child, Miguel, dubious commerce with the Revolutionary Family. A would-be revolutionary fervor converts Miguel into a fanatical defender of truth in its absolute form. And Miguel appears to share the infantilization bound up in Calles's notion of the revolutionary child. Adrift, in need of a father's wise governance, Rubio's son Miguel "vehemently" (*32*; 131) complains and shouts and weeps his way through the play. He refuses to recognize the value of his father's public *or* private motivations. Is Miguel a farcical fool like Alcestes or a praiseworthy warrior like the shade of Cárdenas in *El Presidente*? This, I submit, is the paramount issue at stake in the character Miguel, and the customary suspenseful Usigli ending declines to resolve it. At the last minute, Miguel absconds from the home, having finally mustered the courage that might, just might, betoken the onset of maturity ("He covers his face with his hands for a moment and seems on the verge of surrendering, but he gets up" [*127*; 211]).

Miguel has kept absolutes visible and in motion. He also has acted as a foil for his father, who emblematizes a pragmatic authenticity. César Rubio, in telling contrast to his son, has already entered the public realm—and become an existentialist hero. As an existentialist hero in the European mold, Rubio is free, daring, self-creating, acting in good faith, making choices, profoundly in-situation. As a Mexican existentialist hero, he has realized an ethics of communitarianism, love, and availability to others (disponibilité). On both counts, César Rubio has traded essence for existence, forsaking absolutes in favor of praxis. Usigli's protagonist relocates San Manuel's "good actions, and good deceptions" from Spain to a Mexican domain where the existential hero must grapple with the ubiquitous corruption and lies of a post-Revolution political context. As Usigli puts it: "The truth is inescapable; but, like all countries destined to hardship, Mexico only arrives at its truth through its men's lies" (*TC* 3:463–64). Only by fighting fire with fire, lies with lies, can one implant authentic action in the no-exit scenario of Mexico and comparable sites. Rubio's death at the end, tragic and destabilizing as it may be, proceeds organically from the Sisyphean rhythm of defeat-victory-defeat that falls to an existential hero who acts in a climate lacking absolutes.

Heir and coda to the polemics of *Alcestes*, *El Presidente*, Alarcón, and Molière, *EG* all told emits a defense of pragmatic authenticity that coalesces into a spirited message: If you want to be a major player in a Mexico rife with hypocrisy, if you want to succeed in implementing the goals of the Mexican Revolution, you have to be willing to play the game with all the weapons of the political milieu (lies, demagoguery, blackmail, anything but violence), to get your hands dirty.[27] You have to forfeit Truth with a capital T, which cannot survive in the public arena, and uphold principles instead of Truth. Choose your truth *according to noble standards*, live it authentically. Play the game of Mexican politics but with ethics, daring, and heart.

The twists that *EG* visits on what we could call Bolton's gringo logic underscore Rubio's transformation into a worthy Mexican existentialist protagonist, in the bargain differentiating Mexico from the US. The naivete of Bolton's North American logic prompts Rubio's initial imposture. In the first act, Rubio astutely surmises that Bolton abides by two misguided assumptions: an unshakeable faith in logic consonant with Antonio Caso's merely "economic" positivism (Bolton says, "the truth is always logical" [*43*; 142]) and an exoticizing view of Mexico as marvelous (*33*; 131), a country where truth "is stranger than fiction" (*60*; 156). The at first opportunistic protagonist of *EG* combines the mutually exclusive propositions and sells Bolton the truth to which the North American professor subscribes, in the guise of a logically admissible yet marvelous General Rubio. The second and third acts of *EG* then walk away from both flawed premises of gringo logic. They enter into a supple, pragmatic orbit that operates on passionate, altruistic commitment.

Against the odds, *EG* has worked itself into a space that reaches out to Hiperión and to Mexican identity discourse, even in terms distinct from Paz's *Laberinto*. Usigli not unjustifiably saw himself as a major figure in the conversation on Mexican identity. He had added his voice to the conversation through the essays on Alarcón and on *EG* as well as through *EG* itself, whose proximity to Samuel Ramos's identitary *El perfil del hombre y la cultura en México* Usigli acknowledges (*TC* 3:545).[28] With his habitual immodesty and with Hiperión clearly in mind, Usigli boasts: "Ramos's book, and my 'Epílogo [to *EG*] sobre la hipocresía del mexicano' [Epilogue on the Hypocrisy of the Mexican] . . . were the precursors of the entire enterprise of investigating and searching for Mexicannness that our young intellectuals, psychologists and philosophers, have carried out" (R. Rodríguez 54–55). The "Epílogo" (*TC* 3) to which Usigli refers echoes Ramos's bleak account of his compatriots' inferiority complex and outdoes it, ripping into Mexicans' inveterate hypocrisy, pridefulness, negativity, machismo, brutality, and more. Conspicuous kinship between the cynical "Epílogo" and Ramos's text perforce inscribes Usigli in the line of would-be therapeutic pathologizers and at an obvious distance from Hiperión's more sanguine positions. Directly referring to Usigli, Hiperión's enfant terrible Emilio Uranga *undoes the obvious*. Exploiting the indeterminate aspects we have discerned in *EG*, Uranga constructs an enabling ethos for Mexicans that keeps faith with Hiperión at the same time as it maneuvers within the compass of negative diagnostics. In ways that Usigli himself was unlikely to have apprehended, his grandiloquent boast may well not, we will see, prove quite so outrageous.

In "A propósito de Rodolfo Usigli" [Apropos Rodolfo Usigli] (1950; in *Análisis*), Uranga declares that the Hyperions felt "deeply connected to Usigli's thinking and works" (*Análisis* 202), and that Usigli's epilogue on Mexican hypocrisy is "one of the best treatments of the subject" (201). Uranga digs deeper, into *EG*'s agile version of truth. The Hyperion writes, equally admiringly: "Usigli conceives of Mexican hypocrisy as a necessary conduit to Mexican truth; far from seeing hypocrisy as an inclination totally bereft of positive aspects, our author aptly perceives it as an inexorable component in the dialectic of our character, which makes use of the lie to assert its truth" (201). Invoking both the negative and the positive angles of Usigli's outlook, Uranga here gestures, as it were, to the connections between his own influential contribution to Mexican identity discourse—the dialectical, multilayered *zozobra*—and *EG*.

Uranga primarily elaborates on zozobra in *Análisis del ser del mexicano* (1952). Uranga's usage of the word "zozobra," it is important to note from the first, resists translation into English, or any singular definition. In standard lexical terms, the word has a train of meanings that include unceasing anxiety, insecurity, and a precarious wavering between contrary winds. Uranga's Hiperión-inflected, heroic conception of zozobra yokes it to the ontological state of accidentality. We recall from chapter 2 that Uranga opposes accidentality to substantiality; in other words, contingent, authentic humanity, as represented by non-Westerners like Mexicans, as versus the spurious, unchanging essence that in Uranga and Leopoldo Zea's philosophy the European personifies. Zozobra, then, constitutes for Uranga the *ontic correlate of accidentality*: how ontological accidentality manifests in one's physical, emotional, factual existence.[29] "Concrete phenomena are the embodiment of accidentality," summarizes Uranga (*Análisis* 54). Given the sheer expanse of the ontic and the sheer force of accidentality, zozobra produces effects that encompass the word's multifarious dictionary definitions. Uranga's zozobra inextricably links an oscillation between extremes with the deeply felt and embodied vertigo of uncertainty.

Thrusting zozobra towards the specifically Mexican, Uranga takes care to endow his conception with an autochthonous genealogy. He repeatedly associates zozobra with *nepantla*, which roughly means "in-betweenness." The Nahuatl term first appears in print in early Dominican missionary Diego Durán's *Historia de las Indias de Nueva España* [History of the Indies of New Spain] (ca. 1588) when the friar reports on a conversation with an Indigenous informant who described his people as nepantla, in-between Native and Spanish paradigms. As Uranga tells us, nepantla still serves as a descriptor of Mexican identitary zozobra: "In the state of zozobra, we do not know what to depend on, we vacillate between different 'laws,' we are 'neutral,' 'in-between,' 'nepantla'" ("Optimismo y pesimismo sobre el mexicano," *Análisis* 198).[30] That according to the author of *Análisis* the wavering (between poles whose attributes vary with the times) never ceases, that the dialectic never reaches synthesis but remains churning, constitutes the Mexican's permanent state of becoming and fragility. Uranga portrays zozobra as a vacillating, aporetic identity always in the making, an existential becoming. Grueling as it may be, the byproduct of accidentality that is zozobra comprehends change and thus avoids the bad faith of substantiality.

While *Análisis*, dedicated to Paz, is eminently mindful of the errancy between antithetical domains found in *Laberinto*, it should be clear from the preceding discussion that Uranga's zozobra also intersects richly with

Usigli's stagecraft. Usigli's investments, philosophical and political, in aporia, liminality, and a tensile pragmatism all comport with the bases on which Uranga erects lo mexicano into a radically ex-centric, positive ontology. Rejecting absolutes as does Usigli, Uranga predicates Mexican identity on a relativized, inclusive mode of being that holds opposites in tension rather than resolving them. "Zozobra," Uranga theorizes, "constantly regards the contradictions of life or history" and entails "a dependence on both poles, an accumulation, a not letting go of either extreme" (*Análisis* 94). A restless, unseizable Mexican identity that permanently alternates between extremes ensues from zozobra. On a par with Usigli's in-between Alarcón no less than with *EG*'s acute undecidability, Uranga characterizes Mexican identity as "pendular, oscillating, swinging, zig-zagging" (94). The agility of truth in *EG* for which Uranga applauded Usigli ("far from seeing hypocrisy as an inclination totally bereft of positive aspects, our author aptly perceives it as an inexorable component in the dialectic of our character") accommodates an elastic pragmatism.

Combing through the Mexican Archive, Uranga further harvests his zozobra from the 1919 book of the same title by poet Ramón López Velarde (1888–1921), who, Uranga states, "will always have the last word in my ontology" (*Análisis* 94). Usigli might agree with Uranga in some measure given that two of the dramatist's plays, *El niño y la niebla* and *Corona de fuego* [Crown of Fire], mention López Velarde's *Zozobra*/zozobra. Be that as it may, Uranga highlights Usigli's devotion to the "collective," "society as a whole" ("A propósito," *Análisis* 202), and in *Análisis* the Hyperion extracts a pleading for community from López Velarde that supplements the pacts with the agora and communal good fundamental to *EG*. Uranga premises his intricate argument on López Velarde's poem "La tejedora" [The Weaver] (1916), which the Hyperion adopts as a parable of how zozobra undertakes to weave contraries together.[31] The weaver's efforts originate in a sense of lack, an ontological wound (read: accidentality). They constitute a prayer for completion, for healing an unnameable guilt. In a characteristic existential key, not God but "azar," chance and adventure, moves the weaver's supplication (*Análisis* 96). In a characteristic Hiperión key, only community and intersubjectivity can, as they do in Uranga's version of "La tejedora," heal the voids: "We have said that this primary voice of guilt contains a plea, yet denied that the plea addresses itself to a God. We can clarify the matter by considering that what the weaver seeks is the synthesis of consciousnesses, i.e., *intersubjectivity*. Escape from an insular consciousness and entry into a *communitarian* consciousness. This is the *objective* of the movement to which chance and adventure lend themselves" (*Análisis* 98; emphasis added). Uranga's zozobra, moreover, inclines to an altruism that includes "communion," the relief of one's neighbors' suffering (102*)*, and most of all, "love" (98–99*)*. Uranga adds that zozobra never ceases its fervent, if permanently aporetic, appeals to communion (102). As is the case with Usigli's theater of ideas, we see, zozobra's conflictive energies remain alive and productive.

Unsurprisingly, given his emphasis on altruism, Uranga appraises zozobra and Ramos's *Perfil* as "two portraits of our mode of being that on the face of it are irreconcilable" (*Análisis* 93). Ramos-like disparagement analogous to Usigli's caustic "Epílogo" does nonetheless infiltrate Uranga's roster of Mexican character flaws: desgana, emotionality, resentment, hypocrisy, and cynicism. We know from chapter 2 that in Uranga's system these features all flow from accidentality. And because the accidental manifests in the ontic, as Uranga affirms (99), they both partake of zozobra. Uranga grants that he paints no pretty picture, that zozobra may strike his readers as a negative contribution to "the enterprise of improving ourselves" (105).

The saving graces of zozobra he brings to the fore work to mitigate negative judgments.[32] Not only in ontological terms does "lo mexicano" stand as a model of "lo humano" (*Análisis* 45), in their facticity Mexicans also confront zozobra's challenges head-on and open themselves unstintingly to the human condition. The "Mexican does not flee" from these categories of being. He "stays with them, communicates with them, keeps them at hand, not as innocuous theoretical constructs but as the stuff of life" ("El mexicano y el humanismo," *Análisis* 198). To take ownership of zozobra and push through it in consciousness is to live *authentically*. For Uranga, many Mexicans accomplish that, evincing their signal quality of "valor" (198). The inversion of values that alongside his fellow Hyperions Uranga sponsors vindicates the seemingly pathological. Uranga turns the tables on Ramos and Usigli as well as on zozobra's gainsayers.

Another of Uranga's inversions, a fairly astounding one, magnifies the cynic cum hypocrite into a Hiperión-style Mexican hero. In his deliberations on who might have the courage to replace foreign with autochthonous values, Uranga singles out the cynic as fit for the task.[33] Uranga's cynic, like Jorge Portilla's relajiento, dares to oppose the norm. Distinct from the relajiento, Uranga's cynic does not employ a "rude, hard, vulgar, and brutal hand" (*Análisis* 75) but acts in a refined manner, with a well-calibrated hypocrisy. "*In the cynic, hypocrisy is thus a modus operandi of sagacity and prudence; the cynic tries to approach his prey as stealthily as possible. Then he zeroes in on his target, and demolishes it*" (76). Circuitous yet focused, sounding more and more like César Rubio, the Hyperion's knight of accidentality shrinks neither from his responsibility nor his transcendence. Instead, "owing precisely to his authenticity," Uranga's chosen Mexican *existentialist* hero "does battle and commits himself to capitalizing on the autonomy of which he, as the incarnation of accidentality, is made" (77). The cynical hypocrite, possessed of valor, strives not to "save" others but to "liberate" them, wherein liberation involves providing a mission and a meaning for life (77). In one fell swoop, Uranga has tacitly redeemed himself, enfant terrible; Usigli the contrarian; and Usigli's trenchant hypocrite, César Rubio. Still, Uranga registers that cynics' idealism may eventually plunge them into bitterness and tragedy (78).

Usigli himself also pinpointed valor as Mexicans' signal quality (*TC* 3:414), a quality that César Rubio models for his fellow citizens. *And yet*, corroborating Uranga's dire predictions, Rubio suffers and dies. In Usigli's own existential framework, Rubio's suffering has heightened standing. Rubio does not insouciantly glide into his new identity, which would invite accusations of a pragmatic *in*authenticity and fraud. Instead, act 2 shows the protagonist falling victim to his own crime. Tortured by guilt, Rubio cannot spend the blood money he has obtained from imposture. Usigli's protagonist emerges from the trauma purified. When he enters act 3, the stage directions read: "He has experienced an impressive transformation in the last few weeks. The agitation, the excess of controlled nervous energy, the fever of ambition, the struggle against fear have all given a noble serenity to his countenance, a clarity to his gaze, an almost incredible self-assurance" (*91*; 181). The anguish of the Unamunian agonista, the passion and suffering of the hyper-conscious Nietzschean dissimulator, and a value-rich pragmatism all congregate here to ratify Rubio as authentic, an existentialist hero. However ephemeral the value of his death, in the post-Revolution, post-factual climate he inhabits, Rubio has died for a cause. Such, we might conclude, are the anchors of an ethical, humanistic truth in a world divorced from absolutes.

Chapter Four

Excavating Comala

The Existentialist Juan Rulfo, the Grupo Hiperión, and *Lo Mexicano* in *Pedro Páramo* (1955)

In the first pages of Juan Rulfo's protean *Pedro Páramo*, Juan Preciado meets his half-brother Abundio Martínez at a crossroads called "Los Encuentros." Abundance, crossroads, encounters: all three come to characterize the novel itself, which majestically burgeons into a meeting place of paths as varied as myth, theology, history, and ideology and thus into an all-time classic of Mexican literature. This chapter argues that among the multiple paths converging in *Pedro Páramo* we may count existentialism, predominantly as it impacted formulations of lo mexicano circulating in Rulfo's milieu at the time of the novel's gestation.

To align Rulfo's work with existentialism is a tricky business, splashed with pitfalls as well as promise. After all, to my knowledge neither the author's own statements nor extant scholarship has associated him with the Grupo Hiperión.[1] Yet Rulfo's self-mythmaking displays a penchant for fabulation and withholding (García Bonilla 45), and Carlos Blanco Aguinaga has deemed him one of the best-read men in Mexico (16). In order to truly understand Rulfo, comments Elena Poniatowska, "one must dig and dig" (*Ay vida* 135). Granting the slipperiness of their territory, the dialogues that "Excavating Comala" mounts between Rulfo and existentialism operate under a key caveat. Evidence of Rulfo's involvement with several forms of existentialism, as we will see, is not lacking, but what follows does not always intend to unearth proof of the elusive author's direct engagement with Hiperión. It simply contends that *Pedro Páramo* resonates, sometimes quite closely, with currents in Mexican existentialism, and that they not merely dimensionalize but indeed illuminate the novel, especially in terms of racial issues. On its own and as a gateway to articulations of *mestizaje* [racial mixture] and Indigeneity in Mexico, Hiperión's work helps root out *Pedro Páramo*'s subterranean claims for lo mexicano. That is: What lies buried deep in Comala, in Mexican history, and in the collective DNA of Mexicans? Whether kinships with Hiperión constitute direct influences on Rulfo's novel is to a degree immaterial, for in toto I wish to demonstrate—more interestingly, perhaps—that setting it in conversation with Hiperión helps excavate these crucial, enigmatic zones of the many-voiced *Pedro Páramo* (henceforth, *PP*).

An Existentialist Rulfo?

Whereas associating Rulfo with Hiperión requires some finesse, it takes little maneuvering to insert *PP* in the broad existential Weltanschauung that had captivated Western literary production of the era.[2] Anguish, bad faith, and alienation, largely as a result of Pedro Páramo's iniquitous regime, suffuse the text. When Pedro says to his henchman, "What law, Fulgor? From now on, we're the law" (English *40*; Spanish 107), he seizes the godlike position Fyodor Dostoevsky's world-shaking "if God does not exist, everything is permissible" darkly heralds ("A Hymn and a Secret" in *The Brothers Karamazov*). That Pedro co-opts the Church symptomatizes the novel's interrogation of Christianity, a fundamental impulse of existentialism with which the novel pervasively makes common cause. *PP* assails the immorality of an institutionalized religion that monetizes salvation, religion dependent on the unyielding, dogmatic code that damns the forlorn inhabitants of Comala who believe "out of superstition and fear" (*71*; 140). The novel traffics heavily in theological allusions only to ironize and degrade them systematically. Adam and Eve (Donis and his sister), the Fall (Pedro's destruction of Comala after his wife Susana's death), the Flood (the omnipresent rain that never purifies), and heaven (a dystopia for Dorotea when it crushes her hopes for a child [*60*; 129]) undergo a transvaluation that strips them of transcendence. By endowing its most sinful characters with the names of Peter and Michael, *PP* utterly ravages those biblical figures.

Two considerably more ambiguous, and more philosophically gripping, protagonists dominate the existential landscape of *PP*. At the center of the novel's theological polemics stand Susana San Juan, a blasphemous nonbeliever, and Father Rentería, a doubting priest; the text constantly throws them together. As Rentería attempts to console her for a series of deaths, the sensualist Susana profanes him and religious rites by mentally frolicking with her deceased husband Florencio. Susana's erotic trances, madness, and "alienated discourse" (Bastos and Molloy, "El personaje" 7) parody one of her namesakes, the mystic Saint John of the Cross, and disavow God: "Oh, God! You do not exist. I asked you to protect him [Florencio] . . . . But all you care about is souls. And what I want is his body" (*100*; 170). Of all the women in Comala, only Susana escapes the Church's sway (Valdés 47). Written by a lapsed Catholic and anti-Cristero, *PP* complicates Susana's flagrant transgressions (Cruz; Poniatowska, *Ay vida* 148). The novel twice floats the iconoclastic question of whether Susana is an innocent or a sinner. Two devout women with symbolic names, Ángeles and Fausta, wonder if madness does not absolve people like Susana of sin (*112*; 182), which echoes Rentería's own suspicions: "Perhaps there was nothing for him to pardon" (*114*; 170).

Although Father Rentería perseveres in administering the rites to Susana, throughout the text he wavers between an orthodox and an existential sense of his mission. Rentería effectively rents the church to Pedro and pays for it with the tortured interiority that makes the priest the conscience of the novel. Blaming himself for the dire straits of his parishioners, feeling guilty for refusing them absolution, Rentería begins to doubt the Catholic code (*30–32*; 95–97). Susana, lucid despite her madness (Bastos and Molloy, "El personaje" 12–15), asks him: "Why do you come see me, when you are dead?" (*93*; 162). Rentería's conflicted faith leads him to replicate the negotiations with Christianity of the anguished priest in Miguel de Unamuno's proto-existential *San Manuel Bueno, mártir*. As we recall from chapter 3, Don Manuel cannot bring himself to believe in God, but for the sake of his town he assiduously performs his pastoral duties. By the same token, when Rentería returns to Comala after being denied absolution by a senior priest in Contla, he continues, now illicitly, to confess his demanding parishioners, with the added existential twist that he asks the communicants to judge themselves (*73–75*; 142–44). Rentería's final actions in the novel remain shrouded in ambiguity. He has fled into the hills to fight in the Cristero uprisings—solely as a rebellion against Pedro or, despite the priest's doubts, as a genuine reconsecration to the Church? Earlier versions of *PP* have a prototype of Rentería, Father Sebastián Villalpando, dying in the wars, thereby literalizing the martyrdom that Unamuno's Don Manuel experiences figuratively (Rulfo, *Cuadernos* 73, 83).[3]

The two most existentialist characters of *PP* thus throb with questions. For our purposes, one of them is how Rulfo's novel came to engage several bedrock concerns of existentialism; in other words, whether Rulfo had any actual commerce with existential thinking. Certain benchmarks of his early trajectory establish that he did. Before and while Rulfo worked for the Secretaría de Gobernación, starting in 1936, he attended lectures in the UNAM's Facultad de Filosofía y Letras at its former home in the Mascarones building. There Rulfo attended classes of an Antonio Caso enthused with Kierkegaard. There, too, Rulfo may first have met Octavio Paz (García Bonilla 88).[4] The early 1940s witnessed Rulfo's first publication of the stories that would comprise *El llano en llamas* [The Plain in Flames] (1953), in the Guadalajara journal *Pan: Revista de Literatura* and in the Mexico City journal *América*. *América*, whose editorial board Rulfo eventually joined, focused on Indoamerican, nationalist, and existential topics (López Mena, *Los caminos* 65–67). According to Sergio López Mena, Rulfo's stories well matched the concerns of the journal (67). *El llano en llamas* afforded Rulfo the renown that earned him fellowships to the Centro Mexicano de Escritores between 1952 and 1954. At the Centro, Rulfo had contact with two important figures of the Grupo Hiperión, Agustín Yáñez, a fellow Jaliscan who came to be a friend (Vital 171), and Jorge Portilla, Rulfo's photograph of whom adorned an homage to the author of *Fenomenología del relajo* in the journal *Universidad de México*.[5]

Rulfo's readings, the crux of his intellectual formation, manifest further involvement with existentialism. He credited his knowledge less to formal training than to the fact that he was "an almost pathological reader, capable of reading two books per night" (García Bonilla 89). This prodigious autodidact's library contained up to 10,000 books, hundreds of them philosophical, historical, and international literary works (García Bonilla 274). We know that Rulfo pored over at least one of Dostoevsky's novels during the period in which he audited classes at Mascarones (García Bonilla 88), and that before finishing *PP* he was taken with María Luisa Bombal's proto-existential novel *La amortajada* [The Shrouded Woman; 1939] (García Bonilla 137; Carballo, "Revisión" 23). Rulfo admired José Revueltas, the premier Mexican existentialist cum Marxist writer of the time, to the extent that he reportedly wrote a story for *El llano en llamas* with a character based on him (Lezama 43; unfortunately, Rulfo never published the story). The first review of Rulfo's novel compares it to Revueltas's 1943 *El luto humano* [Human Mourning] (García Bonilla 146; Valadés 1), and with good reason. The ghostly towns, death-centered narrative, cosmic imagery, cynicism regarding the Mexican Revolution and Cristero Wars, and devastations of theology in Revueltas's novel all dovetail with *PP*.[6] At some point, harder to determine, Rulfo's existentialist readings also included Sartre's *Nausea* (López Mena, *Los caminos* 44) and Alejo Carpentier's *Los pasos perdidos* [The Lost Steps; 1953] (García Bonilla 82; Poniatowska, "Agente" 1).

Four pieces of Rulfo's *El hijo del desaliento* [The Child of Despair], his earliest but unpublished novel, offer striking proof that the Mexican author both read and *wrote* appreciably existentialist literature prior to *PP*. Scholars date Rulfo's *El hijo* to the start of the 1940s, an incandescent period for existentialist literature because *Nausea*, Albert Camus's inaugural works, and, in Latin America, Juan Carlos Onetti's *El pozo* had recently been published. Rulfo would ultimately disavow his *El hijo* as cerebral, bombastic, and conventional (López Mena, *Los caminos* 45), but he did publish one fragment of it in 1959 as the story "Un pedazo de noche" [A Slice of Night]. The posthumous issuing of Rulfo's *Cuadernos* [Notebooks] brought other pieces of the novel to light, they being the fragments the editor titled "Mi tía Cecilia" [My Aunt Cecilia], "Cleotilde," and "Ya no habrá quien nos odie" [Then There Will Be No One Who Hates Us] (36–43). In the aggregate, the four known pieces of *El hijo* revolve around the loss of the mother, as would *PP*. They melodramatically recount the death of the narrator's mother-substitute aunt, his marriage to a prostitute who refuses to forsake promiscuity ("Un pedazo de noche" gives her backstory), and the narrator's murder of his wife, catalyzed by her defamation of his aunt's sacred memory. The degraded, embittered narrator who defiles a prostitute unmistakably reincarnates Dostoevsky's underground man, and the guilt that torments the narrator reverberates with his *Crime and Punishment*.

The existentialism of Rulfo's fledgling novel does not end there. For especially "Cleotilde" (*Cuadernos* 38–43) turns out to be Rulfo's rewrite of Onetti's *El pozo*. Onetti's text permeates Rulfo's, sometimes verbatim. The Mexican author's complex yet obvious transposition of *El pozo*, upon which as far as I know no one has commented, deserves a study unto itself. In brief, though, Rulfo's "Cleotilde" recapitulates the brutality, the objectifying gaze, and primarily the notion of woman as a source of salvation in the absence of God that distinguish the trailblazing *El pozo*. Rulfo at the same time shifts the lost innocence of *El pozo*'s Cecilia, narrator Linacero's wife, onto the lost aunt Cecilia. He compacts Onetti's prostitute Ester and the adolescent Ana María whom Linacero rapes and figuratively kills into the prostitute wife whom the narrator of "Cleotilde" murders. Onetti's sordid *El pozo*, of course, inscribes itself in and reinvents Dostoevsky's squalid

Notes from Underground. Triangulating with foundational literary works, the portions of Rulfo's *El hijo del desaliento* that have come down to us form a hefty existentialist constellation.

That Rulfo's masterpiece, *PP*, dialogues with Octavio Paz's 1950 *El laberinto de la soledad* has far-reaching implications for an "existentialist" *PP*. *Laberinto*'s "Día de los muertos" chapter, which illustrates the intimate relationship of Mexicans with death, almost inevitably brings the living dead of Rulfo's novel to mind. Indeed, Emil Volek calls *PP* an "appendix to, and sly rebuttal of, Paz's famous *El laberinto de la soledad*" (552). In its role as an appendix to the existentially oriented *Laberinto*, *PP* portrays the solitude of Comala's alienated Mexicans, disaffected in life by Pedro's contemptible regime and still estranged in death. What Paz sees as the defining Mexican condition of solitude touches even Pedro, unexpectedly nuancing the sinister character. Consigned to solitude by a chain of traumatic deaths and an unattainable love, Pedro in some measure shades into an unstable combination of relatable melancholy versus abhorrent evil. Whatever sympathy for Pedro this zozobra of sorts might engender in the reader, however, quickly wanes as we realize that Pedro sublimates his anguish into the entrenched masks of machismo and despotism. The despot then recreates the Conquest of Mexico by fathering scores of *chingados*: Pedro's orphaned, illegitimate children and by extension the people of Comala, whom he ruthlessly "screws over." Rulfo so thoroughly deplores Pedro's hegemony that he denies fiestas the consoling potency Paz assigns them. *PP* does contain fiestas, notably the misguided carnival that occurs upon Susana's death (*115–17*; 185–87), but they backfire into tragedies. When after that macabre event Pedro swears revenge on Comala (*115*; 187), he initiates the death of the town and carries Rulfo's rebuttal of *Laberinto*'s fiestas to a chilling peak.

An Unresolved Past

Be it by fleshing out or contesting *Laberinto*, Rulfo clearly adopts Paz's treatise as one template for his novel. In so doing, he writes *PP* into the discourse of lo mexicano that the Grupo Hiperión had propagated from Mexico, in the intellectual climate Rulfo imbibed. The past, which *PP* revivifies through the undead Comala, beckoned to Hyperion Leopoldo Zea as an integral part of Mexico's Dasein. Zea's *Dos etapas del pensamiento en Hispanoamérica: Del romanticismo al positivismo* [Two Stages of Spanish-American Thought: From Romanticism to Positivism] (1949) frames the vexed relationship of Mexico, and of Latin America at large, to their respective histories in Hegelian and existential terms. The programmatic first chapter of Zea's *Dos etapas* alleges that Latin America has not yet assimilated its colonial past, its Spanish past. Latin America has not "authentically," as Zea says, assimilated the problematic aspects of its background, an assimilation that would install them in the dialectics of History, transform them into a true past, and enable them to be transcended. Instead, Latin Americans have tried to "amputate" the past (21). That is, they have overleaped it, accumulating new "presents" rather than resolving the past in a dialectical fashion. Zea emphatically maintains that *because the past must be assimilated instead of amputated and because that has not occurred, the past ends up constantly obtruding in Latin America's present*. As Latin Americans fall back on European institutions, the unsavory modes that the Conquest introduced endure. From Zea's perspective, the inevitable return of what Latin America has inauthentically repressed tethers it to the past and condemns it to endlessly repeating the ways of a past it wishes to bury.

In order to escape the vicious cycle, Zea urges that Latin America, once it has acknowledged the re-petitions of its history, devise Latin American, not European, solutions to Latin American problems: "It would seem that Spanish Americans keep posing the same problems and seeking the same solutions they have learned from European culture. But the truth is that, no matter what we imagine, the problems are not the same, nor are the solutions. Reality is always stronger, and it obliges us to pose Spanish American problems and to seek our own solutions to them" (20). Only then, according to Zea, will Latin America have an authentic History. Zea's pan–Latin American solution to the unresolved past, it is important to register, has a specifically Mexican genealogy. In *El problema de México* (1924) Antonio Caso broaches the dilemma, its remedy, and other main pressure points of Zea's argument. For instance, Caso observes: "Instead of following a uniform, gradual, dialectical process, Mexico has proceeded accumulatively" (69), to the effect that "the problem of the conquest" has not yet been laid to rest (70). Among its various meanings, the venerable slogan of "wings and lead" that Caso coins in *Problema* reflects his conviction that Mexicans should stay faithful to "what is their own, their vernacular" (71). Zea cements the parallels between *Dos etapas* and *Problema* in his prologue to the 1976 edition of *Problema*, where he picks up Caso's claims that accord with his and mingles his voice with his forebear's. Thus Zea reissues Caso's call for Mexican models with the words: "Wings to fly, but also the lead that binds man to his native reality" (xxii).

Anchored in an illustrious Mexican tradition as Zea's picture of history is, not by chance does it recall Paz's *Laberinto* or, for that matter, *PP*. *Laberinto*, we know, contends that Mexicans still exist in an alienation and inauthenticity that stem from their past. Chapter 7 of *Laberinto*, on Mexican intellectuals, in fact expounds Zea's ideas, which pervade Paz's text explicitly and inexplicitly.[7] More vital to the lines I am developing here is the centrality to *PP* of the ideas that Zea and Paz share. By this I mean that although *PP* dramatizes several features of *Laberinto*, the *overarching* scenario of the novel reflects the dimensions of Paz's argument most akin to Zea. It is impossible to determine if Rulfo had direct knowledge of Zea's writings, or if he just imaginatively embellished upon the Zea-esque aspects of *Laberinto*. Whatever the case, *PP* evidences a profound investment in the ideas that Hiperión's leader championed.

Rulfo's profound investment in history drives the kinship. He first engrossed himself in the chronicles of the colonial period when working as an archivist at the Secretaría de Gobernación, later sketched out a novel on eighteenth-century Jalisco ("La cordillera"), and his last publication was a preface to sixteenth-century missionary Bernardino de Sahagún's ethnography of the Aztecs.[8] Akin to Zea, Rulfo has lamented that disowning its colonial past has led Mexico to repeat the barbarity of the Conquest "in a kind of eternal return that can only cease when, with no self-deception, we dare to face down our history" (Jiménez 19). In Rulfo's view, the Conquest had especially dire consequences for his home state of Jalisco, where it resulted in the extermination of Indigenous peoples and in the descendants of the conquerors considering themselves "absolute masters" of the land (Sommers 107). Whence Pedro Páramo himself, whom Rulfo explicitly identifies as a "cacique," the prototypical representative of the "old colonialism to which we are still subjected" (Rulfo, qtd. in Vital 200).

For who is the Pedro who shuts out memory (English 67; Spanish 136) if not "living bile" (6; 68), and what is his regime if not the persistence in modern Mexico of the colonialism and its perpetual iterations that the Revolution labored to unseat? Pedro has hijacked all the land and has arrogated total, merciless power. He has imprisoned Comala in an economy based on usufruct and on the commodification of human beings that mirrors the worst of the Conquest. The novel insists that the Mexican Revolution, which aimed to undo the colonial past, changed nothing.[9] Pedro exploits what Rulfo portrays as a shambolic, energetic hulk of a war and buys it, as the landowner had bought everything else. The Revolution leads only to a new eruption of atavistic violence in the Cristero Wars. Equally impactful,

PP reifies the image of the past as the living dead that Zea advances and that William Faulkner famously encapsulates in the words, "the past is never dead, it's not even past" (73). The Comala that Juan Preciado meets is a ghost town, *un lugar de mala muerte*, a purgatory inhabited by revenants who had colluded with the cacique Pedro Páramo voluntarily or otherwise. Their souls haunt Comala in search of someone to pray for them (e.g., *59*; 128). Rulfo's Mexicanized hauntology, in short, delivers a mise-en-scène of the unburied, still-living past that Zea and Paz assail.

At least one component of Zea's essay that *Laberinto* does not take up has a strong presence in *PP*. Zea highlights the spurious lure of utopias, which breed the illusion that one can always start over again from a tabula rasa, eschewing the past. Rulfo's text begins and ends in utopias, in Dolores's vision of Comala as paradise and Pedro's concluding vision of Susana and the Paradise tree (*123*; 193). The body of the text, though, steeps us in the real, dystopian Comala to which Dolores sent her son Juan. That dystopia leaves us with one of the novel's greatest enigmas, namely, if the paradisiacal, idyllic Comala with which Dolores enthralled Juan ever actually existed, or if it was literally a u-topia, a merely notional place.

Textual evidence does not allow us to resolve the enigma, but reading *PP* alongside Zea elucidates it. Inserted in Zea's framework, Dolores's possibly egregious lie emerges as a means of seducing her son to assume the burden of the past. His burden, sadly, proves lethal. The murmurs of the ghosts kill Juan (*58*; 127); having shunted the burden of the past onto him, Dolores arguably experiences an apotheosis ("Her voice seemed all-encompassing. It faded into distant space" [*57*; 127]). In his quest to rescue a utopian Comala, Juan has looked back at the true past, which engulfs and undoes him. Throughout the second half of the novel, nevertheless, Juan Preciado and Dorotea channel the repressed stories of the townspeople, insinuating the dynamic hope that perhaps, just perhaps, the understanding of the past that the stories bequeath readers of *PP* can free Comala's wandering souls from their purgatory and Mexico from the re-petitions of its history. Suggestively, Pedro himself dies in the wake of Abundio Martínez's pleas for the "charity" that the novel solicits (*121*; 191).

The Orestes of Sartre's play *The Flies* (1943), a character to whom Juan Preciado bears an uncanny resemblance, models the salvation of a community that *PP* would thus augur.[10] Prodigal son Orestes has returned home to Argos. He goes "down into the depths" of his community to reclaim his place in it (90). On the Day of the Dead in which ghosts torment the Argives for their crimes, Orestes absorbs his brethren's sins and frees them from the tyranny they have condoned. When in his final speech Orestes entreats his fellow citizens, who no longer need fear the dead, to reshape their lives (123), he tenders a prospect of communal redemption that flows from Argos to Comala. Orestes exits *The Flies* as a Pied Piper whose songs rid the town of its afflictions, as, with the reader's complicity, may the stories Juan Preciado transmits.

Excavating *Lo Indígena*

Therein, imminently, lies one hope for Mexico that *PP* extends to readers. Another—fleeting but palpable and powerful in ways that I believe interpretations of the novel have yet to fully excavate—emanates from the Indigenous peddlers from a different town, Apango, who briefly enter Comala in the forty-eighth section of the novel (*86–87*; 155–56).[11] All the other characters, Rulfo has importantly confirmed, are mestizos (García Bonilla 146; González Boixo). The mestizo Pedro stands in for the criollos who perpetuated the foreign ways of life that according to Zea and Rulfo have affected it so deleteriously. By contrast, the "indios" from Apango endow *PP* with an autochthonous dimension that yields a salutary, authentic Mexico, a Mexican paradigm of the sort Caso and Zea enjoin. Among Rulfo's many photographs of Native artifacts, one particularly speaks to the role of *lo indígena*—Indigenous peoples and cultures—in *PP* that the remainder of this chapter strives to uncover. Rulfo's photograph of a small bas-relief from a Franciscan chapel in Texcoco (*Juan Rulfo's Mexico* 187) portrays an Indigenous man as Atlas, holding up the world as I maintain the Indigenous characters from Apango (for the sake of convenience henceforth I take the liberty of naming them "the Apangans") hold up the novel in ideological and existentialist terms.

One naturally wonders if the few, laconic pages of *PP* on the Apangans can carry so much weight. Given that after publishing the novel Rulfo would devote much of his life to Mexico's Indigenous peoples in his work for the Instituto Nacional Indigenista (the INI), it also seems quite curious that Indigenous characters make so scant an appearance in the novel.[12] Rulfo's declarations and photographs respond to such issues tellingly. The author has repeatedly attributed the scarcity of Indigenous figures in his literary writings to respect for Mexico's Native peoples, whose hermetic mindset Rulfo does not arrogantly presume to comprehend. For example, he has claimed that "despite heading the Departmento de Publicaciones of the Instituto Nacional Indigenista, and having brought to press more than 80 studies of social anthropology, I still do not know how and why the Indigenous mind works" ("Notas" 5); "all I came to know, all that one can know about them [the Indigenous peoples] is what one sees, not how they think" ("Rulfo examina" 876). The second statement points to the fact that starting in the late 1940s Rulfo reached out to Indigenous milieux through photography. Photography functioned as a supplement to writing: Rulfo's son Juan Pablo remarked that an exhibit of his father's photographs could be an image "of what *he did not write*" (García Bonilla 322; emphasis added). And Rulfo's copious, stunning photographs of Indigenous communities more than compensate for his reticence to embody them in literature. Rulfo's photographs enshrine the continuity of the past in the present, Mexico's atemporal infrahistory. Though numerous, the photographs cluster around the themes of ruins, sacred spaces and festivals, single and collective portraits, and the nature that still reigns over many Indigenous peoples' lives. Not entirely abandoning his respectful trepidation, Rulfo often photographed his Indigenous subjects from behind, as unobtrusively as possible (Billeter 40; Amador Tello).

This said, we can survey the tantalizing cameo of the Indigenous group in *PP*. On a Sunday, under a torrential rain, the Indigenous peddlers from Apango descend into the marketplace of the novel's mestizo town, Comala. The "indios" spread out their herbs and other wares in the central square (where Juan Preciado would later die) and await customers. The Apangans fear it is an "ill-fated day" (*86*; 155) for sales and correctly so, because their potential customers are out in the fields of Comala trying to salvage their crops from the rain. Quickly resigning themselves to the situation, the Apangans "tell jokes and laugh" ("sueltan la risa") (*86*; 156). Justina, Susana's nursemaid, approaches them, crossing herself when she passes the church. The outsiders submit Justina to intense scrutiny as she purchases rosemary from them. Justina then goes off to bring Susana the rosemary. The traders gather their wares, and stop by the church to pray to the Virgin and offer her a bunch of thyme. They then set out for Apango, again "telling jokes and laughing" ("soltando la risa") (*87*; 156).

Read over against Luis Villoro's watershed treatment of contemporary indigenism in *Los grandes momentos del indigenismo en México* (1950), the preceding deceptively simple cameo begins to reveal its magnitude for Rulfo's novel at large in ways that will percolate throughout my subsequent arguments. The final movement of *Grandes momentos* deals with twentieth-century indigenismo, under the heading of "Lo indígena manifestado por la acción y el amor" [Lo Indígena as Manifested in Action and Love]. While indigenismo's love for "Lo indígena" remains decidedly circumscribed, Villoro's knows fewer limitations. He completed *Grandes momentos* in 1949, a year after the founding of the INI during Lázaro Cárdenas's administration; in order to promote the assimilation and economic development of Indigenous communities, President Miguel Alemán continued to support the INI. An exposé, as we know, of the positions on Mexico's Indigenous peoples that omit those of the Indigenous peoples themselves (in indigenismo, lo indígena materializes "as an always revealed, but never relevant, reality" [292]), *Grandes momentos* shores up the INI's diametrically opposed position. Villoro's unmasking of indigenism as a "*false* consciousness" (9) also bears a dire cautionary message for anyone who would objectify or instrumentalize the Indigenous peoples. I note that, by the same token, not just the revisionary *Grandes momentos* but also the raft of Hiperión texts that will come into play here gainsay Ana Santos Ruiz's allegations that Hyperions fixated on their own class and race to the disregard of Indigenous concerns.[13] On the contrary, the Mexican existentialists—and Rulfo—gravitate from indigenism to Indigeneity and an Indigenous inflection of lo mexicano.

Santos Ruiz decries the Hyperions' "mestizofilia" (64), which can mean, as it seems to for her, exalting mestiz@s over other races in keeping with Alemanismo's Mexicanidad, or can betoken a doctrine of nation-building predicated on the mestiz@ as a vehicle for unifying a diverse Mexico (Stern 160). Villoro's account of twentieth-century indigenismo delves into the nation-building aspects and attends minutely to evolving notions of mestizaje. According to Villoro's analyses, from the dawn of the century onward indigenists anointed racial mixture the driver of national unity: Indigenous communities would be modernized and Indigenous peoples absorbed into an ethnically blended, holistic Mexico. The ultimate eradication of the Indigenous race and culture that José Vasconcelos prophesied in his controversial *La raza cósmica* [The Cosmic Race] (1925) represents the extreme edge of this platform on mestizaje.[14]

On the other side of mestizaje's early fault lines was Manuel Gamio (1883–1960), progenitor of Mexican anthropology, director for many years of the Instituto Indigenista Interamericano, and a lodestar of Mexico's racial politics through to Rulfo's times. Gamio's *Forjando patria* (1916), *La poblacion del valle de Teotihuacán* (1922), and *Consideraciones sobre el problema indígena* (published by the INI in 1948), while still prescribing the Indigenous peoples' economically advantageous entrance into modernity, reflect the valorization of lo indígena that the Mexican Revolution had incited. *Grandes momentos* informs us that after the Revolution lo indígena began to occupy a leading place in Mexico's self-conceptualization, as the wellspring of the nation's specificity, its uniqueness. For example, in 1948 Manuel Gamio wrote that the Indigenous peoples are the "purest fount of Latin Americanness" (Villoro, *Grandes momentos* 235). Villoro comments that perspectives such as Gamio's rendered the Indigenous worlds "one root of our most authentic specificity, our 'Latin Americanness'" (235). Albeit symbolically, new attitudes towards the Indigenous peoples had removed them from margins and situated them at the center of national autognosis.

Whence the "indigenist mestizo," for Villoro the most recent development in the discourse of mestizaje. Those mestizos (always generic/masculine in Villoro's book) of the mid-twentieth century who propound the foregoing attitudes resite themselves vis-à-vis lo indígena, "nucleus of authentic Latin Americanness" (235). Villoro describes the new indigenist mestizos as intent on reclaiming the authentic Indigenous core that lies deep inside themselves and that also, as Agustín Yáñez affirmed in the foundational definition of Mexicanidad Alemanismo had distorted, "subsists within the national soul" (1942; *Mitos* xxv; Villoro 236). "To grasp the indígena" within, says Villoro in a key assertion, means indirectly capturing "a dimension of one's own being" and thus "recovering one's own 'I'" (272). Villoro clarifies that the present disposition of "the Mexican spirit" (275) regards the Indigenous core as "the community, the ancestral past, the land," the latter being the "telluric principle that binds us to nature" (274). Subscribing to this slate of Indigenous values will further the mestizos' freedom and transcendence (294). Villoro also adduces that, as indigenist mestizos would have it, only *they* possess the mobility and vision to serve as agents of change for a repressed, authentic Indigenous Mexico (269–70 and passim).

In his role as exegete, Villoro refrains from critiquing the blatantly inauthentic facets of the indigenist mestizos' self-interested, bounded mestizaje. Emilio Uranga catches some of them in his 1952 "Ensayo de una ontología del mexicano" (in *Análisis*), which indicts fetishizing the indígena within as another form of substantializing; for his part and for the most part, Villoro honors the love for lo indígena that propels contemporary mestizos.[15] The Marcelian Villoro emphasizes the admirable ways in which the mestizos' indigenism, as versus earlier indigenist enterprises, is geared to intersubjectivity.

However, the unusual penultimate chapter 13 of *Grandes momentos*, "Lo indígena como principio oculto de mi yo que recupero en la pasión" [Lo Indígena as Hidden Principle of My 'I' That I Reclaim in Passion] forcefully articulates what has gone unsaid. This semi-conclusion to the book deviates from the scholarly, exegetical modus operandi that has characterized *Grandes momentos* and takes a more personal tack. Villoro steps away from the indigenist mestizo's discourse on its own, self-stated terms to push hard on the indígena within. In so doing, the author exposes what he considers to be the fallacious premise on which the notion rests: the inability of Westernized mestizos to grasp the Indigenous "hidden principle" that would allegedly heal their "I." Villoro attributes the unknowability of the Indigenous "hidden principle" to the inadequacy of Western reason, which he terms "reflection" ("reflexión"): "there is always an underlying meaning that remains unknown and irrational, impossible for reflection to express" (273). Risking essentializing to make a weighty philosophical point, Villoro suggests lo indígena to be something of an obscure, almost Dionysian life form that resists the Apollonian Western mind. The Latin American existentialist dispute between reason and emotion surfaces here as Villoro maintains that only through "love" (283)—the passion to which his chapter title refers—can one hope to commune with the unfathomable other.

The formal "Conclusión" of *Grandes momentos* repeats Villoro's overall quarrel with indigenism, its exclusion of Indigenous writers themselves. Villoro then returns to his passionate theme of the enigmatic Indigenous other and would-be brother. The final paragraph of *Grandes momentos* underscores that the Indigenous heart of the Mexican self "harbors a hidden and mysterious reality that we can never grasp," though it "captivates us" (295). These words pointedly recall Rulfo's attitude towards writing about Indigenous peoples.

Deep Mexico and Racial Politics

To enter *PP* through the debates *Grandes momentos* filters through Hiperión's prism, is, first off, to recognize the existentialist implications of the novel's Indigenous characters. Through Villoro we have witnessed a movement that acclaims lo indígena as Mexico's authentic core and distinguishes nature as one of its signal features. As Yáñez stated, Mexicanness finds its spirit in "the magnificent panorama of Mexican nature" ("Introducción" x). *PP* associates the Indigenous Apangans with nature. They sell the products of the earth; rain, reminiscent of the ancestral god Tláloc and of the Aztecs' paradise Tlálocan (Lienhard 849), defines their day in Comala. The enmeshment with nature imputed to the Apangans, as any reader of *PP* will have observed, saturates the novel. Comala may have died out, but the four elements and natural flora and fauna endure inalienably. They imbue the otherwise stark narrative with a lush lyricism and unite the local with the cosmic. The rain that leads into most chapters serves as the hinge between past and present. Susana derives erotic delight from water, the sea (*95*; 165). Rain triggers Fulgor Sedano's erotic thirst—*sed*, hence his name—for the very land around which all of Pedro's nefarious designs revolve (*61–62*; 130–31).

PP thus immerses us in the deep structures of Mexico, the atemporal heart of the heart of the country. It is familiar territory for a Latin American existentialism whose followers, including and beyond the Hyperions, have tended to site authenticity in the telluric properties and Indigenous peoples of their nations or continent.[16] Rulfo joins the current with a vision of Mexico's authentic core that precisely anticipates "México profundo," or "deep Mexico," a construct Guillermo Bonfil Batalla (colleague of Villoro and friend of Rulfo) framed in 1987. Bonfil Batalla distinguishes "México profundo" from "México imaginario," a European-leaning Mexico like that which capitalist Pedro imposes on Comala, Zea's *Dos etapas* denounces, and the Hyperions, prompted by Samuel Ramos, scrutinize. As opposed to "México imaginario," "México profundo" privileges and incorporates Indigenous mores—the respect for the community, the ancestral past, and the land to which Villoro referred. Rulfo has observed of what he dubs the Indigenous "infraworld" (Thakkar 193) that "there is something distinctive in the Indians, something new and very old that we have not succeeded in appreciating and from which we have not duly benefited" (López Mena, "Juan Rulfo" 108). Behind these words there conceivably lurks a critique of the regard for "México profundo" that Alemán sought to quash through modernization (Vital 107), thereby reversing Cárdenas's support for the traditional collective *ejido*. In *PP*, significantly enough, the Apangans appear not as individuals but as a group, a community that speaks in an unindividuated collective voice. Rulfo's photographs augment the novel's slim portrait by frequently focusing on Indigenous collectivity in scenes of families, marketplaces, pilgrimages, rituals, and so forth. His photographs of individual Natives, moreover, often depict them as melting into the landscape.

Minimalist as it is, *PP*'s cameo of the Indigenous traders amply conveys the estrangement of an authentic, deep Mexico from the mestizo community. The cameo occupies a distinctive textual space in the novel. Embedded neither in a grave nor in any identifiable mestiz@ character's memory, the Apangans reach the reader as an unmediated, living body. The fact that *PP*'s Indigenous characters literally and figuratively operate outside Pedro's economy reinforces their separatism.[17] Practical necessity may lead the Indigenous actors to intersect with mestiz@s in the marketplace, but the shortage of customers barely perturbs them. Rather, as the text twice tells us, the Apangans tell jokes and unleash (as seen above, the text both times uses the verb *soltar*) their laughter. The Apangans' response to the unpropitious situation is truly arresting. It signals their distance from the economy and values of "Imaginary Mexico," and it contains the text's sole untainted laughter. As such, the scene acquires tinges of the relajo that Rulfo's friend, Hyperion Jorge Portilla, formulated.[18] A small revolution, relajo deploys humor to repudiate a value of the dominant society amid that society's members. Relajo, we know from chapter 2, obstructs "seriousness" (i.e., adherence to a worthy value) and weakens community by nullifying a value without offering another to replace it. In *PP*, on the other hand, Indigenous laughter itself entails a value, an ethic of detachment and freedom. Fittingly, *PP*'s Apangans enact their relajo in the public square of Comala.

The Natives' transient penetration of the mestizo stronghold and their glaring separation from it in *PP* raise the issue of mestizaje. In this respect, I hold, Rulfo Mexicanizes the miscegenation that powers his novel's underlying model, Faulkner's *Absalom, Absalom!* One of the fundamental matters at stake in the vibrantly Mexican *PP* is therefore Vasconcelos's problematic ideology of racial intermixing. Vasconcelos's *La raza cósmica* notoriously advocates the submersion of Mexico's Indigenous peoples into a "fifth universal race, the fruit of previous races and surpassing all that preceded it" (5), a fusion of races in which a "superior form of being will absorb the lower forms of the species" (27). For Vasconcelos, that "superior form of being" would be whites and Europeanized mestizos (Manrique).[19] A militant social Darwinism generally discredited by the 1950s informed the denigration of Indigenous peoples that led Vasconcelos to endorse their de facto eradication. Vasconcelos's project, too, rests on the contention that history, "being transformation and innovation, does not recur" (27), which annuls the return of the repressed so essential to Zea's *Dos etapas* and to *PP*.

Rulfo strikingly disrupts the racial hierarchy that underlies Vasconcelos's mestizaje by setting *PP*'s happy, insouciant Apangans against an array of wretched mestiz@s. Dependent upon Pedro, standard-bearer of the never-ending colonial past no less than of capitalism, Comala's inhabitants lead lives of uremitting misery. A pernicious mix of feudalism and modernity contaminates them all, except Susana and Fulgor, who take their pleasure from unadulterated nature. *PP* thereby begs the question: what would Indigenous peoples gain from mestizaje? Manuel Gamio, whose 1922 ethnography of Teotihuacán Rulfo published in his INI book series (Amador Tello), charts a more moderate, balanced course than Vasconcelos. Gamio's program, writes Villoro, aimed to "preserve and stimulate autochthonous, natural customs and respect the traditions and personality of Indigenous peoples; but, at the same time, ensure economic and cultural progress" (*Grandes momentos* 240). Like the Apangan traders, marginally involved with capitalism but not in its thrall, the Indigenous peoples could reap some benefits from a limited, economically modernizing mestizaje. Yet the rain that inundates Comala on the "ill-fated day" of the peddlers' arrival betokens the biblical Flood and gestures towards the annihilation (influenced by the Apagans' presence?) of a mestizo, not Indigenous, group.

Although Rulfo may not be going quite so far, he envisioned Mexico as steadfastly pluricultural: "I'm not a prophet, but I believe that for many years to come our country will be one of many languages, many different cultures" (Lopez Mena, "Juan Rulfo" 108). He also spoke out about the negative mestizaje with which *PP* shadowboxes. In his 1985 essay "México y los mexicanos," Rulfo remarks that the previous year's economic crisis prompted a resurgence of works on Mexicanness such as those published thirty-five years ago, which imagined that mestizaje would resolve the "tremendous ethnic, economic, social, and regional differences" of Mexico's Indigenous peoples (400). He then declares: "Today we know that mestizaje was a strategy devised by criollos in order to unite a heterogeneous nation, confirm their dominion, fill the power void the Spaniards had left" (400). Doing the math, we realize that Rulfo's first statement targets Paz's 1950 *Laberinto*, a work that praises Vasconcelos and *La raza cósmica*.[20] Here Rulfo swerves from both Paz and Vasconcelos on mestizaje; the presentation of the Apangans in *PP* as an authentic, deep Mexico equates to Gamio's and Villoro's stances.

Deep Magic: Finale

The connection Rulfo establishes in *PP* between the Apangans and Christianity unsettles that equation by intimating a turn towards the assimilation Vasconcelos sponsored. As did Justina, on Sunday the peddlers pay their respects to the Christian church. Rulfo's photographs, I indicated above, pay theirs to Indigenous participation in Christian rites. The novel's interrogation of Christianity renders its Indigenous characters' allegiance to the Church all the more cryptic. We find a means of addressing the contradictions in Amit Thakkar's observation that "the two communities" of the Christians and the Indigenous "have a spiritual need which happens to coincide in Catholicism" (205). To Thakker's analysis I add that Yáñez and Julio Jiménez Rueda (whose classes Rulfo audited) foregrounded Indigenous spirituality, viewing religion as a cardinal feature of pre-Hispanic culture (Yáñez, *Mitos* x–xi; Jiménez Rueda 381; both from 1942). It follows that whereas the Apangans' contact with the Hispanicized mestizo world in the marketplace of *PP* fulfills a utilitarian need, their homage to the Church and the Virgin meets essential autochthonous and atavistic spiritual needs. Both Gamio, in his 1922 monograph, and Caso, in *El problema de México*, had commented on the syncretic nature of Mexican Christianity that derives from such needs. Furthermore, consistent with his sense of the Indigenous peoples' hermeticism, Rulfo has noted that what outsiders interpret as Natives' Christian or syncretic religious modes may be unalloyed Indigenous practices ("Rulfo examina" 877).[21] The foregoing matters would lead *PP* to valorize Indigenous spirituality, whatever shape it might assume, while spurning full-on mestizaje.

Magic, emblem of ancestral Indigenous spirituality with its attendant imponderable mysteries, offsets Christianity in both Mexican existentialism and *PP*. Let us remember Villoro's characterization of mestizos' yearned-for Indigenous quintessence as "a hidden and mysterious reality that we can never grasp," though it "captivates us" (295). Villoro's parting salvo comports with Jorge Carrión's appraisal of magic in *Mito y magia del mexicano* [Myth and Magic in the Mexican] (1952), published after *Grandes momentos* as the third contribution to Zea's "México y lo mexicano" series.[22] Born, he tells us, "in an Indian village" (58), the then psychologist, later anti-imperialist agitator Carrión burrows into the Mexican psyche. Whereas Paz and Ramos shrink from elaborating on the "true" Mexican behind the masks, Carrión unabashedly identifies the authentic, sublimated entity as Mexico's Indigenous soul, a "maternal matrix" (20) composed of *magic, transrationality, and emotion*. These dwell in the Mexican unconscious and insistently leak into would-be scientific, technological modern life. As does Zea vis-à-vis obtrusions of the colonial past that need to be acknowledged and dispelled, Carrión devotes his book to examining the leakages. Yet Carrión urges that, far from being dispelled, the mother lode of lo mexicano his book identifies should come into its own. He acclaims present-day mestizos for undertaking the task: "Fortunately the mestizo—a bridge suspended between the two positions—is now becoming aware of the urgent need to unite emotion and magic with logical thought, thus casting Mexican nationality as a broad stream" (21). As *Mito y magia* lobbies for Mexico's "unfathomable," "indeterminate" Indigenous matrix (54), the book carries prior mestizo indigenism into Hiperión's purview. Together, Villoro and Carrión seed a reading of the ancestral, deep magic that clandestinely rules *PP*.

Anthropologically minded scholars have demonstrated that numerous vestiges of pre-Hispanic Mexican culture make their way into *PP*.[23] Nonlinear time harking back to Aztec religion is one vestige. Magic, which far from playing a decorative role in *PP* indexes a "communitarian worldview" and religious syncretism (Stanton, "Estructuras" 858), is another. The "Indigenous time" that Rulfo says his works employ (Orrego Arismendi) patently dictates the logic of *PP*; magic, on the other hand, intervenes stealthily in the text.

It does so via the small, unassuming conduit of the rosemary that Justina buys from the Apangans, whose herbs eventually provide an antidote to the evil "weed" ("mala yerba"; English *69*; Spanish 138), Pedro. The Spanish word for rosemary, *romero*, also means "pilgrim," and Justina's pilgrimage produces immediate results. For once Susana receives the rosemary a series of magical events—embedded within the scene of the Apangans to which the text returns at the end of the segment, bracketing it (*91*; 161)—transpires. The ghost of Susana's father Bartolomé appears first to Justina (*87–88*; 157) and then, in the form of a cat, twice to Susana. This pivotal narrative unit also encompasses the flashback that divulges the source of Susana's madness: when her father lowered his young daughter into a mine to search for gold, she stumbled on a terrifying skull and lost consciousness (*90–91*; 160–61). Now recognizing the cat as her father's ghost ("I knew it was you, Bartolomé" [*91*; 161]), Susana emits wild guffaws, an echo and distortion of the Apangans' laughter. All three apparitions have taken place within twenty-four hours of their foray into Comala, under the selfsame torrential rain.

The herbs have set off a chain reaction that connects the two mestizas, Justina and Susana, to the Indigenous characters and to magic. Susana, "a woman who was not of this world" (*108*; 178), emerges formidably in the latter third of the novel as the locus of the connections. The sensuous pleasure she gains from nature and *Flor*encio [flower] unites her with the happy, telluric Apangans. Susana's erotic trances allow her to occupy, as do the Apangans, a domain that escapes Pedro's sphere of influence, to erect a zone of resistance to him. By repeatedly intersplicing the sections on Susana with those on the Revolution, the novel counterposes her to a vast yet ineffectual zone of resistance. The Revolution fails to overturn Pedro, but Susana succeeds in unhinging the despot. He watches his wife helplessly from the sidelines of her universe, incapable of reaching her and haunted by her until the end of his days. Susana dies in a fetal posture

(*115*; 185), head on belly, closed in on herself and always already giving birth to her hermetic, resistant preserve. As the famous lines of *PP* read: "But what world was Susana living in? That was one of the things that Pedro Páramo would never know" (*95*; 165). Through textual transference, the unknowable, authentic Indigenous peoples whom Rulfo demurs from narrating attain fuller expression in an authentic, unseizable (for Pedro) Susana. Inchoately, suggestively, the cameo of the Apangans has ascribed a host of characteristics to its Indigenous figures and then played them out expansively through Susana.

Her multiple, auspicious correspondences with the Apangans parlay the mestiza Susana into an avatar of the indígena within that racial politics of Rulfo's era celebrated. Decamping from rationality and facticity, Susana has crossed over to a dream world, the "maternal matrix" that Carrión limns. Susana's transcendence, in both the existentialist and ordinary meanings of the word, bewitches Pedro. Great love for her fractures the monolithic persona of a man whose name connotes *piedra*, stone. "Help me, Susana," beseeches Pedro when the text first discusses his impossible love (*12*; 76). The stakes for Pedro, and lo mexicano, heighten as Pedro's memory continues to revive Susana. Pedro's second crystallization of his wife depicts her as hiding "in God's immensity" (*13*; 77). Subsequent recollections juxtapose her with the Paradise tree. Shortly before his demise, Pedro watches the Paradise tree's leaves fall and remembers the last time he saw Susana. His final, almost mystical, evocation of her exquisitely projects Susana San Juan onto a luminous moon and stars, blotted out by the sun (*123*; 194). The various images of the heroine envelop her in a saintly aura, a throwback to the woman as source of salvation that Rulfo's existential "Cleotilde" debuted. With the vilified, colonialist Pedro who quests for a redemptive, Indigenous-allied Susana, *PP* has afforded its readers two paradigmatic and contrasting yet symbiotic mestiz@ protagonists.

Rulfo's orchestration of his heroine through the imagery of moon, stars, and sun heightens the stakes for lo mexicano even further by planting a link between Susana and the Marian Virgin of Guadalupe, whose iconography features precisely these three elements. Described by Carrión as the totem who gathers Mexicans' "religious and magical inclinations, symbol of their submerged archetypes, the land, the rain, and emotional attachments" (25), the Virgin of Guadalupe is of course the quintessential Mexican icon of religious and racial unity as well as of Mexico's Indigenous birthright. A sheaf of clues in *PP* bolsters the link between the Mexican Mary and Susana. Susana dies on December 8, feast day of the Immaculate

Conception; the bells commemorating her death ring for more than three days, thereby extending into December 12, the Virgin of Guadalupe's feast day (*116*; 186). Only *Juan* Preciado, not Dorotea, can hear the voice of Susana San *Juan* in the grave (*78, 80*; 147, 149): the name "Juan" thus associated with otherworldly communication invokes John the Evangelist, whose vision in Patmos (Rev. 12) underpins the Guadalupan iconography. Three female characters share attributes of the Virgin Mary: Eduviges *Dyada* wears a Marian medal inscribed with the epithet "Refuge of Sinners" (*16*; 81); Dolores is the Mater Dolorosa; the sea-loving Susana correlates to Mary's symbolic identity as fountain.

Last but hardly least, Rulfo had long intended to title *PP* "La estrella junto a la luna" [The Star Next to the Moon] (García Bonilla 117).²⁴ Though the title fell away, the metaphor graces the text at crucial points. Beyond Pedro's closing evocation of Susana, the moon, stars, and sun infiltrate the scene with Donis's sister that heralds Juan Preciado's death (*54*; 121). The episode directly precedes Juan's loss of contact with his mother's voice (*56–57*; 124–25), which clears space for Susana to replace Dolores as Juan's Comala "mother." Juan ceases to intervene in the text after it narrates Susana's death. He dies qua narrator with her (*115*; 185).

A web of magic that fans out from the Apangans and Susana to Dolores enhances the correspondences between Pedro's two wives, both of whom eluded his grasp.²⁵ Here again herbs function as a bridge. We learn at the outset that when she left Pedro to live with her sister away from Comala, Dolores kept a photograph of herself in a clay pot "filled with herbs," among them "castilla blossoms" (*6*; 68)—perhaps an allusion to the famed Guadalupan roses of Castile. Fraught with mystery, as are Susana and the Apangans, the photograph has a hole where the heart should be. We subsequently learn that Dolores had dark skin (at least darker, more "morena," than Eduviges [*17*; 82]), and that a "guard of cats" surrounded her when she lived in Comala (*18*; 83). This confederates Pedro's first wife, respectively, with the Apangans and with Susana, whose father returned in the form of a cat. All of the tell-tale signs animate the enigmatic photograph of Dolores, "riddled with pinpricks" (*6*; 69). They hint that Dolores, who considered photography to be a "tool of witchcraft" (*6*; 69), may have done violence to her inherently "*sweet*" (*11*; 74) nature by employing the photograph riddled with pinpricks and the herbs in a magical effort to conjure up a rhapsodic, seductive Comala. The Dolores who had once requested conjurer Inocencio Osorio's assistance for her wedding night with Pedro would now exercise her own magic on her son, enticing him to complete after her death the task of making Pedro pay that we know Pedro's second wife Susana had so efficaciously discharged before *her* death.

The web of magic continues to expand. It enfolds secondary characters and locates them on a spectrum of resistance and collusion, the novel's integral motors. Susana's helpmeet Justina is privy to the magical visitation of Bartolomé's ghost. Dolores's partner in crime for the wedding night, Eduviges, possesses a magical "sixth sense" (*21*; 86) that puts her in touch with the dead. The obsequious head servant of Pedro's estate, Damiana Cisneros, by contrast, has no magical commerce (*42*; 109). Among the male characters, Abundio Martínez certainly does. Son of Pedro, directly or indirectly responsible for his father's death and himself some kind of apparition, Abundio ushers the living Juan into the underworld, where the prodigal son channels not Pedro but Susana. Amid these agents of good or evil, Inocencio Osorio practices a two-faced magic. One the one hand, he leads Susana to sabotage Pedro's wedding night (and Pedro perhaps murders him).[26] On the other, the diabolical magician uses his spells to beguile female clients into erotic acts, which vitiates magic with self-interest. The necessary purity of magic drives home that while Rulfo has consistently mated magic with resistance, he has primarily sited the two energies in female characters thematically or structurally related to Susana, whom the text has linked to the Apangans, and by extension, as I have sought to develop, to the redemptive indígena within.

Inocencio Osorio's none too innocent name, if not actions, helps me bring this chapter to a close. The name Osorio rings with Osiris, the Egyptian god of the underworld. When Osiris died, his body was scattered over the four corners of the earth. His wife Isis reunited the fragments and resurrected Osiris. As suggested above with regard to *PP* and Zea, Rulfo's death-haunted novel performs a similar act in uniting the dispersed, submerged fragments of the past. On a larger scale, this chapter has undertaken to establish the ways in which existentialism and lo mexicano constitute related pieces of *PP*'s own past that deserve restoration. A literary conclusion ensues from the restoration. When read as the foregoing pages propose, *PP*'s Indigenous characters and magic acquire an unsuspected lineage, one that unfastens them from the magical realism Rulfo disparaged and couples them with the discourses of lo mexicano and existentialism.[27]

The myth of Osiris and Isis, moreover, has implications for the future. As the legend goes, Isis, goddess of wisdom, magic, and the earth, resurrected Osiris so that they could have a child, Horus. Horus the falcon—hence the birds with which *PP* teems?—traditionally signifies healing and renewal. Our excavations of Comala via the Grupo Hiperión have disclosed real rather than mythical possibilities for renewal, for Mexicans to secure "*a present and future that truly belong to them*" (Villoro, *Grandes momentos* 290). Interestingly, though, it is around the question of the future that correspondences between the heroine and the Indigenous characters break down. Despite Susana's undeniable positive attributes, the protagonist's introverted *desgana* and death caved in on herself signal that the mode of existence she has adopted cannot provide a viable model for the future.[28] The childless Susana may contain the mother lode of Mexico, the *indígena* within, but given her alienation she will not birth a future. In the end, the vivacious, enterprising Apangans for whom Susana otherwise fronts offer more potential for what lies ahead than the equivocal heroine.

What *PP* does unequivocally hold out to its readers is an ethical pact with History such as that which Villoro unfolds in "Lo indígena como principio oculto de mi yo que recupero en la pasión." Villoro inveighs against historians who recover the past inauthentically, by means of a priori assumptions and schemas bent on objectifying. They leave the past dead, disengaged from the present. Villoro, having brought Zea's *Dos etapas* into *Grandes momentos* (139), propounds a way to unblock and unlock history: approach it as a living body full of mysteries to be interrogated in a good faith perplexity. Let it speak, and enter into a kind of loving "I-Thou" relationship with it. For, Villoro argues, the past "is not something alien, stone-like, and distant . . . ; it is ours, constitutive of our 'I'" (280). *PP*, one can easily conclude, both de-petrifies the past and literalizes Villoro's plan for assimilating history. The novel resuscitates Comala as a full-bodied community, giving rein to the sundry, divergent voices of its inhabitants ("in *Pedro Páramo* an entire town speaks" [Poniatowska, *Ay vida* 137]). They speak not just beyond the grave but also beyond the pale of the regime that suppressed them. Most germane to History per se, *PP* offers itself up as an entity shimmering with mysteries. Like the past, the novel is an irresistible sphinx and an ongoing oracle.

Chapter Five

"Christs for All Passions"

José Revueltas's *El luto humano* [Human Mourning]

Atheist, Marxist, and existentialist that he was, José Revueltas did not shrink from conceiving a world saturated with God in his renowned title story "Dios en la tierra" [God on Earth] (1944). The story tells us that when federal troops invade a small Mexican town of Christian zealots during the Cristero Wars, God was there, clenching all of life in His fist and radiating so thunderously from the village's closed doors that not even a nonbeliever could fail to recognize Him (367). God comes down to earth in "Dios en la tierra" as the grounded phenomenon Revueltas's theology dictates. He has stated: "God is a social and historical entity in addition to an ideological one . . . . This entity governs the social and historical relationships of human beings and is thus indispensable, whether or not one is a believer" (*Conversaciones* 192). Accordingly, in his story and elsewhere Revueltas tethers an inalienable God to earth, the Mexican author's overriding, most passionate sphere of concern. Embedding religion in the kingdom of this world, Revueltas recruits theology for the situated activism that invigorates his entire oeuvre.[1]

In "Dios en la tierra" God enters Mexico as a monstrous, demonic life form: "God's hatred" (367). Revueltas's hate-filled God reifies the fanaticism of the institutionalized Church, which the Cristero wars have revealed as a power-mongering fury that strips human beings of their potential, freedom, and compassion. Echoing the Cristero slogan's name for Christ, Revueltas calls this will-to-power "Cristo Rey" [Christ the King]. The Christ of "Dios en la tierra," he comments, "is the taciturn, aggressive, rabid Christ of the

Cristeros. Cristo Rey comes to life in the Cristero movement not as a metaphysics, nor as a theological entity, but as an objective reality" (*Conversaciones* 40). The zealous Cristeros, Cristo Rey, deny the parched federal troops the water a benevolent teacher from the town had promised them. Water, "[e]quivalent to life itself" ("Dios en la tierra" 372), escalates into the Living Water of Christ (John 4:10) and into all that Cristo Rey controverts—the true doctrine of Christ, caritas, love for humankind. As the teacher whom the Cristeros execute on a "stake" (373) comes to represent the ethos of an authentic Christ, a genuine Christ on earth, Revueltas fragments Christ into Christs, *plural*. "God is defending his Church, his Church that has no water" (372): the antidote to a hateful God on earth, water incarnates a thirst for the absent other Christ, a desideratum both earthly and ethical. "Dios en la tierra" coils into the tale of two Christs and a parable that denounces an appalling lack of caritas.

If, as it appears, the splintered Christs of "Dios en la tierra" map Søren Kierkegaard's distinction between an institutionalized visible Church and an interiorized, authentic Church militant (*Practice* 211–24) onto a Mexican context, the story also evokes a Kierkegaardian closer to home, Antonio Caso. Guiding light for the Grupo Hiperión, champion of caritas, Caso tailored Kierkegaard's double-edged Christianity to Mexico in his essay "Ideas que construyen e ideas que destruyen" (*El problema de México*). The essay outlines how colonialism, Liberalism, and positivism devalued the Mexican Church from a noble, constructive idea, "Cristo *pueblo*" [Christ, the people], into a destructive one, "Cristo *Rey*" (82–84). As we heard in chapter 2, Caso urges Mexico's return to a constructive Christianity, not "Christ the King, but Christ the people: here we have the dictum and the action that can save us" (84). Taking its cue from the humanized Christ whom Caso especially venerates (e.g., *Existencia* 104; 1919, 1943), "Cristo pueblo" will honor the cardinal value of "love for one's fellow human beings" (*Problema* 84). While with regard to religious belief per se Revueltas and Caso were worlds apart, with regard to ethics the two intellectuals—together with Hiperión—espoused a philosophical Christianity predicated on a caritas that translates into intersubjective solidarity.

A key term in Revueltas's conceptual and textual lexicon, *religare*, points more strongly yet to his ties with Caso. Supremely loaded, the term religare gave rise to the word "religion." It also comprehends a chain of meanings, including "bind fast (to God)" "recover," and "to treat carefully." Caso, no doubt aware of its many splendors, construes religare as a "relationship of individual spirits, indissolubly bound together in a spiritual community" and "a communally assumed bond" (Caso, *Sociología genética y sistemática*, qtd. in Krauze 163). Revueltas builds on the communitarian, ethical implications of religare that Caso's statement contains. For instance, when Elena Poniatowska asked Revueltas if he had a religious vocation, he replied: "Of course I do, if we take the word 'religion' in its broad sense: *religare*='unite.' Unite the genus of humanity. Transferring religion to human relationships provides a kind of solution" (*Conversaciones* 141). Then again, when in his novel *El luto humano* Revueltas examines a priest who has left traditional religion behind, the author drills deep into religare: "Religion had a strict, literal meaning for his [the priest's] church: *re-ligare*, to bind, to tie, to be reborn, to go back to one's origins, or to reach a destination" (*Human Mourning* 25; *Luto humano* 29). Both Caso and Revueltas, we see, seize on religare as a locution expressing unification.[2] At heart, their definitions align religare with its elementary meaning in Spanish of "to bind or solder."

A ravaged Mexico that has forsaken Cristo pueblo desperately needs to be drawn into unity and plenitude. Activist José Revueltas assumes the mission, and this chapter the mission of investigating his multifaceted program of renewal. Through the lens of existentialism, Revueltas proposes a renewal of Christianity. True to the spirit of Caso and Hiperión, he envisions a human confederation that renews Mexican ethics. Revueltas pulls Mexican history, identity, and politics into his vision. More overarchingly, the author regenerates existentialism itself by fusing it with intensely disparate ideological and philosophical currents proper to the Latin American situation. Religare, in sum, voices the authentic bonds that Revueltas strives to forge and that we will explore.

> "Le daban duro con un palo y duro"
> [They struck him hard with a stick, so hard]
> (César Vallejo, *Poemas humanos*,
> "Piedra negra sobre una piedra blanca")

Literary and political passions rose to a fever pitch when José Revueltas published his third novel, *Los días terrenales* [Earthly Days], in 1949 in Mexico. The novel had launched an attack on the rigid, inhuman, and inauthentic dogmatism of the PCM, the Partido Comunista Mexicano [Mexican Communist Party] from which Revueltas had been expelled six years earlier. A public uproar ensued, a preview of the hostility unleashed on Heberto Padilla when he criticized the Cuban Revolutionary government in 1971

(Valenzuela 41). Mexican communists excoriated *Los días terrenales* and its author in a spate of articles that reached even the pages of the hallowed newspaper *Excélsior*. Yielding to the savage attacks, the Revueltas who never abandoned his fundamental commitment to Marxism publicly denounced his novel and withdrew it from circulation.[3]

Surprisingly or not, rather than confronting head-on Revueltas's denigration of the party, its members virulently targeted the Sartrean existentialism of *Los días terrenales* (henceforth, *LDT*). The novel appropriates the battles with commitment that Mathieu wages in Jean-Paul Sartre's *Roads to Freedom* trilogy of the late 1940s. Thick with despair, teeming with bodily sordidness, *LDT* counterposes protagonist Gregorio's anguished quest for an authentic life as a militant and love for the other, however repugnant, to the bad faith of party acolyte Fidel. As Mexican communists scapegoated Revueltas's adherence to Sartre, they catalyzed a major crisis in Latin American existentialism. Evodio Escalante, who coordinated the critical edition of *LDT*, flatly declares: "*Los días terrenales*, a novel that leftists of the time unanimously condemned for its relationship with existentialism, is in fact a denunciation of the Stalinist practices and intellectual atmosphere the party apparatus promoted" (xxix). In covenant with the Stalinist "Zhdanov Doctrine," which had recently condemned Sartrean existentialism for its departures from socialist realism (Koui 222), the storm that gathered around *LDT* threw a highly problematic construction of existentialism into the public eye.

Revueltas himself keenly assessed the narrow, jaundiced profile of existentialism the debates brought to the fore. He noted in 1962 that critics had associated "'existentialism' with a particular atmosphere, one of sordidness and of dark, despairing human relationships, which reflected an essentially disillusioned humankind" ("Sobre mi obra," *LDT* 427). As one example among the many that confirm Revueltas's appraisal, writing in 1950 under the name Juan Almagre, the communist critic Antonio Rodríguez said of the parallels between Sartre's works and *LDT*: "Both are products of the same social decomposition; the same putrefaction, the same lack of faith in man that, ultimately, amounts to a lack of faith in oneself" (*LDT* 383). Obviously, the combination in *LDT* of anti-PCM attitudes and Sartrean existentialism had proved lethal, mostly to the latter.

Over the years, Revueltas completely reversed his position on Sartre. If in the 1950s he disavowed Sartre, in the 1960s he recanted his abjuration as forced and repeatedly professed himself honored by comparisons to the French existentialist.[4] Yet, had Revueltas's detractors read *LDT* without blinders, they might have realized that in it he had already taken Sartre to task, as a whipping boy. Having conceivably been arrested by Revueltas's damning equation of the PCM with Sartrean bad faith, leftist critics appear not to have registered the acerbic satire of the Sartrean gaze in chapter 7 of *LDT*. There readers meet Jorge Ramos, a bourgeois intellectual and a communist "sympathizer" (134), not a card-carrying party member. *LDT* parodies this specious fellow traveler by weaponizing an earlier Sartrean text, the "Concrete Relations with Others" section of *Being and Nothingness*. Like Hiperión, Revueltas zeroes in on Sartre's portrayal of human interactions as sadistic gambits, emblematized in the objectifying gaze, to posses the freedom of others. *LDT* marshals a truly twisted scenario when from the "Olympian" lookout of his high-rise apartment and thinking himself a "god" (109, 117), Ramos casts a perverted gaze on two girls. "They were his, totally his" (117), he concludes. Ramos, in the grip of a "sick excitement" (119), witnesses one of them kill herself. His wife, whom Ramos wishes to possess as an "object" (121), in turn watches him watch. Cinching the satire, the depraved mise en abyme of voyeurism sexually arouses both Ramos and his wife.

The parodic signposting of *Being and Nothingness* in a novel that champions human solidarity brims with irony and, further, gestures towards the several, more fraternally oriented existentialisms that inhabit *LDT*. André Malraux's *Man's Fate* (*La Condition humaine*, 1933) bears so heavily upon *LDT*'s structure and preoccupation with existential choices that, according to Florence Olivier, Revueltas could have titled his novel *Los días terrenales: La condición humana* (253). Albert Camus's *The Plague* (1947) surfaces in chapter 6 of *LDT* when, contemplating human excrement, a character struggles to fight past a repugnant corporality into kinship with others. Camus's arguments against suicide in *The Myth of Sisyphus* ring through Gregorio's harangue to Fidel that only coming to terms with the absence of absolutes, and not the eradication of classes for which communism stands, suffices as a reason to exist (*LDT* 131). Fyodor Dostoevsky, Lev Shestov (see Negrín 171 75), and César Vallejo's meditations on incarceration imprint the ending of *LDT*, which closes with Gregorio, who has made good on his quest, in jail awaiting more torture yet accepting that "[t]his was his truth. He was all right" (170). It emerges that tendentious leftist misprisions of *LDT* had foreclosed Revueltas's ecumenical existentialism and reduced the novel to an easily reviled, sordidly Sartrean enterprise.

The existentialism of Revueltas's previous novel, *El luto humano* (1943), which features a socialist hero par excellence named Natividad, elicited quite a different response. While rife with the despair and sordidness for which critics had pilloried *LDT*, *El luto humano* received the foremost Mexican literary prize in the year of its publication.⁵ Written before the heyday of French existentialism in Mexico and far less affected by the Sartre at the time identified with *Nausea* than *LDT* was by the next Sartre, *El luto humano* (henceforth, *ELH*), boasts a powerful, ecumenical existentialism of its own. Indeed, I will argue in what follows that although less of a cause célèbre, a less conspicuous flashpoint for the history of Latin American existentialism, *ELH* constitutes a richer, more productive enactment of existentialism for Latin America at large than Revueltas's subsequent novel. *ELH*, I believe, rates this claim because it weaves into a whole a Latin American precursor, the Peruvian César Vallejo, and the seemingly immiscible elements of existentialism, Christianity, Marxism, and lo mexicano. No one of them sufficing on its own to convey the ethico-political platform that Revueltas fervently wishes to advance, the elements of the constellation he mounts enter into a dynamic synergy, a *religare*. As *ELH* bodies forth "the Christs for all passions" (Revueltas, "Arte" 192), the novel configures a template for a distinctively Latin American existentialism: whereas Usigli seeded a distinctively Mexican existentialism, *ELH* seeds a Latin American one. *ELH*, we will see, turns the shortly-to-be-scapegoated Revueltas of *LDT* into an abiding paragon for his existentialist compatriots.

> "Su cadáver estaba lleno de mundo"
> [His corpse was full of world]
> (César Vallejo, *España, aparta de mí este cáliz*, "III")

In August of 1939, a year after Vallejo's death, Revueltas published a short article in the leftist journal *El Popular* titled "Arte y cristianismo: César Vallejo."⁶ A critically neglected gem, the essay provides a gateway into the existentialism of *ELH* that holds such resonance for other Latin Americans. Revueltas begins the article by lauding activist artists as veritable new saints. Writers like Dostoevsky, Revueltas notes with admiration, give over their lives to expressing humankind's pain and grievances (*LDT* would accuse party leaders of falsely positioning themselves as saints). What are the artist's weapons? In a remarkable, watershed formulation, the Marxist Revueltas advocates the special currency of Christianity for the new artist-saint: "Why then should we be surprised by the presence of Christianity in art? We are talking about an art that battles a 'Christian' society, and up to now, artists have mustered Christianity against that society . . . . Artists have utilized all the venerable values of Christianity—the struggle against the powerful, the defense of sinners, and the fundamental value, expiation—as a resource, a rationale, a foundation" ("Arte" 193–94). Revueltas then consecrates Vallejo's work as exemplifying a "Christian poetry that renews Christianity," because it expiates guilt, returns spirituality to daily life, and utilizes a Christian language of tribulation to impart the Indigenous peoples' misery (194).

The essay coheres around suffering. And well it might, given the importance of suffering to Vallejo and Revueltas. The Vallejo whose writings chorally orchestrate the leitmotif of "Mas sufro. Allende sufro. Aquende sufro" [But I suffer. I suffer beyond. I suffer here] (*Complete Poetry, Trilce*, "XX," 204) calls out to the Revueltas who obsessively dwells on suffering, tackling its social, historical, philosophical, theological, and ideological dimensions.[7] Vallejo, reader of Søren Kierkegaard (Franco 15), and Revueltas, reader of Vallejo, elevate suffering into something akin to the Danish philosopher's notion of "demonic despair" (*Sickness unto Death*, part 1, "In Despair to Will to Be Oneself: Defiance"). So total, omnivorous, and inalienable is the type of despair Kierkegaard brands as demonic that it defines the self and becomes a god unto itself.[8] Riveting the Mexican novelist and the Peruvian poet alike, demonic despair serves as a matrix for the ensemble of attributes that Vallejo—a tremendous precursor of Latin American existentialism in his own right—offers *ELH*.

Simply and functionally put, the despair of Vallejo's proto-existentialist *Los heraldos negros* [The Black Heralds] (1918) centers on the loss of God. Its title poem encapsulates the forlornness of a poetic speaker hollowed out by life's blows, crazed with incomprehension, and awash in the "caídas hondas de los Cristos del alma" [deep falls of the Christs of the soul] (25)—likely the inspiration for Revueltas's "the Christs for all passions." Jean Franco states that the fall of the "'soul's Christs' introduces a plurality of saviors which destroys the belief in a unique Creator" (33). Vallejo, painfully caught in the interstices of belief and nonbelief, creates a personal, interiorized God joined to the traditional deity through love. Vallejo's lines in "Dios" [God] read: "Oh, Dios mío, / recién a ti me llego, / hoy que amo tanto" [Oh, God of mine, I have recently brought myself to you, today when I love so much] and "Yo te consagro Dios, porque amas tanto" [I consecrate you God, because you love so much] (144). Over the course of the book's six sections Vallejo temporizes with the absent or plural God. The poet attempts to vest the sacred in the beloved and nature. He imports theological concepts like love and charity into a desacralized world, to test their purchase there. Hence, exactly recalling "Dios en la tierra," a poem titled "Ágape" bemoans the lack of fraternal caritas the poetic speaker experiences when he steps outside his door.[9]

As Revueltas had signaled in lauding the broad reaches of Vallejo's religious idiom, the poet's dislocation of Christianity implicates his country's Indigenous peoples. "Lábrase la raza en mi palabra") [My word cultivates the race] ("I," 76), writes Vallejo in the "Nostalgias imperiales" section of *Heraldos*, which compares the deplored lost paradise of Christianity to the grief of dispossession that Peruvian Natives underwent after the Conquest. The Peruvian José Carlos Mariátegui, whom Revueltas deems "the Latin American Marxist par excellence" ("Arte" 194), enshrined Vallejo precisely as a poet of the Indigenous peoples. Commenting on *Heraldos* in 1926, Mariátegui applauded Vallejo for inaugurating a poetry "of a lineage, of a race," where "for the first time in our literature, we find a pristine expression of the Indigenous soul" (259). Revueltas rightfully discerns that Mariateguí "short shrifts the Indigenous peoples by reducing them to an emblem of Vallejo's pessimism or his Christianity" ("Arte" 194). Nonetheless, the shorthand allows Mariátegui presciently to tease a Marxist message out of Vallejo's early *Heraldos*.

Mariátegui, unfortunately, would not live to see Vallejo's Marxism reach fruition in works like *España, aparta de mí este cáliz* [Spain, Take This Chalice from Me; 1939] the corpus truly "full of world" from which I derive this section's heading. In *España*, as Vallejo addresses the Spanish Civil War so paramount to everything he held dear, more than Marxism comes together. *España* uses a Christian language to tell a Marxist tale (see Paoli 364–70); one thinks of Vallejo's "Traspié entre dos estrellas" [Staggering between Two Stars] (478–80), which implants the Beatitudes of Matthew ("Blessed are . . .") in Spanish Republican battlefields. As Jean Franco explains, the loss of the Christian Logos that *Heraldos* and *Trilce* dramatized resolves in *España*, where the Republican cause "becomes the new Logos" (233), a value-challenging scenario that induces Vallejo to recuperate Christian symbols. "Christianity," Franco writes, "no longer promises an afterlife but it does provide a moral ideal" (157). That moral ideal, as apposite to the Gospel as to Marxism, is comprised of human love and solidarity. Love and solidarity reach a stirring peak in Vallejo's parable "Masa" [Mass], based on the biblical Lazarus. In "Masa" all of humankind united by love raises a soldier from the dead (*España* 610). "Considerando en frío, imparcialmente" [Considered Coldly, Impartially], from *Poemas humanas* (like *España*, published in 1939), elucidates the complexities of attaining love and solidarity, a matter on which *LDT* enlarges. At first objectively registering the "encontradas piezas," or paradoxes, of attraction and repugnance that accepting his fellow man entails, the poetic speaker of "Masa" overcomes them and, "Emocionado" [Profoundly moved], embraces him (404). Thus, in brief, does Vallejo achieve a Christian *and* Marxist poetry that renews Christianity.

"propensiones de trinidad"
[propensities for trinity]
(César Vallejo, *Trilce*, "V")

El luto humano, only Revueltas's second novel, is packed to excess with weighty concerns. The novel acts upon Vallejo's already loaded project and roots it in a veritable compendium of lo mexicano. Most saliently, from beginning to end *ELH* unfolds against the backdrop of a tragic, death-involved Mexican consciousness that dates back to the Aztecs. Infant Chonita's death in Nuevo León, Mexico, in the 1930s unites the characters: "Chonita had not mattered when she was alive. She mattered now that she was simply a link to the beyond, profoundly uniting their destinies" (*Human Mourning 94*; *Luto humano* 87). Chonita's death brings preexisting tensions to crisis and augurs the group's doom. Having assembled in Chonita's home to mourn her, the child's parents, Cecilia and Úrsulo, along with Adán, Calixto, Jerónimo, and Marcela prepare to flee a flood rapidly encroaching on the house, a disaster from which they will not escape alive. Death "was like a special, hyperbolic life of consciousness" (*195*; 175): this dense, liminal moment revives the characters' backstories and inspires the prises de conscience that are the very stuff of the novel.

The memories that arise from the characters' vitalized being-towards-death so center on another limit situation, the Mexican Revolution, as by turns to form a novel within the novel. Cognizant of the Mexican Revolution's shortcomings, Marxist Revueltas strives to treat it evenhandedly, employing his technique of "critical realism" ("La novela, tarea de México," *Visión*). Quite distinct from socialist realism, Revueltas's critical realism purveys multiple viewpoints on an event. *ELH*'s version of the Revolution therefore both showcases its barbarism, à la Mariano Azuela, and lionizes Emiliano Zapata, whom Azuela excludes: "Zapata was of the people, the pure and eternal people, in the middle of a savage and just revolution" (*161*; 145).[10] A patchwork of flashbacks recounted in an overblown yet often wrenchingly beautiful, numinous language, *ELH* impacted the Mexican scene not only as a nuancing of *Los de abajo* but also as a precursor of *Pedro Páramo* and an heir to Agustín Yáñez's *Al filo del agua*.

Inserted in the same historical terrain as *Pedro Páramo*, *ELH*'s flashbacks segue from the Mexican Revolution to the Cristero Wars. The latter conflagration then impinges on the more recent present of the novel. Close up, the novel deals with a peasant strike led by Natividad against a government irrigation program that paid workers unconscionably low wages. Workers shut down the irrigation system, the government violently crushes the strike, and everyone except the small group that remains at Chonita's house abandons the area. The iron fist of hegemony kills off the town, as it did Comala. At wider range, the focal setting of *ELH* proves to be as laden as other aspects of the explosive novel. Its fraught scenario conflates events from the regime of Plutarco Elías Calles's last puppet ruler, Abelardo Rodríguez, with those of Lázaro Cárdenas's presidency. *ELH* thereby encompasses the default of the Maximato on the goals of the Mexican Revolution and the Maximato's persecution of communists; renewed hope for agrarian reform and the communists under Cárdenas; and ultimate disillusionment with Cárdenas's administration as it ceded to capitalist interests.[11] From the death of Chonita to the collapse of Cárdenas's promise, *ELH* vents a host of Mexican mournings.

Among its many imperious agendas, *ELH* lays claim to the Bible. Jorge Ruffinelli remarks that the novel erects "a dense system of biblical references, the likes of which Mexican literature had rarely seen" (53). *Al filo del agua*, of course, had steeped the Mexican Revolution in religious baggage. Unlike Yáñez's text, *ELH* works theology existentially, shifting it into transvaluation, Vallejian *"propensities* for trinity" (emphasis added). In fact, the motor of *ELH*—what enables it to fuse lo mexicano, existentialism, Christianity, and Marxism—lies in transvaluation, the reterritorializing of theology. Transvaluation in *ELH* involves advances, retrenchments, and enmeshments, but all spring from the vacating of belief in God for which its nameless priest, an axial figure of the text, serves as vehicle. *ELH*'s priest has been divested of his faith by the misery surrounding him: an Indigenous man sobbing in church (*74–75*; 70–71), the depravity of the would-be righteous Cristero Wars (*196*; 176), the forces of evil incarnated in Natividad's assassin Adán, and more. "All has been consummated, lost," the priest laments (*72*; 68). When he cries out for God and receives no answer, the priest recognizes that suffering, a demonic despair, has become "the Good" and his God (*72*; 68). He says to himself, "what you truly love is your suffering" (*73*; 68). Out of love for his fellow human beings, counterintuitively and shockingly the priest kills the heinous Adán. Forlorn, a sinner, the priest surrenders to the floodwaters engulfing the town, basically committing suicide.

The core of the novel having debunked or at least monumentally shaken Christianity through the figure of the priest, *ELH* effectively animates the undying post-metaphysical life of religion. While Revueltas's novel repudiates the afterlife, as mentioned above its author believes that God remains essential even to a postmodern age.[12] *ELH* therefore interpellates religion for existentialism, rewriting the Bible within the real-time history and space of an "earthly religion" (Enríquez 269). Does Revueltas leave us with a desacralized world, or does he infuse the human with the sacred? Impossible as the question may be to answer, it hovers over Revueltas's concerted use of religion as a vestigial yet living language. The Bible in *ELH*, like allegory in Walter Benjamin's explication of German tragedy, "is conceived from the outset as a ruin, a fragment. Others may shine resplendently on the first day; this form preserves the image of beauty to the very last" (235). Established religion affords Revueltas, Vallejo, and countless other writers a capacious, mobile tradition that can function in multiple systems simultaneously.

As Ruffinelli suggests, *ELH* engages biblical tradition with a vengeance. The entire framework of the novel rests on not just New but also Old Testament topoi. They reflect Revueltas's predilection for the existentially charged Cain and Christ, as well as for the Flood and Exodus. Though extremely ponderous, Revueltas's biblical references are also agile: they harbor paradoxes.[13] The flood in *ELH* relieves a longstanding drought but kills the villagers. The exodus from the flooded village betokens redemption and revenge and death. The new saint, Valentín, a martyr of the Revolution, is a criminal (*197*; 177). Extended and disrupted, Revueltas's religious allusions morph into pulsating contradictions. Such contradictions constitute the "absurd" for Revueltas, an absurd that veers away from the sense of life's fundamental meaninglessness with which Sartre and Camus endow the term. Revueltas's "absurd" instead has more in common with Kierkegaard's "Absolute Paradox," based on the human-superhuman Christ whom a Kiekegaardian Caso dubbed a glorious "*symbol of contradiction*" (*Existencia* 105; 1919, 1943). Kierkegaard's version of the absurd privileges the sublimely contradictory Christ as the foundation of faith and truth (e.g., *Concluding* 217). As Vallejo put it, "Absurdo, sólo tú eres puro" [Absurdity, only you are pure] (*Trilce*, "LXIII," 14).

On the other hand, Revueltas keeps his principal biblically named characters, Adán and Natividad, didactically Manichean. Premised on their biblical identities, Revueltas renders the characters exemplars of evil and good. *ELH* parlays the mestizo Adán, embodiment of Fallen Man, into the quintessence of evil. Adán acquires associations with Judas, Huitzilopochtli,

Prometheus, and primarily with Cain, instigator of postlapsarian strife (see Negrín 77–80). Whereas Revueltas overdetermines Adán, impugning the Old Testament along with him, the author assigns socialist hero Natividad the single, shining, allegorical identity of Christ (Negrín 81). When Adán kills Natividad, *ELH* cements the equation of its hero to Christ: "Natividad would die, pierced, crucified" (*182*; 164). The novel idealizes Natividad into an implausibly larger than life figure. Murdered by Adán for organizing the socialist strike, Natividad lives only in the characters' memories, as more of a symbol than a person (Montoya 70; Negrín 81). Furthermore, and unusually, readers learn little about the hero's background beyond the requisite fact that he fought in the Revolution. The novel specifies neither his race nor his class (Montoya 71). Natividad comes to us nearly pristine, *almost* pure allegory—which well suits the novel's layering of existentialism, Christianity, and Marxism.

The flawed, profoundly human characters who outlive Natividad flail about in a landscape of loss, yet they are buttressed by what the ideal but absent Christ figure and an abdicated Christianity bequeath to them, an *ethics*. Ignacio Sánchez Prado understands Revueltas's fiction as a supplementary space that allows the author to circulate an ethics alien to and irreconcilable with the political discourse of the time, be it the state's, the code of Stalinist Marxism, or the author's own ("Bienaventurados" 158–62). The solution that according to Revueltas the displacement of religious values onto human relationships may produce ("Transferring religion to human relationships provides a kind of solution") leads *ELH* to propound love and solidarity, the heart of Christ's ministry (Mark 12:28–31) no less than of Vallejo's moral code. Religare here claims its partnership with morality.

Every so often, then, flashes of love and solidarity break through the grim terrain of *ELH*. Chonita's death sets them off, for as the novel's epigraph proclaims, "death is infinitely a loving act." Her demise draws people into community, "as if death had spread a strange bond of love between them" (*40*; 42). The conclusion of the novel again exalts solidarity, now in an abstract, inspirational vein: "Those four human beings who were still alive, children of women, examples of mankind, links in our immense, beloved, and human chain" (*203*; 182). Between the bookends, glimmers of positive values punctuate the text. We witness the astounding epiphanies in which hitman Adán and the wife he abuses, La Borrada [She who has been erased], feel the stirrings of love. "So she loves me," thinks Adán of La Borrada, and for "the first time in his life he felt tenderness, happiness, a confident abandon" (*199*; 178). Revueltas, in Dostoevsky's footsteps, presents the prostitute Eduarda as a beacon of compassionate altruism, "an immaterial saint, celestial, ancient, young, full and fruitful" (*82*; 76). Hagiographic allusions notwithstanding, no leap of faith unto God is necessary—or forthcoming from the novel—in order to ratify the secularized values that in a renewal of Christianity *ELH* submits as the desired endpoint of transvaluation.[14]

> "¡Ay la llaga en color de ropa antigua, /
> cómo se entreabre y huele a miel quemada!"
> [Ay, wound in the color of ancient garb,
> how it opens just a bit and smells of burnt honey]
> (César Vallejo, *Los heraldos negros*, "Absoluta")

If love and solidarity make but a few soulful appearances in the lives of *ELH*'s earthbound characters, the positive aspects of Mexico vanish almost completely from the text. For instance, parting ways with the telluric, a staple of Latin American identity discourse, *ELH* delivers just one homage to the land as the pith of Mexico. On the road to the capital Calixto fleetingly discerns "Deep Mexico" ("México profundo"), "the pure impetus of the country" (*112*; 102). Much more important to Revueltas's overall concept of lo mexicano are the *impure* forces of history that have robbed people of land and, interestingly enough, of authentic spirituality. *ELH* amounts to a literary mise-en-scène of the polemical articles on Mexico's history as well as economics, politics, and sociology that Revueltas published from 1939 to 1945 (collected in *Ensayos sobre México*). As do the articles, the eclectic vision of Mexican Christianity developed in *ELH* yokes Mexicans' vexed spirituality to the Conquest. *ELH* weds philosophy and theology to history, suffusing a potentially notional existentialism with concrete facticity.

The nostalgia for God that, as Vallejo's *Heraldos* poignantly illustrates, can inflect existentialism, plays a key role in *ELH*'s picture of lo mexicano. An essayistic interlude of the novel conveys the crux of the picture as it relates to spirituality. Revueltas strikingly characterizes Mexicans as:

> a people lacking religion in the strict, pragmatic sense of the word, but nevertheless a religious, fervent, devout people, more in search of divinity, their own divinity, than already in possession of it, than proprietors of their own god. The Spaniards blundered when they destroyed the pagan temples in order to construct Catholic churches in their place. This never resulted in

the extinction of one religion so that another could replace it, but, rather, in the extinction of all religion, all religious feeling . . . .

Something was lost to the people since then. Land, god, Tláloc, Christ, yes, land . . . . But wherever one looks—in Tlatelolco, in Puebla, or in Oaxaca—one spies amid the stones, climbing with ecstatic slowness, with eyes, a serpent of sad nostalgia exhaling its interrogation, an impossible breath that asks where and in what place. (*190–91*; 171–72)

Christianity emerges from Revueltas's reading as an imposed, hollow religion, a void and a necessity. Mourning for the absent spiritual center cascades into mourning for the lost origins of Mexico itself.[15] And around Christianity in *ELH* crowd the traces of Mexico's ill-fated ancestral gods: Mexicans "do not believe only in Christ, but also in their own inanimate *Christs*, in their own formless gods" (*19*; 23; emphasis added). Historicized, "the Christs of all passions" here speaks to Mexico's syncretic Christianity. Revueltas molds this topic of Mexican identity discourse familiar to us from my previous chapter into a yearning for "divinity" that Christianity could not satisfy. In keeping with his logic, Christianity can only, or at best, authentically function as an ethics in Mexican society.

No mere serpent of nostalgia, the traumas of the past at once urgently demand and block the ethics *ELH* espouses. Revueltas argues that Mexico's past bears down on its mestizos, that they carry the violence of the Aztecs, the serpent, and the predatory aggression of the Conquest, the eagle, into the present. Held hostage to accumulated lacerations not of their making, mestizos infect Mexico with hatred and strife: "As long as the tragic symbols of the serpent and the eagle, symbols of venom and rapacity, persisted, there would be no hope" (*32*; 36). *ELH*'s mestizos, it is clear, are a far cry from those of Luis Villoro's *Los grandes momentos del indigenismo* who seek to heal the past by reclaiming the indígena within.[16]

The array of negative biblical and nonbiblical personas attached to Adán now intersect with a historically conditioned, racialized one—mestizo—and with Mexico's twentieth-century history. Adán's crimes span the historical arc of *ELH*. The contract killer has done the dirty work of the government from the Revolution on into the 1930s. Brutalizing insurgents, Natives, socialists, a priest, and his wife alike, mestizo Adán epitomizes the toxic combination of the serpent and the eagle. Adán's wife, la Borrada, then focuses the tragic results of the mestizaje that colonialism pressed on Mexico. *ELH* equivocally suspends la Borrada's racial identity between Indigenous and mixed-race, two groups colonialism abased: "She was an Indian woman, perhaps with some non-Indian blood ["mestiza" blood] through one of her ancestors, who had been given to Adán by a mountain chief when Adán was municipal agent in the Indigenous camps" (*131–32*; 119). Compared at length, as the quote suggests, to Malinalli/La Malinche ("Malintzin" in the text, *138–40*; 125–28), la Borrada stands in for the erasure and deracination to which the Mexican people were prey. She falls victim to the beatings that Adán continuously inflicts on her, which she passively endures.

The tragedy of the paradigmatic la Borrada—also an image of Indigenous and mixed-race Mexican *women*—establishes that the atavistic violence of the mestizo finds a domestic outlet in machismo. The Hegelian "Lord-Bondsman" dynamic ensuing from the Spanish Conquest replicates itself in machismo, "power isolated in its own potency" (Paz, *Labyrinth 82*; *Laberinto* 220), and machismo pervades *ELH*. Further exposing the horrific residue of Spanish domination, every one of the novel's leading male mestizos (Adán, Calixto, Úrsulo) assaults his female partner. The name "la Borrada" becomes something of a misnomer because rather than being erased, she is a tormented vessel for the past. Revueltas's interpretation of gender relations, we see, radically departs from Vallejo's attempts to resite the sacred in woman.[17] Intent on exposing the wounds "in the color of ancient garb" that still plague Mexico, *ELH* swerves from Vallejo's woman as repository of a benign, existential will-to-God into woman as object of a violent will-to-power.

> "¡Ah querer, éste, el mío, éste, el mundial, /
>   interhumano y parroquial . . . !"
> [Ah to love, this, mine, this, the world's,
>   interhuman and parochial]
>   (César Vallejo, *Poemas humanos*)[18]

The Revueltas who insistently promotes a local agenda also envisages a Mexican Marxism. His Marxist project takes its cue from another Latin American, Mariátegui. As Revueltas declared in 1967, "Mariateguí has always been my teacher, at least in terms of ideology. It was he who made my generation realize that we needed to adapt Marxism to our nation, that ours should not be an imported Marxism" (*Conversaciones* 37). Revueltas's 1945 essay "Caminos de la nacionalidad" [Paths of the Nation] (*Ensayos*), for example, unmistakably reprises and Mexicanizes Mariátegui's *7 ensayos de interpretación de la realidad peruana* [7 Interpretive Essays on Peruvian Reality] (1928). *7 ensayos*, the same book that praised Vallejo, conducts a Marxist analysis of Peruvian history and proposes a country-specific Marxism. Mariátegui not unexpectedly inveighs against the Conquest, colonialism, feudalism, and imperialism. He agitates for the Indigenous peoples and agrarian reform. Less predictably, Mariátegui views Christianity with some favor, esteeming the good works of colonial missionaries. Revueltas does not share the Peruvian's equanimity towards the historical role of the Church in Latin America. However, Mariátegui's conviction, based on "recent historical experience," that "present-day revolutionary or social myths can root themselves as deeply and fully in our consciousness as ancient religious myths" (160) lays tracks for the literally unholy alliance of Marxism and Christianity *ELH* engineers.

Revueltas regards alienation and freedom, linchpins of existentialism, as the core of his Marxist problematic (*Conversaciones* 49). Alienation and an obstructed freedom certainly inhere in the plight of the Indigenous peoples for whose welfare both Mariateguí and Revueltas campaign. Revueltas maintains that the Indigenous peoples are "the cornerstone of Mexico," and that their "resurrection" would mean "the advent of the true and definitive Mexican nation" (*Ensayos* 20). *ELH* portrays Indigenous groups in desperate need of a resurrection that would shake them out of alienation. Yet, the novel flouts the socialist mandate to idealize the masses, opting instead to depict Indigenous peoples as abject.[19] La Borrada, qua Native, again stands in for a greater body. Her disturbing compliance with Adán's abuse symptomatizes the overall condition of the Indigenous peoples in *ELH*, as crushed and inert: "not bloodthirsty, nor cruel, nor rebellious; on the contrary they were spiritless, sad, hardworking, peaceful and full of fear" (*132*; 119). Only once do the text's Natives cast off their passivity. The government's attempt to enlist the Indigenous peoples as strikebreakers by inebriating them backfires, and galvanized, the formerly inert group rallies to the socialist cause that Natividad captains (*175–80*; 158–62).

The more *ELH* abjects its Indigenous characters, the more it foregrounds the ability of Marxism to break the cycle of alienation and suffering through collective action. In the novel's only mention of Soviet Russia and in a rare first-person intervention, the narrator ardently links "this, mine" and his "I" to "this, the world's," that is, to the masses, Mexico, and Stalin (before his crimes became notorious). The narrator rhapsodizes: "The multitude surrounds me in my solitude, in my refuge, the pure multitude, war, the multitude of Mexico hoarse with hidden tears, the profound, inflamed Soviet multitude that surrounded Stalin, that surrounds me, that surrounds you" (*200*; 179). With this, solidarity realizes its full potential as a conduit for Christianity, existentialism, and Marxism.

So does Natividad, "child of the masses" (*200*; 180), especially by virtue of his association with the Christ who rose from the dead. Through Natividad, the undying spirit of Christ aligns with the irrepressible spirit of revolution to give *ELH* a Sisyphean rhythm of downfall and re-"nativity." The Mexican Revolution has stumbled, the strike has miscarried, and Adán has executed Natividad, but as the text repeatedly comments, the ethos of revolution that the socialist hero incarnates will not die. For example: "Men like Natividad would rise up one morning throughout the land of Mexico; it would be a morning of bright light . . . . And then no one would be able to stop them because they would be all enthusiasm and definitive emotion" (*199*; 179). Revueltas's messianic prediction and his undying Natividad endow *ELH* with a transcendence, or "propensities for trinity," that writes beyond the novel's fatalistic, death-ridden ending. Moreover, transcendence inscribes *ELH* in Marxist dialectics and Christian eschatology, confederating the two passions; Natividad bequeaths the world a politics as well as an ethics. Only an activist new saint pledged to Sartrean transcendence, projects that act on a situation, could accomplish so redemptive a religare.[20]

A final locus of braided passions in *ELH* encompasses what Natividad elides, flawed mortals in history and the Old Testament. Revueltas pits Natividad against ordinary, imperfect individuals, personified in mestizos Calixto and Úrsulo, the "bitter, blind, deaf, complex, contradictory transition toward something that waited for them in the future" (*208*; 186). The Cristero Wars that defended the Church with the fanatical violence "Dios en la tierra" dramatizes exhibit the same liminal, absurd profile as *ELH*'s mestizos. Ancient violence, the Mexican serpent, comes to a head with the post-Revolution Cristero conflict. The serpent of *ELH*, exacerbated by the undead Aztec gods of war it carries in tow, blights the Christian cause and again transforms its standard-bearers into Cristo Rey, such that "*Cristo Rey* reached every corner of Mexico" (*189*; 170). As in "Dios en la tierra," Cristo Rey emanates from a vengeful deity comparable to the God of the Old Testament.[21] The deity unleashes what Vallejo would call "golpes como del odio de Dios" [blows like those of God's hatred] ("Los heraldos negros" 24), sows discord, and creates Adam, Cain, and Abel. Having demonized these Old Testament shades, *ELH* leaves the emblem of Cristo Pueblo, the non-supernatural Natividad, affiliated with a secularized, heroic Christianity and with socialism.

Natividad's stature grows, but the Cristero Wars raise issues that complicate *ELH*'s unholy alliances. Even more so than the Mexican Revolution, the Cristero Wars present a knotty situation for Revueltas's account of lo mexicano. Why, according to the logic of the novel, would Mexicans defend an imposed, hollow Christianity? Or, according to the novel's theology, a God? And what could possibly vindicate what Revueltas views as the absurd, depraved Cristero conflict? Revueltas salvages the Cristero Wars and, indeed, the whole spectrum of broken, failed insurrections that *ELH* narrates by underscoring their supreme, Marxist motivation. He contends that the actions of the proletariat in the Cristero Wars stem from "the radical and definitive dispossession man had been forced to endure." If a dispossessed man "defended God," alleged "master of the Church" and of the land and truth, he did so out of mourning for "what he had never possessed" (*191*; 172). Adán, Fallen Man, and Natividad, Christ and the spirit of revolution, *ELH* infers, will forever be locked in mortal combat until the socialist state arrives. Then, and only then, Revueltas asserts in his 1947 essay "Crisis y destino de México," will Mexico fulfill the promise of its Revolution, consummate its progressive energies, and thereby live up to the mission that its Revolution heralded, of serving as a model for Latin America (*Ensayos* 125).

> "quiero / saber de estar siquiera"
> [I want at least to know about being here]
> (César Vallejo, *Trilce* "XLIX")

While the politics Revueltas endorses await their day, the *religare ELH* effects succeeds in providing a robust model for a specifically Latin American existentialism. Heightening the Marxist component already latent in Usigli, Revueltas's situated, transvaluating, *activist* existentialism captures a sweep of vital Latin American preoccupations; the synergies Revueltas enacts form a roadmap for a holistic Latin American existentialism. Individually and conjointly, the passions that *ELH* merges have appeared in an abundance of works. Therefore, to evidence that *ELH*'s *religare* embodies certain *differentia specifica* of Latin American existentialism, I will focus here on test cases in literature and philosophy of a particular, particularly compelling, sort. Involving braided passions and activism, they revolve around the ineluctable matter of a Latin American *estar*, a plenary being-there, in-situation—as versus the ontological "being" that the verb *ser* signifies—such as Revueltas probes vis-à-vis the Mexican Dasein. The fact that several cases have to do with mid-twentieth-century Argentine culture, an unlikely arena thanks to

Jorge Luis Borges and company's famous otherworldly literature, should truly put to the test my claims for Revueltas's generative existentialism.

The first case study, nonetheless, returns to Mexico and places Revueltas over against Hiperión. Despite the numerous considerations that as we have seen Revueltas shares with Hiperión regarding identity, ethics, and community, in 1950 he lit into the Mexican existentialists.[22] Hiperión had invited Revueltas to speak at a conference on lo mexicano, and he delivered a lecture subsequently published under the title "Posibilidades y limitaciones del mexicano" (*Ensayos*). "Posibilidades" assails Hiperión's ontological efforts to define *the* Mexican, in Revueltas's view a betrayal of Mexicans' diversity and an ever-changing estar. It is impossible, he holds, to formulate a profile that obtains for all of Mexico's diverse citizens under all circumstances (*Ensayos* 41). From his existentialist cum Marxist position, Revueltas emphasizes praxis: one surely cannot "conceptualize Mexicans' existence as something emerging and transpiring outside of *praxis*, that is, outside of the necessary, obligatory reciprocity between subjects and their circumstances" (42). And yet, Revueltas concludes "Posibilidades" by tendering his own roster of Mexicans' invariable characteristics, their "own physiognomy" (56–57). Revueltas's excursion into the essentialism for which he had attacked Hiperión rests on a grounded estar consistent with Marxism. Ana Santos Ruiz notes that "Revueltas did not object to reflecting on Mexicanness at large, nor did he dismiss the possibility of detecting specifically Mexican forms of behavior; he just thought that such forms must find their explanation in the inherently mutable historical, economic, and sociological conditions" (376). Be that as it may, any reader of *ELH* will perceive Revueltas's fondness for monumentalizing statements on lo mexicano.

Equally imposing, we know, is Revueltas's investment in an activism freighted with transvaluation. Anchored in Christian existentialist Gabriel Marcel, Julio Cortázar's essay "Existencialismo" (1947; *Teoría del túnel* in *Obra crítica*) theorizes an activism geared to altruism. The Argentine writer rescues existentialism from the solipsism of which it was often accused and relocates the movement in Marcel's co-esse, the estar-in-community that Hiperión had fitted to Mexico. Cortázar proclaims: "Existentialism does not cultivate solitude as an authentic human condition; rather, existentialism accepts solitude in order to transcend it; therein lies the struggle, therein the glory. Man suffers diabolically from angst because he *knows* that he can be more, be himself and an other, be in-the-other, escape solipsism" (112). "As Gabriel Marcel teaches," continues Cortázar, "individuality is impossible without community" (114). Cortázar's *Teoría del túnel* has illuminated paths out of the tunnels that imprisoned Onetti and Sábato's protagonists. In foregrounding the caritas integral to authentic community, Cortázar has also coincided with Christianity. To do so while not debunking Sartre, whose *Existentialism Is a Humanism* afforded Cortázar a guiding light (122, 124), "Existencialismo" conflates Sartre's humanism with Marcel's co-esse. Cortázar makes short shrift of the breach between the two philosophers that in decrying Sartre's "egocentric topography" Marcel had glaringly evidenced (*Philosophy* 41, 54).[23] Marcel and a Marcelian Sartre dominate "Existencialismo"; parallel to Hiperión, Cortázar has stretched Sartre's early essay beyond its bounds.

Johnny, the reinscribed Christ figure we met in Cortázar's existentialist novella "El perseguidor," together with Revueltas's Natividad, usher us into a paramount forum for the merger of activism and transvaluation. I refer to the swath of existentialist saints who populate mid-twentieth-century Latin American fiction. Keeping faith with Christianity if not always with God, Latin American authors fashion a pantheon of new saints. Albert Camus's question in *The Plague*, "Can one be a saint without God?" (225), articulates what propels the Latin American literary saints at issue (we recall from chapter 2 Mario Vargas Llosa's preference for Camus over Sartre). The quandary of how to be a saint on earth leads several authors to commandeer the venerable *imitatio Christi*.

Take, for instance, Brazilian João Guimarães Rosa's parable-like story "The Hour and Turn of Augusto Matraga" (*Sagarana*, 1946), with its prototypical Christian existentialist hero. Having narrowly escaped death, sinner Augusto Matraga undergoes an incremental rebirth that lodges his holy grail, his destined "hour and turn," on earth rather than in heaven. Matraga first aims for heaven, and to assure his seat in the next world he follows the ascetic route of the traditional saint. Little by little, though, the protagonist awakens to the telluric beauty of his native backlands, the *sertão*. "He no longer thought of dying or about going to heaven" (292): Matraga exchanges the hagiographic imitatio Christi for the life in tune with a Godly natural world that *Sagarana* offers up as the quintessence of Brazilianness. Roaming the sertão at "peace with God" (296), mounted on a donkey (a "holy animal, closely associated with episodes in the life of Jesus" [294]), Matraga attains an ethical saintliness worthy of Christ. He dies, presumably gaining heaven, in a courageous struggle to avenge an injustice to a backlands family.

Guimarães Rosa's fellow Brazilian writer Clarice Lispector problematizes the imitation of Christ by embedding it in a mobile *estar*. Deeply mindful of the conventional roles that so many Brazilian women assumed at the time, Lispector's *Family Ties* (1960) devises a feminist activism suited to the "practical and living attitude toward the problems posed by the world" with which Simone de Beauvoir accredits existentialism (*Philosophical Writings* 324). *Family Ties* frames a pragmatic, nuanced feminism that moves beyond a standard female liberation narrative into a volatile existential flow. In solitude the collection's heroines do experience destabilizing epiphanies, but the revelations are simply catalysts. For what matters to Lispector, as to Camus's Sisyphus, is the *return* after the revelation—in *Family Ties*, the return to the still beloved home, crucible of authenticity. Lispector's protagonists discover authenticity within themselves and attempt to inject it into family ties.

Unusually for *Family Ties*, Laura, the reluctant saint of "The Imitation of the Rose," cannot externalize a more authentic self. Back at home after a stay in a psychiatric hospital, the protagonist faces an existential crisis: Laura's whole being comes to hinge on the choices a bouquet of roses foists upon her. She can decide to keep the roses, choosing risky selfhood, or to give them away, choosing a socially approved "feminine" selflessness. A third path outside her volition nevertheless presents itself to Laura. She can, and does, imitate the roses by internalizing them (69). Her internal imitation of the roses brings into play Thomas à Kempis's fifteenth-century devotional handbook *The Imitation of Christ*, which Laura read somewhat obtusely (55).[24] Laura has her doubts about imitating Christ and His perfection: "she had felt that anyone who imitated Christ would be lost—lost in the light, but dangerously lost. Christ was the worst temptation" (55). Imitating Christ/the perfect roses swirls Laura back into a hermetically sealed madness that ruptures family ties. The imitatio Christi has imploded the life of an existential crusader. Laura may have saved her self but she is indeed lost in the light.

A line from another *Family Ties* story lays bare the gist of Argentine David Viñas's sinuous Sartrean novel, *Un dios cotidiano* [An Everyday God] (1957): "Ah! It was easier to be a saint than a person," exclaims Lispector's Anna ("Love" 45–46). *Un dios cotidiano* scrutinizes protagonist Carlos Ferré's theological reflections over the course of a year in the 1930s. A novice priest obliged to spend the year as a teacher at a harsh Salesian preparatory school on the outskirts of Buenos Aires, Ferré wrestles with the themes of freedom, responsibility, authenticity, and choice that vivify Sartre's *Roads to Freedom* series.²⁵ These converge in the principal quest Ferré undertakes. He seeks to replace the absolute, static God whom orthodox Christianity worships with a flexible, existential, loving God who adjusts to the evolving situations of everyday life—in other words, a God of the *estar*, a sanguine "Dios en la tierra." As Jorge Eduardo Noro observes, Ferré desires "an everyday God, an absolutely incarnated God who is committed to reality and enables each day to yield new faith and a new form of commitment" (4). Ferré's particular imitatio Christi then strives to instantiate his God through the elastic modus operandi of adjusting to the circumstances ("adecuarse") and acts of loving kindness.

Ferré's quest ultimately fails due in no small part to the ironclad tendencies the protagonist's name connotes. The task of materializing an amorphous God into a praxis that rights the moral wrongs the school perpetuates in the name of Christianity overwhelms Ferré. "I don't have the formula. I'm tearing myself apart," he tells his friend Porter (148), much as Cortázar's Johnny might have told Bruno. Unlike Johnny, Ferré reflexively defaults to a conventional hagiographic script, with its readymade, Manichean prescriptions for good and evil. Porter admonishes him: "One shouldn't insist on being so pure. It can turn a person into an abstraction" (74). Porter later adds: "Your charity is a bit repulsive" (114). Ferré stubbornly disregards his friend's opinions, and the novel ends with a damning vignette. On the blackboard of his classroom the protagonist spots "a grotesque drawing. Of me. A ridiculous cartoon, a little disgusting. Below it they had written, *Father Ferré plays the saint*" (189). Betraying the authentic "everyday God," Ferré's reversion to a hard line imitatio Christi contorts into bad faith.

Viñas's text projects Ferré's existential dilemma onto a political canvas shot through with the warring factions of the Spanish Civil War—the only precise historical referent in *Un dios cotidiano*. The novel shapes its Salesian school into a microcosm of the tensions between fascism and communism that ricocheted from Spain to Argentina. An ultra-Catholic fascism prevails in Spain as well as in the Argentine school, whose director converts it into a hotbed of fascism. He rallies the students against the communists who have assailed the Church, for example, by touting Francoists victories: " 'Terrific news,' he said almost constantly. 'In a couple of months, they'll have eliminated the whole problem' " (28). His pupils applaud. As a microcosm of battling pressures, the school in fact and significantly does triple duty. It mirrors not only the shock waves of the Spanish Civil War but also those of Argentina's coeval "infamous decade," in which a military dictatorship overthrew Hipólito Yrigoyen's democratic regime, *and* the Peronist fascism that had lately dominated Argentina (Noro 7). *Un dios cotidiano*, we see, fires several guns simultaneously. The novel's layered protocol surreptitiously equates Ferré's lapse into a bad faith rigidity with Argentina's collapses into fascism.

Viñas's activist leanings will not surprise anyone familiar with the radical journal *Contorno* that he and his brother Ismael Viñas founded. The Buenos Aires journal published ten issues of fiction, literary criticism, and political commentary from 1953 to 1959. In addition to the Viñas brothers, *Contorno*'s leading members included Tulio Halperín Donghi, Adelaida Gigli, Noé Jitrik, Adolfo Prieto, León Rozitchner, Juan José Sebreli, and, for a time, Rodolfo Kusch.[26] What unites the variegated group of intellectuals was the distinctive Argentine situation of Peronism. Beginning as it does in the last two years of Perón's first administration and continuing into the presidency of Arturo Frondizi (1958–1962), *Contorno* challenges Peronism. At first wary of retaliation from Perón, *Contorno*'s contributors limit their activism to the literary realm, where they circumspectly attempt "a marriage of artistic and political, aesthetic and ethical considerations" (Katra 26). After Perón was deposed in 1955, *Contorno* shifts from the politics of literature to politics per se. David Viñas may have confined his articles for *Contorno* to literary criticism, but as *Un dios cotidano* demonstrates, his creative writing manifests *Contorno*'s signature field of interests.

Accordingly, David Viñas makes common cause with the Marxist perspective of *Contorno*. More than the transvaluated theology that permeates *Un dios cotidiano* and that *Contorno* tends to eschew, the majority of Viñas's fiction adopts Marxist György Lukàcs's historical approach (Roca 46). For its part, *Contorno* disseminates the work of Argentine Marxists Sebreli, Carlos Correa, and Oscar Masotta; Ismael Viñas has openly declared his Marxist orientation ("Prólogo" v–vi). *Contorno*'s authors turn away from dogmatic, organized Marxism to chart an independent course based on the relationship between middle-class intellectuals like themselves and the working class (see Katra, ch. 2). The journal's Marxist proclivities set it sharply at odds with the at least seemingly apolitical literature that the Argentine journal *Sur* [South] (1931–1992) promoted and that Borges epitomizes. Hence, *Contorno* styles itself as a kind of anti-*Sur*. The "parricides" of the socially engaged *Contorno*, to use Emir Rodríguez Monegal's oft-cited epithet for the group's members, pitch themselves against what they saw as *Sur*'s fanciful creations.[27]

Revueltas's fiction, on the other hand, easily meets *Contorno*'s criteria. With *Contorno*, the imitatio Christi drops off the map, but it gives way to a different coupling of the passions *ELH* had aligned. When in the first issue of *Contorno* Ismael Viñas announces, "[t]he world, this world around us, our country, our city, all press us to take responsibility for them" (*Contorno* 2), the code word of "responsibility" signals the Sartrean existentialism that informs *Contorno* along with Marxism. The two currents organically intersect in their mutual attention to the "situation," or, as the group's name blazons, the *contorno*. Beatriz Sarlo describes *Contorno* as exuding a "family resemblance" to Sartrean existentialism, the "source of its formulas, its style" (803). The chief "formulas" the journal derives from Sartre are the situationally oriented themes of commitment, social transformation, and the intellectual's responsibility. These stomping grounds distance *Contorno* from Eduardo Mallea's introverted, soul-searching Argentine existentialism. More important for the big picture, they reveal a gulf between the Argentine existentialist *Contorno* and the Mexican existentialist Grupo Hiperión, which ended just before *Contorno* began. *Contorno*, dedicated to its specific circumstances, concretizes *another* Sartre than that of Hiperión: the engaged, post-*Being and Nothingness* Sartre of *Anti-Semite and Jew* (1946), "Materialism and Revolution" (1946), and *What Is Literature?* (1948). Privileging Argentina's political situation, *Contorno* abstains from the ontological investigations that, as Revueltas had objected, engrossed Hiperión. Logically, then, Revueltas provides a more apt channel from Mexican to Argentine existentialism.

Philosopher Rodolfo Kusch, however, confronts *lo argentino* as assiduously as Hiperión and Revueltas confront *lo mexicano*; he performs a religare of identity discourse and existentialism. A contributor to just two early issues of *Contorno*, the Argentine Kusch exercises the journal's "parricidal" bent not on *Sur* but on Domingo Faustino Sarmiento's esteemed Argentine identity treatise, *Facundo: Civilización y barbarie* [Facundo: Civilization and Barbarism] (1845). Kusch's first book, *La seducción de la barbarie* [The Seduction of Barbarism] (1953), as its title implies, upends Sarmiento's valorizing of the city and disparagement of the "barbaric" rural interior. Inveterate contrarian Kusch redeems barbarism even more forcefully in *América profunda* (1962). A stunning work of philosophical anthropology, *América profunda* doubles down on Mallea's rural "invisible Argentina," problematic for *Contorno*.[28] Kusch puts his stamp on Mallea's formulation by consecrating the Indigenous cultures located in Latin America's rural zones as the very essence of Latin Americanness. Throughout *América profunda* Kusch elevates Indigenous cultures and an Indigenous mentality into models for "civilization." In so doing, *América profunda* quite obviously paves the way for Guillermo Bonfil Batalla's *México profundo* (1987), itself something of a sequel to Luis Villoro's *Los grandes momentos del indigenismo en México*.

In *América profunda* Kusch says of Villoro: "This author certainly inhabits a far more robustly Indigenous environment than do we in South America, except in Bolivia or Peru" (196). Argentina in particular lacks an Indigenous heritage tantamount to that of certain other nations, so Kusch draws sustenance from the Indigenous cultures of Bolivia, Mexico, and Peru. The material circumstances and the ideological currents that inhere in these countries shape Kusch's thinking on Indigeneity. Above all, he strikes back at coloniality as well as at a colonialist mindset that still subalternizes the Indigenous worlds (see, for example, Derbyshire; Mignolo). A couple of idiosyncratic keywords exemplify Kusch's militant decolonizing stance. First, *lo hediento*, the "stinking" earthiness a sanitized Latin American middle class identifies with the Indigenous peoples: the shocking descriptor throws into relief Kusch's attempts to transform a putative heart of darkness into the authentic heart of Latin Americanness.[29] "As is obvious," Kusch writes, "my deliberate intention was to bring out the deeply positive meaning of this alleged stench" (3). Second, *fagocitación* (phagocytosis), a biological process in which one cell assimilates and destroys another: utterly reversing colonialist projects that would subsume Indigenous cultures into Western mores, Kusch maintains that Indigenous people have stayed true to their culture. Instead of being culturally cannibalized, as, for one, José Vasconcelos's *La raza cósmica* prescribes, Native peoples have cannibalized the culture that purports to dominate them, overcoming it (195). Kusch's stance concertedly undercuts the treacherous indigenism Villoro recounts (185).

No two keywords, in any event, define *América profunda* more than *ser* and *estar*. Through complex operations to which I cannot do ample justice here, Kusch makes an existentialized ser vs. estar the axis of the entire book: "The insight that I work through here swings between two poles. One is what I call the *ser*, or being-someone, which I discover in sixteenth-century European bourgeois culture; and the other, the *estar*, or being-here, which I view as a profound modality of pre-Columbian culture" (5). Kusch plays out his thesis by largely construing ser as a capitalist, urban, and individualistic *Western* mode of being. The text's estar, which according to Kusch (109) has its origins in Heidegger's Dasein, conversely represents a state of being affiliated with nature and community—an *Indigenous* mode.[30] Kusch states that "the solidity of [Indigenous] culture, its cohesion and tenacity, lies in what we have called the estar, which lacks any transcendent reference to the world of essences . . . and which has led its tremendous life in resolute commitment to the 'here and now' " (190–91). As the quote intimates, the decolonizing *América profunda* opposes the essentialized ontological plenitude of the Western *ser* to the authentic *estar* of the Indigenous peoples in ways that recall Emilio Uranga's "accidentality." Kusch, moreover, opposes the sanitized civility of the West to the chthonian Indigenous peoples, at home with sexuality, the land, and love. A panegyric to the love and peace that restoration of the communitarian Indigenous *estar* portends (254) closes *América profunda*.

Clearly, Kusch has taken us far afield from Revueltas's vision of the Indigenous peoples. In a broader sense, though, with Kusch et alia we have landed in a place *ELH* limns and authorizes. The novel enacts a situated, pragmatic existentialism that has enormous potency for Latin American writers. Supple, philosophically eclectic, and multidimensional, it invites them to imagine an existentialism within the compass of Latin America, an existentialism of *religare* that can act as Christs for all passions. If, to paraphrase Camus's *The Rebel*, others at this meridian of thought, rejecting divinity in order to share in the struggles and destiny of their compatriots, choose to imagine different routes to the same goal, then the rebel Revueltas would likely welcome their interventions.[31]

Chapter Six

Rosario Castellanos's Freedom

Yo soy un ancho patio, una gran casa abierta [I am a broad courtyard, a great wide-open house]

—Rosario Castellanos, "Toma de conciencia,"
Materia memorable

And then, always already, the question of woman: where is she in mid-twentieth-century reflections on Mexican identity? Though the question is predictable, even clichéd, the almost total muteness on women of the Grupo Hiperión prods one to ask it. The inattention to women in Samuel Ramos's 1934 *El perfil del hombre y la cultura en México*, a product of its times, disappoints modern readers; we could expect more from Hiperión's newest wave, expansive cosmopolitanism. Yet, besides appraising women's involvement with machismo, Hiperión's principal adherents fail to make specific provision for the feminine. Perhaps to a degree as fallout from their sweeping ontological approach, the Hyperions subsume woman into a collective, generic, Mexican "he."

Two texts by writers friendly to Hiperión do, from its perimeters, pay dedicated attention to Mexican women. In his rigorous sociological analysis, *Imagen del mexicano* (1948), José Gómez Robleda scientifically diagnoses the Mexican condition. Gómez Robleda's contestation of Mexicans' alleged inferiority shines a light on his country's women and Indigenous peoples, both of whom he lauds for possessing a "practical-realist" disposition worthy of emulation, not subordination (e.g., 73–74). María Elvira Bermúdez's *La vida familiar del mexicano* (1955), which I introduced in chapter 2, comprises the sole female-authored text in Leopoldo Zea's "México y lo Mexicano" book series. Bermúdez unveils the tribulations of Mexican women from myriad socioeconomic strata, tribulations that derive from machismo and result in women's stunted *hembrismo*. By hembrismo, the female counterpart of machismo, Bermúdez means women's exaggerated capitulation to the patriarchy, including hostility towards other women (93).

Sociologists, rather than philosophers, that they were, Gómez Robleda and Bermúdez hardly give the lie to Guillermo Hurtado's sharp pronouncement that "the philosophy of lo mexicano was created by men and was about men—never about the woman's vision of Mexican reality" ("Dos mitos" 284). More disruptive to the norm Hurtado so aptly formulates is the distinguished philosopher, essayist, novelist, poet, playwright, short-story writer, *and* feminist Rosario Castellanos, an intellectual vitally connected to Hiperión. Philosophically and personally wrangling with Hiperión's staunch Sartrean, Ricardo Guerra, Castellanos counted among her friends and colleagues Hiperión's Jorge Portilla, Emilio Uranga, Luis Villoro, Agustín Yáñez, and Leopoldo Zea (along with Octavio Paz). She dedicated her *Mujer que sabe latín* [The Woman Who Knows Latin] (1973) to Villoro, who shared her commitment to the Indigenous peoples and equitable alterity. Castellanos not only commended the search for Mexican identity (*Juicios Sumarios*, in *Obras II* 520), she also reminded her readers of Hiperión's "phenomenological-existential" efforts to carry it into concrete situations à la Sartre (*El mar y sus pescaditos*, in *Obras II* 821).[1]

When asked for her own stance on Mexican identity, Castellanos replied with "La tristeza del mexicano" [Mexicans' Sadness], an essay that the newspaper *Excélsior* published on January 30, 1971 (republished in *El uso de la palabra*). Announcing it will "place in crisis" a series of truisms in Mexican identity discourse, Castellanos's article holds that Latin America has yet to "know" or "acknowledge" its identity (*El uso* 175). For Mexico to do so, it must reject deterministic, self-defeating myths. While pre-Hispanic myths per se and the nation's colonial history are two such impediments that Mexican identity discourse has propagated, Castellanos focuses on the commonplace of Mexicans' sadness (we think of Paz's *Laberinto*, the Hyperions' interest in desgana, and Roger Bartra's *La jaula de la melancolía*). Accepting the commonplace simply generates low expectations and, paradoxically, because melancholy has an inalienable beauty, a congratulatory self-justification. Given that neither attitude will stand Mexico in good stead, Castellanos in effect asks Mexican identity discourse to remove *its* masks.[2]

Castellanos performs that task by bringing Mexicans into then-current feminist conversations. Moreover, as I principally wish to demonstrate, she tools herself into a "broad courtyard," a broad thinker who enters into ever more freeing dialogue with Hiperión, Hiperión's Ricardo Guerra, Jean-Paul Sartre, and Simone de Beauvoir. To view Castellanos through the various existentialisms that so impacted her on enmeshed philosophical, personal, and social levels, as this chapter will at heart do, is to reveal her writings as an agora and a battleground. "I've turned into an agora, a battlefield, a no one's land" (60), declares the semi-autobiographical protagonist of Castellanos's novel *Rito de iniciación* [Rite of Initiation] (60). Castellanos's hard-won intellectual freedom allows her, post-Hiperión, to erect a "great wide-open house," a magnanimous existentialist ethos for Mexicans, from women to all.

The Eternal Feminine

Bermúdez remarks that "Emilio Uranga regards the oscillations of Mexican being as a clear and categorical ontic reality," a "nepantla." "Well," Bermúdez comments ironically, "in his amorous and family relationships, the Mexican man is undoubtedly nepantla. He oscillates between Woman and women" (100). Bermúdez's quip signals the sway that hidebound archetypes such as Woman in capital letters—aka the Eternal Feminine—continued to exercise on Mexican male writers in the 1950s, the decade in which their female compatriots at long last received the federal right to vote. Carlos Fuentes's 1962 novella *Aura* (though by no means representative of all the female characters in his vast, imbricated fictions) illustrates what could and did happen when male writers of the times focused on the feminine, siting identity discourse in "her." Published the same year as *La muerte de Artemio Cruz*, Fuentes's intensely existential novel on the Mexican Revolution and its aftermath, *Aura* pivots into a magical world reflective of Zea's thesis that Mexico must authentically assimilate its past in order to move forward. *Aura* rehearses the version of Zea's thesis that Fuentes later spells out in "Kierkegaard in the Zona Rosa [of Mexico City]" (*Tiempo mexicano*; 1972). There Fuentes writes that for Mexicans "all times are still alive, all pasts are present," and that "no Mexican time has yet reached completion. Because the history of Mexico is a series of 'subverted Edens' . . . to which we at once wish to return and wish to forget" (9–10). A novelistic prequel to *Tiempo mexicano*, Fuentes's Gothic *Aura* proposes an ethereal erotics of assimilation and consolation that runs roughly as follows.

Felipe, a historian who has cloistered himself in the home of the aged Consuelo Llorente to translate her husband's memoirs, falls in love with Aura, a phantasmagorical emanation and resurrection of Consuelo's youthful selves whom she conjures up through ritual sacrifices. As Consuelo's magical machinations synchronize with Felipe's chronological reading of General Llorente's memoirs, they produce encounters between Felipe and Consuelo/Aura from successive periods of the dowager's life. In tandem with translating the General's narrative on the nineteenth-century French rule of Mexico, the young historian advances his own work on the Spanish Conquest. The concurrent projects bring him into contact with the two empires that dominated Mexico in the past. Resuscitating and unblocking Mexican history, Felipe arrives at a stunning realization. His true identity, his "real face" and forgotten "ancient countenance" (57), is that of the General. Felipe's fantastic anagnorisis as an other incarnates Indigenous cyclical time, according to Fuentes the true Mexican time (*Tiempo mexicano* 40). Felipe then disavows chronology, history, and rationality (*Aura* 57), hoping to revive a liaison with Aura that merges the past with the present in loving union.

The *Künstlerroman* and *Bildungsroman* of sorts that is *Aura* clearly hinges on Aura herself, a mythified, chimeric figure. Among the manifold sources that inform Fuentes's house-based novella (as intertextually capacious as Castellanos's "house"), the one that most defines the myth of the eternal feminine in *Aura* is Jules Michelet's *Satanism and Witchcraft* (*La Sorcière*, 1862).[3] *Aura* opens with an epigraph by Michelet: "Man hunts and fights. Woman schemes and dreams; she is the mother of fantasy, of the gods. She has a second sight, wings that enable her to fly towards an infinity of desire and imagination. . . . The gods are like men: they are born and they die on a woman's breast . . ." (7; ellipses in the original). Innumerable aspects of *Aura*, from the comprehensive to the minute, are rooted in Michelet's portrait of the "Witch"/"Wise Woman"/"Good Lady" (x) as a fount of healing, a subversive alternative to the institutionalized Church (see Alazraki). One gathers that Michelet, and by extension, Fuentes, aim to valorize the feminine. However, to state the painfully obvious, their valorization is riddled with problems. In the space of matriarchal worlds and texts they have implanted an essentialized conceptualization of the feminine, a mythified, polarized, male-justifying fantasy. As Beauvoir reminds us, "when terrified by the dangerous magic woman possesses, [the male] posits her as the essential, *it is he who posits her*" (*The Second Sex* 82; emphasis added). Fuentes in particular has allegorized the phantom Aura—who barely speaks, who is mostly erotic body but not even that—out of any actual existence.

Aura so abounds in delights and deep structures that I would refrain from critique were it not for the fact that the novella emblematizes the proclivity of Hiperión-orbit literature for magical women together with magical thinking around women. Consider, for example, the most prominent, powerful female character we have encountered, Juan Rulfo's Susana San Juan. Magical, radical Other, solipsistic and hermetic, Susana brings to literary life the image of woman-as-enigma that Paz limns in *Laberinto*: "Woman, another being who lives apart, is also an enigmatic figure. Indeed, she is the Enigma" (*66*; 203); "[s]he is an idol, and like all idols she is mistress of magnetic forces whose efficacy and power increase as their source of transmission becomes more and more passive and secret. There is a cosmic analogy here: woman does not seek, she attracts" (*37–38*; 173). We meet the cosmic feminine again in José Revueltas's *El luto humano*, where she takes the form of Úrsulo's Indigenous mother ("Úrsulo was the son of the obsidian dagger, and his mother was the goddess herself, a young goddess" [*64*; 62], the very image of a woman "with powers over destiny, untouchable and magical" [*159*; 145]). When the iconic "Máscaras mexicanas" chapter of *Laberinto* attempts to come down to earth and grapple with women of flesh and blood, it still serves up the instrumentalized, mythified subjectivity of the woman whom man fallaciously parses into the good/passive and bad/active Mother (*35–37*; 173–75). In either mystified guise, like Susana San Juan and Aura and Úrsulo's mother, woman exercises a magically fearsome, outsize influence on man. While, as distinct from Hiperión, the above writers grant some space to the feminine, their treatment of "her" remains multiply bound to what Wendy Faris neatly calls the "terminal magic" of *Aura* (70).[4]

Paz, to his credit, hazards in *Laberinto* that one might ask Mexican women themselves how they feel about the double-edged, ultimately subjugating respect men afford them. Instead of being pigeonholed as symbols and functions, might not women prefer greater freedom and authenticity (*38*; 173–74)? Castellanos dedicates much of her professional life to addressing a query of that nature. Mexican women writers surged in the 1950s, with such authors as playwright Luisa Josefina Hernández battering away at mystifications of the female; Castellanos would soon take the lead in these efforts. For her generation and going forward, she became "the national standard-bearer of feminism" (Poot Herrera 52–53).[5]

Castellanos's play *El eterno femenino* [The Eternal Feminine] (1975) condenses the fruits of her rousing, decades-long thought on women's freedom, or their lack thereof, into a single, outrageous package.[6] As Castellanos has said, every word in *Eterno* "accords with my truest convictions, my most profound experiences, and my most habitual observations" (Anhalt 75). Begun in Mexico and completed in 1973 in Jerusalem, Castellanos's new home as Mexico's ambassador to Israel, *Eterno* systematically and categorically debunks Mexican myths of the eternal feminine. Castellanos states in the play (*Eternal*, in *A Rosario Castellanos Reader, 351*; *Eterno* 182–83) that she borrows the work's title from Goethe's *Faust*, where it refers to the archetypal ideal woman, impossibly angelic and pure. *Eterno* decimates the archetype with a chain of biting caricatures that descend from the heavens into terrain that Rodolfo Usigli had previously carved out. Having studied theater with Usigli, and having written a play for his course that she destroyed after recognizing it as an "exact copy" of *El gesticulador* (Seale Vásquez 33), Castellanos favors middle-class settings and characters, hallmarks of the male dramatist's work. *Eterno* thus takes place in a middle-class, Mexico City hair salon, an unlikely setting for a shock and awe campaign but one perfectly suited to the Medusas who populate the farce.

The play immediately catapults us out of the ordinary with its far-fetched science fiction premise. Lupita, who has come to have her hair styled for her wedding, will sit under an experimental hair dryer that programs women's dreams. Concocted by men to keep women from entertaining dangerous antisocial thoughts, the magical-thinking apparatus has the opposite effect on Lupita. In act 1, the device that has gone catastrophically awry regales her with scenes that shatter patriarchal myths of marriage. Dreaming an alarmingly possible, nightmarish future, Lupita experiences a honeymoon in which the bride's zestful sexuality collides with her husband's expectations for a blushing virgin, followed by a pregnancy that deteriorates into a power grab between husband and wife. The motherhood that Mexicans glorify then collapses into a chaos of fractious children and into deception, when Lupita's husband takes a mistress. (Quite unlike Castellanos, as we will see,) Lupita murders both offending sides of the love triangle. Older age finds the widowed Lupita transformed into a gesticulator of sorts who in public adopts the hallowed mask of the good mother that wins her kudos, all the while gleefully celebrating at home her deliverance from traditional roles.

Act 2, very much in the mode of 1970s feminist literature, exercises its spleen on a gamut of historical female personages. Still bewitched by the wayward apparatus, Lupe enters a "freak show" in a fair (*297*; 72). She watches wax museum statues of Eve, La Malinche, Rosario de la Peña, Sor [Sister] Juana Inés de la Cruz, Josefa Ortiz de Domínguez, Empress Carlota of Mexico, and Adelita come alive and reveal the untold determining roles they played in Mexico's past. As the revived statue of proto-feminist colonial writer Sor Juana states: "Because they have made us submit against our will to a stereotyped, official version of history . . . now we are going to present ourselves as what we were. Or, at least, as what we think we really were" (*305*; 87). The repressed returns to assail official history by exposing the ways in which the erstwhile submissive, "eternal" females wrested power and agency from men in Mexican politics, war, and love.

Act 3 deflates the triumphant ascendancy of the feminine with a dismal overview of the independent woman in Mexico. As Lupita tries on various wigs, each of which projects her into a different script for an autonomous woman, the play rolls out a series of caustic revelations. Unmasked, the potentially admirable lives of the single woman, the teacher, and the nurse disintegrate into voids of loneliness. Far from gloriously autonomous, the lives of the prostitute and, yet again, the mistress prove to gyrate around men, as do those of its maverick female celebrities. We hear *Eterno*'s successful female politician, scientist, artist, and writer, ostensible exemplars for their fellow women, pay obeisance to the patriarchy. The end of *Eterno* finally slips out of caricature and stages a mini-agora. In her last apparatus-generated role, Lupita teaches a cultural enrichment course for bourgeois homemakers. Spurred by nothing less than a recent performance of *El eterno femenino*, Lupita proposes the discussion topic of Mexican feminism. The heated debate she sparks resounds with female voices that eviscerate the play's author for having divorced. They defend the patriarchy, which affords women status and security. Tying Lupita-the-opportunistic-gesticulator from act 1 to the defrocked female mavericks of act 3, and dealing a coup de grâce to act 2's reempowered historical figures, this band of female voices exposes the complicity of Mexican women in their own subordination, one of Castellanos's key contentions with respect to gender.[7]

As even the preceding minimal summary should indicate, *Eterno* assumes the cast of a feminist manifesto, a gendered Mexican identity treatise. Its encyclopedic range aims to fill in a mountain of blanks, to slap all manner of magical thinking, male and female, in the face. And, cannily, Castellanos has selected farce, an unconstraining genre that accommodates everything from comedy to tragedy (Meléndez, ch. 1), as *Eterno*'s vehicle. Qua farce, the play at once blunts the blows that might alienate the public it wishes to recruit while still unleashing the gaze of Medusa full tilt. *Eterno* in fact represents the feminist Castellanos at her most free, her most iconoclastic. Castellanos's self-caricature in the play confirms it: *Eterno*'s author "takes advantage of being out of the country, and therefore believing she is beyond good and evil, out of the critics' reach . . . casts the stone" (*351*; 184). Offering Mexico her credo, her summa, and, grievously, her swan song (she died from accidental electrocution at home in Israel the next year), Castellanos loads *Eterno* with so many scenarios and Lupitas as to render it practically unstageable, not to mention utterly scandalous. Overburdened as the manifesto-like play is, *Eterno* does not stoop to conquer. Though it could easily have indulged in facile gibes at the patriarchy, *Eterno* delivers adept, original, eminently hilarious tableaux that bear out Castellanos's theories on the liberating forces of humor.[8]

A jocular take-off on Sor Juana's renowned philosophical summa, the "First *Dream*" ("Primero sueño"; emphasis added), *Eterno* cements the status that Castellanos had by the 1970s achieved as high priestess of contemporary Mexican feminism. Castellanos, who taught comparative literature at the UNAM, earned the status of Mexico's premier feminist in part by purveying international women's culture to Mexico. Her essay collection *Mujer que sabe latín* displays the wide-ranging knowledge that enabled this feat and many others. Enjoying a huge print run as a book that the Secretaría de Educación Pública brought out to demonstrate the open-mindedness of President Luis Echeverría's administration, *Mujer que sabe latín* reviews scores of women writers, from Sor Juana to Betty Friedan. The book's literary portrait gallery endows Mexico with a woman-oriented rendition of the Argentine journal *Sur*, the famed cultural clearing house led by Victoria Ocampo. Prodigiously learned as Castellanos was, she wears her erudition lightly. To best fulfill the mission of disseminating women's culture to a broad audience, as distinct from the predominantly arcane Hiperión writers Castellanos approaches her subjects straightforwardly and nontechnically.

Mujer que sabe latín also straightforwardly expounds the feminist agenda that *Eterno* would escalate into a primal "laugh of Medusa." The book's programmatic opening essay, "La mujer y su imagen" [Woman and Her Image] (republished verbatim from the 1966 *Juicios*) consolidates various planks of the platform that girds *Eterno*—a platform that may sound hackneyed now but that introduced a veritable sea change to Mexico. As the play has led us to expect, "La mujer" condemns the reduction of women to myths, which spotlight female characters as "the incarnation of some principle, a generally malefic, fundamentally antagonistic one" (*Mujer* 7–8). Men, Castellanos laments, invert the actions of Pygmalion by turning real women into statues, manufacturing them as absolute Others (12). The author urges women to break away from entrenched social models such as the self-abnegating "angel in the house" (12) and a fetishized, compulsory maternity. Against these detrimental templates Castellanos pits the rebellious woman, capable of forging an "authentic image" (19). When "La Mujer" concludes that it is incumbent upon women to "*become what they are*" (20), readers recognize the magnetism for Castellanos of Beauvoir's *The Second Sex* (1949; henceforth, *TSS*). Gendering Pindar's "become such as you are," *TSS* rallies around the notion that one is not born but becomes a woman, whether through individual choices or the pressures of social constructions.[9]

Indeed, according to her *Cartas a Ricardo* (Guerra) [Letters to Ricardo] Castellanos had first read the myth-disabling Beauvoir in Spain at the start of 1951 (97). Castellanos's 1966 essay, "El amor en Simone de Beauvoir" [Love in Simone de Beauvoir] (*Juicios*), eloquently summarizes certain aspects of *TSS* that resonated with her and that, we deduce, she sees as having special relevance to Mexico. They include multiple patriarchal mythifications of the eternal feminine, like those Paz laid out; male dominance as expressed in machismo; love as abjection for women; society's tolerance for adultery; maternity as the woman's escape from loveless marriage; the need for motherhood to be a choice, not an obligation; and the dead-end paths for the independent woman. "La mujer," like *Eterno*, does not fail to ponder women's complicity with subjugating marriage, their ready abdication of freedom.

This staple of Castellanos's agenda, it is well worth noting, stems from bedrock tenets of *TSS*. If the start of its first volume expatiates on *Mitsein* in keeping with Heidegger's abstract ontological view that we are thrown into the world together with others, Beauvoir adapts Heidegger's being-with-others to the stuff of *TSS*, darkly. The Mitsein that prevails in *TSS* regards the couple—for better or worse, the male-female couple—as "a fundamental unit with two halves riveted to each other" (*TSS* 9). Man and woman cleave to each other by nature, but patriarchy skews the social relationship into one that posits males as essential, females as the inessential Other. Patriarchy mystifies the unnatural relationship of subjection into a seeming organic one. The confluence of Mitsein, mystification, and genuine socioeconomic necessity then weighs so heavily on women as to convert them into "[h]alf victims, half accomplices" (*TSS* 277; a line from Sartre's *Dirty Hands*) of the patriarchy. A pernicious mix akin to Bermúdez's hembrismo, it also ravages female solidarity, producing the deplorable situation in which those who most furiously resist feminism are women themselves (Castellanos, *Juicios* 653).

Castellanos's versions of *The Second Sex*, "lite" in *Eterno* and probing in the essays, joined with the circumstance that she had explored women's support of the patriarchy *before* reading Beauvoir, point to the important fact that the Mexican feminist was a serious, broadly trained philosopher. Quickly abandoning a plan to study law at the university, and then put off by an arid literature curriculum that skirted "the big questions" (*Mujer* 205), Castellanos cast her lot with philosophy. "And I don't regret it," she later said ("Narradores," in *Obras II* 1012), in spite of her distaste for philosophy's abstruse terminology (*Mujer* 205). Castellanos earned bachelor's and master's degrees in the field. She went on to feed her philosophical bent by writing, reading, and teaching on the subject. Philosophy and literature fused naturally for her: "More than anything else, writing has been a way of explaining to myself things I don't understand" (Carballo 422). Moreover, Castellanos's profile as creative writer, philosopher, and comparatist well positioned her to engage an existentialism that intrinsically overruns disciplinary and national boundaries, while still having a special tie to Mexico thanks in part to Hiperión. Engage existentialism Castellanos did, well beyond *TSS* and, ultimately, beyond gender.

Castellanos's investment in existentialism, I will argue over the course of what follows, yields a robust program of freedom. Freedom for women, to be sure, but also personal freedom, philosophical freedom, and freedom of praxis, that is, freedom to embrace a collective Other. The itineraries I will detail, continuing to peel back the layers of *Eterno*, take their cue from the personal trajectory Castellanos articulated: "I underwent a very slow evolution from the most circumscribed subjectivity to the disquieting discovery of the existence of the other and, finally, to relinquishing coupledom as a model and opening onto society at large, which is where poets define themselves, understand themselves, and express themselves" (*Mujer* 203). Though the phases can overlap in her writings, these are the chief roads to freedom that Castellanos travels, each one imprinted by existentialism, many of them richly developed in her less familiar texts. Starting with the unexpected matrix of her letters to Ricardo Guerra, Castellanos elaborates the love triangles on which *Eterno* dwells and which emerge as a center of gravity for the author's meditations on freedom. Because Castellanos's ongoing accounts of *ménages à trois*—real and fictional, her own and Beauvoir's—enclose *philosophical* triangulations of Castellanos/Guerra/Sartre and Castellanos/Sartre/Beauvoir, altogether they enrich not just the gendered but also the ethical cosmopolitanism of works that orchestrate Mexican identity.[10]

Castellanos—Guerra—Sartre

The Rosario Castellanos who would soon embark on new journeys, physical and philosophical, had recently defended her master's thesis at the UNAM. In June of 1950 she presented a thesis titled "Sobre cultura femenina" [On Feminine Culture] (published in 2005 as a book with the same title) to a committee that included Zea and a disciple of Antonio Caso, Oswaldo Robles. No *guerra*/war on men, her inaugural foray into women's issues draws mostly on patriarchal German sources and largely subscribes to their positions. Castellanos reasons that men gain transcendence, in the sense of immortality, by perpetuating themselves in cultural products. Women, by contrast, have at their disposal the more direct route to transcendence of motherhood: "maternity lets women satisfy their need to immortalize themselves" (*Sobre cultura femenina* 216). Innately social, the woman "has no love for solitude" (49, quoting Otto Weininger), which conditions a fierce drive for maternity. Women's metaphysical and biological imperatives thus framed lead to the jarring central premise of Castellanos's thesis, developed in its final two chapters, that what little female culture does exist springs from a *sublimation* of the energies that a woman would normally channel into motherhood. A "haven for those who have been shut out of motherhood" (193), the culture such women produce in essence derives from a pathology. Tongue in cheek? I very much doubt it. Although Castellanos highlights not women's alleged penis envy but men's womb envy of the other sex's ability to procreate, she eventually demeaned "Sobre cultura femenina" as wholly antiquated, unsustainable.[11]

Castellanos's fraught relationship with the then heavily Sartrean philosopher Ricardo Guerra Tejada (1927–2007), whom she met in 1949 when he was an adjunct professor at the UNAM, foists philosophical considerations into the pith of her being, subjecting them to the crucible of lived experience. As Castellanos, embroiled with Guerra, viscerally confronts freedom and attachment, she fights her way towards transcendence, in the *existential* sense of a life-project that transcends facticity—for Castellanos, a project that entails reaching a separate peace with authenticity. Castellanos charts the struggle in letters to Guerra from four periods of her life: (1) a few letters written in Chiapas from the summer of 1950; (2) letters that Castellanos penned from Spain, during the year she spent in Madrid on a fellowship at the Instituto Hispánico, 1950–1951; (3) letters from much later, 1966–1967, after she had married Guerra, when Castellanos spent a year teaching in the US; (4) letters that Castellanos wrote in Mexico in 1967 to Guerra, then teaching in Puerto Rico. The three hundred page epistolary corpus now titled *Cartas a Ricardo* keenly documents Castellanos's *Bildung*. Signaling the importance she attached to the letters, Castellanos requested that they be published after her death (Ascencio 9). Guerra (none of whose missives appear in the collection) and Gabriel Guerra Castellanos, their son, honored the request. The letters in *Cartas a Ricardo* are published exactly as she wrote them.

A brief recap of the couple's relationship sets the scene for the existential issues it calls into action.[12] Guerra and Castellanos had their first affair in 1950. She was twenty-five and he twenty-three, yet it was she who lost her virginity to him (*Cartas* 38). After spending only fifteen days romantically and sexually entwined with Guerra, she left for Chiapas and soon boarded a ship for Spain. Castellanos's ardent letters to Guerra sailed across the Atlantic, but he married artist Lilia Carrillo in 1951 and broke up with Castellanos in 1952 (the peculiar chronology will be explained shortly). Guerra and Carrillo divorced in 1957. Meeting again at a party that Usigli's wife had organized, Castellanos and Guerra renewed their affair. They married in 1958. An onslaught of tragedies blighted the early years of their marriage. Suffering miscarriages and the death of a prematurely born daughter, Castellanos plummeted into dependency on drugs, attempted suicide, and psychiatric hospitalization. In an effort to recover apart from Guerra, she accepted visiting professorships at three US universities; the six-year-old Gabriel joined her.

The letters copiously register Castellanos's affective life, to the exclusion of much else. She almost entirely brackets out her illustrious literary achievements and the fame that burgeoned from 1950 to 1967. With her intellectual depths generally reduced to a mere chronicle of external factors, Castellanos consecrates the letters to searing self-analyses, emotional catharses. Elena Poniatowska suggests that a psychiatrist could have a field day with the letters ("Del 'Querido Niño'" 11), for, especially in Spain, Castellanos abjects herself to a staggering degree. On the altar of love, she sacrifices her self. Inventories of her flaws—she denounces herself as a rancorous, useless, ignorant, ugly "monster"—litter the early correspondence. The author of "Sobre cultura femenina" here epitomizes the self-abnegating dimensions of the "eternal feminine." On the other side of the equation, Castellanos idolizes Guerra as marvelous, brilliant, perfect, the height of goodness. She desires wholly to relinquish her subjectivity to him, the master, to be only and exactly what he wishes her to be, evaporating "all my independence, my convictions, and even more so, my opinions" (136). Engrossed in the writings of Saint Teresa of Ávila, Castellanos pledges herself to a kind of hagiographic path of perfection for self-improvement, with Guerra as her tutelary deity. Long after the initial phase of enamorment, as Poniatowska notes (*Ay vida* 71–73), Castellanos persists in self-flagellation and self-abnegation.

Even as she inscribed herself in a venerable Christian narrative of female submission, Castellanos was absorbing French existentialism. Two of her first published book reviews, from 1948, dealt with Sartre's *Nausea* and *No Exit*, respectively.[13] During the year in Spain, Castellanos stretched her sights to Beauvoir, Albert Camus, and Gabriel Marcel, whose works she gamely essayed to read in French (*Cartas* 97; she does not seem to have continued with Camus). When Castellanos traveled to Paris, Mexican ambassador Octavio Paz introduced her to Jean-Paul Sartre and Beauvoir. "I almost dropped dead," she exclaims of their meeting, in a 1951 letter (97). At that time, too, despite her university degrees and master's thesis, Castellanos attributes her interest in philosophy to Guerra: "I'm glad you're a philosopher . . . . Thanks to you, I might even get interested in philosophy" (29). She entreats him to share the key to existentialism that Uranga has reportedly discovered (140). We might therefore assess in Sartrean terms Castellanos's total capitulation to Guerra. Sartre's *Being and Nothingness* (henceforth, *BN*) puts forth the renowned premise that the gaze of the Other holds the secret to the self. The gaze of the Other "makes me be and thereby he possesses me" (364). Castellanos surrenders to the force of the Sartrean look, feeling it bear down upon her: "whenever I'm faced with another person, I put myself in their place, I look at myself as I imagine that person would, and I immediately begin to act in accordance with that person's gaze" (175). The Other's gaze arrests and defines her.

With regard to Castellanos's extravagantly significant Other, what precisely is that gaze? Lacking Guerra's letters, the question cannot be answered in any full-fledged manner. However, Castellanos's letters and Guerra's own work allow us bit by bit to tease out the contours of his gaze, which, in any case, enters the letters most conspicuously as an exasperating absence. The silences of Castellanos's interlocutor play a determining role in their exchanges. Guerra's shortcomings as a correspondent during their entire time together send Castellanos into paroxysms of anxiety. He does not reply to her letters, or he assuages her with the negligible responses like postcards (in fairness, it would have been difficult to match Castellanos's sometimes daily, prolix letters). According to Castellanos, "foolish words and deaf ears seem to be the hallmark of our epistolary relationship" (310). Though she often trembles with elation upon receiving the slightest word from him (e.g., 29, 75, 154), this "Penelope" (147) cajoles, pleads, and guilts Guerra in protracted, futile attempts to decimate his silences.

The backstory of Guerra's letters accounts in no small measure for his egregious inadequacies as a correspondent. Perpetually running off-scene are the love triangles that Guerra sustained while involved with Castellanos. An inveterate philanderer, Guerra led a complex, secretive life that encompassed affairs not just with Lilia Carrillo but also, before and after Castellanos's self-exile to the US, with actress Selma Castillo Beraud. In 1973, in the eminent *Excélsior* of all places, Castellanos disclosed: "I entered into a marriage that was strictly monogamous on my end and totally polygamous on my husband's end" (republished in *El uso* 257). Among many deceptions, Guerra proposes marriage to Castellanos in April 1951 but marries Carrillo that same year, only informing Castellanos of the event after she returns from Spain in 1952. In 1967 Castellanos learns from her son Gabriel that he and her husband have been living with Castillo Beraud. "All of this is implicit in the letters," remarks Poniatowska; she "does not discuss it" outright ("Del 'Querido Niño'" 16). The letters of both parties may interdict overt references to Guerra's cheating, yet the secrets and lies form a palpable subtext of Castellanos's letters to the man she often affectionately addresses as her "rotten" ("infecto") "little boy Guerra."

Simmering with repression, the letters turn into a cliffhanger that for readers conversant with Castellanos's feminism hinges on whether she will come into her own and resolve into the liberated woman her writings advocate.[14] The author does take heartening steps in that direction. By December 1951, having gone back to the still-married Guerra, Castellanos throws off his persistent criticism of her "egotism" and "inveterate severity," her lack of "the most basic generosity" (*Cartas* 178). In January 1952 she shuts down the relationship (181). Castellanos makes great strides towards self-actualization and autonomy in the US after her marriage and breakdown: "I no longer want to feel that I'm guilty, a victim, or anything of the sort, just free and mature and responsible, as I've felt here" (June 1967; 266). Following suit, the final letters display an impressively capable Castellanos. Back in Mexico, with Guerra off teaching in Puerto Rico, Castellanos cares for the couple's two homes and Gabriel, frequently together with Guerra's two children from his previous marriage. Not long after the last letter in the book (December 11, 1967), Castellanos asks Guerra for a divorce. From Jerusalem she proclaims her happiness, saying, "I have in my grasp that new treasure called freedom" (Poniatowska, *Ay vida* 68).

The arc just traced certainly provides ample wherewithal to view the life story that Castellanos conveyed in her letters—which, we remember, she wanted publicly circulated—as a narrative of liberation.[15] Nevertheless, the letters resist being subsumed into an exemplary tale because in them Castellanos only goes out so far. Her profound alliance with Guerra thrusts Castellanos into anguished, vexed contact with the cardinal existential precept of freedom and into de facto dialogue with Hiperión and Sartre. As a philosophical issue, freedom twists into a Gordian knot, the crux, sine qua non, and occlusion of the couple's adultery-ridden relationship. To better appreciate what was at issue, we make a short side trip into Guerra's exposition of Sartrean freedom.

While Castellanos was in Spain, Guerra wrestled with his master's thesis, "Crítica a las teorías de lo mexicano." As an integral part of the thesis work, he immersed himself in Sartre's *BN* and Sartre's great theme, freedom. Hiperión's inaugural year, 1948, witnessed one fruit of Guerra's studies, an article titled "Jean-Paul Sartre, filósofo de la libertad: Intento de aproximación esquemática a una filosofía" [Jean-Paul Sartre, Philosopher of Freedom: Attempt at a Schematic Approach to a Philosophy], published in the UNAM journal *Filosofía y letras*. Translating into Spanish and explicating portions of *BN*, Guerra stages himself as the foremost emissary to Mexico of Sartre, whom he labels the "principal representative of French existentialism" (295). Guerra divides the article's ontological explorations into three parts: (1) "In search of being"; (2) "Human reality"; (3) "The theory of freedom." The dense commentary, obviously aimed at specialists, homes in on many of *BN*'s most grueling, technical concepts. It quickly launches from basic phenomenology and the essential Sartrean "in-itself" versus the "for-itself" into the intricacies of nihilation.

No simple primer of Sartre, the essay does not simply grandstand, either. Rather, we can surmise that Guerra concentrates on the thickest Sartrean propositions because he believes them to be the most productive for Mexican identity. In other words, they help Guerra build an ontological case for freedom that can furnish an auspicious paradigm for Mexico. Hence the thesis of the article: "Man, the 'for-itself,' qua freedom, is the foundation of the world and of values" (299). Hence, as well, Guerra's emphasis on nihilation, construed as how the "for-itself" is free to create the world.[16] The Sartrean situation (Guerra cites Sartre: "I am absolutely free and responsible for my situation" [312]), facticity, commitment, and transcendence-as-project that Guerra goes on to discuss further elucidate the mechanics of freedom. Though, unlike his master's thesis, Guerra's article nowhere mentions Mexican identity or identity discourse per se, his meditations on the past speak vitally to ideas that as we have seen were percolating in the Hyperions' minds. According to Sartre via Guerra, instead of being prisoners of history, we choose our past—in situation, in freedom—and from it freely construct a future. "[T]he fundamental project that is my 'I,'" Guerra writes, again citing Sartre, "absolutely determines the meaning the past can have for me and for *others*" (310; emphasis added). Like Sartre's, Guerra's rebuttal of determinism extends to dismissing the sway of the Freudian unconscious (308), which would undermine Ramos's psychoanalytical interpretation of Mexicans.

Before moving back into *Cartas a Ricardo*, let us consider the potential implications for Castellanos of the article we have just surveyed. If, as I have suggested, Guerra's Sartrean essay ramifies into a latent meditation on Mexican identity, it dramatically amplifies the stakes of freedom. More intimately germane to Castellanos, Guerra has plighted his troth with Sartrean freedom in a language and on grounds at variance with her paramount concerns. The abstract, cerebral essay, replete with Sartre's trademark obscurity, could inspire both reverence and alienation in Castellanos. A stone wall, the essay has no truck with the intersubjective issues that most crucially, well-nigh exclusively, affect her vis-à-vis him. Guerra twice declares (302, 310), almost boastingly, that he eschews Sartre's thinking on human relationships and morality in favor of "the grand themes of his philosophy" (302). Guerra thereby proscribes existentialism from supplying a language for the emotions.[17] Nor does Guerra's denial of psychoanalysis offer much promise for comprehending human interactions. What works for Mexican identity here works against relationships. To the extent that the article's treatment of freedom infiltrated their personal lives, Castellanos could on more than one level rightfully pronounce their correspondence a transaction between "deaf ears."

Under such auspices, freedom becomes the embattled language of love for Castellanos and Guerra. In one of the last letters she reminds him that their "essential conflict has revolved around your lack of freedom" (325). The conflict, we realize by now, has commingled Guerra's philosophical tenets with his personal proclivities, Sartrean with sexual freedom. Someone as well-versed in Sartrean philosophy as Guerra could easily maneuver the subjectivist vagaries of existential ethics into a justification for objectionable behavior. Whether first and foremost Guerra instrumentalizes philosophy to exculpate his infidelities must remain unresolved, but the letters leave little doubt that he employs it as a weapon with which to coerce Castellanos into accepting his polyamory. As we glean from Castellanos's comments cited above, Guerra wraps the personal into the philosophical by deprecating his partner's selfishness and rigidity. He can sound manipulative, controlling: "You once told me," writes Castellanos, "that as long as I refused to abate my egotism, as long as my love wasn't stronger than my egotism, it wouldn't be real love" (120). In the midst of his diatribes on the lover's "project of absorbing the Other," Sartre at least emphasizes that the lover "wants to possess a freedom as a freedom" (*BN* 364, 367); a Sartrean sword in hand, Guerra browbeats Castellanos into forsaking what by her lights amounts to an untroubled freedom.

Castellanos succumbs. At three points in their epistolary relationship, she lays out plans for revamping traditional marriage into the "wide-open house" that Guerra desires and requires. In the first effort, she responds to his marriage proposal of 1951 with a vow to surmount her "horrible egotistic zeal for possession and domination" (113), a self-criticism that ripples through the letters. She has hopes that he, too, will reform and convert their life together into something "morally admirable" (117). Those hopes dashed, she feels, by her mental illness (rather than by Guerra's ongoing liaison with Castillo Beraud), in October of 1966, from the US a Castellanos wracked with guilt sends Guerra a detailed blueprint for their subsequent coexistence. "You've always complained that you don't feel free" (205), she writes, so her plan for their lives in Mexico will cater to his every need for freedom. He will have a room of his own, they will sleep in separate spaces unless he wishes otherwise, his room will always be readied at night with a robe and slippers, he can come and go at will, and he can use the Cuernavaca house for whatever he wishes (205). Castellanos will be not just the angel in the house but also what Saint Teresa's contemporary Fray Luis de León called in his treatise of the same title the "perfect wife," albeit in an unconventional marriage.

Exceptionally unconventional, it turns out, for in addition to a room of his own Castellanos grants Guerra a romantic/sexual life of his own. In thrall to love and to his philosophical rationales, in the name of freedom, Castellanos obliges herself to countenance Guerra's straying. Throughout, accruing into a belabored refrain of the missives, she dwells on his freedom and swears to honor it no matter what anguish the endeavor occasions in her. She who authored the stridently feminist *Eterno* emits such martyrly, moving pleas as: "I have to be able to do it, I have to be able to love you without limiting your freedom, without any restraints or disputes. I'm trying, my love, have patience with me. Love whomever you want. That's fine, since you're free to do so. Just let me love you, let me keep on learning, little by little, to respect you, understand you, complement you. You don't have to love me" (October 1966; 210). Castellanos's resolve to enable (in both senses of the word?) Guerra's autonomy comes to a head at a critical point in her life. Right before leaving the US, she had for once forcefully defended her prerogative to "choose and exercise my freedom" (269). Still, two months later their relationship has fallen back into its habitual patterns, with the notable difference that Castellanos, previously apprehensive of eroticism, is discovering "the delights of sexuality" (274). Aflame with this newly invigorated ardor, her letters to Guerra away in Puerto Rico repeat and embellish the scheme for an open marriage that Castellanos had spelled out in October of 1966. August 1967 finds her stating, "I have also given much thought to the matter of fidelity. By no means do I want to, should I, nor can I ask you to be faithful" (273). In a barrage of similar statements, Castellanos emphatically reaffirms her commitment to Guerra's freedom.

Most noteworthy for our concerns, the letters reframe marriage a third time, in *existential* terms. Castellanos drills down on the bad faith of boxing their relationship into so rigid a mold as traditional marriage (215), an idea she had broached in October 1966. By late summer of 1967 onward, writing to a Guerra teaching Sartre abroad, she emulates her husband's "penchant for abstraction" (282). Castellanos beseeches him to reconceptualize marriage as a free partnership of lovers rather than as an institutionalized union of spouses. "*Apply your Sartrean doctrines*, don't regard me as an object," she urges him, because "I'm not the incarnation of the institution that you reject" (274; emphasis added). In the throes of her recently enlivened sexuality, Castellanos asks him to consider her not as his wife but as his lover and "companion" (273–75). She envisages that the unorthodox arrangement they are jointly devising—he has recommended that she, too, take a lover (274)—will capitalize on their mutual unconventionality (327). It will grow Guerra's extreme test case for freedom into a good faith form of co-being.

Castellanos demonstrates to an equally extreme degree that she will walk the walk. When at the end of the letters it seems that Castillo Beraud is pregnant (ultimately a false alarm), Castellanos musters a heroic gesture. For the first and last time, she deals with the love triangle directly: both women know "that the relationship exists" (324). Castellanos pledges to help however she can, whether by divorcing Guerra and/or subsidizing the Cuernavaca house where he and Castillo Bernaud may live ("Cuernavaca is the place to be free" [325]). Accepting adultery as somehow fundamental to marriage (326), she accepts the role of mistress to which the new circumstances would consign her ("You and I will flirt . . . and occasionally we'll end up two-timing your partner the same way that you two-timed me with other women" [325]), a literalization of her desire to be lover rather than wife.[18] Although in the last letter, as she definitively splits from him, Castellanos acknowledges that her concessions to Guerra's ultimately insatiable appetite for freedom have gone for naught, the final flourish does not eradicate what preceded it. The brunt of *Cartas*'s denouement evidences a kind of zozobra, an unsettled mix of self-effacement and self-assertion. Even as she abases herself, Castellanos brandishes her integrity, the strength of her convictions on freedom. Reconciling the jagged pieces, we might conclude for the moment—to be revisited later—that Castellanos chooses to exercise her own freedom by maintaining Guerra's. She enacts an authentic, if not unreservedly liberating, project.

Castellanos's novel *Rito de iniciación* retools the nexus of Guerra and Sartre into an unequivocal, wish-fulfilling manual of liberation. She drafted the novel at the nadir of her troubles, between 1965–1966. The devastating feedback on the manuscript Castellanos received from friends around 1969 allegedly convinced her to suppress the entire novel except for the chapter titled "Álbum de familia," a satire of women writers that reappears in the book of short stories *Álbum de familia* (1971) and seeds *Eterno*. Eduardo Mejía discovered the typescript of *Rito*, which he published in 1997.[19] Both Mejía and Castellanos arguably made wise decisions. On the one hand, *Rito* fashions what for the Mexican context was an innovative female subjectivity and supplies missing links in Castellanos's philosophical development. On the other, the 370-page novel tends to fall into excess, into ponderous, overwrought minutiae. The two poles coincide in *Rito*, at least for one reason, because the text unmistakably works through and labors to discharge an array of issues that we heard plague Castellanos in the letters. Castellanos doubles back on her youth and overlays it with issues from her present, as she does in the semi-autobiographical novel *Balún-Canán* [The Nine Stars] (1957).

Rito scrutinizes the formative years, or "evolution from the most circumscribed subjectivity," of Cecilia Rojas, a Mexico City university student in the 1940s. A transparent avatar of *R*osario *C*astellanos, *C*ecilia *R*ojas mirrors the author's journey from the provinces to the capital and studies at Mascarones, alongside the fear of sex, insecurities, self-hatred, marginalization as a pariah or "monster," and so on familiar to us from the letters.[20] Excessive but never literarily crude, Castellanos distributes portraits of herself in *Rito* between the young Cecilia and the mature Matilde Casanova, a half-psychotic, half-inspired, renowned writer who, like Castellanos, began her career by working with Indigenous peoples. Castellanos apportions qualities of Ricardo Guerra between Cecilia's two love interests, Enrique early on (e.g., "again and again and again . . . Enrique's hostile silences, his inattentive absences" [16]), then, at the university, Ramón (among many examples, Cecilia says that Ramón analyzes her jealous complaints "systematically, demonstrating that they are baseless, her assertions tenuous and, ultimately, fallacious" [235], which may further round out Guerra's gaze in the letters). Offsetting the book's autobiographical elements, Castellanos pronouncedly inscribes it in two consecrated novelistic forms, the Bildungsroman and Künstlerroman. Cecilia evolves from a flailing innocent dependent upon men into a free, independent woman. She inches towards the triumphant affirmation of her vocation as a writer.

Like *Eterno*, and with the same caveats, today *Rito* can come across as hackneyed, indeed, as downright cloying.[21] More pathbreaking and riveting, again for our concerns, is the as yet unnoticed story this coming of age novel encloses, a tale of Castellanos's *philosophical* coming of age. Her most existentialist novel, *Rito* teems with alienation, gazes, and choices. A forum of French existentialisms, it puts Sartre and Beauvoir into a conversation that shows Castellanos masterfully taking possession of a (of Guerra's?) Sartrean topography and amplifying it with that of Beauvoir. The novel comprises a phenomenal, phenomenally creative, mash-up of Sartre (*BN*; *Nausea*; and *The Age of Reason*, the first novel in his *Roads to Freedom* trilogy) and Beauvoir (*Memoirs of a Dutiful Daughter*, the first volume of her autobiography; the novel, *She Came to Stay* [*L'Invitée*]; and *TSS*). To duly unpack the interfaces would require a chapter unto itself, but we get a fair taste of them in the ending, Cecilia's arrival at freedom.

Rito's overladen, multipart, final movement starts with Cecilia abjuring the gaze of the Other in favor of autonomy. Ramón, who had wheedled Cecilia into sexual relations by outlining a relationship "that does not curtail anyone's freedom" (184), has served as the heroine's tutelary figure and catalyzed her induction into the war of subjectivities (he kindles Cecilia's thirst for "absolute domination, for total power over the other, even the annihilation of the other" [232]). At a farewell party for Ramón, about to depart for a year in Europe, Cecilia decides that she can extricate herself from his sphere (320–22), that she needs no Pygmalions to forge her being. Sergio, a member of their circle, intrudes on Cecilia's musings and puts her decision to the test. He outs himself as gay and offers Cecilia, whom he believes to be lesbian or bisexual, a marriage of convenience that will allow them both freedom from a homophobic society (341).

Castellanos raises the then taboo for Mexico subject of homosexuality in a literary context that had witnessed Sartre's *The Age of Reason* (1945). Sartre's novel ends with Daniel, a gay man, volunteering to marry protagonist Mathieu's pregnant lover, Marcelle. By committing to Marcelle when Mathieu, unable to act, would not, Daniel models choice and freedom ("He is free," thinks Mathieu enviously [394]). Sergio's scheme in *Rito*, conversely, radiates bad faith. He and Cecilia will dissimulate (336) and utilize masks, to the extent that Sergio will condone a love triangle in which Cecilia secretly continues her affair with Ramón (346–47). Cecilia rejects Sergio's proposed charade with umbrage. Much as his plan to reform marriage, a debased iteration of Castellanos's in the letters, might release Cecilia from social imperatives like bearing children, she protests that the two of them would be "colluding in a lie" (344). Sergio's tainted design, we see, entails freedom but not authenticity, a net pragmatism but not pragmatic authenticity.

Castellanos infuses the grand finale of the novel (353ff.) with a burst of Sartrean and Beauvoirian energies. After three hundred turgid pages, Cecilia at long last experiences the epiphany that crowns *Rito* and epitomizes its disposition as a philosophical agora. The epiphany throngs with resonances of Sartre's *Nausea*, paradigmatic novel of awakening as well as redoubtable combination of Bildungsroman and Künstlerroman. Alone, like *Nausea*'s Roquentin, Cecilia enters a city park that cannot help but recall the Bouville park whose chestnut tree led Sartre's protagonist to understand existence. *Rito*'s locale features a "labored root," trees "resurrected, in silence, from the total eclipse they had borne during the day," and the wind that summons Roquentin to adventure (*Rito* 353). The primeval garden of *Rito* brims with portent, which materializes into Cecilia's exultant affirmation of her freedom and self. "Behold, I am free"; "[h]appiness, the happiness of being myself" (354), proclaims Cecilia, glossing these revelations at length. As any reader of *Nausea* will realize, Castellanos has traded Roquentin's belated philosophical awakening to the contingency of existence for Cecilia's similarly delayed personal awakening. *Rito* has put Sartre's epiphanic moment to work for women's/her own freedom.[22] As an attentive reader of *TSS* will realize, *Rito*'s garden also evokes the rush of freedom that according to Beauvoir woman can experience in solitary communion with nature, specifically in the "forest"—an affirmation of self and a unity with "the riches of the world" (*TSS* 376). No less has Castellanos textually implanted in a Sartrean park a parable of woman spurning the treacherous Mitsein that *TSS* thoroughly incriminates.

Castellanos then keys *Rito*'s coda, outside the park, to the Künstlerroman ending of Sartre's novel. With the hope of justifying his existence,

Roquentin abandons the planned historical biography of Rollebon that objectifies the past in order to write a novel as supple as a jazz tune (178). Cecilia, having earlier declined to study history ("dynamism congealed into rigidity" [96]), now one by one casts off the false models of her past (355–60) and wittily sketches out scripts for transposing her life into fiction (365–68). Like the open endings of Sartre's literary works that Castellanos describes as charged with "doubts, delays, unfinished matters" ("Cuando Sartre hace literatura" 23), *Rito* leaves Cecilia on the brink of carrying out her projects, yet "totally happy" as she assumes her freedom (368). At the risk of overplaying *Rito*'s personal wagers, one might see a certain elegant revenge in Castellanos's act of both giving (again, Guerra's?) Sartre the last word and hijacking it for Cecilia's rebirth.

Simone—Jean-Paul—Olga

From beneath its hide-and-seek games, *Rito* attests to Castellanos's growing involvement with Beauvoir's works. Castellanos's *Juicios sumarios* [Summary Judgments] published in 1966 and therefore presumably written in the midst of *Rito*'s genesis, contains four substantial essays on the French author.[23] Referencing all of Beauvoir's works to date (among them, *She Came to Stay* [1943], *Pyrrhus and Cineas* [1944], *Memoirs of a Dutiful Daughter* [1958], and *The Prime of Life* [*La Force de l'âge*; 1960]), *Juicios* confirms that by the time Castellanos wrote not just *Rito* but also the last two sets of letters she had steeped herself in Beauvoir's oeuvre. The first *Juicios* essay, "Simone de Beauvoir o la lucidez" [Simone de Beauvoir: Lucidity], maps out some of Beauvoir's allure for Castellanos. Castellanos culls from Beauvoir's *Memoirs of a Dutiful Daughter* the portrait of a kindred soul: free, strong, and rebellious, raised Catholic but a convinced atheist, a passionate reader with a "theoretical bent" (628–32). Moreover, the essay voices what will be Castellanos's primary affinity for Beauvoir outside the feminism of *TSS*, namely, that Beauvoir countermands Sartre's infamous "Hell is other people." Beauvoir, announces Castellanos, knows that "hell is other people, but also that they are the only road to salvation" (634). For Beauvoir, "the Absolute was therefore happiness, which entailed love, companionship, service to others" (632).

Predicated on the foregoing appeal, in its ordinary and its specialized meaning of intersubjectivity, Beauvoir's work on ethical, compassionate relations with the Other ascends to prominence in Castellanos's repertoire.

I hasten to observe that Castellanos's preoccupation with such matters does not *arise from* Beauvoir. It flows logically from her assertions on women's innate sociability in the pre-Beauvoir "Sobre cultura femenina." More prominently, a burning social consciousness drives Castellanos's novels on Chiapas, *Balún-Canán* and *Oficio de tinieblas* [Tenebrae] (1962). In both texts, President Lázaro Cárdenas's reform program fans existing tensions between Indigenous peoples and the higher social class *caxlanes*. The novels showcase Hegelian "Lord-Bondsman" dramas of incomplete recognition: if Cardenismo represented a possible will-to-recognition between racial or social groups, Castellanos's Chiapas demolishes that potential. Rifts, hatred, will-to-power, and violence persist, seemingly irremediably. The last chapter of *Oficio* thunders: "Always defeat and persecution. Always the master whom neither the most abject obedience nor the most servile humility can placate. Always the whip lashing the submissive back. Always the knife stabbing the least gesture of rebellion" (362). Castellanos's novels convene frictions that several of our authors have brought out—Revueltas's poisonous mestizos, Rulfo's disastrous fiestas, Usigli's ironic rants on socialist education, Zea's disquiet with foreign models, Indigenous religion versus Christianity—and weave them into a litany of lamentations, a roster of wounds with no clear and present remedy.

Beauvoir's work helps Castellanos break the stalemate by furnishing a channel out of unrelenting hatred and power relations into intersubjectivity and altruistic solidarity with one's fellow human beings. Castellanos's migration to Beauvoir carries no small weight for the Latin American philosophical panorama of the times. Whereas many Latin American intellectuals invested in ethics can *sound* like Beauvoir by virtue of magnifying Sartre's lesser concern for his fellow human beings in the early works into a de facto replica of his partner's greater one, Castellanos engages Beauvoir outright. Locally for Mexico but no less momentously, in embracing Beauvoir's ethics Castellanos supplements both Hiperión and Sartre on grounds broader than gender. An examination of the love triangles in Beauvoir's *The Prime of Life* and *She Came to Stay* as they pertain to the Mexican author's writings will flesh out my claims regarding Castellanos's arrival at a more complete recognition of the Other.

Beauvoir's first novel, *She Came to Stay* (henceforth, *SCS*), reached publication the same year as Sartre's *BN*, 1943. *SCS* bodies into fiction the experiment that Beauvoir and Sartre performed in real life, which she discusses in the second volume of her memoirs, *The Prime of Life* (1960). Marriage, writes Beauvoir, "offended our principles" (*Prime* 66); further,

"Sartre was not inclined to be monogamous by nature" (23–24). To uphold "freedom," their own "most passionately held conviction" (110), Sartre and Beauvoir settled on a "morganatic" modus operandi (21). "What *we* have," Beauvoir famously reports Sartre as stating, "is an *essential* love; but it is a good idea for us also to experience *contingent* love affairs" (24). Accordingly, in what became an acute test case of freedom, Sartre and Beauvoir welcomed Olga Kosakievicz, originally Beauvoir's student at a Rouen lycée, into their emotional (but, Beauvoir disingenuously insists, not sexual) life in Paris. *Prime* recounts the harrowing vicissitudes that the love triangle underwent as Sartre, architect of the affair, grew more and more possessive of Kosakievicz, Kosakievicz more deranged, Beauvoir more distressed by the experiment. Though the arrangement eventually failed, the two women preserved their friendship for decades.[24]

While still actively involved in the dangerous triangular liaison Beauvoir imported it, thinly veiled, into *SCS*, written between 1938 and 1941. There, novelist Françoise Miquel stands in for Beauvoir, theater director Pierre Labrousse for Sartre, and the unbalanced young Xavière Pagès for Kosakievicz. Françoise and Pierre, predominantly of one mind on the morganatic scheme and each a willing participant in it, form an implausible five-year covenant of exclusivity with Xavière. Beauvoir's four hundred page novel, likely a model for the exorbitantly granular *Rito*, tracks every permutation and emotional nuance of the always metamorphosing triangle, destabilized by a center that would not hold. What rescues the, for Beauvoir "cathartic" (*Prime* 270), *SCS* is its philosophical heft. Beauvoir parlays the Simone—Jean-Paul—Olga transactions into a sweeping philosophical disquisition on *la conscience d'autrui*, awareness of the Other.

To wit, *SCS* commences with an epigraph from Hegel, "Each consciousness pursues the death of the other," and proceeds to impart a literally lethal mis en scène of the war of subjectivities. The trio's would-be joyful practice of freedom degenerates into sadomasochism as *SCS* runs through the gamut of moves that Sartre describes in the chapters on "being-for-others" of *BN* (Barnes 129). For instance, we recall from chapter 2 Sartre's synoptic "While I attempt to free myself from the hold of the Other, the Other is trying to free himself from mine; while I seek to enslave the Other, the Other seeks to enslave me" (*BN* 364). Heightening the dramatic quotient of the Sartrean scenario, Beauvoir has her novel's infuriatingly willful Xavière emblematize an unconquerable, all-conquering freedom. Pierre, seeking to dominate Xavière, falls prey to a "mania" for victory, acts like a "madman" (166, 303). It is to Françoise, nonetheless, that the young woman poses the greatest existential threat. Françoise feels Xavière's "sovereign reality" devour her freedom: "The entire universe was engulfed in it, and Françoise, forever excluded from the world, was herself dissolved in this void" (291). Awakening to a dire, consummate awareness of the Other's gaze, Françoise realizes that "she would have to choose herself" (291). Françoise's Bildung surges to an astounding climax in which she kills the freedom-engulfing Xavière—a heinous outcome, no doubt, but one totally consistent with the preeminence of freedom and the precarious ethics ingrained in early Sartrean existentialism.

Beauvoir's *SCS*, in sum, manifestly traverses Sartrean terrain. Yet the simultaneous genesis of *SCS* with *BN*, which Beauvoir read in draft form, affords her an opportunity to incorporate *and* contest Sartre's thinking on relations with Others. A trained eye can therefore unearth from the horrorscape of *SCS* Beauvoir's seminal attempts to release being-with-others from its shackles. *SCS* sets Pierre and Françoise at philosophical odds in a conversation on the arrangement with Xavière. Pierre: "What surprises me, is that you should be affected in such a concrete manner by a metaphysical problem." Françoise: "But it is something concrete . . . . to me, an idea is not a question of theory. It can be tested or, if it remains theoretical, it has no value" (301). The gap between the two characters' positions widens and transfigures relations with the Other, for over against power-mongering, Françoise posits a model of reciprocity, friendship. In friendships, she says, each person "renounces his pre-eminence" (302) and respects the Other's freedom. Françoise achieves a relationship of this sort, mingling it with romantic love, in a dalliance with the playwright Gerbert near the novel's close. She remarks to Gerbert, "it's wonderful for us to love one another so much and still remain free" (391). Françoise and Pierre's original relationship also exemplified reciprocity, albeit complacently. The love triangles disrupt the couple's self-satisfied equilibrium, and their companionate love survives the trials, which imbue it with authenticity. While the Olga experiment that Pierre, theorist and theater director, had commandeered disintegrates, were it not for the Sartrean pressures that induce Françoise to commit a metaphysically freighted murder, she would have emerged wholly triumphant.

Through Françoise, it is clear, Beauvoir begins to take ownership of a different form of Mitsein: not Heidegger's ontological "being-with-others," Sartre's tenuous "we," or his power-mongering, but concrete reciprocity, the loving relationship of equals and ethical responsibility to an Other. Sartre's contemporaneous *Notebooks* were already beginning to envision a more benign intersubjectivity; yet *No Exit*, which Castellanos reviewed, purveys an unregenerate Mitsein.[25] A buoyant, humanistic Mitsein does thread its way into *The Second Sex* with such inspirational axioms as: "Authentic love must be founded on reciprocal recognition of two freedoms . . . . For each of them, love would be the revelation of self through the gift of the self and the enrichment of the universe" (706). Amid the strained love triangles of *SCS*, Beauvoir debuts that Mitsein.

Saturated with issues that strike Castellanos at her core, *She Came to Stay* transfixed the Mexican author. All of Castellanos's essays on Beauvoir besides "Simone de Beauvoir o la lucidez" deal with the novel's love triangle and matters related to it. Philosopher that she was, despite the triangle's intimate pertinence to her circumstances, Castellanos reads it impersonally, as an existentialist and feminist. Beauvoir's plans to reform marriage, a "life project" (*Juicios* 657), rate Castellanos's closest attention. She extols Beauvoir and Sartre's unconventional partnership as a perfect marriage of minds and a repudiation of social norms. Castellanos pays special homage to the raison d'être of the couple's triangular arrangements, their ethical, philosophical motivations. With respect to Beauvoir's memoir, she writes: "Olga, Simone, and Sartre resolved to form a trio that would exclude jealousy, partiality, possessiveness, rivalries. It would be a relationship based on respect for the other, companionship without reservation, and a caring friendship" (641). Castellanos applauds *SCS*'s trio for its attempts to negotiate the difficult balance between freedom and fidelity (656).[26]

Castellanos also catches the malignancies of Sartrean relations with the Other. The brutal war of consciousness that *SCS*'s epigraph announces does not escape her scrutiny or deploring comment (641). Hard hit by the novel's ending, Castellanos berates it for engraving Françoise in readers' minds as an assassin (641–42). Nor do Beauvoir and Sartre's divergent stances on being-with-others go unnoticed. In addition to the potent comments in defiance of "Hell is other people" quoted above, Castellanos adduces Sartre's "cold bloodedness" (636), the fixation on abstract thinking that Françoise and Pierre had debated. The intersubjectivity that Beauvoir and Sartre achieve in their relationship nonetheless earns Castellanos's unmitigated admiration. Above all, she praises what Sharon Larisch calls their "*ethical* erotic relationship" (112), which has endured for thirty years, withstood social opprobrium, and let Beauvoir flourish intellectually and personally.

"Apply your Sartrean doctrines," Castellanos had entreated Guerra in the letters (274), urging him to rethink their marriage. How do Castellanos's triangular dilemmas, intensely congruent with those of Simone-Françoise, look when we apply *Beauvoir's* "doctrines" to them? Quite different, I believe.

As Castellanos's guiding light, Beauvoir supplies an escape from the Sartrean prison house, with its dead-end interactions and the assaults on his partner's freedom that the Sartrean Guerra exacted.

Consubstantially, Beauvoir's rehabilitated Mitsein heightens the philosophical stakes of an open marriage, ennobling them. Seen through a Beauvoirian lens, a marriage that admits a third Other becomes more of an ethical opportunity than a site of abjection. Castellanos matches the fungibility between life and fiction in Beauvoir's works by taking the philosophical quest deep into her own existence, as her project. Decoupling Beauvoir and Sartre, laying claim to some independence from Sartre, Castellanos conceives for herself and Guerra a "wide-open house," physical and figurative, that an ethical subject can inhabit. One need not, however, hold with polyamory or open marriage to accept the altruism that Castellanos gleans from them. In an analysis of Robert Musil's character Ulrich, she says that although love "is a moral phenomenon, we must remember that morality is not only a series of commandments and prohibitions . . . . but an attitude of accepting the world and people in their plenitude" (*Juicios* 682). It stands to reason, then, that Castellanos would rebuke *SCS*'s deadly Sartrean ending and strive in her own life to maintain ethical relationships that surpass it.

Castellanos—Beauvoir—Sartre

In *The Prime of Life*, Beauvoir herself roundly critiques the finale of *She Came to Stay* for defaulting on human coexistence (270). Beauvoir's critique betokens the expanded consciousness that *Prime* intently chronicles. At the decades' remove that lets Beauvoir endow her life with a crisp story-shape, *Prime* recounts the transformation she underwent between 1929 and 1944 from self-absorption to social engagement. Beauvoir plots *Prime* as a conversion tale in which World War II jostled her from an "individualistic, antihumanist," "autonomous and self-sufficient project" (285, 296) such as *SCS* dramatizes into a wide compass that linked her "every nerve . . . to each and every other individual" (295). Hence the epigraph from Dostoevsky of her 1945 novel *The Blood of Others*, "Each of us is responsible for everything and to every human being," as well as the novel's central female character Hélène, who has learned "the meaning of solidarity" (*Prime* 429). Beauvoir's horizons irreversibly enlarged, she hereafter champions solidarity with the *collective* Other. For Castellanos's part, in contrasting *Prime* with *SCS* she registers Beauvoir's transition to what above I called a freedom of praxis: "Simone de Beauvoir increasingly opened herself to the world, to solidarity with everyone, no matter what their location or race" (*Juicios* 634). This insight, a lever for Castellanos's full-grown relinquishing of "coupledom as a model and opening onto society at large," caps her engagement with French existentialism. Triangles, affective and philosophical, now come to a head in the constellation of Castellanos—Beauvoir—Sartre, *inflected towards Beauvoir and her broad social compass.*

Castellanos's literary works and essays persistently strike certain stock existential chords that are generally, and appropriately, identified with Sartre but that Beauvoir in fact shares. They include themes upon which we have touched: the situation, authenticity, the gaze, choice, and, almost needless to reiterate, freedom.[27] Each and every one of them has an obvious connection to Castellanos's overriding preoccupation with alterity. Maureen Ahern, editor of *A Rosario Castellanos Reader*, summarizes that the "exploration of the other, whether that other be woman, indigenous culture, language, silence, or writing itself" underlies "all [of Castellanos's] verse and prose" ("Reading" 8). Though a treatment of Castellanos's verse lies beyond my scope, the programmatic "Poesía no eres tú" [You Are Not Poetry] (1972; *En la tierra de en medio*, in *Obras II* 98–99) so encapsulates her solidarity with Beauvoir's altruism that it warrants a brief reading. Castellanos chose *Poesía no eres tú* as the title for her collected poetry (1972); the author's introduction to the volume, republished in *Mujer que sabe latín*, contains the statement on her personal trajectory from a singular to a collective consciousness that I have sought to orchestrate herein. The poem "Poesía no eres tú" reflects on an ideal couple, profoundly united and profoundly receptive to the world. They walk together, "las dos cabezas juntas, pero no contemplándose / (para no convertir a nadie en un espejo)" [their two heads together, but not looking at each other, so as not to make anyone into a mirror]. Forswearing the objectifying gaze, they look straight ahead "hacia el otro," "mediador, juez, equilibrio / entre opuestos;" "la mudez que pide voz" [towards the other; mediator, judge, balance of opposites; muteness that asks for a voice]. The binding of the pair to something larger than themselves not only contravenes the Sartrean gaze, it also purposefully breaches Gustavo Adolfo Bécquer's Romantic "Poesía eres tú" [You Are Poetry], which locates poetry solely in the beloved. Castellanos has panned from a discrete to a limitless intersubjectivity. She accordingly seals her poem with a fervent credo worthy of César Vallejo: "El otro. Con el otro / la humanidad, el diálogo, la poesía, comienzan" [The other. With the other, humanity, dialogue, and poetry begin].[28]

An impactful about-face from the "Lord-Bondsman" quagmire of the novels on Chiapas, the Beauvoir-inflected outlook that "Poesía no eres tú" distills to its essence infiltrates the novel, *Rito*, and even the farce, *Eterno*. In an autobiographical cameo of the novel, Castellanos ascribes social impulses to Matilde Casanova. Like Castellanos herself, Matilde forsakes an isolating absorption in poetry to work with Indigenous peoples, which taught her the "moral rule" of "considering the other," whom "only love renders visible" to her (*Rito* 277). *Eterno* leads up to a communitarian gesture that challenges Mexican women to devise their own brand of feminism. When her students balk at the North American feminism they consider rather extreme for their country, Lupita outlines paths for a feminism tailored to a Mexican context (193). Here Castellanos seizes on another early divide between Sartre and Beauvoir. As befits a situationally oriented feminist, Beauvoir opposed Sartre's initial belief in radical freedom—inviolable freedom no matter what the circumstances—with an awareness that contexts limit choices.[29] Castellanos, too, acknowledges the constraints a situation places on freedom. Freedom, she stresses, can only be "enacted within specific circumstances" (*Juicios* 627). With an eye to the dynamics of the Mexican situation, a student in *Eterno* then asks: "Isn't there a third way for those of us who belong to the Third World?" (*356*; 193). The curtain falls on Lupita as she bids farewell to the hair salon and tosses the challenge out to her community, the play's audience and readers. *Eterno*'s unresolved, Usiglian ending convokes women's solidarity with their Dasein and solidarity amongst women, the absence of which *TSS* decried.

All the more does solidarity with a Beauvoirian agenda pervade Castellanos's essays, venue of preponderance for Mexican identity discourse. According to Mexican critic Joaquín Blanco, resentful of the Mexican intelligentsia that denied a feminist her due, Castellanos courted fame by styling herself as the Beauvoir of her country (qtd. in Poniatowska, *Ay vida* 128). Blanco's assertion, if we can put aside its jaundice, finds sustenance in Castellanos's essays. An article she wrote for *Excélsior* in 1964, "Elogio de la amistad" [In Praise of Friendship], tenders a paean to friendship reminiscent of Beauvoir's *SCS* and *Pyrrhus and Cineas*. The article lauds friendship's capacity to make the Other our neighbor, which can extend to fraternity with all humankind (*El uso* 71–74). In one of the *Juicios* essays on Beauvoir, Castellanos broadcasts the inspirational side of *TSS*'s Mitsein, reminding her readers that Beauvoir espouses "a more just and more egalitarian treatment of all constitutents of the human race" (634). Throughout *Juicios*, in fact, Castellanos lends her knowledge as a literary comparatist to an existentialist campaign with Beauvoirian hues. *Juicios* performs the tour de force of applying an existentialist optic to a spectrum of often non-existentialist European and Latin American writers. The collection scans authors as remote from existentialism as Jorge Luis Borges, Pierre Choderlos de Laclos, Sor Juana, Saint Teresa, and Virginia Woolf for what their works have to say about solidarity, the Other, and similar matters. Keeping faith with the writer's "inescapable responsibility" to society and the power of literature to serve as "an apt instrument . . . for achieving the ideals of freedom and justice, and for overcoming ignorance" (*Juicios* 502) that arguably motivates Castellanos to act as a cultural clearing house, *Juicios* accomplishes a signal pedagogical mission. It teaches the Mexican public to read existentially, and to read existentially beyond Sartre.

Indeed, when we survey Castellanos's essays from *Juicios* (and thus *Rito*) onward, Sartre *per se* turns out to have a scant presence in them. I indicated above that Castellanos mobilizes stock, diffuse topics of French existentialism. Largely folding Sartre into the warp and woof of existentialism or relegating him to incidental mentions, Castellanos's essays show no cognizance of post-*BN* developments in his ethics. Her final, as far as I can tell, word on Sartre, in the 1973 "Cuando Sartre hace literatura" [When Sartre Writes Literature], concretizes him as precisely that, a writer of literature focused on freedom, the situation, and action (23–24). She refers to Sartre's works of fiction up to 1949 and to *The Words* (1960), Sartre's autobiography of his formative years. Fossilized and vestigial, Sartre has nearly fallen off Castellanos's map.

Pulling free from Sartre's bleak picture of human relations, Castellanos's ethical cosmopolitanism offers object lessons to an identity discourse like *El laberinto de la soledad* that blazons Mexican solitude. If Castellanos's most explicit contribution to Mexican identity discourse reproaches the myth of Mexicans' sadness, Beauvoirian existentialism gives her a formidable weapon with which to combat the sorry condition that Paz imputes to his compatriots in "Máscaras mexicanas": all the Mexican attitudes he has described, "however different their sources, testify to the 'closed' nature of our reactions to the world around us or to our fellow men" (*40*; 175). We remember that on Paz's interpretation the historically damaged, hermetically sealed Mexican recoils from others, retreats into protective solitude. Committed as she is to intersubjectivity and the collectivity, Castellanos pushes back against endemic Mexican alienation.

She also redefines solitude as a *disponibilité* compatible with Gabriel Marcel's thinking. Castellanos writes in an essay on Mexican poet José

Gorostiza: "Solitude, yes, but not isolation, nor the closed doors of egotism, ignorance, and contempt; rather, availability [disponibilidad] to life's essentials" (*Juicios* 731–32). Castellanos construes solitude existentially, as the space in which writers incubate ideas at liberty and authentically, untethered from social dictates (*Juicios* 732–33). That in honoring their "inescapable responsibility" to society (*Juicios* 502) writers then set those ideas into circulation reimagines solitude as a productive way station, a conduit to the collectivity. At the close of *Rito* Cecilia envisages her future as a "tunnel" towards freedom, "an internal imperative that takes me as its instrument" (363); thanks in no small part to her interactions with Beauvoir, the Mexican author has transformed the internal into the external, the tunnel into an agora. She has, one might say, succeeded in exchanging Sábato's lonely Sartrean tunnel for Cortázar's fraternal one (man "*knows* that he can be more, be himself and an other, be in-the-other, escape solipsism" [*Obra crítica*, 112]). In so doing, the Castellanos who has surmounted mourning, melancholia, and seemingly insuperable tensions aligns Mexico with preeminent currents of Latin American existentialism.

Coda: Mexican Mitsein

Whereas at the outset of this chapter we heard *Rito*'s protagonist declare that she has been "turned into an agora, a battlefield, a no one's land," we now realize that Castellanos's no one's land comes into rhythm with the heartbeat of Mexican existentialism, literary and philosophical. Far from a no one's land, Castellanos's chosen territory pulsates with the altruistic ethos that Mexican existentialists had adapted from Antonio Caso. Their and her "being-with-others," bound up in the Golden Rule and community, is a Mexican Mitsein, a being-there that is an ethical being-with. When Castellanos, after Hiperión disbanded, advocates for intersubjectivity and solidarity with the Other, she susses out and expands the group's beneficial Mexicanizing of existentialism, as had the creative writers whose texts we have visited. Unlike Castellanos, these many free thinkers—"broad courtyards" and "wide-open houses"—charted their own path, without a Beauvoir to lean on or into. One and all, they go a long way towards fulfilling Uranga's appeal for a "wide-open plaza, an all-embracing space for humanity in its plenitude" (*Análisis* 55).

Notes

Chapter One

1. When titles of works in Portuguese and French differ greatly from their published English translations, I provide the published English title as well.

2. To do its job, this chapter—and indeed, parts of the entire book—rehearses some material that will be familiar to experts in the fields at issue. I beg such readers' indulgence with foundational information, whose purpose is to render the book accessible and meaningful to the host of constituencies it seeks to engage.

3. Throughout the book, I do not interfere with the generic/exclusive "man" nor with other similarly problematic language that appears in the original texts. My own writing, though, employs a more gender-inclusive language.

4. For an introduction to the resurgence of existentialism in post-continental philosophy, see Maldonado-Torres; also see Gratton's summary of contestations and reaffirmations of Sartre in recent years.

5. Astrada expounds on the humanism of freedom in *Ser, humanismo, "existencialismo"* [Being, Humanism, Existentialism] (1949), *La revolución existencialista* (1952), and *Existencialismo y crisis de la filosofía* (1963). On Astrada's trajectory as a whole and for bibliography, see David's massive *Carlos Astrada, la filosofía argentina*.

6. Along with Astrada, others whom Heidegger had trained such as the Peruvian Alberto Wagner de Reyna returned to Spanish America in the 1930s. They invigorated study of Heidegger and phenomenologist Edmund Husserl, portions of whose work were then being published in Spanish by the Argentine journal *Sur* and Ortega y Gasset's *Revista de Occidente*. Existentialism began to catch on in Brazil with the publication of Christian existentialist Eurialo Canabrava's *Seis temas do espíritu moderno* (1942). See Jalif de Bertranou for a synopsis of Latin American existentialist philosophers in various countries.

7. For an overview of Latin American positivism and antipositivism, see Stabb's old but authoritative powerhouse of a book.

8. However, as the reference to Getúlio Vargas's regime suggests, antipositivism did not gain a strong foothold in Brazil, where positivism and positivists

were associated with the founding of the Brazilian Republic. The positivist motto "Ordem e progresso" still appears on the Brazilian flag.

9. See Toledo's essay for a valuable treatment of Latin American Christian existentialism, its notable practitioners, and the influence of Gabriel Marcel and Max Scheler (whom we meet later in this book).

10. Toledo states: "The centrality of community in the development of the person in the Catholic heritage explains the alternative route of Latin American existentialism compared to some of the more solipsistic European versions" (223). As should be evident, I do not use "transvaluation" in the Nietzschean sense of transcending—that is, leaving behind—life-denying Christian values. I do, instead, have much in mind Bellos's fine, pertinent observations on Camus: "There's no point doubting Camus's agnosticism. At the same time, we do have to recognize that Camus's fiction is built on premises and couched in language that constantly imply the presence, not the absence, of Christian discourse and of its religious presuppositions. This is not just because of Camus's initial training in Christian theology, in his master's thesis on St Augustine; it is also because it spoke eloquently to Camus's first audience, large sections of which were still, in mid-twentieth century, straining to free themselves from the mental and moral authority of the church" (xx).

11. The second part of Hurtado's *Dialéctica del naufragio* [Dialectics of a Shipwreck] (2016), a book that my next chapter discusses, joins forces with Habermas's postsecularism and defines it as follows: "The essays of the book's second part are inscribed in the philosophical current known as *postsecularism*. This intellectual movement maintains that it behooves the West to imbue the structures of secularism with the values of the Judeo-Christian traditions" (12); "I consider my work to form part of a larger project, perhaps one of the most urgent tasks of present-day philosophy: to restore the eroded meaning of the keywords of our civilization" (13). I should note that, apart from brief discussions of postsecularism and a few other matters, in order to rein in what could have been too vast a territory for a single book, I generally *do not examine recent outgrowths of existentialism*. Had I done so, the work of Emmanual Levinas, for example, would have been an apt place to go.

12. As Aníbal González keenly notes, "in a small but significant number of [Latin American] narratives from the 1930s until after World War II, one finds an overt appropriation of ideas and motifs associated with religion and theology and an attempt to link them organically . . . to the novel's discourse about the nation" (27); further, "with all of them the incorporation of religious elements in a secular key is a fundamental narrative resource" (83).

13. When Mallea dropped out of law school in Buenos Aires he became involved with a literary magazine, the *Revista de América*, that espoused Rodó's vision of Latin America (Lewald 23). Further, there is a notable congruence between *Ariel*'s parable of the "interior kingdom," an inner preserve of autochthonous values, and Mallea's "invisible Argentina."

14. From a wider perspective, though, Latin American existentialist and fantastic literatures have several deep structures in common. Both test limits, interrogate givens and norms, heighten the role of the reader, and flout the sovereignty of reason—in sum, valorize freedom.

15. We may think of the pronouncement in Borges's "El milagro secreto" [The Secret Miracle]: "Hladík praised the verse form, because it makes it impossible for spectators to lose sight of irreality, an essential principle of art" (*Obras* 510).

16. "El escritor argentino y la tradición" was first published 1953. It was republished in the journal *Sur* in 1955 and in the second edition of Borges's *Discusión* in 1957. For more details, see Balderston's article on versions of the essay.

17. Aside from Unamuno, whom I discuss in chapter 3, Spanish literary existentialism appears not to have had a great influence on Mexican literature. Interestingly, Marías's book contends that French existentialism hardly impacted Spain because Spain already possessed its own existentialism in the prior form of Unamuno and Ortega y Gasset. Regardless of this explanation, it comes as little surprise that, in a postcolonial context, Mexican existentialists would turn away from Spanish literature.

18. Sartre and Bergson link up here around freedom. As Bergson wrote in *Time and Free Will*: "To act freely is to recover possession of oneself, and to get back into pure duration" (231–32).

19. For instance, Johnny calls himself "a poor devil with more plagues under my skin than the devil himself" (243), and the "weird blotches" on Johnny's legs inspire "infinite disgust" in Bruno (228). Cortázar's much earlier, more or less fantastic story, "Las puertas del cielo" [The Gates of Heaven] (*Bestiario*, 1951) exquisitely echoes part 4, ch. 6, of Camus's *The Plague* when it portrays a moment of communion between Mauro and Marcelo, prototypes for Johnny and Bruno.

20. Latin American existentialist philosophy has fared considerably better; to wit, the studies by David, Gracia, Jalif de Bertranou, Sánchez, Sánchez and Sanchez, Stabb, and Toledo I list in "Works Cited."

21. In the penultimate paragraph of Onetti's novella we read: "Everything is useless and one must at least have the courage not to use pretexts. I would have like to pin the night onto paper like a great nocturnal butterfly. Instead, it was night that lifted me into its waters like the livid body of a dead man and drags me through cold, vague foam, inexorably, down with it" (45–46).

22. Pérez Monfort situates Fuentes in the Medio Siglo group of the 1950s. According to Pérez Monfort, the group included Víctor Flores Olea, Sergio Pitol, Arturo González Cosío, Genaro Vázquez Colmenares, Carlos Monsiváis, Juan Bañuelos, Salvador Elizondo, and Javier Wimer Zambrano (on Mexican women writers of the 1950s, see my last chapter). They, too, strike at the Revolution and its aftermath (xvi–vii). Castellanos calls attention to the other pole of the mid-twentieth-century literary landscape, José Juan Arreola's fantastic literature. She writes in 1966: "Until

very recently, it was impossible to read a page of narrative literature without immediately asking oneself which of the two adversaries it had taken as a model: Juan Rulfo or Juan Arreola" (*Juicios sumarios*, in *Obras II* 491).

23. Alive to the grip of religion on Mexico, Yáñez's novel does put forth a modernizing program for the Church through the young priest, Abundio Reyes. Yáñez, we will later see, was also involved with the existentialist Grupo Hiperión.

24. A prominent omission that ensues from my criteria is Fuentes's much-studied, overtly existentialist *La muerte de Artemio Cruz*.

25. Domínguez Michael, too, describes the Revolution as "the somewhat clandestine partner of the philosophy of lo mexicano" (206).

26. According to Bartra's brilliant revisionist study, Mexican identity discourse represents the country as an axolotl, a larval salamander whose development ceases before the creature reaches full maturity. Bartra discerns in identity treatises a typology of the Mexican that turns on melancholy, idleness, fatalism, inferiority, violence, sentimentalism, resentment, and evasion (192). All of this, Bartra argues, clearly meets the needs of the state's self-legitimation. For a useful summary of diagnostic Mexican identity treatises from 1901 onward, see Lipp, chs. 1–2; Ochoa's excellent book considers the diagnostic, productive aspects of failure in Mexican identity discourse.

27. Ramos's allies, including Juan Hernández Luna, Adela Palacios, and Rubén Salazar Mallén, accused Paz of plagiarizing *Perfil* (Domínguez Michael 203); Emilio Carballo's negative review of *Laberinto* criticized its author for insufficiently acknowledging Ramos's work (Santí 58).

28. In the second (1957) and subsequent editions of *Laberinto*, Paz makes this argument in the last paragraph of ch. 8. In the first edition of *Laberinto* (1950), ch. 8 concluded the entire book. On the numerous editions and revisions of *Laberinto*, see Hurtado, "Octavio Paz," and Santí (55–56). The Santí edition of *Laberinto* from which I cite is based on the 1957 edition.

29. Sánchez Prado states that "the 1940s and 1950s cannot be studied separately," among various reasons because the Hyperions' teacher José Gaos "introduced a series of themes that literature and philosophy developed in parallel" (*Naciones* 140). Sánchez Prado, concerned with the hegemonic and anti-hegemonic "discourses of the nation" (*Naciones* 140), mostly follows through on his claims by examining several works by Paz. My next chapter has much to say about Gaos.

30. I thank my colleague Kenneth Haynes for helping me to crystallize this formulation. On other migrations of existentialism, their commonalities and differences, see Judaken's introduction to *Situating Existentialism: Key Texts in Context*. The pathbreaking edited collection has essays on existentialism in France, Germany, the Hispanic worlds, Great Britain, Russia, and the US. With regard to Brazil, see Romano.

31. As will be discussed later, Beauvoir's *Pyrrhus and Cineas* (1944; in *Philosophical Writings*) transcends Sartre's jaundiced picture of human relations

and defends generosity, affirmation of the other; Carlos Sánchez refers to Uranga's "generosity-narrative" (*Contingency* 128).

Chapter Two

1. When I cite Uranga's *Análisis*, I am citing Hurtado's 2013 edition, *Análisis del ser del mexicano y otros escritos sobre la filosofía de lo mexicano (1949–1952)*. Hurtado's edition helpfully contains several hard to obtain texts by Uranga with which my chapter deals (but not all of them): the book, *Analisis del ser del mexicano per se* (33–109); "Ensayo de una ontología del mexicano" (113–25); "Optimismo y pesimismo del mexicano" (147–61); "Dos existencialismos" (173–77). When no other title is specified, references are to the book *Analisis del ser del mexicano* per se. Translations of Uranga are mine, but readers will certainly profit from Carlos Sánchez's English version of Uranga, *Emilio Uranga's Analysis of Mexican Being: A Translation and Critical Introduction*.

2. Uranga observed of Gaos in 1952: "He has geared all his activity to the service of Mexico, in a cordial, visceral spirit of 'compatriotism' " (*Algo más*). Other notable Spanish philosophers who took refuge in Mexico included Eduardo Nicol, José Gallegos Rocafull, Juan David García Bacca, Joaquín Xirau, and María Zambrano.

3. The same years that Zea submitted his MA and doctoral theses, they were published as books: *El positivismo en México* (1943) and *Apogeo y decadencia del positivismo en México* (1944), respectively.

4. Spanish exiles Juan David García Bacca and Eduardo Nicol were also teaching Heidegger in Mexico at the time.

5. Gaos here again teams up with Ortega y Gasset. As Zea mentions: "Some years ago, the Spanish philosopher José Ortega y Gasset had acutely disputed European culture's pretensions to universality" (*Conciencia* 8, with reference to the Spanish philosopher's *Las Atlántidas*, 1924).

6. The Hyperions rejected Gaos on other fronts. In 1958 Hyperions Guerra, Uranga, and Villoro, as well as Alejandro Rossi, having returned from their studies in Europe, regrouped in a private seminar with Gaos on modern philosophy. Published in 2012 as *Filosofía y vocación: Seminario de filosofía moderna de José Gaos*, the essays and commentaries on a philosophical vocation that the seminar generated contain harsh attacks on Gaos, especially his personalismo.

7. On Gaos's critiques of Hiperión, see Uranga's "Advertencia de Gaos" [Gaos's Reprimands] in *Análisis* 232–40. In *Análisis de ser del mexicano* per se, Uranga recounts Gaos's comment that formulating "a Mexican ontology was, in his opinion, impossible; the most one could do is to speak of a Mexican *ontics*" (78).

8. *La filosofía de lo mexicano* (1960) by Abelardo Villegas, Zea's student, treats the paradox of Mexican circumstancialismo: how to formulate an ontology of the

Mexican that also resonates with the universal. Only he himself, Villegas says, has been able to resolve the paradox (rather confusedly, I believe).

9. In "White Mythology: Metaphor in the Text of Philosophy," Derrida writes: "Metaphysics—the white mythology which reassembles and reflects the culture of the West: the white man takes his own mythology, Indo-European mythology, his own *logos*, that is the *mythos* of his idiom, for the universal form of that he must still wish to call Reason" (213). Young's *White Mythologies: Writing History and the West* (1990) placed contestation of Western logocentrism front and center in postcolonial theory.

10. It stands to reason that Zea would be the spokesperson for Hiperión. Already well established, Zea had been teaching the philosophy of history at the UNAM since 1944 and had gained renown for his work on positivism. He served as Secretario General de la Facultad de Filosofía y Letras between 1948 and 1953, the years of Hiperión's activities. Zea, I note, tended to reiterate not only Hiperión's ideas but also his own. Extremely prolific, he was also extremely repetitive. Thus, *Conciencia* also synthesizes the text by Zea we join in chapter 4, *Dos etapas del pensamiento en Hispanoamérica: Del romanticismo al positivismo* [Two Stages of Spanish-American Thought: From Romanticism to Positivism] (1949). As Lipp benevolently observes: "Many of [Zea's] works represent an amplification of themes dealt with in earlier volumes, and an attempt to unify them into a single, comprehensive whole" (60).

11. Similarly, Valero Pie remarks that Gaos taught Heidegger "with an eye to Mexico," emphasizing the potentially useful rather than the pessimistic aspects of his work (119).

12. Hurtado writes: "It is possible that if today we no longer concern ourselves with lo mexicano in the same ways as fifty years ago, or if we do not find the matter quite so pressing, it is because somehow—deliberately or unintentionally—Hiperión helped dissipate or alleviate lo mexicano" ("Introducción" xxxiv).

13. I thank Carlos Sánchez for this insight and for guiding me through Uranga's thorny concept of insufficiency via truly generous personal communications. Any anomalous interpretations are mine.

14. The downsides (which, it should be said, Uranga does not belabor) commonly imputed to the Mexican character additionally include resentment, cynicism, and anxiety; the upsides include compassion and a vigorous conscience.

15. In an interview with Santí, Paz stated that he and his generation had already read parts of Heidegger by the time Gaos arrived in Mexico (Zamorano Meza 78). Díaz Ruanova remembers a lecture on Heidegger that Paz gave at Mascarones in the 1950s (99). Also on Paz and existentialism, see Santí's magisterial introduction to his edition of *Laberinto*.

16. Here, it is clear, Paz turns identifiably and darkly Sartrean. A later section of the present chapter addresses the Sartrean gaze.

17. In *Laberinto* Paz writes of Hiperión: "Other younger writers are studying the meaning of our attitudes towards life. The greatest virtue of many of these efforts

lies in the writers' anxiety to understand what we are, and to understand clearly and without complacency. Nevertheless, most of the members of this group—especially Emilio Uranga, its principal inspiration—have realized that the theme of Mexicanness can only be a part of a larger meditation on a much vaster theme: the historical alienation of dependent peoples and of mankind in general" (*171*; 317). We return to *Laberinto*'s affinity with Zea in chapter 4.

18. As versus Santos Ruiz, who states that Paz took up "the philosophy of Mexicanness in the same terms that Hiperión had proposed" (37).

19. Formed practically on the eve of the Mexican Revolution, the Ateneo dispersed during the upheaval. While the majority of its members went into exile at some point in the turmoil, Caso stayed in Mexico (Stabb 50).

20. Stehn, expanding Zea's work on the subject, demarcates two phases in Mexican positivism: first, Barreda's more humanistic version and, second, that of the Porfirian *científicos*, with their adherence to the survival of the fittest. Stehn writes: "it is too simplistic to say that Sierra came to oppose positivism. He had only come to realize that its vision stood in opposition to the ideology of Porfirism, which needed to be fought with the help of other philosophical traditions" (59).

21. I quote from the editions of *Existencia* that appear in Caso's *Obras completas*, vol. 3, which *only includes the 1916 and 1943 editions*, supplemented by a table detailing the contents of the 1919 edition. In the body of my text, I list the edition(s) in which the cited lines appear; page numbers reflect the *first* time that the quoted lines from *Existencia* appear in the *Obras completas* volume. The 1916 edition runs from pp. 3 to 22 there.

22. Ortiz Guadarrama states that in *Existencia*, Caso "aims to recover the basic aspects of Christianity and purge them of the variants, dogmatisms, and imperatives they have acquired over time, with the goal of demonstrating that the essence of Christianity not only meets the needs of human self-fulfillment, but also that it emphasizes the possibility of a way of life distinct from the egotistic logic that permeates the human world."

23. On Caso and Heidegger, see Krauze 226–30. A statement from Caso's 1944 article "San Agustín y Heidegger" demonstrates the Mexican philosopher's principal critique of Heidegger and appears to include French existentialism: "And since contemporary philosophers have painstakingly omitted from their (otherwise remarkable) thinking all references to another world, to another region of reality that gives meaning to existence, they offer us the Heideggerian 'man-in-nothingness' or 'for-nothingness,' a 'being-towards-death,' none of which, in sum, is the true man or true being!" (171).

24. According to Hurtado, Caso's *Problema* offers a moral basis for Mexican democracy that would transcend and heal ideological rifts (*Búho* 57, 79). Further, according to Hurtado Caso's philosophy of the Mexican Revolution in *Problema* dovetails with that of the idealistic Francisco Madero who overthrew Porfirio Díaz: "Madero sacrificed his life for freedom and for democracy, but what motivated him

above all was love for his fellow human beings; the same Christian charity that Caso defended. If this dimension of Madero's thought and action goes unrecognized, one cannot understand the Mexican Revolution" (*Búho* 83).

25. In the prologue to the 1951 edition of *Perfil*, Ramos explains the shift from *Perfil*'s specificity to *Hacia*'s abstraction. He tells us that he composed *Hacia* having understood that beneath *Perfil*'s references to a new humanism lay "a question about the essence of man that warranted broad discussion," an issue "that had to be treated in the abstract, *without reference to any specific case*" (17; emphasis added).

26. Sartre has portrayed *The Flies* as an allegory of the French Resistance during the German Occupation. For Sartre, Orestes's flagrant rejection of remorse intended to convey this message: "I was saying to my fellow Frenchmen: You do not have to repent, even those of you who have in a sense become murderers; you must assume your own responsibility for your acts, even if they have caused the deaths of innocent persons" (*Sartre on Theater* 194).

27. Similarly, in *Anti-Semite and Jew* (1946), Sartre writes: "To be a Jew is to be thrown into—to be *abandoned* to—the situation of a Jew; at the same time it is to be responsible in and through one's own person for the destiny and the very nature of the Jewish people" (89).

28. Villoro translated Marcel's *Position et approches concrètes au mystère ontologique*, an appendix to the play *Le Monde cassé* (1933), as *Posición y aproximaciones concretas al misterio ontológico*, 86 pp.

29. With regard to Hiperión and values, see especially Sánchez's accounts of the group's earliest contributions in ch. 1, the discussion of Portilla in ch. 2, and of Uranga in ch. 5 of *Contingency*.

30. At the end of *Nausea*, as he has before, Roquentin listens to a jazz tune sung by a Black woman and written by a Jewish man. Roquentin, transported by the music, concludes that it has rescued them both from merely existing: "So two of them are saved [sauvés]: the Jew and the Negress. Saved. Maybe they thought they were lost irrevocably, drowned in existence." In fellow feeling with the rescued parties, Roquentin joyously imagines writing a novel that would be "above existence," create bridges between himself and his potential readers, and let them perhaps think of Roquentin's own life "as something precious and almost legendary" (177–78).

31. Born in Spain, raised in Mexico, Luis Villoro (1922–2014) continually opened up new fields of investigation in books such as *El proceso ideológico de la revolución de Independencia* (1953), *Estudios sobre Husserl* (1975), *Creer, saber, conocer* [Believe, Know, Recognize] (1982; a work of analytic philosophy), *El poder y el valor: Fundamentos de una ética política* (1997), and *Estado plural, pluralidad de culturas* (1998). Villoro taught at the UNAM. He received several major national prizes. He also served as president of the Asociación Filosófica de México, as Mexico's ambassador to UNESCO, and as a member of the Consejo Nacional para el Desarrollo de los Pueblos Indígenas [National Council for the Development of Indigenous Communities].

32. Hiperión's softening of the lines between ontology and ontics may relate to that of Marcel. As Tattam notes: "In practice, intersubjectivity's dual status simply seems to grant Marcel a license to discuss the ontology and ethics of intersubjectivity simultaneously, making it almost impossible to separate the two and leaving one to wonder whether Marcel does not, at times, simply confuse or conflate the two issues" (69–70).

33. Portilla's "Comunidad, grandeza y miseria del mexicano" (1949), which contemplates desgana, wishes to "disclose present-day advancements in thinking about our own values" (120). Portilla praises community in a Marcelian vein and extols Mexicans' dedication to "the living and true relationship between man and his fellow man, in which an 'I' addresses a 'you' [the informal "tú"] from whom he obtains a response" (137), even if such relationships have not yet come to full fruition. Mexican personalismo—an anthropomorphic conception of the community as person—facilitates fulfillment of the quest (123). Whence the tendency to form the "inter-individual relationships of friendship" that "set the tone for politics and everything else, even culture" (130). Mexican community may still be "disarticulated" (130) by phenomena like desgana, but it possesses the wherewithal to create an "authentic community" (137).

34. "Seriousness" for Portilla is explicitly the opposite of the Sartrean "spirit of seriousness" (bourgeois, self-congratulatory, bad faith complacency). In *Fenomenología del relajo*, the bourgeois *apretado*, another antagonist of community like the relajiento, stands in for the "spirit of seriousness." Apretados, loosely translated as "snobs," think they *are* the value, the incarnation of it—a conviction that threatens the freedom of others. Portilla writes: "Relajientos and apretados constitute two poles that threaten this difficult task we all have undertaken: the creation of a Mexican community, an authentic community, not a society split into property owners and the dispossessed" (95).

35. "Hell is other people" in *No Exit* also reverberates with Heidegger's Mitsein insofar as the characters recognize that they are inalienably joined to one another (29). It is worth noting that Sartre's *What Is Literature?* sketches out a more benign intersubjectivity, between authors and readers. For example, Sartre writes: "There is no art except for and by others" (43); "the writer appeals to the reader's freedom to collaborate in the production of his work" (46), and "reading is a pact of generosity between author and reader. Each one trusts the other; each one counts on the other, demands of the other as much as he demands of himself" (55). As Bergoffen comments: "Here the other is no longer the one who steals my world from me, but the one with whom I build a world" (107).

36. On p. 409 of *BN* we see how thoroughly Sartre forecloses altruism: "It does not follow, however, that an ethics of '*laisser-faire*' and tolerance would respect the Other's freedom any better." "Charity, *laisser-faire*, tolerance—even an attitude of abstention—are each one a project of myself which engages me and which engages the Other in his acquiescence." In sum, "respect for the Other's freedom

is an empty word: even if we could assume the project of respecting this freedom, each attitude which we adopted with respect to the Other would be a violation of that freedom which we claimed to respect."

37. Research for the present book has turned up no substantial treatments of Beauvoir in Mexico by then-contemporary authors except Rosario Castellanos.

38. My chapter on Castellanos discusses the wider Mitsein of Beauvoir's *The Second Sex*. In any case, numerous scholars have studied Beauvoir's defections from Sartre around intersubjectivity. I have gained particular insight on the matter from Bauer, Eshleman, Gothlin, Kruks, and Weiss.

39. Beauvoir's focus on the question of the neighbor in *Pyrrhus* displays strong connections with Kierkegaard's *Works of Love* (1847).

40. It lies beyond the scope and concerns of my chapter to detail the mutations that Sartre's thinking underwent in the posthumously published *Notebooks* and his later works. On this, see Anderson's book. For instance, Anderson intimates—without, sadly, any mention of Beauvoir—how in the *Notebooks* Sartre edges towards her ideas on intersubjectivity. Anderson writes: "unlike *Being and Nothingness* where only subject/object relations were possible, *Notebooks* asserts that we can apprehend each other as both freedom and object at the same time. The narrow alternatives of his earlier work 'may be transformed through conversion,' Sartre confirms" (79–80). "For Sartre, this sympathetic engagement in the freedom of the other involves a unity between persons that was totally missing in *Being and Nothingness*" (80). On the transition from the *Notebooks* to the *Critique*, also see Orlando.

41. In *Pyrrhus* Beauvoir states: "One never arrives anywhere. There are only points of departure" (110).

42. The relationship between Hiperión's platform and the recent works mentioned, as well as with the liberation theology of Enrique Dussel (originally from Argentina but working in Mexico), is well worth further study. I leave that to another writing, or another scholar.

43. Others who assail Hiperión along similar lines as Santos Ruiz include Paz apologist Domínguez Michael; Valero Pie (conceivably harboring umbrage at Hiperión's betrayal of Gaos, but not condemning the group as virulently as Santos Ruiz, who read Valero Pie's book in manuscript and draws on it); and Hyperion Sánchez MacGrégor, in a 1952 course that rebuked his fellow members' collaboration with the government (Hurtado, "Introducción" xxxii). On the other hand, Sánchez Prado has credited Hiperión's philosophical discourse, particularly Villoro's and Zea's, with taking over from literature the creation of an autonomous, counterhegemonic space. If nationalistic tropes permeate the dissentient "intellectual nation" of Hiperión, he maintains, it is because they had become so diffuse and persistent as to be practically unavoidable (*Naciones* 203).

44. Nonetheless, it is difficult to quarrel with Ruiz Santos's evidence of Zea's close ties to Alemán's ideology. At points in her text we encounter smoking guns corroborating that Zea bought into Alemanismo's racial homogenization and the prime role it allotted to the bourgeoisie (e.g., 349, 353, 354).

45. A monumental case-in-point of literature's independence from Alemanismo is Carlos Fuentes's first novel, *La región más transparente* [Where the Air is Clear] (1958). Over the course of some 450 pages, the novel satirizes Alemanismo's grasping venality. Though not an existentialist novel, *Región* assimilates the busy Mexican existentialist arena that the foregoing chapter has considered. As Reeve demonstrates in "Octavio Paz and Hiperión," the novel reflects on certain discourses of lo mexicano circulating at the time by means of the character Manuel Zamacoma, a mestizo intellectual. For some scholars, Zamacoma represents Paz (when *Región* first appeared Fuentes was accused of plagiarizing *Laberinto* [Reeve 14]). Anyone familiar with Hiperión, however, will hear unmistakable echoes of Zea in Zamacoma. Indeed, in a fine avant la lettre response to Santos Ruiz, the lengthy conversation between pro-Alemán banker Federico Robles and Zamacoma in *Región* pits the two men against each other as polar opposites (389–98).

Chapter Three

1. Key to Usigli references in this chapter: *EG* is *El gesticulador* (Meyran's annotated edition); *Corona* is *Corona de luz* (Usigli's *Teatro completo* omits the play's important prologues); *JR* is *Juan Ruiz de Alarcón en el tiempo*; *TC* 3 is volume 3 of Usigli's *Teatro completo*; *TC* 5 is volume 5 of Usigli's *Teatro completo*. References to all other plays by Usigli that I treat correspond to volume 1 of his *Teatro completo*. Page numbers for the English version of the play derive from Ramón Layera's translation of *El gesticulador*, *The Imposter*. To enhance readability, *The Imposter* at times takes appreciable liberties with the original. Therefore, in several cases I have brought the translations closer to the original, which bears out my arguments.

2. Paz writes: "Every moment [the Mexican dissimulator] must remake, re-create, modify the personage he is playing, until at last the moment arrives when reality and appearance, the lie and the truth, are one" (*40*; 176).

3. I borrow the term "aporetic theater" from Náter (24).

4. In "Ideas sobre el teatro," Usigli mentions Beauvoir, along with Sartre and Camus (1969; *TC* 5:636–37); Beauvoir's essay pulls theater into the compass of the metaphysical novel (*Philosophical Writings* 270). To be fair, it should be noted that in writing on theater Sartre quickly followed Beauvoir's cue. From 1947 onward, he theorized a theater of situations that "does not give its support to any one 'thesis' and is not inspired by any preconceived idea" (*Sartre on Theater* 38).

5. In "Juan Ruiz de Alarcón: Una mentalidad moderna," Rosario Castellanos observes of *La verdad sospechosa*: "Oh, the gusto and art with which García constructs his fragile edifices of deception! It is interesting that the more the narration deviates from the truth, the more lyrical, more spangled with lovely metaphors, more rich in literary techniques it becomes" (*Juicios sumarios*, in *Obras II* 558*).*

6. Unpublished letters from Usigli to Caso reveal important connections between the two men. Usigli had already met Caso by 1929, when he addresses him

in a letter as "my beloved teacher" (though he likely awards Caso the title more in solidarity than in point of fact, because Usigli had studied at the National Conservatory). Further, Caso sponsored Usigli for diplomatic service in 1930, supported the publication of his *México en el teatro* in 1932, and recommended Usigli for the fellowship at Yale that the dramatist assumed in 1936–1937. Writing to Caso from New Haven on January 21, 1936, Usigli declared him the fountainhead of Mexican philosophy, "the only Mexican who teaches such things." Without Caso, Usigli says, rationalism would have "killed off the spiritual side of Mexico." Profound thanks to Carly Sentieri, former Curator of Special Collections at Miami University, for sending me Usigli's letters to Caso (dated 1929, 1930, and 1936) and related materials from the Rodolfo Usigli Archive.

    7. García Máynez characterizes Caso's pragmatism as "the humanistic and Christian pragmatism of existence as charity, not the myopic pragmatism of existence as economy" (56). On Caso's humanistic pragmatism also see Krauze (53, 72–75, 92, 269–70). In Hurtado's *Dialéctica del naufragio* (2016) we encounter a latter-day resurgence of pragmatism that reverberates with Caso, James, Hiperión, and Usigli. Hurtado writes, for instance: "Beyond the classic definition of truth as consistent with reality lies the ancient idea that truth—eluding error and defying the lie—leads us to that which holds the greatest value for reality. Therefore, we can say that an ideal is truthful because it guides our lives like a beacon that illuminates our path" (141–42).

    8. Usigli discusses Nietzsche's *The Birth of Tragedy*, for one, in "Notas a *Coronas de fuego*." A mixture of the Apollonian and the Dionysian, in Usigli's opinion, constitutes what the German philosopher calls "the delight of tragedy" (*TC* 3:793).

    9. On the thick matter of Nietzsche's and James's pragmatic approaches to truth and for bibliography on the topic, see Fabbrichesi; Sinhababu. The two scholars suggest that whereas Nietzsche jettisons pure truth, James retains belief in it yet considers it beyond our grasp, constantly subject to adjustment.

    10. Starting in 1896 and for the rest of his life, Unamuno read and quoted James. His published works include thirty-two citations of James, over half of them from James's *The Will to Believe* (Nubiola 26). Unamuno's penchant for the North American philosopher has received much scholarly attention; see, for example, Farré's study.

    11. Usigli's book-length essay, "Una comedia shaviana. *Noche de estío*" (1933–1935; *TC* 3:303–416), and his "Ensayo sobre la actualidad de la poesía dramática" (1947; *TC* 3:495–531) are indispensable sources on the author's political views. Beardsell, Meyran, Moraña, and Swansey have addressed, in varying ways and degrees, Usigli's post-Maximato agenda. Vevia Romero inventories Usigli's political plays. As far as I know, though, scholars have not probed most of the intersections between Usigli's post-Maximato agenda and *EG* that the present chapter unpacks.

    12. When Beardsell notes Usigli's belief that "Mexico needed to aim at an integrated society in which each social class retained its essential characteristics"

(27), he touches on an intriguing aspect of the dramatist's political thought that merits a study unto itself. For instance, Usigli's revisionist socialism would not hand government over to the peasant class (*TC* 3:380). Rather, as he writes: "Mexico is a just country that calls for the consolidation of each social class in its own body and essence rather than for a lame socialism" (*TC* 3:400). Usigli's *La familia cena en casa*, along with his introduction to the play (*TC* 3:606–19), flesh out their author's notions of class, authentic class consciousness, and socialism.

13. On his stint as chief of Cárdenas's press department, Usigli informs us: "my good friend Pedro Arena, who headed the president's office, asked me to serve as chief of the press department. I hope that the former members of the Presidential General Staff—as well as the President himself—will remember the Usiglian cast of my reports. I pride myself on the fact that the president was kept well informed. I resigned after six months because I had finished writing and wanted to publish and stage my *Tres comedias impolíticas*, and some of my friends thought that the plays could cause problems" (*TC* 3:599–600). However, remarkably or unremarkably, the three plays were *not* published at the time, nor in 1950, despite Caso having sponsored their publication by the Editorial Stylo (Layera 187, 189). Only in vol. 1 of Usigli's *TC* (1963) did the *Tres comedias* first reach publication.

14. Qtd. in R. Rodríguez 51. Beardsell (ch. 2), Meyran (34–36), Swansey (92), and Layera (51–52) all examine political allusions in the *Tres comedias impolíticas*, of which Meyran also says: "These three plays can certainly be read as works by an organic intellectual fighting for Cárdenas and against the 'Supreme Chief,' Plutarco Elías Calles" (22–23).

15. On Calles's involvement in the assassination of Obregón, see O'Malley (15, 16, 29, 55). As O'Malley discusses on p. 16 and passim, belief that Calles had engineered the assassination of Obregón contributed to a major uprising, the 1920 Escobar Rebellion in northern Mexico.

16. We return to Castellanos's novels on Chiapas in chapter 6. Regarding fallout from the socialist education program, see Medin, *Ideología*, ch. 7, and Buchenau, ch. 6.

17. Usigli further attributes his resignation as Cárdenas's press secretary to the "desire to publish my impolitic comedies without compromising the supporters of Cárdenas to whom I owed my job" (R. Rodríguez 59).

18. This counterface to Alcestes's inflexibility reminds us of Leon Trotsky's aphorism: "A means can be justified only by its end. But the end in its turn needs to be justified" (48). Still, I consider it unlikely that Usigli's endorsement of pragmatism relates in any fundamental way to Trotsky's aphorism. The horrors of Stalin's political repression (1936–1938) that concretized "the ends justifies the means" were occurring as Usigli wrote and would have disillusioned anyone but a hard-line party member. As a left-leaning moderate who subscribed to "Ibsen's stand against membership in any given party and, personally, as someone who leans both right and left" (Usigli, qtd. in Meyran 54), Usigli was not that sort of socialist. To

wit, he wrote: "Forcibly making Mexico socialist is not much better than forcibly making it Catholic" (*TC* 3:368).

19. We may, though, admire Alcestes's choice of prison over collusion. Alcestes receives an offer to join the government if he promises to collude with it, abandoning his principles. Of course, he refuses. The last lines of the play hint that Alcestes may heroically confront the police with the truth: "The officials keep one waiting, but they do not wait. So, fine, let them come in. I'll start with the police" (*TC* 1:169).

20. Swansey considers the threshold to be a defining conceit of Usigli's life and works (23). He discusses the deferral of freedom experienced by Usigli's characters poised on the threshold, the "doubt about their possible liberation, always postponed or mistaken" (20) and "the precarity of the interior space, always about to flounder" ("a punto de zozobrar"; 98).

21. Son David, perhaps dying of tuberculosis, imparts that existentialist message to his family, as when he tells his sister: "Everything going on with you, Enriqueta, has to do with being scared. You'd come up with a fixed idea of life and you're seeing it collapse, because life isn't fixed, it's always changing" (*TC* 1:541).

22. To my knowledge, previous scholars have not associated *EG* with the Revolutionary Family. Buchenau (ch. 6) is an excellent historical source on the Revolutionary Family per se and Zolov a terrifically suggestive one.

23. Zolov 4; phrases in single quotes cite O'Malley 47, 85. Buchenau describes the script's conflation of leaders in slightly different terms: "Exploiting the martyrdom (or sacrifice) of these leaders, the new ruling party combined Villa's and Zapata's agrarian aims with Carranza's and Obregón's economic nationalism and Madero's commitment to effective suffrage and political democracy" (156). In any event, Thomas Benjamin reproduces an image from the PNR's 1934 *Calendario Nacionalist y Enciclopedia Popular*, "an idealized portrait of the Revolutionary Family including Carranza, Zapata, Ángeles, Obregón, Calles, and Cárdenas" (88) that exactly illustrates the purported new unity of revolutionary fathers.

24. Thomas Benjamin has much of interest to say about how the institutionalization of the Revolution produced the depersonalized Revolutionary Family and *Monumento a la Revolución* that breached commemorative tradition. See, for instance, ch. 5, where he states: "The Monument to the Revolution, a reaction against personalism and factionalism in the Mexican collective memory, would ignore the revolutionary factions and their chiefs altogether and glorify only *la Revolución* itself" (132). That Cárdenas was reluctant to fund the monument, which was finally completed in 1938 but had no official inauguration (T. Benjamin 132, 194n74), and that he repersonalized the Revolution by electing Zapata as its symbol (O'Malley 64) was perhaps to be expected.

25. Significantly, *EG* does not spell out Rubio's exact political platform nor identify him with Cárdenas. In sharply contrasting Rubio to other leaders and emphasizing the fervor he inspires, the play impresses on its audience the (*still-*) unequaled fidelity of this new revolutionary father to the Revolution's most righteous drives.

Hence the generalized "today" with which the play begins. Similarly, the sequel to *EG* that Usigli projected in 1961, *Los herederos* [The Heirs], would have dispelled any expectations for latter-day redemption that the 1938 play's liminal ending may have raised. The sequel to *EG* that Usigli outlined relaunches the idealist Miguel as a corrupt politician, Navarro as a governor who wields absolute power, and Julia as Navarro's wife (*TC* 3:565). Upon hearing Usigli recount the plot of *Los herederos*, Alfonso Reyes asked him: "So, do you see any hope for us?" Usigli replied, "in all sincerity," that he did not (*TC* 3:566).

26. Julia's role in *EG* materializes the convictions of feminist Claudina in *Alcestes*: "The world's greatest men, Shaw among them, agree that women can embrace all male professions, be intelligent, independent, lead" (*TC* 1:139).

27. I purposely evoke Sartre's play *Dirty Hands* (1948), subsequent to *EG* but a lightning rod for later "Dirty Hands" theorists like Michael Walzer who treat issues inherent in Sartre's play such as consequentialism, pragmatic ethics, deontological ethics, and situational ethics. Germane in a broad sense to Usigli's pragmatic authenticity as these areas may be, they are anachronistic to my focus, the contextualizing of *EG*'s seminal existentialism. Given that Sartre's play *was* available to Hiperión, it is worth noting that Sartre's *Dirty Hands* targets the very same dilemma as Usigli's early political theater, the purist versus the pragmatist. Sartre showcases the purist Hugo, who sacrifices his life for the Truth, as over against the pragmatic Hoederer, willing to lie in order to achieve his ends. Consistent with his critique in "Materialism and Revolution" (1946) of neo-Stalinist Marxism for its pretensions to an absolute, objective truth that extorts an absolute, unquestioning allegiance, Sartre seems to be coming out for Hugo and individualistic dissent. (See Drake on Sartre's early post-Liberation efforts to inject the Stalinist French Communist Party with humanism.) Nevertheless, that Hoederer's program has merit unto itself—because it saved hundreds of thousands of lives (238), because Hoederer "dies for his ideas, for his political program; he's responsible for his death" (241), and more—muddies the waters. Wittingly or not, the inconsistencies complicate Sartre's exalting of Hugo. They render *Dirty Hands* more a "theater of situations" than a mere theater à these and could thus, for Hiperión, align Sartre's play with Usigli's mobile, pragmatic-leaning *EG*.

28. Schmidhuber several times associates Usigli with Mexican identity discourse and rues that the dramatist's contributions to the field have not received sufficient attention (81). Vieyra begins to fill the gap (77–79). On Uranga and Usigli et alia, he writes: "Uranga's study of Mexican being relies on, and fully comes to grips with, the precedents of Ramos and [José Gómez] Robleda's psychological studies, Usigli and Yáñez's censorious notes, and Paz's brilliant essay" (79). Beyond the connections with Uranga that I lay out, it would be worthwhile to explore links between the relajo of Portilla's *Fenomenología* and Usigli's notion of critical laughter (e.g., Usigli's search for "a Mexican-style laughter, neither vulgar nor bloody" [*TC* 3:580] that turns Mexican tribulations into entertainment, into "a Mexican-style theater that reflects Mexicans themselves" [*TC* 3:588]).

29. Uranga's category of "insufficiency," which I analyzed in chapter 2, is one form of accidentality.

30. On nepantla in terms particularly relevant to Uranga's, see Maffie, ch. 6.

31. In his prologue to *Análisis*, Hurtado comments on Uranga's perhaps individualistic interpretation of López Velarde: "Whether Uranga to some extent projected his own philosophical ideas onto López Velarde's poems, or whether he truly found in them a wellspring of primary intuitions that coincided with his theses on Mexican being is open to question. Be that as it may, the result is entrancing. To this day, Uranga's philosophical venture stands as a model for creating a Mexican philosophy from Mexican literature" (20).

32. Sánchez concludes: "The point of all this then, is not to thrust the Mexican into an irreversible pessimism; rather, the point is to bring them to an awareness of their own-most accidentality so as to better survive and redeem their accidental being" ("Heidegger" 454).

33. According to Uranga, cynicism is "*the conscious acceptance of an inversion of values*" (*Análisis* 75).

Chapter Four

1. For instance, after listing several authors Hiperión influenced, Hurtado adds: "The name of Juan Rulfo is conspicuous by its absence from this list" ("Introducción" xvii).

2. Klahn discerns certain existentialist traits in *PP*: "Rulfo's narrative subverts the logical-rationalist premises of positivism. Rulfo delves into the individual 'I,' opens up unwonted existential spaces in human beings, and from there, treats the anguish of solitude and death" (424).

3. Previous versions of *PP* have much to say about the Rentería figure, generally called Padre Villalpando. Magnifying his ambiguity and moral import, they present the priest as Pedro's own son. At one point, they confirm the priest's disbelief in the afterlife (Rulfo, *Cuadernos* 55), which further inserts him in the lineage of Unamuno's *San Manuel*.

4. On Rulfo's studies at Mascarones see García Bonilla 88–89; López Mena, *Los caminos* 44; Vital 55, 59. Rulfo himself refers to Caso's *El problema de México* ("México" 400). A clarification on citations from García Bonilla's book: *Un tiempo suspendido: Cronología de la vida y la obra de Juan Rulfo* weaves hundreds of works by and about Rulfo into a narrative compendium of sources that proceeds chronologically. The book is tremendously useful but problematic to cite because García Bonilla often lists all the sources in which the information appears, resulting in the citation of multiple sources that can be difficult to identify in the book's bibliography. Further, it is not always clear which information pertains to which source, and given the complexities of obtaining older Mexican journals, I was not always

able to consult the original sources. I therefore provide double references—to García Bonilla and to the original, as cited in *Tiempo suspendido*—when García Bonilla's original source is clear. When it is not, I simply reference García Bonilla. In other words, readers should be aware that García Bonilla is *almost always citing another source and should consult his book.*

5. According to Zepeda, Rulfo's uncredited photo of Portilla illustrated the issue of the *Universidad de México* published in April, 1966 (43). Another photo of Portilla by Rulfo can be found in Vital 86.

6. See pp. 633 and 638–39 of Agustín's "Epílogo" to the second volume of Revueltas's *Obra literaria*. In it, Agustín rather extremely calls Rulfo's works "poor mirror images" of Revueltas's *El luto humano* and *Dios en la tierra* (633), texts I treat in chapter 5.

7. An example from *Laberinto* that keys us into its general affinity with Zea's *Dos etapas* would be: "The Revolution became an attempt to integrate our present and our past, or—as Leopoldo Zea put it—to 'assimilate our history,' to change it into a living thing: a past made present" (*144*; 289).

8. "Sahagún y su significado histórico" [Sahagún and His Historical Significance], Rulfo's short, factual prologue to an edition of Sahagún's *Historia general de las cosas de la Nueva España*, was published the year before *PP*'s author died. Fell reprints it (393–94).

9. Here Rulfo parts ways with Zea and Paz, both of whom have deemed the Revolution the moment when Mexico came into its own.

10. Although to my knowledge there is no proof that Rulfo read *The Flies*, so notable are its similarities to *PP* that one cannot help but wonder if the Mexican author had Sartre's play in mind. Consider, in addition to the similarities registered above, pronouncements by Orestes in *The Flies* such as: "I want my share of memories, my native soil, my place among the men of Argos" (88) and, "mind you, if there were something I could do, something to give me the freedom of the city; if, even by a crime, I could acquire their memories, their hopes and fears, and fill with these the void within me, yes, even if I had to *kill my own mother*" (61; emphasis added).

11. According to Amit Thakkar: "Over 50 years since the publication of Juan Rulfo's masterpiece, the novel *Pedro Páramo* (1955), publications on the writer are as prolific as ever. Few of these have shed light on the text of his one fictional treatment of indigenous people, and none has done so in the context of his thoughts as editor of anthropological works for the Instituto Nacional Indigenista (1962–86)" (191). Thakkar's own reading of the scene with the Apangans greatly helps fill the critical void and contains the insights I reference.

12. Shortly after finishing *PP* and up to 1956, Rulfo worked for the Comisión de la Cuenca de Papaloapan, investigating the Indigenous populations of the regions that the Papaloapan dam affected. Throughout the latter third of his life, from 1962 up to his death in 1986, Rulfo served the Instituto Nacional Indigenista in various

capacities. They included writing numerous anthropological and archeological studies of Indigenous groups and editing an extensive book series on the subjects. For a summary of these activities, see Vital 165–68.

13. Santos Ruiz repeatedly makes assertions in the tenor of: Hiperión's "philosophy of Mexicanidad took the mestizo, especially the urban mestizo, as its focus. It continued to view the Indian as part of the landscape, unfazed, stone-like"; and, for "Hiperión, Mexico was a mestizo nation, that is, Mexican was synonymous with mestizo. Not only because Mexico's majority population was mestizo, but also because so were Mexico's institutions and because identifying itself as a mestizo nation should be the way to unite Mexico" (63). The second assertion, as I indicated in note 44 to chapter 2, may hold for Zea, but Santos Ruiz reads Villoro's survey of indigenism as representing his *own* ideological partiality for mestizos/mestizaje (108). Further, she describes Carrión's *Mito y magia* as arguing that "Mexicans' lives featured primitive thought and a magical bent that hindered the nation's development" (37; we see later in this chapter that her description is patently incorrect).

14. Despite the fact that in *Grandes momentos* he treats many issues directly implicating Vasconcelos, Villoro only names the author of *La raza cósmica* once (218)—a remarkable omission. Might it be that Villoro hesitated to address so major or so controversial a personage, still alive at the time of *Grandes momento*'s publication?

15. *Grandes momentos*, published a year before Uranga's "Ensayo de una ontología del mexicano," anticipates Uranga's notion of zozobra when, for example, Villoro sees present-day indigenists as turning their gaze inward and discovering "instability and contradiction within themselves" (275).

16. One thinks of the Argentine philosophers Carlos Astrada (*Tierra y figura*, 1963) and Rodolfo Kusch (*América profunda*, 1962). As I mention in chapter 5, Kusch refers to Villoro, and Bonfil Batalla's *México profundo* unmistakably references Kusch's *América profunda*. I thank Brown University student Ana-Irma Patete for enlightening me on the "telluric existentialism" of Latin American writers. Moreover, Villoro's later *El poder y el valor: Fundamentos de una ética política* (1997), which chapter 2 briefly examined, at times parallels Bonfil Batalla's *México profundo*. The section of Villoro's book titled "Comunidades indias" observes that some Latin American communities still uphold the pre-Hispanic privileging of the "totality over individual interests" and that for society in general this authentic communitarianism "remains an ideal yet to be achieved" (368).

17. Thakkar calls *México profundo* a "promising framework" for analyzing the section on the Apangans and their separation from the "de-Indianised mestizo peasantry" (198, 197). Thakker's article also provides the guiding light for my point on the detachment of the Indigenous traders when it describes the scene in which they figure as "a fragment of poetic lucidity in which indigenous society is presented as a world-in-itself, running parallel to but somehow radically disconnected from Comala" (192) and as a world whose values "co-exist *side-by-side* with those of the

mestizo majority rather than being *subordinated* by them; the two towns of Apango and Comala seem to 'function' independently without much in common except the Sunday market" (193).

19. Although Portilla's work on relajo only reached publication after his death, he had been working on Mexicanness since 1947 and perhaps discussed relajo at the Centro Mexicano de Escritores, where he coincided with Rulfo. I am grateful to Carlos Sánchez for information on this matter.

19. As Stavans neatly concludes: "Vasconcelos attempted to develop a philosophy of race and ended up with a racist tirade" (18). That Vasconcelos virulently opposed existentialism (Díaz Ruanova 89) would also not have endeared him to Hiperión.

20. Paz praises Vasconcelos in *Laberinto* as an "extraordinary man" who possessed a "unity of vision" (*152*; 296). He describes the philosophy of *La raza cósmica* as "the natural and ultimate consequence of Spanish universality, child of the Renaissance" (*154*; 298). The conflicts between Paz and Rulfo that developed as the latter gained renown may also have propelled Rulfo's critique of Paz in 1985. García Bonilla (210–11) presents various testimonies to the two men's vexed relationship, including Tomás Segovia's opinion that Paz, seeing Rulfo as competition, did not give Rulfo his due.

21. In a discussion with Venezuelan university students in 1974, Rulfo reiterated: "The mindset of Mexican Indians, like that of all Indians, is very hard to understand; it is very difficult to penetrate their mindset." As an example, he cites the Indigenous people of Tenexapa who appear to be praying to the crosses at the city gates but are actually respecting the ancient custom of asking their gods to open the gates; they are not praying to the Christian God ("Rulfo examina" 876–77).

22. An ancillary Hyperion who speaks the language of psychoanalysis more than that of existentialism, Carrión accords with the Grupo Hiperión on various planes. He draws on characterological and phenomenological methodologies (104–05); foregrounds mestizos' precarious, oscillating identity; and analyzes (blockages to) community. When it comes to literature that bridges the external and the internal dimensions of lo mexicano, Carrión especially singles out the works of Revueltas and Usigli (74–75).

23. See Lienhard, Orrego Arismendi, and Stanton ("Estructuras").

24. Jiménez de Báez points out that "la estrella junto a la luna" could derive from John Millington Synge's play *Riders to the Sea*, where it refers to the death of a son (588). Also see Bastos and Molloy's "La estrella" for a pathbreaking analysis of "the star next to the moon" in *PP*, as well as of the novel's Marian dimensions.

25. In their 1978 article, Bastos and Molloy characterize Dolores Preciado and her avatars as emblems of Susana San Juan ("polestars of the morning star that slowly approaches the moon, Susana San Juan") and Susana as a "constellation" ("El personaje" 24).

26. Donis describes a "divine," or seer, who lived in Media Luna and whom Pedro killed: what the seer "never 'divined' was that he was going to die as soon as the *patrón* 'divined' what a bungler he was" (55; 122). Wouldn't this trickster be the seamy Inocencio Osorio?

27. In his 1965 lecture "Situación actual de la novela contemporánea" Rulfo states: "The novel today, all over the world, marches under the banner of magical realism"; it is a hard course to travel and basically "one that leads nowhere" (379).

28. For an acute reading of Susana's introversion see Valdés 42ff.

Chapter Five

1. A shorter, substantially different version of this chapter was published in the *Revista Hispánica Moderna*. Warm thanks to Hernán Díaz and the anonymous referee of the article for their excellent suggestions.

2. Negrín explains that by religare Revueltas means "the potential for unity, for establishing fraternal bonds among men," and that the word encloses "a whole array of human values." As such, she concludes, the religare of *ELH* "fully and consciously accepts religion" (254).

3. A summary of the scandal, the texts of the principal attacks, and Revueltas's responses to the affair can be found in the "Dossier" section of *LDT*. Revueltas's famous retraction of 1950 appears on pp. 387–89 of the section. For more on the scandal, see Campos and Valenzuela. In the critical edition of *LDT* from which I cite, the actual text of the novel runs from pp. *1* to *170*. *All other page numbers listed refer to the edition's critical apparatus.*

4. For example, in 1950 Revueltas wrote: "Nothing is further from true and noble commitment than Sartre's literature" (*LDT* 407), and "I object to being labeled an existentialist" (408). In 1962 he expressed his admiration for Sartre (422) and stated of his 1950 predicament: "In a country like ours, with a colonial mentality . . . . I was in no position to defend myself; my hands and feet tied, I was kicked around and, moreover, found myself absolutely alone" (423).

5. Cheron does register some grumblings from a PCM member about the dark cast of *ELH* (212).

6. The article has been reprinted in Revueltas's *Visión del Paricutín*, from which I cite. I have not found any in-depth treatments of the essay or of Revueltas vis-à-vis Vallejo.

7. I quote all of Vallejo's texts in Spanish from Eshleman's splendid Spanish-English edition of the Peruvian poet's works. Page numbers reference the Spanish originals in Eshleman's edition. The prose translations are my own, though at times they necessarily coincide with the most literal of Eshleman's renditions.

8. On demonic despair and authorship, see Butler. With regard to Revueltas's treatment of suffering, Ruiz Abreu comments that the author "seeks a center that

would unite all the shattered pieces. He seems to have encountered that 'center' in suffering; from an early age, he had learned that only through pain can one achieve true freedom" (44).

9. The poetic speaker of "Ágape" fervently desires, like Christ, to give his life for humankind but finds this desire frustrated: "He salido a la puerta, / y me da ganas de gritar a todos: / Si echan de menos algo, aquí se queda!" [I've gone out to the door, and it makes me want to shout to everyone, if you're missing something, it's left here with me] (102).

10. Revueltas sees Azuela's portrayal of the Revolution as too negative and one-sided. He believes that *Los de abajo* omits "the people, victorious despite all odds; men's blind, unarticulated hope; in a word, everything redeeming and heartening." Revueltas's more well-rounded critical realism strives to produce not a work *about* the Revolution but in his parlance a "revolutionary" writing: to treat the events of the Revolution "in a revolutionary manner would mean reflecting the scope of reality itself, an independent and autonomous reality, not that of the artist" ("La novela," *Visión* 235–36).

11. See Negrín, pp. 123–34, for an important elucidation of *ELH*'s historical setting. Revueltas outlines his disillusionment with Cárdenas in the 1944 essay "Hay que resolver la crisis del movimiento revolucionario" [The Crisis of the Revolutionary Movement Must Be Resolved] (*Ensayos*). For its part, *ELH* tells us that an "agency of the Agricultural Bank, in combination with a high-ranking agency of the Ministry of Agriculture, financed the tenant farmers, who paid off the loan by giving over to the bank the products of the land, most of which was destined for the Yankee market" (*146*; 132).

12. Revueltas's resoundingly existentialist negation of the afterlife in *ELH* reads: "I exist and this fact is communicated to me by my body and my spirit; both of which will soon cease to exist; I have participated in the unspeakable miracle, I have belonged" (*99*; 91).

13. The examples that follow are but a few of the paradoxes that fill the novel and that form the bedrock of Negrín's indispensable 1995 book. I also call attention to Bosteels's more recent analysis of Revueltas's *Los errores*, which reads the novel through the lens of melodrama. Suggestively for *ELH*'s explosion of biblical references, Bosteels demonstrates that *Los errores* breaks down melodrama's unequivocal moralizing.

14. Enríquez appraises "Revueltas's desire for a Christ liberated from God" (270) and notes that this Christ's "ethical dimension, which encompasses nonbelievers, is an essential motor of Revueltas's thinking. When Christ is understood as an ethical position taken by Man, one need not believe in any specific religious content in order to believe in him" (267). Negrín affirms: "Christianity, incarnated in Natividad, represents human solidarity and love" (109).

15. Paz says of *ELH*: "Religious concerns constantly invade the work: Mexicans, devout by nature and enamored with blood, have been stripped of their

religion, and Catholicism has not satisfied their stone-like thirst for eternity" (*México* 576).

16. For example, in stark contrast to Villoro Revueltas declaims: "Adán had that poisoned *sangre mestiza*, or mixed blood, in which the Indians saw their own fear and discovered their own undying nostalgia, their retrospective terror, the shipwreck they could not forget" (*11*; 18).

17. If in Vallejo one encounters a "longing for a mother love which might have the totalizing force of divine grace" (Franco 71), Revueltas skews the mother into someone who "triggers an alienating anguish that irremediably imprisons the child" (Ruffinelli 109) and, in *ELH*, into an Aztec goddess of brutality and death (*66–67*; 62–63).

18. Untitled poem. Its first line is "Me viene, hay días, una gana ubérrima, política," and the line quoted appears two stanzas below (520).

19. Having critiqued Azuela's version of the Revolution as overly negative, Revueltas also objects to how other authors idealize the masses who participated in the uprising: "this is not correct, it is not honest, it is not revolutionary, because the people have vices and virtues, great defects and great qualities; and our tragic Mexican masses are simultaneously splendid and savage, heroic and cowardly, capable of great undertakings and of great monstrosities" ("La novela," *Visión* 239).

20. Despite paying much illuminating attention to Natividad, Negrín rejects the possibility of transcendence in *ELH*, be it Sartrean or otherwise. She avows: "After Nativity's death, the characters seem irremissibly condemned to suffer the biblical curse placed on Cain and shared by Adán: to live as 'fugitives and vagabonds'" (91). To my eye, it is unfortunate that instead of giving French existentialism the wider berth it warrants, Negrín polarizes existentialism and Marxism into solitude versus solidarity. Paz, on the other hand, understands that Marxism, Christianity, and atheism can join forces in Revueltas ("Christianity and Revolution" xv–viii).

21. The first paragraph of "Dios en la tierra" expounds on "God's hatred," "such a Godly hatred." Asking, "from where does it come?," the story responds, from "the Bible, from Genesis, from the darkness, before light" (367). On Old Testament aspects of the story, see Sarfati-Arnaud.

22. Montoya delineates several possible points of contact between Revueltas's positions on Mexicanness and those of Hyperions Uranga and Zea. Revueltas, nonetheless, places much weight on his polemic with Hiperión. He republished "Posibilidades" several times; see Orduña Carson, p. 43, for the publication history of the essay. I cite "Posibilidades" from *Ensayos sobre México*.

23. Cortázar writes: "Sartre was quite right when he insisted that existentialism is a humanism, even though he does not refer to the *social* transcendence of angst. Existentialism is a humanism insofar as existence can confer being, a being that (according to Marcel's axiom, which I do not hesitate to repeat) is all the greater when it accedes to being-with" (*Obra crítica* 122).

24. In short, at least for our purposes, *The Imitation of Christ* (1418) emphasizes interior life and withdrawal from the world, a total surrender of the self and will to God.

25. The Sartrean, prizewinning *Un dios cotidiano* (Kraft Prize, 1957) and Mario Vargas Llosa's Sartrean, prizewinning *La ciudad y los perros* [The City and the Cadets] (Biblioteca Breve Prize, 1962), both of which deal with dystopian boarding schools that represent their respective societies, beg to be compared. There are multiple similarities between the two novels; in terms of our focus, transvaluation, *La ciudad y los perros* worries the relationship between its boarding school's military personnel and Catholic confessors. The military officers refuse the role of confessor, but Lieutenant Gamboa eventually assumes it, which leads to an ethical crisis.

26. *Contorno* had more women in its ranks than Hiperión (my chapter 6 discusses women and Hiperión). Susana Fiorito and Ismael Viñas cofinanced *Contorno*; Adelaida Gigli served on the editorial board and contributed articles to the journal; Regina Gibaja and Marta Molinari also published in it.

27. *Sur*, of course, was radical in its own way. Just when Argentina was becoming more militantly nationalist and populistic, *Sur* began to sponsor a cosmopolitan, elite literature. Ismael Viñas, among others, disputes the blanket application of "parricides" to *Contorno*'s members. He terms *Contorno* "a denuciatory journal" but argues that "as distinct from what Uruguayan critic Rodríguez Monegal seemed to think when he labeled us 'parricides,' it was not entirely negative. We did vindicate certain works and authors, in part or completely" ("Prólogo" vi). Viñas adds: "Despite all my critiques and my disagreements with Borges and Lugones, I truly enjoy their work" (viii).

28. That Peronism had co-opted Mallea's "invisible Argentina" for its populist program (see Rodríguez Monegal, *Juicio*, ch. 2) would hardly endear *Una pasión argentina* to *Contorno*. Yet *Contorno*'s specific quarrel with Kusch, and Kusch's with *Contorno*, had to do with the anti-rational, spiritual aspects of Mallea's thinking (Katra 92). In his first article for *Contorno*, "Inteligencia y barbarie" (1954), Kusch urges a return to "Mallea's 'invisible Argentina,' understood as "what is unintelligible to rationalist norms, what goes beyond rationalist norms." Doing so, he says, requires a "leap into the absurd, a leap of faith." While valorizing "invisible Argentina," Kusch still considers Mallea too abstract and classist to do full justice to the notion (*Contorno* 30–31).

29. In like manner, Cuban author Alejo Carpentier's Sartrean novel *Los pasos perdidos* (1953) reverses colonialist standpoints on barbarism and civilization by transforming tribal life a into a wellspring of the authenticity that modern society lacks.

30. Kusch notes: "This is the same as Heidegger's concept of *Dasein*, always rendered as 'being-there,' except that *Dasein* has the sense of 'just being,' that is, of 'throwness.' Let us remember that the verb *estar* does not exist in German. Therefore, when translating *Dasein* into Spanish, we can make the mistake of considering it

a composite of the verb *ser* [*sein* in German]" (109). Although *América profunda* sidesteps outright references to Sartre, Kusch's estar clearly falls in line with the Sartrean "for-itself" and his ser with the Sartrean "in-itself."

31. Camus writes in the conclusion to *The Rebel*: "At this meridian of thought, the rebel thus rejects divinity in order to share in the struggles and destiny of all men" (306).

Chapter Six

1. Castellanos's *Obras II: Poesía, teatro, y ensayos* contains the following works that this chapter cites: *Al pie de la letra* (1959; 105–26), *Materia memorable* (1969; 145–76), *En la tierra de en medio* (1972; 177–99), *Juicios sumarios* (1966; 457–746), *El mar y sus pescaditos* (published posthumously in 1979; 747–874), and an interview with Castellanos, "Los narradores ante el público" (1966; 1008–17). All citations from these texts—not to others by Castellanos—correspond to the *Obras II* edition. I also note that Castellanos's two novels on Chiapas, discussed later in this chapter, have been translated into English under somewhat different titles: *Balún-Canán* as *The Nine Guardians* and *Oficio de tinieblas* as *The Book of Lamentations*.

2. See Rivera-Rodas, who states that Castellanos utilizes sundry genres to create "a model for *identity discourse*" (294). In *Cartas* Castellanos writes, "Octavio Paz isn't fond of me" (294).

3. In "On Reading and Writing Myself: How I wrote *Aura*," Fuentes lists several sources for *Aura*'s magical women, among them Michelet, Henry James's *Aspern Papers*, Francisco de Quevedo, the film *Ugetsu Monogatari*, and the mythological figures of Circe and Medusa.

4. Castellanos, too, sets her hand to the magical woman. *Oficio de tinieblas* gives a leading role to the priestess Catalina Díaz Puiljá, who attempts to revive ancient Indigenous gods. Yet *Oficio* tarnishes and demythifies the female prophet, showing her to be contaminated by a will-to-power.

5. The 1950s ushered in a wave of professional, published women writers, launching stellar figures like Castellanos, Luisa Josefina Hernández, and Josefina Vicens. Hernández was the first woman to receive a fellowship, in 1952–1953, from the prestigious Centro Mexicano de Escritores, followed by Castellanos in 1953–1954. Vicens's novel *El libro vacío* [The Empty Book] (1958), which received the Xavier Villaurrutia Prize in 1958, and the early plays of Hernández, who would become Mexico's most prolific female dramatist, perpetuate various hallmarks of existentialism (see Poot Herrera, from whose excellent article I draw the foregoing information). Hernández's *Los frutos caídos* [The Fallen Fruit] (1958), for example, trades in choice, courage, freedom, responsibility—and women's difficult lot. A student of Usigli and a friend of Castellanos, Hernández focuses her play on truth-telling in a middle-class household replete with "caged" females. While thus maintaining some of Hiperión's

pursuits, this watershed period for Mexican women's writing opened the doors to a modern feminism, with Castellanos in the vanguard and as the leader.

6. A translation of *El eterno femenino* as *The Eternal Feminine* (plus translations of numerous essays, poems, and stories) appears in *A Rosario Castellanos Reader*, from which I cite. Though painstaking and accurate, the translation of *Eterno* does not, understandably enough, entirely convey the brilliance of the play's colloquial, slangy humor. References to the Spanish original of the play correspond to the more complete first edition of *Eterno*, not to the second volume of Castellanos's *Obras*.

7. Castellanos first discusses Mexican women's adherence to the patriarchal marriage system in her 1950 "Sobre cultura femenina," which I examine later. She lists the benefits women believe they obtain from matrimony: "they may not make it to heaven, and that does not matter, but they will make it to marriage, a more effective and immediate heaven. They will gain a man who protects them . . . A man who works for them, thinks for them, and feels superior to them. The man and the woman will form a couple, a household, a family" (175–76).

8. Castellanos treats the liberating force of humor in such essays as "La participación de la mujer en la educación formal," " 'Por sus máscaras los conoceréis . . .': Karen Blixen-Isak Dinesen" [By Their Masks You Will Know Them: Karen Blixen-Isak Dinesen], and "Si 'poesía no eres tú,' entonces ¿qué?" [If Poetry Is Not You, Then What?], all in *Mujer*. Humor, she observes, "is the most immediate form of liberation from what oppresses us" (*Mujer* 39). And reminiscent of Jorge Portilla's relajo: "Therefore, you have to laugh. And laughter, as we know, is the first mark of freedom" (*Mujer* 207).

9. Scholars have frequently noted that Castellanos gleans numerous staples of her agenda from Beauvoir's pathbreaking treatise. On Castellanos and *TSS* see Ahern, Ansoleaga, Cano, Larisch, Poniatowska (*Ay vida*), and Underwood.

10. Despite the existentialist nature of Castellanos's triangles and the abundant desire they encompass, I do not view them as Girardian. Girard's triangles of mimetic desire need a model and a mediator; in Castellanos's triangles, as we will see, everyone is flawed, and morality is open to (re)definition.

11. Expectably and reasonably, scholars find it difficult not to consider Castellanos's arguments in "Sobre cultura femenina" ironic. See, for example, Schwartz 40. O'Connell's substantial analysis of "Sobre" asserts that "Castellanos's text is ironic, subversive, and the text that emerges from her reading is productive of a 'double-voiced discourse' " (67–68). She also calls "Sobre" "a text divided against itself" (41), "marked by profound ambivalence, motivated by a powerful but never clearly articulated rejection of the misogynist tradition of Western European thought, yet still closely bound up in the concepts and values of that tradition" (27). Poniatowska believes the arguments of "Sobre" should be taken at face value (*Ay vida* 87), and Castellanos's later denial of the work would support that perspective.

12. In addition to the copious personal information in Castellanos's letters and Poniatowska's introduction to them, I draw on Muñoz's interview of Ricardo

Guerra. With regard to Guerra himself, I note that he was a distinguished professor and philosopher who studied with luminaries like José Gaos, Samuel Ramos, and Ramón Xirau at the UNAM, Maurice Merleau-Ponty and Jean Hyppolite in Paris, and Heidegger in Freiburg. He met with Sartre in Paris. Guerra went on to teach in and chair the Facultad de Filosofía at the UNAM. He founded two schools in Morelos as well as philosophy departments at universities in Guanajuato and Guadalajara. Although writing was not perhaps his greatest strength, Guerra authored *The Problem of the Body in the French Philosophical Tradition* (1956; his doctoral dissertation, written in French), *Filosofía y fin de siglo* [Philosophy and the End of the Century] (1996), and *Actualidad de Nietzsche* (2006). He collaborated with Wenceslao Roces on the translation of Hegel's *The Phenomenology of Spirit* (1966). Guerra also served as Mexico's ambassador to Germany from 1978 to 1983. After his divorce from Castellanos, Guerra married Margarita Moreno and then the philosopher Adriana Yáñez, with whom he coedited *Martín Heidegger: Caminos* [Martin Heidegger: Paths] (2009).

13. Castellanos's " 'La Naúsea' (un síntoma)" astutely summarizes Sartre's novel with attention to its formulations of freedom, choice, and action, as well as to the principal epiphany of *Nausea* that, as we will see, *Rito de iniciación* reprises. Her review of Sartre's *No Exit*, "A puerta cerrada," defines the "horror" of the play's hell thus: "each prisoner has become the torturer of the others" (564).

14. The prizewinning 2017 Mexican film *Los adioses* [The Goodbyes], based on Castellanos's letters, brought precisely this tension to the silver screen.

15. While Poniatowska portrays the letters as representing "a process of liberation and a triumph" ("Del 'Querido Niño' " 19), more in line with my thinking is her verdict, which cites Castellanos's poem "Meditación en el umbral" [Meditation on the Threshold]. "In the end," writes Poniatowska, "it is not Ricardo's continual infidelity nor his lies that matter but how Rosario Castellanos constructs 'another way to be human and free' " ("Del 'Querido Niño' " 21).

16. For instance, Guerra says of nihilation: "Here we thus have two forms of reality: being and nothingness; being is the 'in-itself,' objects, things, and nothingness is 'nihilation,' freedom, in a word, man" (299).

17. As further evidence: when outlining his "concept of philosophy" in 1958, Guerra (somewhat turbidly) remarks that for him philosophy "arises as a 'response,' an 'acceptance,' which constitute its only justification and its fulcrum; even in times of crisis (personal or subjective)," and that philosophy "is not a subjective problem, nor a personal confession" (Gaos et al., *Filosofía y vocación* 46, 48).

18. Castellanos writes: "I have taken for granted that 'the other woman' (whatever form she assumes) is a permanent institution, and I consider her to be a useful complement, necessary for maintaining the harmony of the household" (*Cartas* 326).

19. I base my discussion of *Rito*'s genesis and suppression on the information Mejía provides in his afterword to the novel; Castellanos states in the "Narradores"

interview (which was published in 1966 but might well have taken place in 1965, before she went to the US) that she is finishing the novel (*Obras II* 1017).

20. See Bustamante Bermúdez's article on the autobiographical dimensions of *Rito*. Likewise, *Rito* incorporates and transposes Castellanos's university colleagues. According to the author, her cohort included Emilio Carballido, Ernesto Cardenal, Sergio Fernández, Sergio Galindo, Miguel Guardia, Luisa Josefina Hernández, Sergio Magaña, Ernesto Mejía Sánchez, Augusto Monterroso, and Jaime Sabines ("Narradores" 1013).

21. Mejía mentions that the Künstlerroman, female or male, was hardly common currency in Mexico at the time (377). Both *Rito* and *Aura*, then, would be pioneering fictions for their context.

22. Castellanos's readings of Roquentin's chestnut tree epiphany in her articles "'La náusea'" and "Noche oscura del alma 1970" [Dark Night of the Soul; 1970] (both in *Mujer*) make it clear that she fully grasped Sartre's own argument on contingency. Her reprising of *Nausea* is therefore not a misprision but a conscious departure from Sartre's novel. Castellanos matches *Nausea*'s philosophical apogee with a large-scale conceit of her own: she has Cecilia glimpse the interrelatedness of all things in a Neoplatonic vision that combines two of the author's favorite poets, Sor Juana and Jorge Guillén (*Rito* 353). Intentionally or not, Cecilia's revelation also calls to mind the ending of Bombal's proto-existentialist *La amortajada* (1938) and Lispector's version of the Sartrean park scene in her story "Love" (*Family Ties*, 1960).

23. Castellanos's four essays on Beauvoir in *Juicios* (*Obras II*), in sequence, are: "Simone de Beauvoir o la lucidez" (624–34), "Simone de Beauvoir o la plenitud" (634–43), "La fuerza de las cosas" [The Force of Things; i.e., an essay on Beauvoir's book of the same title] (643–47), and "El amor en Simone de Beauvoir" (647–58). The "Lucidez" essay and several others by Castellanos also deal with the second major Simone in her life, the Christian activist and philosopher Simone Weil (1909–1943). Castellanos both equates the two Simones as strong, free women, and contrasts them: "In many ways, Simone Weil is a medieval figure. On the other hand, Simone de Beauvoir represents modernity, with all its contradictions and doubts, its evolution from a class-based ideology to one that encompasses all of humanity" (*Juicios* 626). She describes Weil as tormented, humble, and solitary but in solidarity with the disenfranchised, and heroic (626). Elsewhere, Castellanos states that while working with Indigenous peoples in Chiapas she read Weil, who opened her eyes to the relations between the oppressed and the oppressors (Carballo, *Diecinueve protagonistas* 420). On Castellanos and Weil, see Larisch and Jörgenson. The intersections of Weil's Christian social consciousness, Beauvoir's existential ethics, and Castellanos's approaches to the subjects certainly deserve further study.

24. Although I limit my analysis to the texts on which Castellanos comments, Beauvoir later extensively discussed the centrality of love/sexual affairs to her relationship with Sartre in *Adieux: A Farewell to Sartre* and *Letters to Sartre*. For a revealing summary, see Menand. The *Letters to Sartre*, unlike *SCS*, disclose

that all three parties had sexual relationships with one another. In terms of the love triangle, *Prime* and *SCS* cover the same ground and fit together inseparably. However, regretting the novel's ending, in *Prime* Beauvoir is at pains to destigmatize and exculpate her dear friend Olga Kosakievicz. She places much of the onus for the experiment's failure on Sartre.

25. Evans submits that Sartre's *No Exit* "is an implicit reply to Beauvoir's novel, *She Came to Stay*" (113). The predominance in *No Exit* of triangular relationships fueled by jealousy and hatred (Florence even kills Inez the same way that Françoise murders Xavier, by lighting the gas) supports Evans's point and mine—that in *No Exit* Sartre reaffirms the positions of *Being*. Bauer's superb "Beauvoir's Heideggerian Ontology" analyzes Beauvoir's reworking of Heidegger's and Sartre's Mitsein, also surveying other significant treatments of the subject.

26. Castellanos does concede that as a social experiment in freedom the "morganatic" relationship (*Juicios* 641) fell short: "The Sartre-De Beauvoir system does not sufficiently improve the current institution of matrimony" (*Mujer* 646). Gesturing to the principles that underlie *Eterno*, Castellanos maintains that, to succeed, private efforts must be accompanied by changes in the institution of marriage. She believes that the institution of marriage "cares more about safeguarding economic interests and social welfare and stability than about the dignity and happiness of the people who enter into this civil state" (*Mujer* 645). No one, she declares along with Sartre, will be saved unless everyone is (*Mujer* 658).

27. The existential situation that Castellanos invokes so frequently lends itself to two further topics she privileges: the concrete (versus the abstract) and the quotidian. For instance, in an essay on Carlos Monsiváis Castellanos asserts: "Viewed through the right lens, employing the appropriate methodology, every moment acquires the privileged status of showing us . . . what we are made of, what defines us, what limits us, what characterizes us" (*El mar* 822). The two topics accord with phenomenology and, once again, with Beauvoir, women's issues, and *TSS*. According to Castellanos, Beauvoir's *Prime* contends that "we learn more from studying a given case than from an abstract and general approach" (*Juicios* 635). *TSS* more fully links the quotidian and concrete to women. In line with the conversation between Pierre and Françoise cited above, *TSS* states that man "recites so-called general ideas," "woman is more attentive than man to herself and the world," and "the objects she touches are precious to her: by not binding them in concepts or projects, she displays their splendor" (662).

28. It would be a pity not to mention Castellanos's poem "El otro" (*Al pie de la letra*, in *Obras II*), which pronouncedly evokes the credo that Beauvoir frames as: "The other is there, before me" (*Pyrrhus* 116). Castellanos exclaims that the Other "está / presente a toda horas y es la víctima / y el enemigo y el amor y todo" [is always present and is the victim, the enemy, and love and everything]; and, "Mira a tu alrededor: hay otro, siempre hay otro" [Look around you: the other is there, always there] (116).

29. In *Prime* Beauvoir writes, "actual concrete possibilities vary from one person to the next. Some can attain to only a small part of those opportunities that are available to mankind at large"; and "I attempted to reconcile Sartre's ideas with the views I had upheld against him in various lengthy discussions: I was establishing an order of precedence among various 'situations'" (434). For a fine account of Beauvoir's divergences from Sartre vis-à-vis the situation and freedom, see Kruks, ch. 1.

Works Cited

Adams, Michael Ian. *Three Authors of Alienation: Bombal, Onetti, Carpentier*. U of Texas P, 1975.
Agustín, José. "Epílogo de José Agustín." *Obra literaria*, by José Revueltas, vol. 2, Empresas Editoriales, 1967, pp. 631–48.
Ahern, Maureen. "Reading Rosario Castellanos: Contexts, Voices, and Signs." *A Rosario Castellanos Reader*, edited by Maureen Ahern, U of Texas P, 1988, pp. 1–77.
Alazraki, Jaime. "Theme and System in *Aura*." *Carlos Fuentes: A Critical View*, edited by Robert Brody and Charles Rossman, U of Texas P, 1982, pp. 95–105.
Alexander, Ryan M. *Sons of the Mexican Revolution: Miguel Alemán and His Generation*. U of New Mexico P, 2016.
Amador Tello, Judith. "Juan Rulfo entre antropólogos." *Proceso*, 26 May 2017, https://www.proceso.com.mx/cultura/2017/5/26/juan-rulfo-entre-antropologos-184939.html.
Anderson, Thomas C. *Sartre's Two Ethics: From Authenticity to Integral Humanity*. Open Court, 1993.
Anhalt, Nedda G. de. "Conversaciones y lectura de Nedda G. de Anhalt con Raúl Ortiz y Ortiz sobre Rosario Castellanos." *Rosario memorable*, CONACULTA; Consejo Estatal para las Culturas y las Artes de Chiapas, 2012, pp. 52–99.
Ansoleaga, Blanca L. "Ser mujer como otro modo de ser." *Rosario Castellanos: De Comitán a Jerusalén*, edited by Luz Elena Zamudio R. and Margarita Tapia A., Tecnológico de Monterrey, 2006, pp. 49–57.
Appiah, Kwame Anthony. *The Ethics of Identity*. Princeton UP, 2005.
Ascencio, Juan Antonio. "Presentación." *Cartas a Ricardo*, by Rosario Castellanos, edited by Juan Antonio Ascencio, Consejo Nacional para la Cultura y las Artes, 1994, pp. 9–10.
Astrada, Carlos. *Existencialismo y crisis de la filosofía*. Devenir, 1963.
———. *La revolución existencialista*. Nuevo Destino, 1952.
———. *Ser, humanismo, "existencialismo."* Kairós, 1949.
Azuela, Mariano. *Los de abajo: Novela de la Revolución Mexicana*. FCE, 1958.

Balderston, Daniel. "Detalles circunstanciales: Sobre dos borradores de 'El escritor argentino y la tradición.'" *Cuadernos LIRICO*, vol. 9, 2013, https://journals.openedition.org/lirico/1111.

Barnes, Hazel E. *The Literature of Possibility: A Study in Humanistic Existentialism*. U of Nebraska P, 1959.

Bartra, Roger. *La jaula de la melancolía: Identidad y metamorfosis del mexicano*. Grijalbo, 1987.

Bastos, María Luisa, and Sylvia Molloy. "La estrella junto a la luna: Variantes de la figura materna en *Pedro Páramo*." *MLN*, vol. 92, no. 2, 1977, pp. 246–68.

———. "El personaje de Susana San Juan, clave de enunciación y de enunciados en *Pedro Páramo*." *Hispamérica*, vol. 7, no. 20, 1978, pp. 3–24.

Baudrillard, Jean. *Impossible Exchange*. Translated by Chris Turner, Verso, 2001.

Bauer, Nancy. "Beauvoir's Heideggerian Ontology." *Philosophy of Simon de Beauvoir*, edited by Margaret A. Simons, Indiana UP, 2006, pp. 65–91.

———. *Simone de Beauvoir, Philosophy, and Feminism*. Columbia UP, 2002.

Beardsell, Peter. *A Theatre for Cannibals: Rodolfo Usigli and the Mexican Stage*. Fairleigh Dickinson UP/Associated University Presses, 1992.

Beauvoir, Simone de. *Adieux: A Farewell to Sartre*. Translated by Patrick O'Brian, Pantheon, 1984.

———. *Letters to Sartre*. Translated by Quintin Hoare, Arcade, 1991.

———. *Philosophical Writings*. Edited by Margaret A. Simons, with Marybeth Timmermann and Mary Beth Mader, U of Illinois P, 2004.

———. *The Prime of Life*. Translated by Peter Green, World Publishing Company, 1962.

———. *Pyrrhus and Cineas*. *Philosophical Writings*, edited by Margaret A. Simons, with Marybeth Timmerman and Mary Beth Mader, U of Illinois P, 2004, pp. 89–149.

———. *The Second Sex*. Translated by Constance Borde and Sheila Malovany-Chevallier, Vintage, 2011.

———. *She Came to Stay*. Translated by Y. Moyse and R. Senhouse, World Publishing Company, 1954.

Bellos, David. Introduction. *The Myth of Sisyphus, The Plague, The Fall, Exile and the Kingdom, and Selected Essays*, by Albert Camus, translated by Stuart Gilbert and Justin O'Brien, Knopf, 2004, pp. ix–xxvi.

Benjamin, Thomas. *La Revolución: Mexico's Great Revolution as Memory, Myth, and History*. U of Texas P, 2000.

Benjamin, Walter. *The Origin of German Tragic Drama*. Translated by John Osborne, Verso, 1998.

Bergoffen, Debra. "Existentialism and Ethics." *The Continuum Companion to Existentialism*, edited by Felicity Josephy, Jack Reynolds, and Ashley Woodward, Bloomsbury, 2011, pp. 98–116.

Bergson, Henri. *Time and Free Will: An Essay on the Immediate Data of Consciousness*. Translated by F. L. Pogson, Unwin, 1910.

Bermúdez, María Elvira. *La vida familiar del mexicano*. Antigua Librería Robredo, 1955.
The Bible. Authorized King James Version, Oxford UP, 1998.
Bieber, León Enrique. *Las relaciones germano-mexicanas*. UNAM, 2001.
Billeter, Erika. "Juan Rulfo: Images of Memory." *Juan Rulfo's Mexico*, by Juan Rulfo, essays by Carlos Fuentes et al., translated by Margaret Sayers Peden, Smithsonian, 2002, pp. 39–43.
Blanco Aguinaga, Carlos. "Prólogo." *Un tiempo suspendido: Cronología de la vida y la obra de Juan Rulfo*, edited by Roberto García Bonilla, Centauro, 2009, pp. 13–17.
Bonfil Batalla, Guillermo. *México profundo: Una civilización negada*. Random House Mondadori, 2005.
Borges, Jorge Luis. *Obras completas, 1923–1972*. Emecé, 1974.
Bosteels, Bruno. *Marx and Freud in Latin America: Politics, Psychoanalysis, and Religion in Times of Terror*. Verso, 2021.
Buchenau, Jürgen. *Plutarco Elías Calles and the Mexican Revolution*. Rowman and Littlefield, 2007.
Bustamente Bermúdez, Gerardo. "Rasgos autobiográficos en *Rito de iniciación* de Rosario Castellanos." *Revista: Literatura Mexicana*, vol. 18, no. 1, 2007, pp. 89–105.
Butler, Judith. "Kierkegaard's Speculative Despair." *The Age of German Idealism*, edited by Robert C. Solomon and Kathleen M. Higgins, Routledge, 1993, pp. 363–92.
Campos, Marco Antonio. "*Los días terrenales* y el escándalo de las izquierdas." *Literatura: Teoría, historia, crítica*, no. 6, 2004, pp. 75–108.
Camus, Albert. *The Myth of Sisyphus*. Translated by Justin O'Brien. *The Plague, The Fall, Exile and the Kingdom, and Selected Essays*, translated by Stuart Gilbert and Justin O'Brien, Knopf, 2004, pp. 489–604.
———. "On Jean-Paul Sartre's *La Nausée*." *Lyrical and Critical Essays*, translated by Ellen Conroy Kennedy, edited by Philip Thody, Vintage, 1970, pp. 199–202.
———. *The Plague. The Plague, the Fall, Exile and the Kingdom, and Selected Essays*, translated by Justin O'Brien, Knopf, 2004, pp. 1–235.
———. *The Rebel: An Essay on Man in Revolt*. Translated by Anthony Bower, Knopf, 1969.
Cano, Gabriela. "*Sobre cultura femenina* de Rosario Castellanos." *Sobre cultura femenina*, by Rosario Castellanos, edited by Gabriela Cano, FCE, 2005, pp. 9–34.
Carballo, Emmanuel. *Diecinueve protagonistas de la literatura mexicana del siglo XX*. Empresas Editoriales, 1965.
———. "Revisión de Juan Rulfo." *unomásuno*, April 7, 1985, p. 23.
Carpentier, Alejo. *Los pasos perdidos*. Edited by Roberto González Echevarría, Cátedra, 1985.
Carrión, Jorge. *Mito y magia del mexicano*. Porrúa y Obregón, 1952.

Caso, Antonio. *La existencia como economía, como desinterés, y como caridad. Obras completas*, edited by Rosa Krauze de Kolteniuk, vol. 3, UNAM, 1972, pp. 1–120.
———. *El problema de México y la ideología nacional. Obras completas*, edited by Rosa Krauze de Kolteniuk, vol. 9, UNAM, 1976.
———. "Ramos y yo: Un ensayo de valoración personal." *Obras completas*, edited by Rosa Krauze de Kolteniuk, vol. 1, UNAM, 1971, pp. 142–57.
———. "San Agustín y Heidegger." *Obras completas*, edited by Rosa Krauze de Kolteniuk, vol. 3, UNAM, 1972, pp. 169–70.
———. "Trascendencia y libertad." *Obras completas*, edited by Rosa Krauze de Kolteniuk, vol. 3, UNAM, 1972, pp. 171–73.
Castellanos, Rosario. "A puerta cerrada." *Suma bibliográfica*, vol. 3, no. 15, 1948, pp. 563–64.
———. *Balún-Canán*. Edited by Dora Sales, Cátedra, 2004.
———. *The Book of Lamentations*. Translated by Esther Allen, Marsilio, 1996.
———. *Cartas a Ricardo*. Edited by Juan Antonio Ascencio, Consejo Nacional para la Cultura y las Artes, 1994.
———. "Cuando Sartre hace literatura." *Revista de la Universidad de México*, vol. 8, no. 4, 1973, pp. 19–24.
———. *El eterno femenino*. FCE, 1975.
———. *The Eternal Feminine*. Translated by Diane E. Marting and Betty Tyree Osiek. *A Rosario Castellanos Reader*, edited by Maureen Ahern, U of Texas P, 1988, pp. 273–357.
———. *Mujer que sabe latín*. FCE, 1984.
———. "'La Naúsea' (un síntoma)." *Suma bibliográfica*, vol. 3, no. 14, 1948, pp. 451–54.
———. *The Nine Guardians*. Translated by Irene Nicholson, Faber and Faber, 1959.
———. *Obras II: Poesía, teatro, y ensayos*. Edited by Eduardo Mejía, FCE, 1998.
———. *Oficio de tinieblas*. Joaquín Mortiz, 1972.
———. *Rito de iniciación*. Alfaguara, 1997.
———. *A Rosario Castellanos Reader*. Edited by Maureen Ahern, U of Texas P, 1988.
———. *Sobre cultura femenina*. Edited by Gabriela Cano, FCE, 2005.
———. *El uso de la palabra*. Edited by José Emilio Pacheco and Danubio Torres Fierro, Ediciones de Excélsior, 1974.
Castro Ricalde, Maricruz. "*Mujer que sabe latín*: Rosario Castellanos y el ensayo." *Rosario Castellanos, perspectivas críticas: Ensayos inéditos*, edited by Pol Popovic Karic and Fidel Chávez Pérez, Miguel Ángel Porrúa, 2010, pp. 169–97.
Cheron, Philippe. "Ficción y encierro: algunas modalidades 'carcelarias' en la obra literaria de José Revueltas." *El terreno de los días: Homenaje a José Revueltas*, edited by Francisco Ramírez Santacruz and Martín Oyata, Porrúa/Benemérita Universidad Autónoma de Puebla, 2007, pp. 207–23.

Cortázar, Julio. *Bestiario*. Sudamericana, 1972.
———. *Obra crítica*. *Obras completas*, edited by Saúl Yurkiévich and Gladis Anchieri, vol. 6, Galaxia Gutenberg, 2006.
———. "El perseguidor." *Ceremonias*, Seix Barral, 1970.
———. *Rayuela*. Edited by Andrés Amorós, Cátedra, 2008.
Cruz, Juan. "Entrevista, Juan Rulfo: 'No puedo escribir sobre lo que veo.'" *El País*, August 19, 1979, https://elpais.com/elpais/2015/07/27/actualidad/143799 1191_012418.html.
Danto, Arthur. *Nietzsche as Philosopher*. Columbia UP, 2005.
David, Guillermo. *Carlos Astrada, la filosofía argentina*. El Cielo por Asalto, 2004.
Davis, Colin. "Existentialism and Literature." *The Continuum Companion to Existentialism*, edited by Felicity Josephy, Jack Reynolds, and Ashley Woodward, Bloomsbury, 2011, pp. 138–54.
Derbyshire, Philip. "Andeanizing Philosophy: Rodolfo Kusch and Indigenous Thought." *Radical Philosophy*, no. 163, Sept.–Oct. 2010, https://www.radicalphilosophy.com/article/andeanizing-philosophy.
Derrida, Jacques. "White Mythology: Metaphor in the Text of Philosophy." *Margins of Philosophy*, translated by Alan Bass, U of Chicago P, 1982, pp. 207–72.
Díaz Ruanova, Oswaldo. *Los existencialistas mexicanos*. Editorial Rafael Giménez Siles, 1982.
Domínguez Michael, Christopher. *Octavio Paz en su siglo*. Aguilar, 2015.
Dostoevsky, Fyodor. *Notes from Underground*. Translated by Mirra Ginsburg, Bantam, 1985.
Drake, David. "The 'Anti-Existentialist Offensive': The French Communist Party against Sartre (1944–1948)." *Sartre Studies International*, vol. 16, no. 1, 2010, pp. 69–94.
Enríquez, José Ramón. "Dios, Cristo y Cíclope en la obra de Revueltas." *Nocturno en todo se oye: José Revueltas ante la crítica*, edited by Edith Negrín, Ediciones Era, 1999, pp. 265–74.
Escalante, Evodio. "Introducción del coordinador." *Los días terrenales: Edición crítica*, by José Revueltas, edited by Evodio Escalante, 2nd ed., ALLCA XXe, 1996, pp. xxix–xxxvii.
Eshleman, Matthew C. "Beauvoir and Sartre on Freedom, Intersubjectivity, and Normative Justification." *Beauvoir and Sartre: The Riddle of Influence*, edited by Christine Daigle and Jacob Golumb, Indiana UP, 2009, pp. 65–89.
Evans, Debbie. "Sartre and Beauvoir on Hegel's Master-Slave Dialectic and the Question of the 'Look.'" *Beauvoir and Sartre: The Riddle of Influence*, edited by Christine Daigle and Jacob Golumb, Indiana UP, 2009, pp. 90–115.
Fabbrichesi, Rossella. "Nietzsche and James: A Pragmatist Hermeneutics." *European Journal of Pragmatism and American Philosophy*, vol. 1, no. 1, 2009, pp. 1–16.
Faris, Wendy B. *Carlos Fuentes*. Frederick Ungar, 1983.

Farré, Luis. *Unamuno, William James y Kierkegaard y otros ensayos*. Editorial La Aurora, 1967.
Faulkner, William. *Requiem for a Nun*. Knopf Doubleday, 2011.
Flynn, Thomas. "Jean-Paul Sartre." *The Stanford Encyclopedia of Philosophy*, edited by Edward N. Zalta, fall 2013, https://plato.stanford.edu/archives/fall2013/entries/sartre.
Franco, Jean. *César Vallejo: The Dialectics of Poetry and Silence*. Cambridge UP, 1976.
Fuentes, Carlos. *Aura*. Ediciones Era, 1962.
———. "On Reading and Writing Myself: How I Wrote *Aura*." *World Literature Today*, vol. 57, no. 4, 1983, pp. 531–39.
———. *La región más transparente*. Edited by Georgina García Gutiérrez, Cátedra, 1994.
———. *Tiempo mexicano*. Joaquín Mortiz, 1971.
Fuentes Mares, José. *México en la hispanidad*. Instituto de Cultura Hispánica, 1949.
Gaos, José. *En torno a la filosofía mexicana*. Porrúa y Obregón, 1952.
Gaos, José, Ricardo Guerra, Alejandro Rossi, Emilio Uranga, Luis Villoro. *Filosofía y vocación: Seminario de filosofía moderna de José Gaos*. Edited by Aurelia Valero, FCE, 2012.
García Bonilla, Roberto. *Un tiempo suspendido: Cronología de la vida y la obra de Juan Rulfo*. Centauro, 2009.
García Máynez, Eduardo. "Antonio Caso, pensador y moralista." *Homenaje a Antonio Caso*, Editorial Stylo, 1947, pp. 41–56.
Girard, René. *Deceit, Desire, and the Novel: Self and Other in Literary Structure*. Translated by Yvonne Freccero, Johns Hopkins UP, 1965.
Gómez Robleda, José. *Imagen del mexicano*. Secretaria de Educación Pública, 1948.
González, Aníbal. *In Search of the Sacred Book: Religion and the Contemporary Latin American Novel*. U of Pittsburgh P, 2018.
González Boixo, José Carlos. Personal interview with Juan Rulfo, Apr. 30, 1983. Unpublished.
González Valenzuela, Juliana. *Ética y libertad*. UNAM/FCE, 1997.
Gordon, Lewis R. *Existentia Africana: Understanding Africana Existential Thought*. Routledge, 2000.
Gothlin, Eva. "Beauvoir and Sartre on Appeal, Desire, and Ambiguity." *Philosophy of Simon de Beauvoir*, edited by Margaret A. Simons, Indiana UP, 2006, pp. 32–145.
Gracia, Jorge J. E., and Elizabeth Millán-Zaibert. "General Introduction." *Latin American Philosophy for the 21st Century: The Human Condition, Values, and the Search for Identity*, edited by Jorge J. E. Gracia and Elizabeth Millán-Zaibert, Prometheus, 2004, pp. 13–22.
Gratton, Peter. "Sartre." *The Continuum Companion to Existentialism*, edited by Felicity Josephy, Jack Reynolds, and Ashley Woodward, Bloomsbury, 2011, pp. 305–10.

Guerra, Ricardo. "Una historia del Hiperión." *Los universitarios*, vol. 12, no. 18, 1984, pp. 15–17.

———. "Jean-Paul Sartre, filósofo de la libertad: Intento de aproximación esquemática a una filosofía." *Filosofía y letras*, vol. 16, no. 20, 1948, pp. 295–312.

Guimarães Rosa, João. *Sagarana*. Translated by Harriet de Onís, Knopf, 1966.

———. *The Third Bank of the River and Other Stories*. Translated by Barbara Shelby, Knopf, 1968.

Hale, Charles A. *The Transformation of Liberalism in Late Nineteenth-Century Mexico*. Princeton UP, 1989.

Harss, Luis, and Barbara Dohmann. *Into the Mainstream: Conversations with Latin American Writers*. Harper and Row, 1967.

Hayden, Rose Lee. *An Existential Focus on Some Novels of the River Plate*. Latin American Studies Center, Michigan State University, 1973.

Heidegger, Martin. *Being and Time*. Translated by John Macquarrie and Edward Robinson, Blackwell, 1962.

Henríquez Ureña, Pedro. *Horas de estudio*. Paul Ollenforff, 1910.

Homenaje a Antonio Caso. Editorial Stylo, 1947.

Hurtado, Guillermo. "The Anti-Positivist Movement in Mexico." *A Companion to Latin American Philosophy*, edited by Susana Nuccetelli, Ofelia Schutte, and Otávio Bueno, Wiley-Blackwell, 2010, pp. 82–94.

———. *El búho y la serpiente: Ensayos sobre la filosofía en México en el siglo XX*. UNAM, 2007.

———. *Dialéctica del naufragio*. FCE, 2016.

———. "Dos mitos de la mexicanidad." *Revista de filosofía Diánoia*, vol. 40, no. 40, 1994, pp. 263–93.

———. "Introducción." *El Hiperión: Antología*, edited by Guillermo Hurtado, UNAM, 2006, pp. ix–xl.

———. "Octavio Paz: *El laberinto de la soledad* (1950)." *México como problema: Esbozo de una historia intelectual*, edited by Carlos Illades and Rodolfo Suárez, Siglo XXI, 2012, pp. 239–55.

———. "Prólogo." *Análisis del ser del mexicano y otros escritos sobre la filosofía de lo mexicano (1949–1952)*, by Emilio Uranga, edited by Guillermo Hurtado, Bonilla Artigas Editores, 2013, pp. 11–26.

Jalif de Bertranou, Clara Alicia. "La fenomenología y la filosofía existencial." *El pensamiento filosófico latinoamericano, del Caribe y "latino" (1300–2000): Historia, corrientes, temas y filósofos*, edited by Enrique Dussel, Eduardo Mendieta, and Carmen Bohórquez, Siglo XXI, 2011, pp. 278–318.

Jiménez, Víctor. *Juan Rulfo: Letras e imágenes*. Editorial RM, 2002.

Jiménez de Báez, Yvette. "Historia y sentido en la obra de Juan Rulfo." *Juan Rulfo: Toda la obra*, edited by Claude Fell, ALLCA XXe, 1992, pp. 583–608.

Jiménez Rueda, Julio. "México en busca de su expresión." 1942. *El ensayo mexicano moderno*, edited by José Luis Martínez, FCE, 1958, pp. 380–87.

Jörgenson, Beth. "Actos de atención: Intersecciones en el pensamiento social de Weil, Castellanos y Poniatowska." *Revista Canadiense de Estudios Hispánicos*, vol. 31, no. 3, 2007, pp. 413–29.

Judaken, Jonathan. Introduction. *Situating Existentialism: Key Texts in Context*, edited by Jonathan Judaken and Robert Bernasconi, Columbia UP, 2012, pp. 1–33.

Katra, William H. *Contorno: Literary Engagement in Post-Peronist Argentina*. Fairleigh Dickinson UP, 1988.

Kierkegaard, Søren. *The Concept of Irony, with Continual Reference to Socrates*. Translated and edited by Howard V. Hong and Edna H. Hong, Princeton UP, 1989. Kierkegaard's Writings 2.

———. *Concluding Unscientific Postscript to Philosophical Fragments*. Translated and edited by Howard V. Hong and Edna H. Hong, vol. 1, Princeton UP, 1992. Kierkegaard's Writings 12.

———. *Practice in Christianity*. Translated and edited by Howard V. Hong and Edna H. Hong, Princeton UP, 1991. Kierkegaard's Writings 20.

———. *The Sickness unto Death*. Translated and edited by Howard V. Hong and Edna H. Hong, Princeton UP, 1980. Kierkegaard's Writings 19.

Klahn, Norma. "La ficción de Juan Rulfo: Nuevas formas del decir." *Juan Rulfo: Toda la obra*, edited by Claude Fell, ALLCA XXe, 1992, pp. 419–27.

Koui, Théophile. "*Los días terrenales*, la novela de la herejía." *Los días terrenales: Edición crítica*, by José Revueltas, edited by Evodio Escalante, 2nd ed., ALLCA XXe, 1996, pp. 215–42.

Krauze de Kolteniuk, Rosa. *La filosofía de Antonio Caso*. UNAM, 1990.

Kruks, Sonia. *Situation and Human Existence: Freedom, Subjectivity and Society*. Unwin Hyman, 1990.

Kusch, Rodolfo. *América profunda. Obras completas*, vol. 2, Editorial Fundación Ross, 2007.

Larisch, Sharon. "Ethics, Eros, and Necessity: Rosario Castellanos on the Two Simones." *Chasqui*, vol. 39, no. 1, 2010, pp. 104–19.

Layera, Ramón. "Mecanismos de fabulación y mitificación de la historia en las comedias impolíticas y las *Coronas* de Rodolfo Usigli." *Latin American Theatre Review*, vol. 18, no. 2, 1985, pp. 49–55.

Leidenberger, Georg. "Samuel Ramos: *La historia de la filosofía en México* (1943)." *México como problema: Esbozo de una historia intelectual*, edited by Carlos Illades and Rodolfo Suárez, Siglo XXI, 2012, pp. 222–38.

Lerner, Victoria. *Historia de la Revolución mexicana (período 1934–1940)*. Colegio de México, 1979.

Lewald, H. Ernest. *Eduardo Mallea*. Twayne, 1977.

Lezama, Leopoldo. *En busca de* Pedro Páramo. STUNAM, 2018.

Lienhard, Martin. "El substrato arcáico en *Pedro Páramo*: Quetzalcóatl y Tláloc." *Juan Rulfo: Toda la obra*, edited by Claude Fell, ALLCA XXe, 1992, pp. 842–50.

Lipp, Solomon. *Leopoldo Zea: From* Mexicanidad *to a Philosophy of History*. Wilfrid Laurier UP, 1980.
Lispector, Clarice. *Family Ties*. Translated by Giovanni Pontiero, U of Texas P, 1972.
López Mena, Sergio. *Los caminos de la creación en Juan Rulfo*. UNAM, 1993.
———. "Juan Rulfo y el mundo indígena." *Fragmentos*, vol. 23, 2002, pp. 103–09.
Maffie, James. *Aztec Philosophy: Understanding a World in Motion*. UP of Colorado, 2014.
Maldonado-Torres, Nelson. "Post-continental Philosophy: Its Definition, Contours, and Fundamental Sources." *Worlds and Knowledges Otherwise*, vol. 1, dossier 3, fall 2006, pp. 2–29.
Mallea, Eduardo. *Historia de una pasión argentina*. Espasa-Calpe Argentina, 1945.
Manrique, Linnete. "Dreaming of a Cosmic Race: José Vasconcelos and the Politics of Race in Mexico." *Cogent Arts and Humanities*, vol. 3, no. 1, 2016, https://www.cogentoa.com/article/10.1080/23311983.2016.1218316.
Marcel, Gabriel. *Man against Mass Society*. Translated by G. S. Fraser. Gateway, 1978.
———. *The Philosophy of Existentialism*. Translated by Manya Harari, Citadel, 1961.
———. *Posición y aproximaciones concretas al misterio ontológico*. Translated by Luis Villoro, Filosofía y Letras, 1955.
Marías, Julián. *El existencialismo en España*. Ediciones Universidad Nacional de Colombia, 1953.
Mariátegui, José Carlos. *7 ensayos de interpretación de la realidad peruana*. Edited by Elizabeth Garrels, Ayacucho, 2007.
Martínez, María Antonia. *El despegue constructivo de la Revolución: Sociedad y política en el alemanismo*. Porrúa, 2004.
Martínez Estrada, Ezequiel. *Radiografía de la pampa*. FCE, 1988.
Medin, Tzvi. *Ideología y praxis política de Lázaro Cárdenas*. 1973. Siglo XXI, 1992.
———. "La mexicanidad política y filosófica en el sexenio de Miguel Alemán. 1946–1952." *Estudios Interdisciplinarios de América Latina y el Caribe*, vol. 1, no. 1, 1999, http://eial.tau.ac.il/index.php/eial/article/view/1308/1334.
Mejía, Eduardo. "El libro de Rosario Castellanos que se no perdió." *Rito de iniciación*, by Rosario Castellanos, Alfaguara, 1997, pp. 369–83.
Meléndez, Priscilla. *The Politics of Farce in Contemporary Spanish American Theatre*. North Carolina Studies in the Romance Languages and Literatures, 2006.
Menand, Louis. "Stand by Your Man." *The New Yorker*, 18 Sept. 2005. http://www.newyorker.com/magazine/2005/09/26/stand-by-your-man.
Mendieta, Eduardo, and Jonathan VanAntwerpen. Introduction. *The Power of Religion in the Public Sphere*, edited by Eduardo Mendieta and Jonathan VanAntwerpen, Columbia UP, 2011, pp. 1–14.
Menéndez Samará, Adolfo. *Menester y precisión del ser*. Antigua Librería Robredo, 1946.
Meyran, Daniel. "Introducción." *El gesticulador*, by Rodolfo Usigli, edited by Daniel Meyran, 2nd ed., Cátedra, 2010, pp. 9–91.

Michelet, Jules. *Satanism and Witchcraft: A Study in Medieval Superstition.* Translated by A. R. Allinson, Citadel, 1939.
Mignolo, Walter D. "Introduction: Immigrant Consciousness." *Indigenous and Popular Thinking in America*, by Rodolfo Kusch, translated by Joshua M. Price and María Lugones, Duke UP, 2010, pp. lv–lxx.
Montoya, Claudia. "El luto humano, una visión mitificada del mexicano y de su historia." *Hispanófila*, vol. 152, 2008, pp. 67–85.
Moraña, Mabel. "Historicismo y legitimación del poder en *El gesticulador* de Rodolfo Usigli." *Revista Iberoamericana*, vol. 55, no. 148–49, 1989, pp. 1261–75.
Muñoz, Miguel Ángel. "Ricardo Guerra cuenta su amor y su vida con Rosario Castellanos." *Crónica*, 28 September 2018, https://www.cronica.com.mx/notasricardo_guerra_cuenta_su_amor_y_vida_con_rosario_castellanos-1094812-2018.html.
Náter, Miguel Ángel, *Los demonios de la duda: Teatro existencialista hispanoamericano.* Editorial Isla Negra, 2004.
Negrín, Edith. *Entre la paradoja y la dialéctica: Una lectura de José Revueltas (literatura y sociedad).* Colegio de México/UNAM, 1995.
Nietzsche, Friedrich. "On Truth and Lying in an Extra-Moral Sense." *Friedrich Nietzsche on Rhetoric and Language.* Edited, translated, and introduction by Sander Gilman et al., Oxford UP, 1989, pp. 246–57.
Noro, Jorge Eduardo. "Vigilancia, castigo y temor en *Un dios cotidiano* de David Viñas." https://www.academia.edu/11772380/41_DAVID_VIÑA_EDUCACIÓN_VIOLENCIA_Y_CASTIGO_EN_UN_DIOS_COTIDIANO.
Nubiola, Jaime. "The Reception of William James in Continental Europe." *William James and the Transatlantic Conversation: Pragmatism, Pluralism, and Philosophy of Religion*, edited by Martin Halliwell and Joel D. S. Rasmussen, Oxford UP, 2014, pp. 15–29.
Ochoa, John A. *The Uses of Failure in Mexican Literature and Identity.* U of Texas P, 2005.
O'Connell, Joanna. *Prospero's Daughter: The Prose of Rosario Castellanos.* U of Texas P, 1995.
Olivier, Florence. "*Los días terrenales*, un debate." *Los días terrenales: Edición crítica*, by José Revueltas, edited by Evodio Escalante, 2nd ed., ALLCA XXe, 1996, pp. 251–75.
Olsen, Patrice Elizabeth. *Artifacts of Revolution: Architecture, Society, and Politics in Mexico City.* Rowman and Littlefield, 2008.
O'Malley, Ilene V. *The Myth of the Revolution: Hero Cults and the Institutionalization of the Mexican State, 1920–1940.* Greenwood Press, 1986.
Onetti, Juan Carlos. *El pozo.* Arca, 1969.
Orduña Carson, Miguel. "José Revueltas: *México: Una democracia bárbara* (1958)." *México como problema: Esbozo de una historia intelectual*, edited by Carlos Illades and Rodolfo Suárez, Siglo XXI, 2012, pp. 140–54.
Orlando, John. "Human Relationships in Sartre's 'Notebooks for an Ethics.'" *Sartre Studies International*, vol. 2, no. 2, 1996, pp. 49–64.

Orrego Arismendi, Juan Carlos. "Lo indígena en la obra de Juan Rulfo: Vicisitudes de una 'mente antropológica.'" *Co-herencia*, vol. 5, no. 9, 2008, http://www.scielo.org.co/scielo.php?script=sci_arttext&pid=S1794-58872008000200005.
Ortega y Gasset, José. "La pampa . . . promesas." *Meditación del Pueblo Joven*, Revista de Occidente, 1962, pp. 2–14.
———. *Meditaciones del Quijote*. Edited by Julián Marías, Cátedra, 1984.
Ortiz Guadarrama, Tania. "Reseña: *La existencia como economía como desinterés y como caridad*." Círculo de Estudios de Filosofía Mexicana, 24 June 2013, https://filosofiamexicana.org/2013/06/24/la-existencia-como-economia-como-desinteres-y-como-caridad-resena.
Pacheco, José Emilio. *Las batallas en el desierto*. Ediciones Era, 1981.
Paoli, Roberto. "España, aparta de mí este cáliz." *César Vallejo*, edited by Julio Ortega, Taurus, 1974, pp. 347–72.
Pappas, Gregory Fernando, editor. *Pragmatism in the Americas*. Fordham UP, 2011.
Paz, Octavio. "Christianity and Revolution: Two Reviews of José Revueltas's *Human Mourning* by Octavio Paz." *Human Mourning*, by José Revueltas, translated by Roberto Crespi, U of Minnesota P, 1990, pp. vii–xxi.
———. *Itinerario*. Planeta, 1994.
———. *El laberinto de la soledad*. Edited by Enrico Mario Santí, Cátedra, 1993.
———. *The Labyrinth of Solitude and The Other Mexico, Retun to the Labyrinth of Solitude, Mexico and the United States, The Philanthropic Ogre*. Translated by Lysander Kemp, Yara Milos, and Rachel Philips Belash, Grove Press, 1985.
———. "Memento, Jean Paul Sartre." *Hombres en su siglo*, Seix Barral, 1984, pp. 111–25.
———. *México en la obra de Octavio Paz*. Vol. 2, FCE, 1987.
———. "Vuelta a *El laberinto de la soledad*: Conversación con Claude Fell." *El laberinto de la soledad*, edited by Enrico Mario Santí, Cátedra, 1993, pp. 417–43.
Pérez Monfort, Ricardo. "Ana Santos y los que miraron desde arriba." *Los hijos de los dioses: El* Grupo filosófico Hiperión *y la filosofía de lo* mexicano, by Ana Santos Ruiz, Bonilla Artigas Editores, 2015, pp. xiii–xviii.
Poniatowska, Elena. "Agente de Migración y vendedor de llantas, antes de ser escritor/ III parte." *Novedades*, 29 Apr. 1980, p. 1.
———. *¡Ay vida, no me mereces!* Joaquín Mortiz, 1985.
———. "Del 'Querido Niño Guerra' al 'Cabellitos de Elote.'" *Cartas a Ricardo*, by Rosario Castellanos, edited by Juan Antonio Ascencio, Consejo Nacional para la Cultura y las Artes, 1994, pp. 11–23.
Poot Herrera, Sara. "Primicias feministas y amistades literarias en el México del siglo XX." *Nueve escritoras mexicanas nacidas en la primera mitad del siglo XX, y una revista*, edited by Elena Urrutia, Colegio de México, 2006, pp. 35–78.
Portilla, Jorge. *Fenomenología del relajo y otros ensayos*. FCE, 1984.
Ramos, Samuel. "Antonio Caso." *Obras completas*, by Antonio Caso, edited by Rosa Krauze de Kolteniuk, vol. 1, UNAM, 1971, pp. 158–67.

———. *Hacia un nuevo humanismo: Programa de una antropología filosófica*. FCE, 1997.

———. *Historia de la filosofía mexicana*. Imprenta Universitaria, 1943.

———. *El perfil del hombre y la cultura en México*. 3rd ed., Austral, 1951.

Reeve, Richard M. "The Making of *La región más transparente*: 1949–1974." *Carlos Fuentes: A Critical View*, edited by Robert Brody and Charles Rossman, U of Texas P, 1982, pp. 34–63.

———. "Octavio Paz and Hiperión in *La región más transparente*: Plagiarism, Caricature or . . . ?" *Chasqui*, vol. 3, no. 3, 1974, pp. 13–25.

Revueltas, José. "Arte y cristianismo: César Vallejo." *Visión del Paricutín (y otras crónicas y reseñas)*, edited by Andrea Revueltas and Philippe Cheron, Ediciones Era, 1983, pp. 192–95.

———. *Conversaciones con José Revueltas*. Edited by Andrea Revueltas and Philippe Cheron, Ediciones Era, 2001.

———. *Los días terrenales: Edición crítica*. Edited by Evodio Escalante. 2nd ed., ALLCA XX, 1996.

———. *Dios en la tierra (cuentos)*. Obra literaria, vol. 2, Empresas Editoriales, 1967.

———. *Ensayos sobre México*. Edited by Andrea Revueltas and Philippe Cheron, Ediciones Era, 1985.

———. *Human Mourning*. Translated by Roberto Crespi, U of Minnesota P, 1990.

———. *El luto humano*. Ediciones Era, 1980.

———. "Sobre mi obra literaria." *Los días terrenales: Edición crítica*, edited by Evodio Escalante, 2nd ed., ALLCA XXe, 1996, pp. 419–28.

———. *Visión del Paricutín (y otras crónicas y reseñas)*. Edited by Andrea Revueltas and Philippe Cheron, Ediciones Era, 1983.

Reyes Nevares, Salvador. *El amor y la amistad en el mexicano*. Porrúa y Obregón, 1952.

Rivera-Rodas, Óscar. "Rosario Castellanos y los discursos de identidad." *Literatura Mexicana*, vol. 20, no. 1, 2009, pp. 89–118.

Roca, Pilar. *Política y sociedad en la novelística de David Viñas*. Editorial Biblos, 2007.

Rodó, José Enrique. *Ariel*. Las Américas, 1967.

Rodríguez, Antonio (aka Juan Almagre). "El arte en México." *Los días terrenales: Edición crítica*, by José Revueltas, edited by Evodio Escalante, 2nd ed., ALLCA XXe, 1996, pp. 382–84.

Rodríguez, Roberto. "Vida y teatro de Rodolfo Usigli: 3 conversaciones." *Tramoya*, no. 13, 1978, http://cdigital.uv.mx/bitstream/123456789/4895/2/197813P45.pdf.

Rodríguez Monegal, Emir. *El juicio de los parricidas. La nueva generación argentina y sus maestros*. Editorial Deucalión, 1956.

———. *Narradores de esta América*. Vol. 1, Alfa, 1969.

Romano, Luís Antônio Contatori. *A passagem de Sartre e Simone de Beauvoir pelo Brasil em 1960*. Mercado de Letras, 2002.

Ruffinelli, Jorge. *José Revueltas: Ficción, política y verdad*. Universidad Veracruzana, 1977.

Ruiz Abreu, Álvaro. "Revueltas, nostalgia por la unidad perdida." *El terreno de los días: Homenaje a José Revueltas*, edited by Francisco Ramírez Santacruz and Martín Oyata, Porrúa/Benemérita Universidad Autónoma de Puebla, 2007, pp. 41–55.
Rulfo, Juan. *Los cuadernos de Juan Rulfo*. Edited by Yvette Jiménez de Báez, Ediciones Era, 1994.
———. "El desafío de la creación." *Juan Rulfo: Toda la obra*, edited by Claude Fell, ALLCA XXe, 1992, pp. 383–85.
———. "Juan Rulfo examina su narrativa." *Juan Rulfo: Toda la obra*, edited by Claude Fell, ALLCA XXe, 1992, pp. 873–81.
———. *Juan Rulfo's Mexico*, by Juan Rulfo, essays by Carlos Fuentes et al., translated by Margaret Sayers Peden, Smithsonian, 2002.
———. "México y los mexicanos." *Juan Rulfo: Toda la obra*, edited by Claude Fell, ALLCA XXe, 1992, pp. 400–402.
———. "Notas sobre la literatura indígena en México." *Los mundos de Juan Rulfo*, special issue of *Inti: Revista de Literatura Hispánica.*, vol. 1, no. 13, 1981, pp. 2–8.
———. *Pedro Páramo*. Edited by José Carlos Boixo, Cátedra, 1999.
———. *Pedro Páramo*. Translated by Margaret Sayers Peden, Grove Press, 1994.
———. "Un pedazo de noche." *Juan Rulfo: Toda la obra*, edited by Claude Fell, ALLCA XXe, 1992, pp. 311–16.
———. "Situación actual de la novela contemporánea." *Juan Rulfo: Toda la obra*, edited by Claude Fell, ALLCA XXe, 1992, pp. 371–79.
Sábato, Ernesto. *El túnel*. Edited by Ángel Leiva, Cátedra, 1976.
Safarti-Arnaud, Monique. "'Dios en la tierra' de José Revueltas." *Nocturno en todo se oye: José Revueltas ante la crítica*, edited by Edith Negrín, Ediciones Era, 1999, pp. 165–72.
Sánchez, Carlos Alberto. *Contingency and Commitment: Mexican Existentialism and the Place of Philosophy*. State U of New York P, 2016.
———. "Heidegger in Mexico: Emilio Uranga's Ontological Hermeneutics." *Continental Philosophy Review*, vol. 41, no. 4, 2008, pp. 441–61.
———. *The Suspension of Seriousness: On the Phenomenology of Jorge Portilla, with a Translation of* Fenomenología del relajo. State U of New York P, 2013.
Sánchez, Carlos Alberto, and Robert Eli Sanchez, Jr. Introduction. *Mexican Philosophy in the 20th Century: Essential Readings*, edited by Carlos Alberto Sánchez and Robert Eli Sanchez, Jr., Oxford UP, 2017, pp. xxi–lviii.
Sánchez MacGrégor, Joaquín. "¿Hay una moral existencialista?" *Filosofía y letras*, vol. 15, no. 30, 1948, pp. 267–78.
Sánchez Prado, Ignacio. "'Bienaventurados los marginados porque ellos recibirán la redención': José Revueltas y el vaciamiento literario del marxismo." *El terreno de los días: Homenaje a José Revueltas*, edited by Francisco Ramírez Santacruz and Martín Oyata, Porrúa/Benemérita Universidad Autónoma de Puebla, 2007, pp. 147–73.

———. *Naciones intelectuales: Las fundaciones de la modernidad literaria mexicana (1917–1959)*. Purdue UP, 2009.
Sánchez Reulet, Aníbal. Introduction. *Contemporary Latin-American Philosophy: A Selection*, translated by Willard R. Trask, edited by Aníbal Sánchez Reulet, U of New Mexico P, 1945, pp. xi–xx.
Santí, Enrico Mario. "Introducción." *El laberinto de la soledad*, by Octavio Paz, edited by Enrico Mario Santí, Cátedra, 1993, pp. 11–132.
Santos Ruiz, Ana. *Los hijos de los dioses: El* Grupo filosófico Hiperión *y la filosofía de lo mexicano*. Bonilla Artigas Editores, 2015.
Sarlo, Beatriz. "Los dos ojos de *Contorno*." *Revista Iberoamericana*, vol. 49, no. 125, 1983, pp. 797–807.
Sartre, Jean-Paul. *The Age of Reason*. Translated by Eric Sutton, Knopf, 1952.
———. *Anti-Semite and Jew: An Exploration of the Etiology of Hate*. Translated by George J. Becker, Schocken Books, 1995.
———. *Being and Nothingness: An Essay on Phenomenological Ontology*. Translated by Hazel E. Barnes, Philosophical Library, 1956.
———. *Existentialism Is a Humanism*. Translated by Carol Macomber, edited by John Kulka, Yale UP, 2007.
———. *The Flies. No Exit and Three Other Plays*, translated by Stuart Gilbert, Vintage, 1989, pp. 47–124.
———. "Materialism and Revolution." *Literary and Philosophical Essays*, translated by Annette Michelson, Collier Books, 1962, pp. 198–256.
———. *Nausea*. Translated by Lloyd Alexander, New Directions, 2007.
———. *No Exit and Three Other Plays*. Translated by Stuart Gilbert, Vintage, 1989.
———. *Sartre on Theater*. Translated by Frank Jellinek, edited by Michel Contant and Michel Rybalka, Pantheon, 1976.
———. *What Is Literature?* Translated by Bernard Frechtman, Philosophical Library, 1949.
Schmidhuber de la Mora, Guillermo. *Apología de Rodolfo Usigli: Las polaridades usiglianas*. Guadalajara UP, 2004.
Schmidt, Henry C. *The Roots of* Lo Mexicano*: Self and Society in Mexican Thought, 1900–1934*. Texas A&M P, 1978.
Schwartz, Perla. *Rosario Castellanos: Mujer que supo latín*. Katún, 1984.
Scott, Niall, and Jonathan Seglow. *Altruism*. Open UP, 2007.
Seale Vásquez, Mary. "Rosario Castellanos, Image and Idea." *Homenaje a Rosario Castellanos*, edited by Maureen Ahern and Mary Seale Vásquez, Albatros, 1980, pp. 15–40.
Sierra, Justo. "Discurso pronunciado en la velada que tuvo lugar en el Teatro Arbeu, la noche del 22 de marzo de 1908, en honor del maestro Dr. Don Gabino Barreda." *Antología del pensamiento de la lengua española en la edad contemporánea*, edited by José Gaos, Editorial Séneca, 1945, pp. 800–812.

Simons, Margaret A. Introduction. *Philosophy of Simon de Beauvoir*, edited by Margaret A. Simons, Indiana UP, 2006, pp. 1–10.
Sinhababu, Neil. "Nietzschean Pragmatism." *The Journal of Nietzsche Studies*, vol. 48, no. 1, 2017, pp. 56–70.
Sommers, Joseph. "Juan Rulfo: Entrevista." *Hispamérica*, vol. 2, nos. 4–5, 1973, pp. 103–07.
Spade, Paul Vincent. "Jean-Paul Sartre's *Being and Nothingness*." http://pvspade.com/Sartre/pdf/sartre1.pdf.
Stabb, Martin S. *In Quest of Identity: Patterns in the Spanish American Essay of Ideas, 1890–1960*. U of North Carolina P, 1967.
Stanton, Anthony. "Estructuras antropológicas en *Pedro Páramo*." *Juan Rulfo: Toda la obra*, edited by Claude Fell, ALLCA XXe, 1992, pp. 851–73.
———. "Una lectura de *El arco y la lira*." *Reflexiones Lingüísticas y Literarias*, vol. 2, *Literatura*, edited by Rafael Olea Franco and James Valender, Colegio de México, 1992, pp. 301–22.
Stavans, Ilan. *José Vasconcelos: The Prophet of Race*. Rutgers UP, 2011.
Stehn, Alexander V. "From Positivism to 'Anti-Positivism' in Mexico: Some Notable Continuities." *Latin American Positivism: New Historical and Philosophical Essays*, edited by Gregory D. Gilson and Irving W. Levinson, Lexington Books, 2012, pp. 49–81.
Stern, Alexandra Minna. "Eugenics and Racial Classification in Modern Mexican America." *Race and Classification: The Case of Mexican America*, edited by Ilona Katzew and Susan Deans-Smith, Stanford UP, 2009, pp. 151–73.
Swansey, Bruce. *Del fraude al milagro: Visión de la historia en Usigli*. Universidad Autónoma Metropolitana, 2009.
Tattam, Helen. *Time in the Philosophy of Gabriel Marcel*. Modern Humanities Research Association, 2013.
Thakkar, Amit. "One Rainy Day: 'Integration' and the Indigenous Community in the Fiction and Thought of Juan Rulfo." *(Re)Collecting the Past: History and Collective Memory in Latin American Narrative*, edited by Victoria Carpenter, Peter Lang, 2010, pp. 191–216.
Toledo, Roberto Domingo. "Existentialism and Latin America." *The Continuum Companion to Existentialism*, edited by Felicity Josephy, Jack Reynolds, and Ashley Woodward, Bloomsbury, 2011, pp. 215–37.
Trotsky, Leon. *Their Morals and Ours*. Pathfinder Press, 1973.
Unamuno, Miguel de. *San Manuel Bueno, mártir*. Edited by Mario Valdés, Cátedra, 1984.
———. *Vida de Don Quijote y Sancho*. Espasa-Calpe, 1961.
Underwood, Leticia Iliana. "The Legacy of Simone de Beauvoir in Mexico: Rosario Castellanos." *Simone de Beauvoir Studies*, vol. 10, no. 1, 1993, pp. 165–73.

Uranga, Emilio. *Algo más sobre José Gaos: Seguido de Una Bibliohemerografía Aproximada*. Edited by Adolfo Castañón, Colegio de México, 2016. E-book ed. EBSCOhost.com.

———. "Antonio Caso y Emile Meyerson." *Homenaje a Antonio Caso*, Editorial Stylo, 1947, pp. 219–53.

———. *Análisis del ser del mexicano y otros escritos sobre la filosofía de lo mexicano (1949–1952)*. Edited by Guillermo Hurtado, Bonilla Artigas Editores, 2013.

———. *Astucias literarias*. Goberno del Estado de Guanajuato, 1990.

———. *Emilio Uranga's Analysis of Mexican Being: A Translation and Critical Introduction*. Translated and edited by Carlos Sánchez, Bloomsbury, 2021.

———. "Maurice Merleau-Ponty: Fenomenología y existencialismo." *Filosofía y letras*, vol. 15, no. 30, 1948, pp. 219–41.

Urrutia León, Manuel María. *Evolución del pensamiento político de Unamuno*. Universidad de Deusto, 2009.

Usigli, Rodolfo. *Corona de Luz: La Virgen*. FCE, 1965.

———. *El gesticulador*. Edited by Daniel Meyran. 2nd ed., Cátedra, 2010.

———. *The Imposter: A Play for Demagogues*. Translated by Ramón Layera in collaboration with Don Rosenberg, Latin American Literary Review Press, 2005.

———. *Juan Ruiz de Alarcón en el tiempo*. Revista de la Universidad, UNAM, https://www.revistadelauniversidad.mx/download/1d7788c2-dbb4-4b11-853b-092d417ec0c0?filename=juan-ruiz-de-alarcon-en-el-tiempo.

———. Letters to Antonio Caso. Rodolfo Usigli Archive, Miami University, Oxford, Ohio. Manuscript.

———. *Teatro completo*. Vol. 1, FCE, 1963.

———. *Teatro completo*. Vol. 3, FCE, 1979.

———. *Teatro completo*. Edited by Luis Tavira, vol. 5, FCE, 2005.

Valadés, Edmundo. "Tertulia literaria: La tinta fresca." *Novedades*, 30 Mar. 1955, pp. 1, 5.

Valdés, María Elena de. *The Shattered Mirror: Representations of Women in Mexican Literature*. U of Texas P, 2010.

Valenzuela, Andrea. "*Los días terrenales* del PCM y José Revueltas: Polémica, poética y el papel del intelectual." *Literatura Mexicana*, vol. 25, no. 2, pp. 39–63.

Valero Pie, Aurelia. *José Gaos en México: Una biografía intelectual, 1938–1969*. Colegio de México, 2015.

Vallejo, César. *The Complete Poetry: A Bilingual Edition*. Translated and edited by Clayton Eshleman, U of California P, 2007.

Vargas Llosa, Mario. *Entre Sartre y Camus*. Ediciones Huracán, 1981.

———. *La ciudad y los perros*. Cátedra, 2021.

Vasconcelos, José. *La raza cósmica*. Porrúa, 2001.

Vevia Romero, Fernando Carlos. *La sociedad mexicana en el teatro de Rodolfo Usigli*. Universidad de Guadalajara, 1990.

Vieyra, Jaime. "El problema del ser mexicano." *Devenires*, vol. 7, no. 14, 2006, pp. 51–100.
Villegas, Abelardo. *La filosofía de lo mexicano*. FCE, 1960.
Villoro, Luis. "La cultura mexicana de 1910 a 1960." *Historia Mexicana*, vol. 10, no. 2, 1960, pp. 196–219.
———. "Génesis y proyecto del existencialismo en México." *Filosofía y letras*, vol. 18, no. 36, 1949, pp. 233–44.
———. *Los grandes momentos del indigenismo en México*. 3rd ed., FCE, 1996.
———. *El poder y el valor: Fundamentos de una ética política*. FCE, 1997.
———. "La reflexión sobre el ser en Gabriel Marcel." *Filosofía y letras*, vol. 15, no. 30, 1948, pp. 279–94.
———. "Soledad y comunión." *La significación del silencio y otros ensayos*. Universidad Autónoma Mexicana, 2008, pp. 25–47.
Viñas, David. *Un dios cotidiano*. Centro Editor de América Latina, 1992.
Viñas, Ismael. "Prólogo." *Contorno: Edición facsimilar*, by Ismael Viñas et al., Biblioteca Nacional, 2007, pp. iii–ix.
Viñas, Ismael, et al. *Contorno: Edición facsimilar*. Biblioteca Nacional, 2007.
Vital, Alberto. *Noticias sobre Juan Rulfo, 1784–2003*. Ediciones RM, 2003.
Volek, Emil. "Mexico: 20th-Century Prose and Poetry." *Encyclopedia of Latin American Literature*, edited by Verity Smith, Fitzroy Dearborn, 1977, pp. 549–55.
Walzer, Michael. "Political Action: The Problem of Dirty Hands." *Philosophy and Public Affairs*, vol. 2, no. 2, 1973, pp. 160–80.
Weiss, Gale. "Freedom F/Or the Other." *Beauvoir and Sartre: The Riddle of Influence*, edited by Christine Daigle and Jacob Golumb, Indiana UP, 2009, pp. 241–54.
Yáñez, Agustín. *Al filo del agua*. Porrúa, 1955.
———. "Introducción." *Crónicas de la conquista*, edited by Agustín Yáñez, 4th ed., UNAM, 1987, pp. v–xv.
———. *Mitos indígenas*. Ediciones de la Universidad Nacional Autonoma, 1942.
Young, Robert J. C. *White Mythologies: Writing History and the West*. Routledge, 1990.
Zamorano Meza, José Manuel. *Existential Octavio Paz or the Poetic Essence of Being*, http://hdl.handle.net/2429/42954.
Zea, Leopoldo. "Advertencia." *La X en la frente*, by Alfonso Reyes, Porrúa y Obregón, 1952, pp. 7–9.
———. "Antonio Caso y la Mexicanidad." *Homenaje a Antonio Caso*, Editorial Stylo, 1947, pp. 95–108.
———. *Conciencia y posibilidad del mexicano*. Porrúa, 2001.
———. *Dos etapas del pensamiento en Hispanoamérica: Del romanticismo al positivismo*. Colegio de México, 1949.
———. "La filosofía como compromiso." *El Hiperión: Antología*, edited by Guillermo Hurtado, UNAM, 2006, pp. 155–67.
———. *La filosofía como compromiso y otros ensayos*. FCE, 1952.

———. "Prólogo." *El problema de México y la ideología nacional*, by Antonio Caso, *Obras completas*, edited by Rosa Krauze de Kolteniuk, vol. 9, UNAM, 1976, pp. vii–xxvi.

Zepeda, Jorge. "Fixing the Boundaries: Juan Rulfo—Writer and Photographer." *Rethinking Juan Rulfo's Creative World: Prose, Poetry, Film*, edited by Dylan Brennan and Nuala Finnegan, Routledge, 2006, pp. 32–50.

Zolov, Eric. *Refried Elvis: The Rise of the Mexican Counterculture*. California UP, 1999.

Index

À Kempis, Thomas, 149, 209n24
Los de abajo [The Underdogs] (Azuela), 22
"Absolute Paradox," 139
the absurd, 15, 98, 139, 209n28
accidentality, 42, 45–46, 101, 103, 104, 154, 202n29, 202n32
Adams, Michael Ian, 15
Los adioses [The Goodbyes] (film), 212n14
Adler, Alfred, 26
The Age of Reason (Sartre), 175
Ahern, Maureen, 182, 211n6
Al filo del agua [The Edge of the Storm] (Yáñez), 22, 23, 137–138
Alarcón, Juan Ruiz de, 79–80, 197n1, 197n5
Álbum de familia (Castellanos), 173
Alcestes (Usigli), 85, 86, 88–90, 98
Alemán Valdés, Miguel, 43, 62, 71, 116
    Mexicanidad and, 21–22, 34, 69
    racial homogenization and, 196n44
alienation, 15–16, 18, 62–63, 112, 184
    freedom and, 144
    masks with, 76
    Paz and, 47
Almagre, Juan. *See* Rodríguez, Antonio

altruism, 49–51, 58, 60, 103, 147, 195n36
América profunda (Kusch), 152, 153–154
"El amor en Simone de Beauvoir" [Love in Simone de Beauvoir] (Castellanos), 163, 213n23
El amor y la amistad en el mexicano [Love and Friendship in the Mexican] (Reyes Nevares), 63
La amortajada [The Shrouded Woman] (Bombal), 108, 213n22
Análisis del ser del mexicano [An Analysis of Mexican Being] (Uranga), 42, 44–45, 101–102, 191n1, 191n7, 202n31
Anderson, Thomas C., 196n40
La angustia [Anguish] (Mallea), 10
Another Spring (*Otra primavera*) (Usigli), 91
Anti-Semite and Jew (Sartre), 55, 152, 194n27
Apogeo y decadencia del positivismo en México (Zea), 191n3
aporetic theater, 77, 197n3
Argentina, 27, 146–147, 152–153
    "infamous decade," 9, 150–151
    "invisible," 10, 152, 188n13, 209n28

The Argentine Writer and Tradition ("El escritor argentino y la tradición") (Borges), 12, 189n16
Ariel (Rodó), 7, 10, 188n13
Arreola, José Juan, 35, 189n22
"Arte y cristianismo" (Revueltas), 134–135
Astrada, Carlos, 5, 187n5, 204n16
Ateneo de la Juventud [Athenaeum of Youth], 48–49, 50, 81, 193n19
Augustine (saint), 51, 188n10
Aura (Fuentes), 157–159
Azuela, Mariano, 22, 137, 207n10, 208n19

Balún-Canán (Castellanos), 177, 210n1
Bañuelos, Juan, 189n22
Barnes, Hazel, 11
Barreda, Gabino, 50, 193n20
Bartra, Roger, 25, 27, 70, 190n26
Bastos, María Luisa, 205n25
Las batallas en el desierto (Pacheco), 22
Baudrillard, Jean, 3
Beardsell, Peter, 198nn11–12, 199n14
Beauvoir, Simone de, 5, 10, 59, 63, 149, 157, 158, 190n31, 196n41
    Castellanos and, 163, 164, 175, 176, 183, 196n37, 213n23, 214nn27–28
    Castellanos, Sartre and, 167, 180–185
    ethics and, 67–68
    "Literature and Metaphysics," 12, 78
    Mitsein and, 163, 175, 179–180, 181, 196n38, 214n25
    Sartre, Kosakievicz and, 176–181
    Sartre and, 213n24, 214nn25–26, 215n29
    theater and, 197n4
    values and, 67–68
    "What Is Existentialism?," 4
Bécquer, Gustavo Adolfo, 182

Being and Nothingness (*BN*) (Sartre), 13, 31, 39, 41, 55, 56, 152, 169
    altruism and charity in, 195n36
    "Concrete Relations with Others," 64–66, 133
    the Other in, 64–65, 167, 178–179
Being and Time (Heidegger), 37, 39, 65
Bellos, David, 188n10
Benjamin, Thomas, 200nn23–24
Benjamin, Walter, 139
Bergson, Henri, 50, 189n18
Bermúdez, María Elvira, 63, 156, 157, 163
Between Sartre and Camus (*Entre Sartre y Camus*) (Vargas Llosa), 11, 68
the Bible, 138–140, 142, 208n21
Bildungsroman, 55, 158, 174, 175
The Birth of Tragedy (Nietzsche), 82, 198n8
The Black Heralds (*Los heraldos negros*) (Vallejo), 135, 136, 141
Blanco, Joaquín, 183
Blanco Aguinaga, Carlos, 105
The Blood of Others (Beauvoir), 181
BN. See *Being and Nothingness*
Bolton, Oliver, 96–97, 99
Bombal, María Luisa, 108, 213n22
Bonfil Batalla, Guillermo, 119, 152, 204nn16–17
the Boom, 12, 15
Borges, Jorge Luis, 11–12, 13, 189nn15–16
Bosteels, Bruno, 207n13
The Boy and the Fog (*El niño y la niebla*) (Usigli), 88, 90, 102
Brazil, 6, 187n6, 187n8
The Brothers Karamazov (Dostoevsky), 16

The Cage of Melancholy (*La jaula de la melancolía*) (Bartra), 70

Calles, Plutarco Elías "Jefe Máximo, Supreme Chief," 20, 22, 26, 43, 85–89, 92–96, 138, 199n15
Camacho, Manuel Ávila, 21
"Caminos de la nacionalidad" [Paths of the Nation] (Revueltas), 143–144
Camus, Albert, 1–2, 10–11, 14–15, 46, 148, 154, 189n19
  absurd creation and, 19
  agnosticism of, 188n10
  engaging existentialism and, 3, 4, 68, 133
  influence of, 167
  on the rebel, 210n31
  Sartre and, 60
  values and, 67, 68
Canabrava, Euríalo, 187n6
Carballo, Emilio, 190n27, 213n20
Cardenal, Ernesto, 213n20
Cárdenas, Lázaro, 20–21, 36, 85–90, 93–96, 138, 177
  Revueltas and, 207n11
  Usigli and, 199n17, 199nn13–14
caridad. See charity
Carpentier, Alejo, 11, 109, 209n29
Carranza, Venustiano, 93–94, 96, 200n23
Carrillo, Lilia, 166, 168
Carrión, Jorge, 122–124, 205n22
Cartas a Ricardo [Letters to Ricardo] (Castellanos), 163–166, 168–173, 180
Casa de España, 36
Caso, Antonio, 6, 29, 46, 48, 50, 83, 193n21. *See also La existencia como economía, como desinterés, y como caridad*
  altruism and, 60
  Christianity and, 51, 52–53, 122, 130, 193n22
  democracy and, 193n24

  formation of Grupo Hiperión and, 54–55
  on Heidegger, 51, 193n23
  humanistic pragmatism and, 198n7
  past and, 111
  patriotism and, 53
  religare and, 130–131
  Rulfo and, 108
  Usigli and, 80–81, 197n6
  Villoro and, 60–61
Castellanos, Rosario, 11, 23–24, 73, 87, 167, 210nn4–5, 211n6
  Beauvoir and, 163, 164, 196n37, 213n23, 214nn27–28
  Beauvoir, Sartre and, 167, 180–185
  Eternal Feminine and, 157–164, 166
  Grupo Hiperión and, 155–157
  Guerra and, 165–176
  Paz and, 167, 210n2
Castillo Beraud, Selma, 168, 172
Catholic Church, 6, 20, 144–146, 150, 158, 188n10, 190n23
Centro Mexicano de Escitores, 24
charity (*caridad*), 50–51, 61, 69, 113, 150, 198n7
  in *BN*, 195n36
  love and, 135, 193n24
The Children of the Gods (*Los hijos de los dioses*) (Santos Ruiz), 69–70, 71–72
The Child of Despair (*El hijo del desaliento*) (Rulfo), 109, 110
Christian existentialism, 8–9, 35, 51, 188n9
Christianity, 8, 51, 58, 80, 83, 130
  art and, 134–135
  the Bible, 138–140, 142, 208n21
  Marxism and, 144, 145
  in *Pedro Páramo*, 106–107, 121–122
  root values of, 52–53, 193n22
  Vallejo and, 136–137

circunstancialismo, 37, 39, 40
La ciudad y los perros (The City and the Cadets) (Vargas Llosa), 209n25
"Cleotilde" (Rulfo), 109, 124
"Una comedia shavian. *Noche de estío*" [A Comedy à la Shaw. Summer Night] (Usigli), 95, 198n11
communism, 85–86, 91, 131–132, 133, 150
community, 51, 59, 66, 188n10, 195n34
  emotion and, 17–18
  solitude and, 47, 58, 60, 61
  values and, 62–63
Comte, Auguste, 6, 49–51
"Comunidad, grandeza y miseria del mexicano" (Portilla), 62, 63, 195n33
Conciencia y posibilidad del mexicano (Zea), 42–43, 45, 62, 63
"Concrete Relations with Others," *BN*, 64–66, 133
the Conquest, 28, 112, 144
Consideraciones sobre el problema indígena (Gamio), 116–117
Contorno (journal), 151–152, 209nn26–28
Corona de luz [Crown of Light] (Usigli), 82, 102
Correa, Carlos, 151
Cortázar, Julio, 8, 11–15, 17, 147–148, 189n19, 208n23
Cortés, Hernán, 28
Cosío Villegas, Daniel, 36
The Cosmic Race (*La raza cósmica*) (Vasconcelos), 116, 120, 121
cosmopolitanism, 9, 41, 60, 154, 164, 184
Crime and Punishment (Dostoevsky), 109
Cristero Wars, 20, 107, 109, 112, 129–130, 138, 145–146

critical realism, 137, 207n10
Critique of Dialectical Reason (Sartre), 55, 68
Crown of Light (*Corona de luz*) (Usigli), 82, 102
Cuadernos [Notebooks] (Rulfo), 109
"Cuando Sartre hace literatura" [When Sartre Writes Literature] (Castellanos), 184
Cuba, 11, 33, 131

Danto, Arthur, 82
Dasein
  alienation and, 47
  Grupo Hiperión and, 39
  Heidegger and, 5, 37, 51, 153, 209n30
  Mexican, 19, 38, 41, 110
  Mitsein and, 65
Davis, Colin, 11
The Death of Artemio Cruz (*La muerte de Artemio Cruz*) (Fuentes), 22, 157, 190n24
deep magic, 121–127
"Deep Mexico" (*México profundo*), 30, 118–121, 141
democracy, 52, 69, 91, 193n24, 200n23
demonic despair, 135, 138, 206n8
Departamento de Asuntos Indígenas [Department of Indigenous Affairs], 20
Derrida, Jacques, 42, 192n9
desgana, 44–45, 72, 103, 127, 156, 195n33
determinism, 6, 7, 46, 170
Deústua, Alejandro, 6
Dialéctica del naufragio [Dialectics of a Shipwreck] (Hurtado), 68, 188n11
Dialectics of a Shipwreck (*Dialéctica del naufragio*) (Hurtado), 68, 188n11

Los días terrenales [Earthly Days] (Revueltas), 131–133
Díaz, Porfirio, 6, 19, 48, 87, 193n24
Díaz Ruanova, Oswaldo, 40, 192n15
"Dios en la tierra" [God on Earth] (Revueltas), 129–130, 135, 145, 150, 208n21
Un dios cotidiano [An Everyday God] (Viñas, D.), 149–151, 209n25
Dirty Hands (Sartre), 201n27
dissimulation, 76–77, 82
Domínguez Michael, Christopher, 27, 190n25, 196n43
Dos etapas del pensamiento en Hispanoamérica [Two Stages of Spanish-American Thought] (Zea), 110–111, 119, 120, 192n10
"Dos existencialismos" [Two Existentialisms] (Uranga), 39, 55–56, 59
Dostoevsky, Fyodor, 16–17, 78, 106, 108–110, 133, 181
"Dudemos" [Let Us Doubt], 48
Durán, Diego, 101
Dussel, Enrique, 196n42

Earthly Days (*Los días terrenales*) (Revueltas), 131–133
Echeverría, Luis, 162
The Edge of the Storm (*Al filo del agua*) (Yáñez), 22, 23, 137–138
EG. See *El gesticulador*
ELH. See *El luto humano*
Elizondo, Salvador, 189n22
"Elogio de la amistad" [In Praise of Friendship] (Castellanos), 183
emotion, community and, 17–18. See also love
The Empty Book (*El libro vacío*) (Vicens), 210n5
En torno a la filosofía mexicana [On Mexican Philosophy] (Gaos), 38

"Ensayo de una ontología del mexicano" [Essay on an Ontology of the Mexican] (Uranga), 44–45
Entre Sartre y Camus [Between Sartre and Camus] (Vargas Llosa), 11, 68
"Epílogo" (Usigli), 100, 103
Escalante, Evodio, 132
"El escritor argentino y la tradición" [The Argentine Writer and Tradition] (Borges), 12, 189n16
Escuela Nacional Preparatoria, 48, 50
España, aparta de mí este cáliz [Spain, Take This Chalice from Me] (Vallejo), 136
Essay on an Ontology of the Mexican ("Ensayo de una ontología del mexicano") (Uranga), 44–45
Estado de secreto [State of Secrecy] (Usigli), 85
Eternal Feminine, 157–164, 166
El eterno femenino [The Eternal Feminine] (Castellanos), 159–162, 164, 183, 211n6
ethics, 4, 33, 55–56, 59, 67, 68, 179
The Ethics of Ambiguity (Beauvoir), 4, 67
ethos. See Mexican existentialist ethos
Ética y libertad (González Valenzuela), 66
Evans, Debbie, 214n25
An Everyday God (*Un dios cotidiano*) (Viñas, D.), 149–151, 209n25
Excélsior (newspaper), 132, 156, 168, 183
Existence as Economy, Disinterest, and Charity (*La existencia como economía, como desinterés, y como caridad*) (Caso), 50–52, 81, 193n21, 200n23
La existencia como economía, como desinterés, y como caridad [Existence as Economy, Disinterest, and Charity] (Caso), 50–52, 81, 193n21, 200n23

"Existencialismo" (Cortázar), 147–148
An Existential Focus on Some Novels of the River Plate (Hayden), 15
existentialism
  in Brazil, 187n6
  Christian, 8–9, 35, 51, 188n9
  EG and, 75–80, 84–85, 88
  engaging, 3–10
  European, 3, 9, 29
  freedom and, 4–5
  God and, 16
  identity and, 6, 7, 10
  literature of possibilities, 10–19
  Mexican platforms, 19–31
  nihilism and, 40
  Rulfo and, 105–110
  Sartre and, 132
  situated, 5, 41, 46
  Situating Existentialism, 190n30
  Western, 12–13
Existentialism Is a Humanism (Sartre), 4, 55, 57, 59–60, 148
The Existential Gambit (*El juego existencial*) (Astrada), 5

Facundo (Sarmiento), 152
fagocitación (phagocytosis), 153
The Fallen Fruit (*Los frutos caídos*) (Hernández), 210n5
La familia cena en casa [The Family Dines at Home] (Usigli), 91, 198n12
family
  Álbum de familia, 173
  dramas, 90–98
  revolutionary, 93–98, 200nn22–24
  La vida familiar del mexicano, 63, 155–156
Family Ties (Lispector), 149
The Family Dines at Home (*La familia cena en casa*) (Usigli), 91, 198n12
fantastic literature, 11, 189n14, 189n22

Farias Brito, Raimundo, 6
fascism, 9, 150–151
Faulkner, William, 113, 120
Faust (Goethe), 160
Fenomenología del relajo (Portilla), 63, 108, 120, 195n34
Fernández, Sergio, 213n20
Filosofía y letras (journal), 35–36, 169
La filosofía de lo mexicano (Villegas), 191n8
Fiorito, Susana, 209n26
The Flies (Sartre), 56–57, 113–114, 194n26, 203n10
Flores Olea, Víctor, 189n22
Flynn, Thomas, 57
Forjando patria (pro-nacionalismo) [Forging a Homeland (Pro-nationalism)] (Gamio), 25, 116
France-Amérique (magazine), 4
Francis (saint), 53
Franco, Jean, 135, 136
freedom, 53, 200n20
  alienation and, 144
  Castellanos and, 159, 164, 168, 170–175, 183
  democracy and, 193n24
  existentialism and, 4–5
  human, 7, 51, 66
  humanism of, 5, 187n5
  "Jean-Paul Sartre, filósofo de la libertad" [Jean-Paul Sartre, Philosopher of Freedom] (Guerra), 169–170
  literature and, 11, 12
  love and, 61, 170–173, 177–178, 180
  moral anarchy and, 57
  of praxis, 164, 181–182
  The Roads to Freedom trilogy, 55
  Sartre and, 40, 59, 189n18
  sexual, 170–172
French Resistance, 194n26
Friedan, Betty, 162

friendship, 63, 68, 179, 183, 195n33
Frondizi, Arturo, 151
Los frutos caídos [The Fallen Fruit] (Hernández), 210n5
Fuentes, Carlos, 11, 22, 25, 157–159, 190n24, 197n45, 210n3
Fuentes Mares, José, 27

Galindo, Sergio, 213n20
Gallegos Rocafull, José, 191n2
Gamio, Manuel, 25, 116–117, 120–121, 122
Gaos, José, 36, 53, 190n29, 192n11, 211n12
    Grupo Hiperión and, 37–41, 54–55, 191n6
    Uranga on, 191n2, 191n7
García Bacca, Juan David, 191n2, 191n4
García Bonilla, Roberto, 202n4, 205n20
García Máynez, Eduardo, 198n7
The Gates of Heaven ("Las puertas del cielo") (Cortázar), 189n19
gender, 63, 143, 161, 163–164, 187n3
"Génesis y proyecto del existencialismo en México" (Villoro), 61
Germanization, of Mexican mind, 38
El gesticulador (*EG*) [The Gesticulator] (Usigli), 29, 82–83, 102, 160, 200n25
    existentialism and, 75–80, 84–85, 88
    pragmatic authenticity and, 89, 99–100
    Revolutionary Family and, 92–93, 96–98
Gibaja, Regina, 209n26
Gigli, Adelaida, 151, 209n26
God, 8, 129–130, 149–151, 207n14, 209n25
    existentialism and, 16
    Usigli and, 82
    Vallejo and, 135

God on Earth ("Dios en la tierra") (Revueltas), 129–130, 135, 145, 150, 208n21
Goethe, 160
Golden Rule, 8, 17, 51–52, 185
Gómez Robleda, José, 155, 156
González, Aníbal, 188n12
González Cosío, Arturo, 189n22
González Valenzuela, Juliana, 66
The Goodbyes (*Los adioses*) (film), 212n14
Gordon, Lewis R., 4–5
Gorostiza, José, 184–185
Los grandes momentos del indigenismo en México (Villoro), 60–62, 115–118, 142, 152, 204nn14–15
Grupo Hiperión, 2, 130, 152, 155
    Castellanos and, 155–157
    Filosofía y letras and, 35–36
    Gaos and, 37–41, 54–55, 191n6
    Heidegger and, 37–38, 39, 46–47
    members, 28–29, 34–35, 54–56, 70, 156, 190n23, 192n10, 196n43, 202n1, 205n22
    Mexican existentialist ethos and, 29, 33–46, 58–69
    Mexican identity and, 33, 35, 41, 52, 76
    Mexicanness and, 34, 110, 192n12, 192n17
    Paz and, 46–48, 68, 73, 192n17
    PP and, 105–106
    Sartre and, 29, 33, 39, 40, 41, 55–57, 59, 60, 64, 72, 157, 168
    values and, 58–69
Guardia, Miguel, 213n20
Guerra, Ricardo, 28, 35, 40, 71, 156–157, 191n6, 211n12
    Cartas a Ricardo, 163–166, 168–173, 180
    Castellanos, Sartre and, 165–176
    on nihilation, 169, 212n16
    on philosophy, 170, 212n17

Guimarães Rosa, João, 2, 11, 18–19, 148–149
Guzmán, Martín Luis, 22, 87

Habermas, Jürgen, 8, 188n11
Hacia un nuevo humanismo [Towards a New Humanism] (Ramos), 27, 53–54, 194n25
Hale, Charles, 50
Half Tones (*Medio tono*) (Usigli), 90–92
Halperín Donghi, Tulio, 151
"¿Hay una moral existencialista?" [Is There an Existentialist Morality?] (Sánchez MacGrégor), 59
Hayden, Rose Lee, 15
Hegel, Georg Wilhelm Friedrich, 37, 111, 143, 177, 178, 183, 211n12
Heidegger, Martin, 187n6, 192n11, 192n15, 193n23
  Dasein and, 5, 37, 51, 153, 209n30
  Grupo Hiperión and, 37–38, 39, 46–47
  Mitsein and, 65, 163, 179, 195n35, 214n25
hembrismo, 156
Henríquez Ureña, Pedro, 48, 81–82
Los heraldos negros [The Black Heralds] (Vallejo), 135, 136, 141
Hernández, Luisa Josefina, 210n5, 213n20
Hernández Luna, Juan, 190n27
hero, existentialist, 56, 99, 104, 148
El hijo del desaliento [The Child of Despair] (Rulfo), 109, 110
Los hijos de los dioses [The Children of the Gods] (Santos Ruiz), 69–70, 71–72
Historia de una pasión argentina (Mallea), 9–10
"Una historia del Hiperión" (Guerra), 71

Homenaje a Caso, 54–55
homosexuality, 24, 175
Hopscotch (*Rayuela*) (Cortázar), 12
"The Hour and Turn of Augusto Matraga" (Guimarães Rosa), 148
Human Mourning. See *El luto humano*
humanism, 4–5, 27, 53–55, 57, 59–60, 87n5, 148
humanistic pragmatism, 83, 84, 198n7
Hurtado, Guillermo, 28, 46, 68, 188n11, 192n12, 202n31
  lo mexicano and, 70–71, 156
  on Madero and democracy, 193n24
  on truth and lies, 198n7
Husserl, Edmund, 50, 187n6

identity, 6–10, 15, 26. See also Mexican identity
  of women, 162–163
Ideología y praxis política de Lázaro Cárdenas (Medin), 21
IFAL (Instituto Francés de América Latina), 35, 39
Imagen del mexicano (Gómez Robleda), 155
The Imitation of Christ (Thomas à Kempis), 149, 209n24
In Praise of Friendship ("Elogio de la amistad") (Castellanos), 183
inauthenticity, 10, 15–16, 47, 62, 76, 104, 112
in-betweenness (*nepantla*), 101, 157
indigenismo, 61, 115–116
Indigenous peoples, 20, 28, 52, 69, 93, 174, 177, 205n21
  Christianity and, 136
  culture, 152–153
  ELH and, 144
  Los grandes momentos del indigenismo en México, 60, 61–62
  lo indígena, 114–118
mestiz@s, 70, 116, 119–120, 124

spirituality and, 122
as worthy of emulation, 155
"infamous decade," Argentina, 9, 150–151
inferiority complex, 26–27, 44–46, 54, 72, 100
INI (Instituto Nacional Indigenista), 114, 116, 120, 203nn11–12
Instituto Francés de América Latina (IFAL), 35, 39
Instituto Nacional Indigenista (INI), 114, 116, 120, 203nn11–12
intersubjectivity, 29, 33, 47, 58, 60–62, 63, 64, 66, 67–68, 102, 117, 176, 180, 185, 196n38, 196n40
Introducción a El ser y el Tiempo de Martín Heidegger (Gaos), 37
inversion of values, 43, 46, 62, 103, 202n33
Is There an Existentialist Morality? ("¿Hay una moral existencialista?") (Sánchez MacGrégor), 59

James, Henry, 210n3
James, William, 81, 82, 83, 198nn9–10
La jaula de la melancolía [The Cage of Melancholy] (Bartra), 70
"Jean-Paul Sartre, filósofo de la libertad" [Jean-Paul Sartre, Philosopher of Freedom] (Guerra), 169–170
Jeanson, Francis, 59
"Jefe Máximo." *See* Calles, Plutarco Elías
Jesus Christ, 8, 140, 145, 149, 207n14
imitation of, 148–150
Jews, 194n27, 194n30
Jiménez de Báez, Yvette, 205n24
Jiménez Rueda, Julio, 122
Jitrik, Noé, 151
"Juan Ruiz de Alarcón" (Castellanos), 197n5

Juan Ruiz de Alarcón en el tiempo (Usigli), 79–80, 197n1, 197n5
Juana Inés de la Cruz, Sor, 160–162, 184, 213n22
Juárez, Benito, 49
Judaken, Jonathan, 190n30
El juego existencial [The Existential Gambit] (Astrada), 5
Juicios sumarios [Summary Judgments] (Castellanos), 176, 183–184

Kerouac, Jack, 13
Kierkegaard, Søren, 8–10, 18, 52, 108, 130, 135, 139
"Kierkegaard en la Zona Rosa [of Mexico City]" (Fuentes), 157–158
Klahn, Norma, 202n2
Korn, Alejandro, 6
Kosakievicz, Olga, 176–181
Krauze, Rosa, 51
Kruks, Sonia, 57, 68
Künstlerroman, 158, 174, 175, 213n21
Kusch, Rodolfo, 151, 152–154, 204n16, 209n28, 209n30

El laberinto de la soledad [The Labyrinth of Solitude] (Paz), 24–28, 33, 43, 75–76, 184, 190nn27–28
alienation and, 47
Grupo Hiperión in, 192n17
PP and, 110, 112
The Labyrinth of Solitude. *See El laberinto de la soledad*
Larisch, Sharon, 180
Layera, Ramón, 82, 197n1
Let Us Doubt ("Dudemos"), 48
Letters to Ricardo (*Cartas a Ricardo*) (Castellanos), 163–166, 168–173, 180
Levinas, Emmanual, 188n11
liberation theology, 5, 196n42

El libro vacío [The Empty Book] (Vicens), 210n5
lies, 76–80, 82–83, 197n2, 198n7
Lispector, Clarice, 11, 149
"Literature and Metaphysics" (Beauvoir), 12, 78
El llano en llamas [The Plain in Flames] (Rulfo), 108–109
lo mexicano. *See* Mexicanness
López Mena, Sergio, 108
López Velarde, Ramón, 102, 202n31
The Lost Steps (*Los pasos perdidos*) (Carpentier), 109, 209n29
love, 65, 66, 135, 193n24, 208n17
    freedom and, 61, 170–173, 177–178, 180
    solidarity and, 136, 140, 141
    triangles, 168, 172–173, 177–181, 214n25
Love and Friendship in the Mexican (*El amor y la amistad en el mexicano*) (Reyes Nevares), 63
Love in Simone de Beauvoir ("El amor en Simone de Beauvoir") (Castellanos), 163, 213n23
Lukàcs, György, 151
El luto humano (*ELH*) [Human Mourning] (Revueltas), 131, 133–134, 143, 154, 159, 208n20
    the Bible and, 138–140, 142
    Cristero Wars and, 145–146
    Indigenous peoples and, 144
    love and solidarity, 140, 141
    Mexicanness and, 137, 138, 141–142
    Paz on, 207n15
    PP and, 108–109
    spirituality and, 141–142

machismo, 26, 100, 110, 143, 155–156, 163

Madero, Francisco, 87, 94, 193n24, 200n23
Magaña, Sergio, 213n20
magic, 121–127, 158–160, 210nn3–4
magical realism, 15, 126, 206n27
Mallea, Eduardo, 9, 10, 16, 152, 188n13, 209n28
Malraux, André, 133
"El mandarín" (Vargas Llosa), 11
Man's Fate (Malraux), 133
Man's Place in Nature (Scheler), 53
Marcel, Gabriel, 8, 58, 60–61, 66, 147–148, 167, 184, 188n9, 195n32
Marías, Julián, 189n17
Mariátegui, José Carlos, 136, 143–144
marriage, 160, 163, 166, 168, 171–172, 180–181, 211n7, 214n26
Martínez de Hoyos, Oliverio, 94
Martínez Estrada, Ezequiel, 27
Marxism, 4, 24, 68, 151, 152, 201n27, 208n20
    ELH and, 138, 140, 144–145
    Gaos and, 37
    Revueltas and, 73, 132, 134, 143, 147
    Usigli and, 85
    Vallejo and, 136
"Masa" [Mass] (Vallejo), 2, 136–137
Masotta, Oscar, 151
Mass ("Masa") (Vallejo), 2, 136–137
Materia memorable (Castellanos), 155
"Materialism and Revolution" (Sartre), 152
"Maurice Merleau-Ponty" lecture, Grupo Hiperión, 39
Medin, Tzvi, 21, 71
Medio Siglo group, 189n22
Medio tono [Half Tones] (Usigli), 90–92
Mejía, Eduardo, 173
Mejía Sánchez, Ernesto, 213n20

Memoirs of a Dutiful Daughter (Beauvoir), 174, 176
Menéndez Samará, Alberto, 61
Menester y precisión del ser [Mission and Rationale of Being] (Menéndez Samará), 61
mestizaje (racial mixture), 106, 116–117, 120–122, 142, 204n13
mestiz@s, 70, 116, 119–120, 124
metaphysical novel, 12, 78, 197n4
Metaphysics (Aristotle), 42
Mexican Constitution, Article 3, 87
Mexican *Dasein*, 19, 38, 41, 110
Mexican existentialist ethos
  arena, 46–57
  Grupo Hiperión and, 29, 33–46, 58–69
  Paz and, 46–48
  weaponizing Mexicanness, 69–73
Mexican Family Life (*La vida familiar del mexicano*) (Bermúdez), 63
Mexican identity, 26–27, 100, 190n26
  Castellanos and, 156–157
  character and, 192n14
  Grupo Hiperión and, 33, 35, 41, 52, 76
  Mexicanness and, 25, 34, 44, 118, 121, 147, 192n17, 193n18, 205n18, 208n22
  Usigli and, 201n28
Mexican *Mitsein*, 185
Mexican Philosophy in the 20th Century (Sánchez and Sanchez), 28
Mexican Revolution, 24–25, 28, 86–87, 208n19
  critical realism and, 137, 207n10
  lo indígena and, 116–117
  politics and, 19–21, 138
  Revolutionary Family and, 90–98
Mexicanidad, 21–22, 34, 69–72, 116–117, 204n13

"La mexicanidad política y filosófica en el sexenio de Miguel Alemán.1946–1952" (Medin), 71
Mexicanness (*lo mexicano*), 79, 110, 156, 192n12
  ELH and, 137, 138, 141–142
  identity and, 25, 34, 44, 118, 121, 147, 192n17, 193n18, 205n18, 208n22
  weaponizing, 69–73
"The Mexican and His Culture," UNAM course, 35
México en la hispanidad (Fuentes Mares), 27
México profundo (Bonfil Batalla), 152, 204nn16–17
"México profundo" ("Deep Mexico"), 30, 118–121, 141
"México y lo Mexicano" book series, 29, 36, 42, 48, 122, 156
Michelet, Jules, 158, 210n3
"El milagro secreto" [The Secret Miracle] (Borges), 189n15
Mill, John Stuart, 49
Le Misanthrope (Molière), 89
Mission and Rationale of Being (*Menester y precisión del ser*) (Menéndez Samará), 61
Mito y magia del mexicano [Myth and Magic in the Mexican] (Carrión), 122
Mitsein
  Beauvoir and, 163, 175, 179–180, 181, 183, 196n38, 214n25
  Heidegger and, 65, 163, 179, 195n35, 214n25
  Mexican, 185
  Sartre and, 66, 67, 179, 214n25
Modern Language Association International Bibliography, 16
Molière, 89, 99

Molinari, Marta, 209n26
Molloy, Sylvia, 205n25
Monsiváis, Carlos, 189n22, 214n27
Monterroso, Augusto, 213n20
Montoya, Claudia, 208n22
Monumento a la Revolución, 94, 95
moral anarchy, 57, 58
morality, 59, 62, 75, 79, 81, 211n10
    altruism and, 49, 50
    Christianity and, 80, 83, 136
"Much Ado" (Guimarães Rosa), 2, 18–19
La muerte de Artemio Cruz [The Death of Artemio Cruz] (Fuentes), 22, 157, 190n24
Mujer que sabe latín [The Woman Who Knows Latin] (Castellanos), 156, 162–163
Muñoz, Miguel Ángel, 211n12
Myth and Magic in the Mexican (*Mito y magia del mexicano*) (Carrión), 122
The Myth of Sisyphus (Camus), 1, 4, 14–15, 68, 133

nationalism, 9, 21, 25, 69, 71–72, 94, 200n23
The Nature of Sympathy (Scheler), 61
Nausea (Sartre), 10, 55, 91, 109, 167, 175, 194n30, 213n22
"La náusea y el humanismo" (Portilla), 60
Negrín, Edith, 206n2, 207n13, 208n20
nepantla (in-betweenness), 101, 157
The Neurotic Constitution (Adler), 26
Nicol, Eduardo, 66, 191n2, 191n4
Nietzsche, Friedrich, 18, 81–83, 198nn8–9
"Nietzsche y el pragmatismo" lecture, 81–82
El niño y la niebla [The Boy and the Fog] (Usigli), 88, 90, 102

No Exit (Sartre), 31, 64, 167, 179, 195n35, 214n25
Noche de estío [Summer Night] (Usigli), 85
Noro, Jorge Eduardo, 150
Notebooks (*Cuadernos*) (Rulfo), 109
Notebooks for an Ethics (Sartre), 55, 68, 179, 196n40
Notes from Underground (Dostoevsky), 16, 110
Nubiola, Jamie, 83

Obregón, Álvaro, 87, 92, 94, 199n15, 200n23
Obregón Santacilia, Carlos, 94
Ocampo, Victoria, 162
O'Connell, Joanna, 211n11
"Octavio Paz y Hiperión" (Reeve), 197n45
Octavio Paz en su siglo [Octavio Paz in His Century] (Domínguez Michael), 27
Oficio de tinieblas (Castellanos), 177, 210n4
Olivier, Florence, 133
O'Malley, Ilene V., 199n15
On Feminine Culture ("Sobre cultura femenina") (Castellanos), 165, 177, 211n7, 211n11
On Mexican Philosophy (*En torno a la filosofía mexicana*) (Gaos), 38
On the Road (Kerouac), 13
"On Truth and Lying in an Extra-Moral Sense" (Nietzsche), 82–83
Onetti, Juan Carlos, 11, 16–18, 109–110, 148, 189n21
"Optimismo y pesimismo sobre el mexicano" (Uranga), 44
"Order and Progress" motto, 6, 187n8
Ortega y Gasset, José, 5, 10, 27, 36–38, 187n6, 189n17, 191n5
Ortiz Guadarrama, Tania, 193n22
Ortiz Rubio, Pascual, 20, 85, 92

Otra primavera [Another Spring] (Usigli), 91
"El otro" (Castellanos), 214n28

Pacheco, José Emilio, 22
Padilla, Herberto, 131
Palacios, Adela, 190n27
Pan (journal), 108
Pappas, Gregory, 81
Parker, Charlie, 13
Partido Comunista Mexicano (PCM), 131–132, 133
Partido de la Revolución Mexicana (PRM), 20–21
Partido Nacional Revolucionario (PNR), 20, 89, 93, 96, 200n23
Partido Revolucionario Institucional (PRI), 20, 69
Los pasos perdidos [The Lost Steps] (Carpentier), 109, 209n29
pathologizing, 25–27, 28, 43, 72, 100
Paths of the Nation ("Caminos de la nacionalidad") (Revueltas), 143–144
Paz, Octavio, 24–26, 33, 43, 108, 167, 184, 190nn27–28. *See also* *El laberinto de la soledad*
    Castellanos and, 210n2
    on *ELH*, 207n15
    Gaos and, 37
    Grupo Hiperión and, 46–48, 68, 73, 192n17
    Heidegger and, 192n15
    on masks of conformity, 28
    Mexicanness and, 193n18
    Ramos and, 27
    Rulfo and, 110, 121, 205n20
    Sartrean gaze and, 192n16
    on truth and lies, 197n2
    Usigli and, 75–77
    women and, 159
    Zea and, 112–113

PCM (*Partido Comunista Mexicano*), 131–132, 133
Pedro Páramo (*PP*) (Rulfo), 105, 108–109
    Christianity in, 106–107, 121–122
    deep magic and, 121–127
    with "Deep Mexico" and racial politics, 118–121
    lo indígena and, 114–118
    past and, 110–114
Pérez Monfort, Ricardo, 189n22
El perfil del hombre y la cultura en México [Profile of Man and Culture in Mexico] (Ramos), 26–28, 43–45, 70, 100, 103, 155, 190n27
Peronism, 151, 209n28
"El perseguidor" [The Pursuer] (Cortázar), 13–15, 17, 148
personalismo, 37, 62, 191n6, 195n33
phagocytosis (*fagocitación*), 153
Pitol, Sergio, 189n22
The Plague (Camus), 68, 133, 148, 189n19
The Plain in Flames (*El llano en llamas*) (Rulfo), 108–109
PNR (*Partido Nacional Revolucionario*), 20, 89, 93, 96, 200n23
El poder y el valor [Power and Value] (Villoro), 68
"Poesía eres tú" [You Are Poetry] (Bécquer), 182
"Poesía no eres tú" [You Are Not Poetry] (Castellanos), 182, 183
politics, 4, 8, 9, 15, 99
    "Deep Mexico" and racial, 118–121
    Mexican Revolution and, 19–21, 138
    Revolutionary Family and, 90–98
    theater and, 84–90, 198n11
Poniatowska, Elena, 105, 131, 166, 167, 168, 211n11, 212n15
Portes Gil, Emilio, 20, 85, 92

Portilla, Jorge, 28, 35, 40, 60, 103, 108
  desgana and, 195n33
  relajo and, 63, 120, 205n18
  Rulfo and, 120, 203n5
  seriousness and, 63, 120, 195n34
"Posibilidades y limitaciones del mexicano" lecture (Revueltas), 147
positivism, 6–7, 8, 37, 48–50, 99, 202n2
  antipositivism and, 6–7, 187n8
  Christianity and, 8, 130
El positivismo en México (Zea), 191n3
postsecularism, 8, 68, 188n11
Power and Value (*El poder y el valor*) (Villoro), 68
El pozo [The Well] (Onetti), 16, 17, 18, 109
PP. *See Pedro Páramo*
pragmatic authenticity, 175
  EG and, 89, 99–100
  Usigli and, 76, 201n27
pragmatism, 199n18
  humanistic, 83, 84, 198n7
  truth and, 81–83
Pragmatism in the Americas (Pappas), 81
praxis
  freedom of, 164, 181–182
  Revueltas and, 147
El Presidente y el ideal (Usigli), 85–87, 89–90, 96
PRI (*Partido Revolucionario Institucional*), 20, 69
Prieto, Adolfo, 151
Primeiras estórias (Guimarães Rosa), 2, 18
The Prime of Life (Beauvoir), 31, 176, 177–178, 181, 215n29
PRM (*Partido de la Revolución Mexicana*), 20–21
El problema de México y la ideología nacional (Caso), 52–53, 54, 111, 122, 130, 193n24

Profile of Man and Culture in Mexico (*El perfil del hombre y la cultura en México*) (Ramos), 26–28, 43–45, 70, 100, 103, 155, 190n27
psychoanalysis, 26, 39, 170, 205n22
"Las puertas del cielo" [The Gates of Heaven] (Cortázar), 189n19
The Pursuer ("El perseguidor") (Cortázar), 13–15, 17, 148
Pyrrhus and Cineas (Beauvoir), 67–68, 176, 183, 190n31, 196n41

Quevedo, Francisco de, 210n3

racial mixture (*mestizaje*), 106, 116–117, 120–122, 142, 204n13
racial politics, "Deep Mexico" and, 118–121
Radiografía de la pampa [X-ray of the Pampas] (Martínez Estrada), 27
Ramos, Samuel, 26, 28, 43–45, 54, 103, 119, 190n27, 194n25
  Ateneo de la Juventud and, 49
  Mexican identity and, 35, 100
  Paz and, 27
Rayuela [Hopscotch] (Cortázar), 12
La raza cósmica [The Cosmic Race] (Vasconcelos), 116, 120, 121
The Rebel (Camus), 154, 210n31
Reeve, Richard, M., 197n45
"La reflexión sobre el ser en Gabriel Marcel" (Villoro), 60–61
La región más transparente [Where the Air is Clear] (Fuentes), 197n45
relajiento, 63, 103, 195n34
relajo, 120, 201n28, 205n18, 211n8
religare, 130–131, 134, 140, 145–146, 152, 154, 206n2
"Religion of Humanity" (Comte), 49–50
Revista de América (literary magazine), 188n13
Revista de Occidente (journal), 10, 187n6

Revista Mexicana de Literatura, 48
Revolutionary Family, 90–98,
    200nn22–24
Revueltas, José, 11, 23–24, 73, 129,
    135–136, 147. *See also El luto
    humano*
  afterlife and, 139, 207n12
  Cárdenas and, 207n11
  critical realism and, 137, 207n10
  Mariateguí and, 143–144
  Mexican Revolution and, 208n19
  religare and, 130–131, 206n2
  Rulfo and, 108–109
  Sartre and, 132–133, 134, 206n4
  suffering and, 206n8
  women and, 143, 159
Reyes, Alfonso, 48
Reyes Nevares, Salvador, 28, 35, 63
Riders to the Sea (Synge), 205n24
Rito de iniciación [Rite of Initiation]
    (Castellanos), 157, 173–176, 178,
    183, 185
The Roads to Freedom trilogy (Sartre),
    55, 132, 149
Robles, Oswaldo, 165
Roces, Wenceslao, 211n12
Rodíguez Monegal, Emir, 151, 209n27
Rodó, José Enrique, 7, 10, 25, 49,
    188n13
Rodríguez, Abelardo, 20, 85, 94, 138
Rodríguez, Antonio (Juan Almagre),
    132
Romero, Francisco, 6
Romero, Vevia, 198n11
A Rosario Castellanos Reader (Ahern),
    182, 211n6
Rossi, Alejandro, 191n6
Rozitchner, León, 151
Ruffinelli, Jorge, 138, 139
Ruiz Abreu, Álvaro, 206n8
Rulfo, Juan, 23–24, 73, 159, 189n22.
    See also Pedro Páramo
  the Conquest and, 112

  existentialism and, 105–110, 202n2
  The Flies and, 203n10
  Grupo Hiperión and, 202n1
  Indigenous peoples and, 114–120,
    205n21
  INI and, 203n12
  magical realism and, 126, 206n27
  Paz and, 110, 121, 205n20
  Portilla and, 120, 203n5

Sábato, Ernesto, 11, 17–18, 148
Sabines, Jaime, 213n20
Saint Manuel the Good, Martyr
    (San Manuel Bueno, Mártir)
    (Unamuno), 75, 83–84, 107
Salazar Mallén, Rubén, 190n27
"San Agustín y Heidegger" (Caso),
    193n23
San Manuel Bueno, Mártir [Saint
    Manuel the Good, Martyr]
    (Unamuno), 75, 83–84, 107
Sánchez, Carlos Alberto, 28, 38, 59,
    189n20, 190n31, 191n1, 192n13,
    194n29, 202n32, 205n18
Sanchez, Robert Eli, 28
Sánchez MacGrégor, Joaquín, 28, 35,
    59, 196n43
Sánchez Prado, Ignacio, 36, 140,
    190n29, 196n43
Sánchez Reulet, Aníbal, 7
Santí, Enrico, 47
Santos Ruiz, Ana, 19, 40, 69–72, 116,
    147, 193n18, 196n43
Sarlo, Beatriz, 152
Sarmiento, Domingo Faustino, 152
Sartre, Jean-Paul, 3, 5, 10, 30, 31,
    44, 91, 113–114, 149, 189n18,
    208n23, 213n22
  on altruism, 195n36
  Beauvoir, Kosakievicz and, 176–
    181
  Beauvoir and, 4, 68, 213n24,
    214nn25–26, 215n29

Sartre, Jean-Paul *(continued)*
  Castellanos and, 167, 174, 175–176, 180–185
  Castellanos, Guerra and, 165–176
  Contorno and, 152
  criticism of, 32, 40, 77
  "Cuando Sartre hace literatura" [When Sartre Writes Literature] (Castellanos) 184
  ethics and, 55–58
  French Resistance and, 194n26
  Grupo Hiperión and, 29, 33, 39, 40, 41, 44, 55–57, 59, 60, 61, 64, 66, 72, 157
  influence of, 109, 148, 168
  intersubjectivity and, 196n40
  on Jews, 194n27, 194n30
  literature and influence of, 11–12, 13
  love and, 65, 66
  Mitsein and, 65, 66, 67, 179, 214n25
  Paz and, 33, 46–47, 68
  Revueltas and, 132–133, 134, 206n4
  Rulfo and, 109, 203n10
  theater and, 77, 197n4
  Vatican Index of Prohibited Works and, 8
Sartrean gaze, 133, 182, 192n16
Satanism and Witchcraft (Michelet), 158
Scheler, Max, 8, 50, 53–54, 61, 188n9
Schmidhuber, Guillermo, 82, 201n28
Schmidt, Henry, 25
Schopenhauer, Arthur, 50
Sebreli, Juan José, 151
The Second Sex (Beauvoir), 63, 163, 164, 176
  Mitsein and, 163, 175, 180, 183, 196n37
The Secret Miracle ("El milagro secreto") (Borges), 189n15

La seducción de la barbarie (Kusch), 152
Seis temas do espíritu moderno (Canabrava), 187n6
seriousness, 63, 120, 195n34
7 ensayos de interpretación de la realidad peruana [7 Interpretive Essays on Peruvian Reality] (Mariátegui), 143–144
The Shadow of the Strongman (*La sombra del caudillo*) (Guzmán), 22, 87
Shakespeare, William, 7
Shaw, George Bernard, 77, 201n26
She Came to Stay (Beauvoir), 177–179, 180, 181, 214n25
Shestov, Lev, 133
The Shrouded Woman (*La amortajada*) (Bombal), 108, 213n22
Sierra, Justo, 48, 50, 193n20
Silva Herzog, Jesús, 21
"Simone de Beauvoir o la lucidez" (Castellanos), 176, 180, 213n23
"Situación actual de la novela contemporánea" lecture (Rulfo), 206n27
"Situación de la novela" (Cortázar), 14
situated existentialism, 5, 41, 146
Situating Existentialism (Judaken), 190n30
"Sobre cultura femenina" [On Feminine Culture] (Castellanos), 165, 177, 211n7, 211n11
socialist realism, 132, 137
"Soledad y comunión" [Solitude and Communion] (Villoro), 61
solidarity, 2, 65, 67, 136, 140, 145, 163, 181, 183, 184
solitude, community and, 47, 58, 60, 61
Solitude and Communion ("Soledad y comunión") (Villoro), 61

La sombra del caudillo [The Shadow of the Strongman] (Guzmán), 22, 87
Spade, Paul Vincent, 57
Spain, Take This Chalice from Me (*España, aparta de mí este cáliz*) (Vallejo), 136
Spanish American War, 7, 81
Spanish Civil War, 2, 36, 136, 150
Staggering between Two Stars ("Traspié entre dos estrellas") (Vallejo), 136
State of Secrecy (*Estado de secreto*) (Usigli), 85
Stavans, Ilan, 205n19
Stehn, Alexander, 50, 193n20
substantiality, 42, 45, 101, 117
suffering, 135, 138, 144, 206n8
Summary Judgments (*Juicios sumarios*) (Castellanos), 176, 183–184
Summer Night (*Noche de estío*) (Usigli), 85
"Supreme Chief." *See* Calles, Plutarco Elías
Sur (journal), 151–152, 162, 187n6, 189n16, 209n27
The Suspicious Truth (*La verdad sospechosa*) (Alarcón), 80
Swansey, Bruce, 198n11, 199n14, 200n20
Synge, John Millington, 205n24

"Tantarum, My Boss" (Guimarães Rosa), 18–19
Tattam, Helen, 195n32
"La tejedora" [The Weaver] (López Velarde), 102
The Tempest (Shakespeare), 7
Teoría del túnel (Cortázar), 8, 148, 185
Teresa of Ávila (Saint), 167
Thakkar, Amit, 121–122, 203n11, 204n17
theater, 9, 17, 29, 66, 197n3
  existentialism and, 76–80
  family plays, 90–98
  French existentialism and, 77–78
  of ideas, 77, 91, 103, 197n4
  Mexican womanhood and, 78, 98
  philosophy and, 80–84
  politics and, 84–90, 198n11
  theatre of values, 9, 17, 66
thesis novel, 12, 78
Third World, 4, 42, 183
Three Authors of Alienation (Adams), 15
Three Impolitic Comedies (*Tres comedias impólíticas*) (Usigli), 85, 86, 88, 92, 199nn13–14
Un tiempo suspendido (García Bonilla), 202n4
Time and Free Will (Bergson), 189n18
Toledo, Roberto Domingo, 188n10, 189n20
"Toma de conciencia" (Castellanos), 155
Towards a New Humanism (*Hacia un nuevo humanismo*) (Ramos), 27, 53–54, 194n25
transvaluation, 49–50, 59, 68, 106, 209n25
  activism and, 147–148
  ELH and, 138, 141
"Traspié entre dos estrellas" [Staggering between Two Stars] (Vallejo), 136
Tres comedias impólíticas [Three Impolitic Comedies] (Usigli), 85, 86, 88, 92, 199nn13–14
Trotsky, Leon, 199n18
truth, 81, 91, 201n27
  lies and, 76–80, 82–83, 197n2, 198n7
  politics and, 99
El túnel (Sábato), 17–18
Two Existentialisms ("Dos existencialismos") (Uranga), 39, 55–56, 59

Two Stages of Spanish-American Thought (*Dos etapas del pensamiento en Hispanoamérica*) (Zea), 110–111, 119, 120, 192n10

Unamuno, Miguel de, 75, 83–84, 107, 189n17, 198n10
The Underdogs (*Los de abajo*) (Azuela), 22
Universidad de México (journal), 108
Universidad Nacional Autónoma de México (UNAM), 21, 35–36, 48, 54, 108, 160, 165, 192n10
Uranga, Emilio, 26, 36, 41, 59, 117, 157, 191n1
  accidentality and, 42, 45–46, 101, 103–104, 154, 202n29
  on cynicism, 202n33
  on Gaos, 191n2, 191n7
  "generosity-narrative" and, 190n31
  Grupo Hiperión and, 28, 34, 35, 39, 40, 42, 44, 48, 54–56, 63, 156, 191n6
  Mexicanness and, 192n17
  Usigli and, 102–104
  zozobra and, 100–103, 110, 173, 204n15
Usigli, Rodolfo, 23–24, 29, 35, 73, 160, 197n1, 197n5. See also *El gesticulador*
  Cárdenas and, 199n17, 199nn13–14
  Caso and, 80–81, 197n6
  existentializing dynamics and, 76–80
  family plays and, 90–98, 198n12
  freedom and, 200n20
  with lies, 78–79
  Mexican identity and, 201n28
  Nietzsche and, 198n8
  Paz and, 75–77
  philosophical drives, 80–84
  political drives, 84–90, 198n11
  pragmatic authenticity and, 76, 201n27
  pragmatism and, 199n18
  theater of ideas and, 77, 91, 103, 197n4
  Uranga and, 102–104

Valero Pie, Aurelia, 36–37, 192n11, 196n43
Vallejo, César, 2, 133, 139, 141, 182
  "Arte y cristianismo" and, 134–135
  Christianity and, 136–137
values
  Christianity and root, 52–53, 193n22
  Grupo Hiperión and, 58–69
  inversion of, 43, 46, 62, 103, 202n33
Vargas, Getúlio, 6, 187n8
Vargas Llosa, Mario, 11–12, 68, 209n25
Vasconcelos, José, 6, 48, 90, 116, 120–121, 153, 204n14, 205nn19–20
Vatican Index of Prohibited Works, 8
Vaz Ferreira, Carlos, 6
Vázquez Colmenares, Genaro, 189n22
La verdad sospechosa [The Suspicious Truth] (Alarcón), 80
Vicens, Josefina, 210n5
La vida familiar del mexicano [Mexican Family Life] (Bermúdez), 63, 155–156
Vieyra, Jaime, 201n28
Villa, Pancho, 93, 94, 96, 200n23
Villegas, Abelardo, 60–61, 191n8
Villoro, Luis, 28, 35, 41, 49, 58, 121, 142, 152, 194n31, 204nn14–15
  Grupo Hiperión and, 60, 68, 156, 191n6
  Indigenous peoples and, 60, 61–62, 69, 115–118
  intersubjectivity and, 64
  magic and, 122–123

Viñas, David, 11, 149–151, 209n25
Viñas, Ismael, 151–152, 209nn26–27
Virgin of Guadalupe, 124–125
Volek, Emil, 110

Wagner de Reyna, Alberto, 187n6
Walzer, Michael, 201n27
The Weaver ("La tejedora") (López Velarde), 102
Weil, Simone, 213n22
The Well (*El pozo*) (Onetti), 16, 17, 18, 109
"What Is Existentialism?" (Beauvoir), 4
What Is Literature? (Sartre), 12, 55, 152, 195n35
"What is the Mexican" lecture, Grupo Hiperión, 35
When Sartre Writes Literature ("Cuando Sartre hace literatura") (Castellanos), 184
Where the Air is Clear (*La región más transparente*) (Fuentes), 197n45
"White Mythology" (Derrida), 42, 192n9
The Will to Believe (James, W.), 198n10
Wimer Zambrano, Javier, 189n22
The Woman Who Knows Latin (*Mujer que sabe latín*) (Castellanos), 156, 162–163
women
  Contorno and, 209nn26–27
  Eternal Feminine and, 157–164, 166
  Grupo Hiperión and, 155–157
  magic of, 158–160, 210nn3–4
  marriage and, 160, 163, 166, 168, 171–172, 180–181, 211n7, 214n26
  patriarchy and, 156, 162–163
  violence against, 16–17, 143
  writers, 162, 210n5
The Words (Sartre), 184

Xavier Villaurrutia Prize, 210n5
Xirau, Joaquín, 191n2
Xirau, Ramón, 211n12
X-ray of the Pampas (*Radiografía de la pampa*) (Martínez Estrada), 27

Yáñez, Agustín, 22–23, 35, 108, 118, 137–138, 156, 190n23
  Mexicanidad and, 69, 117
You Are Not Poetry ("Poesía no eres tú") (Castellanos), 182, 183
You Are Poetry ("Poesía eres tú") (Bécquer), 182
Yrigoyen, Hipólito, 150

Zambrano, María, 191n2
Zapata, Emiliano, 94, 96, 137, 200n23
Zea, Leopoldo, 26, 45, 101, 119–120, 165, 191n3, 191n5, 193n20
  Gaos, positivism and, 37
  Grupo Hiperión and, 28, 35, 40–44, 54–55, 63, 110, 156, 192n10
  with "México y lo Mexicano" book series, 29, 36, 42, 48, 122, 156
  past and, 110–111, 113
  Paz and, 112–113
  racial homogenization and, 196n44
  values and, 62, 63
Zepeda, Jorge, 203n5
zozobra, 100–103, 110, 173, 204n15

www.ingramcontent.com/pod-product-compliance
Lightning Source LLC
Chambersburg PA
CBHW030535230426
43665CB00010B/905